Peter the Great

Peter the Great

A Biography

Lindsey Hughes

Yale University Press
New Haven and London

Copyright © 2002 by Lindsey Hughes
First published in paperback 2004

For information about this and other Yale University Press publications, please contact:
U.S. Office: sales.press@yale.edu   yalebooks.com
Europe Office: sales@yaleup.co.uk.   www.yaleup.co.uk

Set in Garamond by Fakenham Photosetting, Norfolk
Printed in Great Britain by the MPG Books Group

Library of Congress Cataloging-in-Publication Data

Hughes, Lindsey, 1949–
   Peter the Great : a biography / Lindsey Hughes.
      p. cm.
Includes bibliographical references.
   ISBN 0-300-09426-4 (hbk.)
   ISBN 978-0-300-10300-7 (pbk.)
1. Peter I, Emperor of Russia, 1672–1725. 2. Russia—Kings and rulers—Biography.
3. Russia—History—Peter I, 1689–1725. I. Title.
   DK131 .H838 2002
   947'.05'092—dc21   2001007276

A catalogue record for this book is available from the British Library.

10 9 8 7 6 5 4 3

To my father, George Ernest James Hughes

Contents

Illustrations

Illustrations are printed by courtesy of the individuals and institutions listed. Where no acknowledgement is indicated, materials are the author's own photographs or from her own collection.

GRM: Gosudarstvennyi Russkii Muzei, St Petersburg.
SSEES: School of Slavonic and East European Studies, London.

Preface

The back dust jacket of my *Russia in the Age of Peter the Great*, published by Yale University Press in 1998, has an image taken from the side of Carlo Rastrelli's bronze bust of Peter, which shows him as Pygmalion, putting the finishing touches to a statue of a woman. The subject of that book was Peter's New Russia (the sculpture) as much as Peter himself (the sculptor) and its structure reflected this emphasis, with a central core of thematic chapters on war and diplomacy, army and navy, government, economy, society, culture, the court, education and religion sandwiched between an introductory section on Peter's background and youth and a conclusion on his personality, his family and associates and the Petrine legacy. The chronologically arranged chapter on foreign policy provided a framework into which the rest of the reign could be placed, but otherwise the grand narrative and the chronological interconnectedness of life, war and reform were abandoned. This approach had the advantage of allowing detailed analysis of individual topics spread over the whole reign, but it lost something of the dynamics of Peter's personal development, his interaction with other people over time and the evolution of his reforms, even if Peter was a looming presence throughout. I did not set out to write a life of Peter, but apparently this was by no means evident to some of the reviewers, who insisted on calling the book a 'biography', in some cases praising it as a good one, in others finding it somewhat lacking with respect to narrative flow and/or psychological depth. I am therefore grateful to Yale University Press for allowing me a second bite at the cherry in order to write 'Peter the Little', as this smaller book has informally been known while I was writing it, with a different readership in mind. In particular, I hope that this slimmed-down Peter will prove useful to students and other readers who are interested in Peter and his Russia but could not face ploughing through more than 600 densely footnoted pages.

Anyone writing Peter's life – and there have been many attempts – encounters the usual biographer's dilemma of striking a balance between the public man and the 'real', private Peter. The first Russian publications on the topic in the eighteenth century were modelled on Western exemplary lives of monarchs, statesmen and soldiers, which were biographical to the extent that they provided a chronological narrative about the life of a single individual, but concentrated on public rather than private activities, in fact, on the sort of topics Peter himself advocated in 1722 to the compilers of an official history of his reign, whom he instructed to write about

> what was done during this past war and what regulations were made on civil and military order, statutes for both branches of the services and the ecclesiastical regulation; also about the building of fortresses, harbours, fleets of ships and galleys and various manufactures, and about construction work in St Petersburg, on Kotlin island and in other places.[1]

It was widely held that private life was irrelevant to the chronicles of great men. Voltaire, for example, insisted that his own history of Peter's reign was 'the transactions of his public life', not 'the secrets of his cabinet, his bed, or his table'.[2] This approach may work with those world figures (few, surely) who single-mindedly dedicated themselves to pursuing public goals to the exclusion of everything else; but this was patently not the case with Peter, whose life was filled with personal drama and bizarre incident. The hero of Poltava and founder of the Russian navy, the absolute ruler of one of the biggest countries in the world, married an illiterate peasant woman and deferred to a mock sovereign known as Prince-Caesar, signing himself in letters as simple Peter Mikhailov or 'Piter'. His love of inversion and parody, of the 'world turned upside down', was clearly a key element in his style of rulership, not just relaxation or aberration. The man credited with bringing civilisation to Russia numbered among his hobbies extracting teeth, performing autopsies, wood-turning and fire-fighting. The Father of the Fatherland condemned his eldest son to death. The founder of St Petersburg preferred to live in small wooden houses with low ceilings. All this and much more – alcoholic binges, sexual excesses, crudity and violence – co-existed with a life dedicated to duty and crowned with achievements which formed the basis of official biographies of Peter, in both Tsarist and Soviet times. In this book I have tried to show both the private and the public Peter, with the assumption that most readers will find the private Peter interesting primarily *because* he was emperor of Russia.

Readers of *Russia in the Age of Peter the Great* who have come back for more will find much which is familiar – I have found no reason to change my treatment of key issues – and also some passages from the earlier book but, I hope, will discover new emphases and new material. In particular, this book is concerned with Peter's image, in both the literal and the figurative sense. Probably no Russian ruler left and inspired so many physical reminders of his

life and activities. He was the first tsar (perhaps the first Russian) whose likeness was consistently recognisable and he remains one of the few Romanov
rulers whose face Russians today can easily identify, although that may change
as figures more or less consigned to oblivion in the Soviet era, such as
Catherine II, Alexander III and Nicholas II, are rehabilitated. Both written
and visual materials were in turn inspired by Petrine anniversaries, such as his
bicentenary in 1872, which also prompted the creation or preservation of
museum displays and memorial sites. Yet Peter's visual legacy has been studied
much less than the huge body of written texts on his life and reign, to which
several monographs have been devoted. Each of my first ten chapters includes
an examination of key portraits and other images of Peter produced by
Russian and foreign artists, starting with the 'measuring' icon of St Peter
made to mark his birth in 1672 and ending with depictions of him on his
deathbed in 1725. In the penultimate chapter I assess Peter's legacy (the balance sheet of reform) and discuss views of Peter, from immediate reactions to
his death to the fragmentation of opinion which occurred in the last few years
of the Soviet Union. In the final chapter I examine how Peter has been commemorated since his death – by artists and sculptors, in buildings, galleries,
museums and anniversary celebrations – up to the present day, an investigation which remains open-ended as ever more images are generated to meet
new post-Soviet requirements. As this book goes to press, the tercentenary of
the founding of St Petersburg (2003) is approaching, an event which promises to add much in the way of memorabilia and writings.

On one level, my approach has been to dismantle the bigger book and put
it back together in the 'correct' order, discarding much of the finer details of
reforms and historiographical debate and putting Peter more firmly in the
picture. Generally I have cut down on documentation, usually only footnot-
ing direct quotations and relegating most English sources consulted and recommendations for further reading to the Select Bibliography at the end of the
book. Although the main narrative of the little book is based on the same
sources as the big book, the last two chapters contain new material relating to
'Petrine places', statues and paintings, the Petrine collections in the
Hermitage, and recent publications. I have reduced Russian terms in the text,
including transliterated words and phrases in brackets, to a minimum. In
general, I have assumed that Russian-speaking readers who need access to
fuller documentation will consult the big book which also contains a discussion of the major sources for Peter's reign.

For this opportunity to tell Peter's story I am indebted to Robert Baldock,
my ever-patient and supportive editor in Yale University Press's London office
and to his colleague Diana Yeh. The School of Slavonic and East European
Studies, University College London, provided study leave and the British
Academy a research grant to allow me to make visits to St Petersburg and
Moscow in 1999–2000. Although primarily for the purpose of researching a

project on landmarks of Russian visual culture, these trips led to the discovery of interesting new material and provoked fresh thoughts on Peter's reputation and image in Russia today. I am indebted to the following people and institutions: in St Petersburg, Evgeny Anisimov, Elena Mozgovaia, Elena and Mikhail Stolbov; the libraries of the Russian Museum and Academy of Arts; the Department of the History of Russian Culture in the State Hermitage (Viacheslav Fedorov, Irina Kotel'nikova, Galina Moiseeva, Evelina Tarasova) and the 'Palace of Peter I' exhibition; in Moscow, Galina Andreeva, Dmitry Fedosov, Olga Kosheleva, and staff in the State Historical Library. (Acknowledgements for material collected on earlier occasions can be found in the preface to *Russia in the Age of Peter the Great*.) As always, my friends in the Study Group on 18th-Century Russia have provided stimulating ideas and feedback and Caroline Newlove in SSEES gave invaluable practical help. My partner Jim Cutshall has supported me in all sorts of ways, including helping with the index, taking some of the photographs and unearthing some interesting items of Petrine memorabilia during expeditions to antiques and book fairs. Last but not least, my thanks to the cats Sophie and Catherine, who have now seen me through three books and one collective volume on the Petrine era (which, sadly, is not rich in feline themes) and several times that number of articles and papers. One reviewer of *Russia in the Age of Peter the Great* was actually under the impression that Sophie was the author and referred to her as Professor of Russian History at London University but luckily this didn't go to her head. Any errors in this book are, of course, my own.

Note on Transliteration, Dates and Monetary Units

Apart from certain transcribed terms, quotations from Russian sources are given in English translation, in most cases my own, unless otherwise stated. Russian proper names, terms and bibliographic references have been transcribed using a modified Library of Congress system, with further adaptations in the interest of readability in the main text. Feminine proper names, which in Russian have alternative spellings – with a soft sign (Mar'ia) or -iia (Mariia) – are all rendered as -ia, e.g. Maria, Natalia, Evdokia. The -ii and -yi endings of masculine proper names are simplified to -y, e.g. Dmitry, Vasily. Names of some famous individuals are given in their English equivalents, e.g. Peter (Petr), Catherine (Ekaterina), Sophia (Sof'ia or Sofiia), Alexis (Aleksei). In transcribed citations and bibliographical references, however, original spellings are rendered in full.

Dates (days and months) for Peter's reign are usually given in Old Style, i.e., according to the Julian calendar which was in use in Russia until 1918 and in the seventeenth century was ten days and in the eighteenth eleven days behind the New Style Gregorian calendar, which was adopted from the 1590s by many European countries. In a few cases the New Style (NS) date is given in brackets.

Units of currency referred to in the text had the following value:
1 rouble = 100 kopecks
1 Joachimsthaler = about 1 rouble (the value fluctuated)

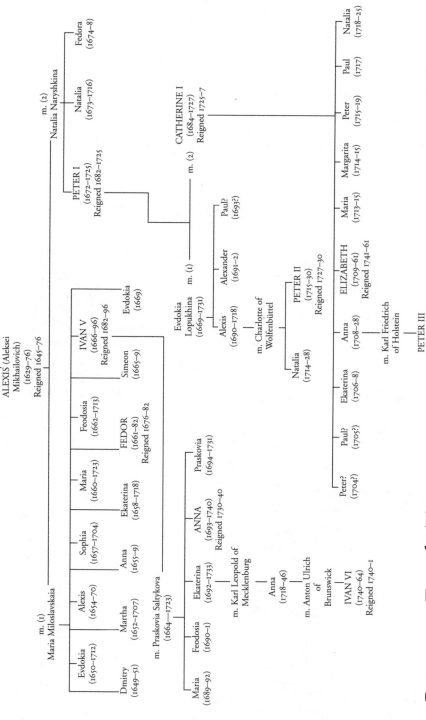

MICHAEL (Mikhail
Fedorovich)
(1596–1645)
Reigned 1613–45

ALEXIS (Aleksei
Mikhailovich)
(1629–76)
Reigned 1645–76

m. (1)
Maria Miloslavskaia

m. (2)
Natalia Naryshkina

Evdokia
(1650–1712)

Dmitry
(1649–51)

Alexis
(1654–70)

Martha
(1652–1707)

Sophia
(1657–1704)

Anna
(1655–9)

Maria
(1660–1723)

Ekaterina
(1658–1718)

Feodosia
(1662–1713)

FEDOR
(1661–82)
Reigned 1676–82

IVAN V
(1666–96)
Reigned 1682–96

Simeon
(1665–9)

Evdokia
(1669)

PETER I
(1672–1725)
Reigned 1682–1725

Natalia
(1673–1716)

Fedora
(1674–8)

m. Praskovia Saltykova
(1664–1723)

Maria
(1689–92)

Feodosia
(1690–1)

Ekaterina
(1692–1733)

m. Karl Leopold of
Mecklenburg

Anna
(1718–46)

m. Anton Ulrich
of
Brunswick

IVAN VI
(1740–64)
Reigned 1740–1

ANNA
(1693–1740)
Reigned 1730–40

Praskovia
(1694–1731)

Evdokia
Lopukhina
(1669–1731)

m. (1)

Alexis
(1690–1718)

Alexander
(1691–2)

Paul?
(1693?)

m. Charlotte of
Wolfenbüttel

Natalia
(1714–28)

PETER II
(1715–30)
Reigned 1727–30

CATHERINE I
(1684–1727)
Reigned 1725–7

m. (2)

Peter?
(1704?)

Paul?
(1705?)

Ekaterina
(1706–8)

Anna
(1708–28)

m. Karl Friedrich
of Holstein

PETER III
(1728–62)
Reigned 1761–2

ELIZABETH
(1709–61)
Reigned 1741–61

Maria
(1713–15)

Margarita
(1714–15)

Peter
(1715–19)

Paul
(1717)

Natalia
(1718–25)

Romanov Family Tree

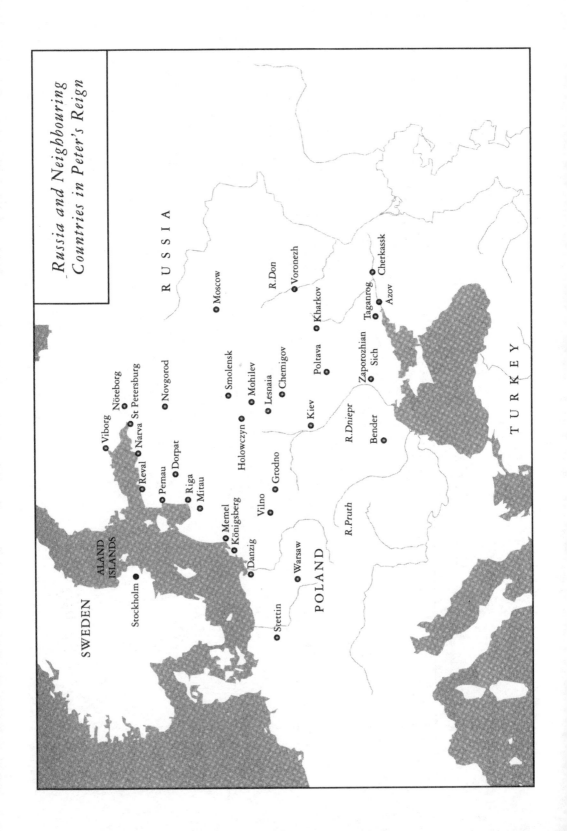

Russia and Neighbouring
Countries in Peter's Reign

SWEDEN

Stockholm

ALAND
ISLANDS

Viborg

Nöteborg

St Petersburg

Narva

Reval

Pernau

Dorpat

Riga

Mitau

Memel

Königsberg

Danzig

Stettin

Warsaw

POLAND

Vilno

Grodno

Holowczyn

Smolensk

Mohilev

Lesnaia

Chernigov

Kiev

R.Dniepr

R.Pruth

Bender

Zaporozhian
Sich

Poltava

Kharkov

R U S S I A

Moscow

R.Don

Voronezh

Taganrog

Azov

Cherkassk

Novgorod

TURKEY

Growing Up
1672–89

Childhood games brought mature triumphs.
(Inscription on an engraving (1722) of Peter's little boat)

A tsar is born

The future Peter the Great was born in Moscow at around one in the morning of Thursday, 30 May 1672, on the feast of St Isaac of Dalmatia. The children of the tsars of Muscovy were usually born in the Kremlin, which is almost certainly where Peter first entered the world, but legends persist that his mother, Tsaritsa Natalia, the second wife of Tsar Alexis of Russia, gave birth to her first child either in the royal palace at Kolomenskoe to the south of Moscow (which a Russian poet later dubbed the 'Russian Bethlehem') or at the significantly named village of Preobrazhenskoe (Transfiguration.) The life and deeds of the tsar, who was later credited with transforming Russia from 'non-existence' into 'being', gave rise to many myths and legends. Later writers, for example, recorded the court poet Simeon Polotsky's prediction of Peter's future greatness, made on the basis of astrological calculations for 11 August 1671, the supposed day of his conception, and quoted his ode to celebrate the birth, which portrayed Peter as the future conqueror of Constantinople and a 'new Constantine', a literary commonplace for praising Muscovite princes.[1] As it turned out, Peter did not fulfil his destiny in quite the way in which Polotsky envisaged. He was to be Russia's first emperor and to found a new capital in emulation of his imperial Roman forerunner, it is true, but his notion of his country's role in world history was to be oriented towards Western Europe rather than the Orthodox East, with immense consequences for Russia.

Opponents of this reorientation towards Western culture and values saw grim portents in the circumstances of Peter's birth. Later in his reign, rumours circulated that Natalia had given birth to a daughter, who was secretly exchanged for a German boy baby from Moscow's foreign community. Others identified the Swiss mercenary Franz Lefort, Patriarch Nikon or other unlikely candidates as Peter's father, on the grounds that a man who destroyed

Russian traditions could not have been the son of the pious tsar Alexis. Even what most people accept as the true facts of his ancestry were interpreted negatively by conservative critics, who argued that as the child of a second wife he was born in sin and as the product of the blood of tsars, 'slaves' (his mother's family, the Naryshkins), and priests (his great-grandfather Filaret was patriarch of Moscow) he was doomed to bring ill fortune to Russia.

All this was in the future, when disillusioned subjects sought explanations for Peter's often bizarre, 'alien' behaviour and unpopular policies. In 1672 the birth of a prince was a reason for rejoicing. The boy was large and healthy, 19¼ inches long according to the measuring icon of his patron saint the apostle Peter, made shortly after the birth in the tsar's workshop to record the infant's length. (Had he measured the 33 inches which some historians erroneously recorded, he would have qualified as one of the 'monsters' which he himself later collected and his mother would hardly have survived to see him grow to maturity.) The healthy male infant was an insurance for the dynasty's future, but he was not the heir to the throne. Peter's twenty-one-year-old mother, Natalia Kirillovna Naryshkina, daughter of a fairly minor military servitor, was married on 22 January 1671 to Tsar Alexis (Aleksei) Mikhailovich, whose first wife Maria Miloslavskaia had died in 1669 at the age of forth-three after giving birth to her thirteenth child. Alexis's first marriage produced five sons, of whom two were still alive in 1672. The heir, Fedor, born in 1661, was intelligent but delicate, while Ivan, born in 1666, was mentally and physically handicapped. In 1672 Tsar Alexis's three sisters – Irina, Anna and Tat'iana – were still alive and six of his eight daughters: Evdokia (the eldest, at twenty-two), Martha, Sophia, Ekaterina, Maria and Feodosia. In 1673 and 1674 Tsaritsa Natalia gave birth to girls, Natalia and Fedora, bringing the tally of princesses to eleven. Fedora died in 1678, Irina in 1679 and Anna in 1692, but all the others survived into the eighteenth century and witnessed at least some of Peter's reforms. The tsarevny (daughters of the tsar) were not regarded as candidates for the succession, nor did they or would they have husbands who could engage in palace politics and children to augment the royal line, for in the seventeenth century a policy emerged of keeping them unmarried; but all enjoyed the sanctity and power which came with royal blood or marriage. Peter could expect to grow up in an extended family dominated by women in which he, as a boy, enjoyed a superior status, but without any immediate prospect of becoming tsar. Given the high rates of infant mortality, even in the royal palace, it is unlikely that anyone formulated an individualised, long-term plan for Peter's future, except within the conventions of raising princes to be good Orthodox Christians.

Russia in 1672

Peter was born in a country which was poised to play an increasingly active role in world affairs but was hampered in many ways from pulling its full weight. In the so-called Thirteen Years or First Northern War (1654–67), Russia had clashed with its old neighbour-enemies Poland-Lithuania and Sweden. War with Poland ended in 1667 to Russia's advantage, with Left Bank Ukraine (to the east of the River Dnieper) and Kiev brought provisionally under the tsar's rule or, in the Muscovite view, *restored* to it, for the tsars of Muscovy regarded 'Little Russia' as their patrimony and its Cossacks as their subjects, as they did all the lands inhabited by Orthodox Slavs who lived under Catholic rule in the Kingdom of Poland and Grand Duchy of Lithuania. Russia gained nothing during the shorter conflict of 1656–61 with Sweden, which had blocked its way to the Baltic since the 1617 Treaty of Stolbovo removed Russia's narrow foothold on that sea. In the south, Russia and Poland vied for possession and domination of the steppes with the Ottoman Turks and Crimean Tatars, who blocked Russia's access to fertile agricultural lands and its advance to the Black Sea. Tatar raids across the Russian and Ukrainian borders exacted a heavy toll in annual tribute, prisoners and livestock, forcing Russia to maintain expensive garrisons. In 1672 Turks and Tatars seized parts of Polish (Right Bank) Ukraine and threatened incursions across the Dnieper into Muscovite territory. It was this crisis which prompted Tsar Alexis in the same year to send envoys to courts all over Europe to seek aid for an anti-Turkish league. In 1676 his successor Fedor found himself at war with the Turks and Tatars. After losing its fort at Chigirin on the Dnieper, Moscow made an uneasy twenty-year truce at Bakhchisarai (January 1681). Thus all three major issues of Muscovite foreign policy – the Polish, Swedish and Turkish questions – remained unresolved during Peter's childhood, with the potential for conflict to flare up along any of the borders. In addition, Muscovy was increasingly involved in Europe-wide diplomatic relations, even though it still did not maintain accredited ambassadors abroad. For their part, many Western countries regarded Russia in terms of commercial opportunities rather than alliances, although this was soon to change.

The population of late seventeenth-century Muscovy has been estimated at about ten million. It was by far the biggest country in Europe, but one of the least densely populated. It is possible to divide the great majority of Muscovy's inhabitants into two very broad categories in terms of their relationship to the state: those who performed military and other forms of service (including churchmen) and – the overwhelming majority – those who paid taxes. There were many variations, for example, non-Russian tribes people, who rendered taxes in the form of tribute (often in furs) or did irregular military service, and foreigners in temporary employment. Some of the tsar's subjects were difficult to pin down, such as the so-called 'men of other ranks' and 'wandering' people unattached to any fixed locality, who were incapable either of performing service or of paying taxes – for example, cripples and 'fools in Christ' – or those who wilfully escaped obligations – runaway serfs, army deserters and religious dissidents. Cossack military communities, originating as refuges from the long arm of government on the periphery of Muscovy, maintained a variety of links with the centre, either bound in service, like the registered Cossacks of Ukraine, intermittently loyal, like the Cossacks of the Don, or persistently hostile, like the Zaporozhian Cossack Host on the River Dnieper.

Peasants accounted for about 90 per cent of the population. Roughly half – the serfs or seigniorial peasants – were the property of the land-owning state servitors; the rest belonged to the church or the royal family or to the state. Serfs fulfilled their obligations by doing agricultural work (*corvée*) on their owners' land, working as domestics in their houses or paying in money or kind (*quitrent*). All peasants were obliged to pay taxes to the state and were liable to be conscripted for military service, which, if they were serfs, freed them from their obligations to their former owners. Tsar Alexis's 1649 Law Code abolished the time limit on owners recovering fugitive serfs, thereby fixing serfdom as a hereditary status in perpetuity. Making peasants stay in one place in perpetuity, however, was another matter, as Peter was constantly to be reminded. Despite their propensity to run away, Russian peasants should not be regarded primarily as 'victims'. Given that the climate and soils of most of seventeenth-century Russia were on the margins of viability for agriculture, the peasant economy was fairly successful in providing subsistence for peasants and a surplus for a state whose policies were determined by the requirements of the growth and maintenance of empire. It was not serfdom as such but the difficult climatic and geographical conditions which brought about generally low productivity, which is not to say that serfdom was good *per se*, that peasants enthusiastically embraced it or that peasant life was easy.

Towns accounted for no more than four per cent of the Muscovite population. The total male registered urban population in the 1670s has been estimated at just 185,000, which comprised merchants, artisans and traders, all of whom had communal tax liabilities to the state. The rest of the town population was variously made up of military servitors, priests and their families, strel'tsy (musketeers), artillerymen and postal drivers, secretaries and clerks working in government offices, household slaves on temporary contracts of bondage and many peasants residing temporarily, while continuing to be registered and pay taxes to their rural communities. In all cases we should add 'and their wives and other female relatives'. Women were not counted in censuses and, with the exception of nuns and some women traders, had no status independent of their male relatives. Russian towns, even Moscow – by far the biggest – lacked indigenous professional people such as bankers, scholars, doctors, teachers, lawyers and actors whom one might have encountered in any sizeable Western European town.

Muscovy was administered by the top layer of the Moscow-based service class, roughly the equivalent of the Western aristocracy, the core of whom enjoyed the privilege of attending and advising the tsar and a few of whom owned tens of thousands of serfs on hereditary estates dotted about the country. The so-called boyar duma or council (never a formally constituted body) in the seventeenth century varied in number from 28 to 153 members and had its own fourfold hierarchy: the boyars proper, sub-boyars or *okol'nichie*, gentlemen and clerks of the council. Membership of the two top groups was determined chiefly by hereditary right. Men from leading families generally became boyars and *okol'nichie* in the course of time according to seniority within their clan. The pecking order also accommodated royal in-laws (marrying a daughter to the tsar or his son considerably boosted a family's fortunes) and a handful of men of lower status who were raised by royal favour. Servitors immediately below the élite advisory council, mostly younger relatives and aspirants to membership, bore the hard-to-translate titles (in descending order) of *stol'nik, striapchii, dvorianin moskovskii* and *zhilets*. In peacetime these Moscow-based servitors in junior ranks performed a variety of duties, perhaps the most important of which was providing 'extras' for the elaborate rituals of the tsars' court. In wartime they went on campaign as cavalry officers.

In 1672 commissions, appointments and other placings, such as seating at state banquets, were still in theory governed by the code of precedence or 'place' system (*mestnichestvo*), which determined an individual's position by calculations based on his own and his clan's service record and his seniority within his clan. It was considered a great dishonour to be appointed or seated below someone who officially merited a lower place. Such insults gave grounds for an appeal to the tsar, who, however, for some campaigns ordered military rolls to be drawn up 'without places'. Defending the honour of one's clan and maintaining its position within the hierarchy of service was regarded as vital, for service to the state was compulsory even for the highest in the land and there were no alternative careers for the élite. The Russian nobility (some historians question the validity of this term in the Russian context) lacked a corporte identity and, apparently, any aspiration towards constitutional power-sharing. Russia had no parliament. There was no legal profession, although state servitors were called upon to administer the law within the government chancelleries. With very few exceptions, even younger sons of noblemen did not enter the Orthodox priesthood, which had developed as a more or less closed caste, although retiring to a monastery in old age was an option. Local politics barely figured as a career path for the upper service class, apart from the handful of men whom the tsar appointed as military governor (*voevoda*). In the countryside the state's business was carried out by the middle service class or gentry, who were privileged in being exempt from tax and labour burdens and holding lands which were granted and held on condition of military service but increasingly were passed on to heirs from generation to generation. These lands were worked by serfs, although many of the lesser provincial gentry owned only one or two peasant households and in some cases cultivated their own plots. Making a full-time career of administering one's estate in person was not possible until after 1762, when the Russian nobility was freed from compulsory service. Landed estates, manned by serfs and slaves (bondsmen), provided the income and the servants which allowed top men to reside close to the tsar in Moscow in order to do their duty, and lesser nobles to feed themselves and their families.

The absence of professions was reflected in the absence of training for professions. There were no universities in Muscovite Russia and no schools, apart from some in-house establishments for lower-ranking chancellery staff in the Kremlin. The gentleman-poet, playwright, astronomer or architect (still less the female of the species) had no place in Muscovite society and in modern histories of science based on great names (Newton, Descartes and their like) seventeenth-century Russia simply does not feature. Of course, we should not exaggerate literacy levels in the rest of Europe or overestimate the number of Westerners who had even heard of Copernican theory or calculus. Then, as now, advanced scientific knowledge was in the hands of a tiny minority and native folk wisdom and skills, passed from father to son or mother to daughter, satisfied most needs. But folk wisdom and peasant crafts did not produce the latest military technology, build seagoing ships or command respect at foreign courts, areas to which Peter was to devote considerable attention.

Awareness of Russia's need to 'catch up' in certain areas did not begin with Peter. The inflated claim which gained momentum after the fall of Constantinople in 1453 that Moscow was the guardian of true Christianity and the culminating point of Christian history was, even in the fifteenth century, tempered by the uncomfortable knowledge that Muscovite armies could prevail (sometimes) against Tatar 'infidels' but rarely against heretical 'Latins and Lutherans'. In the sixteenth century the empire spread inexorably eastwards, but acquisitions in the west, especially on the sought-after Baltic, were generally not held for long. The danger was that technical inferiority coupled with internal instability could lead to foreign subjugation, as underlined by the Time of Troubles (1598–1613), when famine and a dynastic crisis precipitated the collapse of central authority and Russian territory was overrun by Poles and Swedes. Foreign merchants and military advisers first began to arrive in Muscovy in significant numbers for more peaceful purposes during the reign of Ivan IV (1533–84). More came when Peter's grandfather Michael (1613–45), the first Romanov tsar, reorganised certain infantry regiments along foreign lines in the 1630s. To accommodate the growing numbers of military, commercial and diplomatic personnel from Western European countries, in 1652 Tsar Alexis set aside a separate area of Moscow called the Foreign or 'German' Quarter, which also housed a handful of foreign crafts-men and artists. In October 1672 it supplied a director and amateur actors to stage Russia's first theatrical performance, given at Tsar Alexis's command.

With its taverns, shops and Protestant churches (Catholics were allowed to worship only at home) the Foreign Quarter was a small corner of Western Europe which could not fail to excite Russians' curiosity, made even more irresistible because it was out of bounds. Far from being a symbol of Russia's increasing openness to the West, it was actually an attempt to restrict non-Orthodox foreigners and their churches to their own ghetto, away from the city centre where they had lived previously, as well as to stop them getting their hands on prime properties and business premises in unfair competition with local merchants. The Orthodox church warned its flock to regard such foreigners as dangerous heretics and to keep foreign 'novelties' and fashions at arm's length. Joachim, patriarch of Moscow from 1674 to 1690, urged the tsars to expel even mercenaries and to demolish non-Orthodox churches. The church also insisted that Russians be differentiated from Western Europeans, from whom ethnically they are indistinguishable, by their dress and hairstyle. In 1675 the growing practice among some Russian magnates of wearing Western fashions in private prompted the tsar to issue an order that courtiers were 'forbidden to adopt foreign, German and other customs, to cut the hair on their heads and to wear robes, tunics and hats of foreign design, and they are to forbid their servants to do so'.[2]

Shaving the beard, which increasingly became the fashion in the West among urban dwellers during the later seventeenth century, attracted par-ticular disapproval. In this respect Orthodox Russians were guided by the pronouncement of a church council of 1551: 'The sacred rules to all Orthodox Christians warn them not to shave their beards or moustaches or to cut their hair. Such is not an Orthodox practice but a Latin and heretical bequest . . . .'[3] That such warnings had to be issued at all indicates that adherence to tradition was by no means universal.

The Muscovite church found itself fighting a war on several fronts, not least with internal religious dissent, the best known example of which – the so-called Old Believer movement – was a reaction to the programme of reform carried out by Patriarch Nikon in 1652–58 to correct Russian service books on the basis of Greek and Ukrainian texts. At the same time he imposed the sign of the cross made with three fingers (the Greek practice) instead of two (Old Russian) and changed spellings and liturgical practices. Many Christians believed that to wor-ship using the new books and rituals posed a mortal danger to the soul and it was better to die than to submit. These protesters and other schismatics who rejected the authority of the church for all sorts of reasons added to the strong undertow of dissent and flight from obligations which characterised Muscovite Russia.

Religion also dictated strict rules of decorum for women. Married women concealed their hair at all times in public and women of all ages and classes wore loose, layered garments which revealed only their faces and hands. Elite women, both married and unmarried, lived in semi-seclusion in what some later sources refer to as the *terem*, which served both to protect them from illicit sexual encounters and to emphasise their exclusiveness, as well as allowing them access to their own finances and to have their own household administrators and servants. One of the most intriguing features of the Foreign Quarter for Russians was that the inhabitants followed Western conventions regarding fashion, mixed-sex gatherings and courtship, which, as we shall see, was to hold a particular attraction for Peter.

Russians were protected from foreign influences by other controls, too. For example, publishing and printing remained firmly in the hands of the church. In the whole of the seventeenth century fewer than ten non-religious titles were isued by Muscovite presses, which were devoted chiefly to producing liturgical and devotional texts. Even publications from Slavonic presses in Kiev, Chernigov, Vilna and other centres of Orthodoxy were intermittently banned for fear of spreading heresy. Books in foreign languages reached the libraries of a few leading nobles and clerics, but were not freely on sale. The absence of Muscovite printed news sheets, journals, almanacs, histories, plays, poetry and philosophy – the sort of works found in bookshops in London, Paris and other cities – was partly compensated by popular literature in manuscript and a flourishing oral tradition. Private reading of printed books (as opposed to listening to books being read out in church or to stories told by a storyteller) was a minority occupation in Muscovy, and scholarship even at an amateur level was more or less confined to members of monastic orders. The exceptions were some of the government chancelleries in Moscow, which had to cater for state needs in such areas as map-making, building, medicine and gathering foreign news, but their activities hardly reached a wider public.

The Russia into which Peter was born, then, was a country in many ways very distinct from its neighbours in Protestant and Catholic Europe, where Russia was still regarded as a 'rude and barbarous' kingdom, with rulers more akin to the emperors of China or the sultans of Turkey than to European kings. In the year 1672 the birth of a Russian prince went more or less unobserved in the West. There would not even have been much speculation about the new prince's eligibility as a marriage partner, as the Muscovite royal family was known to remain aloof from such contacts. Tapping foreigners' knowledge, marrying his children to them and gaining their respect were to be among Peter's major goals and not the least of the areas in which he tried to 'catch up' was that of chronology and time-keeping. Most sources agree that 30 May was Peter's birthday, as did Peter himself by honouring St Isaac of Dalmatia, later founding a church to the rather obscure saint. But at least one record gives 29 May, following the old Russian practice of starting the new day not at midnight but at first light, according to which calculation 30 May (the nights are short in Russia at that time of year) began an hour or so after Peter was born. For those European countries, mostly Catholic, which had adopted the more accurate Gregorian calendar and so were ten days ahead of those which, like Russia, followed the older Julian calendar, Peter was born on 9 June. Contemporary Russian chroniclers, in the meantime, used not Arabic numerals but Cyrillic letters with numerical equivalents to record the year of Peter's birth as 7180, following the Byzantine practice of numbering years from the notional creation of the world in 5509 BC. The year 7181 was due to begin not on 1 January 1673 but on 1 September 1672, again following the Byzantine practice.

It is appropriate that questions of time and chronology should arise at the very outset of Peter's biography, for he was to be obsessed with time and its passing, believing that 'wasted time, like death, cannot be reversed'.[4] On the eve of the new eighteenth century, which most people agreed started in 1700 rather than 1701, Peter decreed that official records would henceforth keep calendar years from the birth of Christ, as other Christian nations did, whereupon traditionalists denounced him for tampering with 'God's time'. When he died on 28 January 1725, as it was now entered in official records, he had changed much more than the calendar.

Childhood

For the first decade of his life Peter was a junior member of an extended royal household, with his own nursery and servants in the Kremlin palace, which was a warren of chambers and chapels. Materially, he wanted for nothing. His birth was celebrated with a banquet featuring confections fit for a prince: a spice cake in the shape of the Muscovite coat of arms, a sugar duck, parrot, dove and eagles, a whole spun sugar Kremlin with infantry, cavalry and two towers with an eagle soaring above them, and great platters heaped with marzipan, frosted fruits, candied peel, and other sweets, some of which were presented to guests to take home.

Given that the major ingredients had to be imported, this represented conspicuous consumption on a grand scale, even if such festive fare was not served every day. Late Muscovite taste was for colourful ornateness and everything in the royal household was richly decorated: robes embroidered with gold and silver thread and pearls, household utensils and cult objects enamelled in glowing colours, embossed saddles and harnesses, carved and gilded velvet-lined carriages, religious frescos in bright paints with lashings of gold leaf, icons with jewelled casings. The desired effects were achieved by Russian craftsmen in the royal workshops and with imported goods, especially textiles, brought from all over the world.

The royal children were protected from the public gaze, only occasionally making an appearance in written records, often when they were glimpsed by curious foreigners: for example, sightings of three-year-old Peter leaving the Kremlin in a tiny gilded carriage, accompanied by dwarfs, or escaping his mother's grasp to run out from behind a curtain. His early upbringing followed the traditional Orthodox model, based on learning to read from a primer, graduating to the Psalter and Acts of the Apostles, then learning to write and count. Peter received indifferent tuition from Russians seconded from government chancelleries, who apparently failed to inculcate even basic disciplines into their pupil: his handwriting and spelling remained atrocious for the rest of his life and his original autographs are barely decipherable even by specialists. In this respect Peter's education lagged behind that of several of his half-siblings. His brothers Fedor and Alexis (died 1670) were taught by Simeon Polotsky, who gave instruction in Latin, Polish, versification and other elements of the classical syllabus. Polotsky died in 1680 before he had the chance, had it been offered, to tutor Peter, who only ever mastered a few token names and terms from classical languages and had little interest in poetry. His daughter Elizabeth later recounted how Peter often visited her and her sisters at their lessons and told them to be grateful that they were receiving a good education. 'I was deprived of all that in my youth.'[5] Was this a myth of Peter's own making, one wonders, intended to blacken the reputation of relatives who allegedly 'oppressed' him in his youth and to cover up his own difficulties with intellectually challenging subjects? Throughout his life Peter was to be more comfortable with practical skills, such as carpentry and wood-turning, than with theory or academic disciplines. Foreign mentors were certainly to hand but not one was a scholar. The Scottish General Paul Menzies from Aberdeen (1637–94), who went on diplomatic missions for Russia in the 1670s, had connections to Peter's circle through Peter's maternal relatives the Naryshkins and the family of one of their sponsors, Artamon Matveev, the head of the Foreign Office, who were related to the Scottish Hamiltons. References survive to Menzies as Peter's 'tutor', although as a Catholic he would not have been entrusted with traditional literacy teaching through the Psalter and primer. He, like the Dutchman Franz Timmermann who later taught Peter to sail and perhaps gave him lessons in Dutch, was probably most valued as an adviser on military affairs, which soon became one of Peter's major preoccupations.

Later writers credited the infant Peter with extraordinary military prowess, comparing him with the young Hercules who strangled a serpent in his cradle, but these precocious talents were extrapolated from his mature military victories. Even so, military affairs were regarded as the right and proper concern of a tsarevich and like his father and elder brothers before him, Peter played with toy soldiers, miniature forts, cannon, bows and arrows and drums. He learned to ride, to shoot a bow and handle a sword. Toy weapons were supplemented with spades, hammers and mason's tools, which no doubt fostered Peter's love of mechanical crafts. The fiercest of Peter's boyhood passions – his love of ships and the sea – is harder to explain in a country without a seagoing tradition, especially as the young Peter is said to have had a dread of water, the overcoming of which features in a number of anecdotes illustrating his courage and determination. Russia's naval inexperience should not be exaggerated. English vessels had been docking on the White Sea since the 1550s and Tsar Alexis commissioned Dutch shipwrights to build a small fleet on the Caspian in the 1660s. Russians may not have been expert sailors on the high seas, but they knew how to navigate inland waters and the northern coastlines. Peter found no lack of stimulants to the imagination close to hand: toy boats, maps, charts and engravings and what he himself identified as the spark which lit the flame, the old English sailing boat, the 'grandfather of the Russian fleet', which he discovered in the early 1680s in the outhouse of a country estate and which will make several appearances in our narrative.

In January 1676 Tsar Alexis died at the age of forty-seven, apparently from a cocktail of ailments leading to kidney and heart failure. Probably Peter had few personal memories of his father, although later in life he expressed admiration for his achievements. In contemporary documents Alexis was described as 'most quiet' and 'most pious'. Nineteenth-century Slavophile (nationalist) historians regarded him as the ideal ruler, contrasting his cautious approach to government, inspired by piety and respect for tradition, with Peter's obsessive urge to turn everything upside down. The most often reproduced portraits of Alexis tend to confirm the image of a passive man, a static figure in heavy robes, carrying symbols of office, as though about to set forth to attend a church service. But contemporary sources reveal that the 'most quiet', who, in the words of his biographer, 'perceived good order to be the necessary condition of the good life and for success in everything', also had a violent temper, which his son evidently inherited.[6]

If Alexis's mildness has been exaggerated, so too has his reputation as a consistent guardian of national traditions which Peter wantonly destroyed. In fact, in his own way Alexis was a moderniser and Peter himself acknowledged his debt to the father he scarcely knew in two key areas: military reform and the creation of a fleet. Many things which Peter's own publicists and later historians included among the achievements of the Petrine 'revolution' had their roots in his father's and even his grandfather's reign, including a professional army based on infantry, subjugation of the church, use of foreign specialists and imported technology and culture. Even some of the more bizarre aspects of Peter's behaviour as an adult seem to emulate his father. Alexis instituted a method of fines and punishments for courtiers who failed to attend morning prayers or name-day services. He had them ducked in water, like a baptism, then forced to drink three draughts of vodka. Peter was to devise even more inventive penalties. By and large, modern historians regard Alexis as Peter's precursor rather than his antithesis.

Fourteen-year-old Fedor succeeded his father. Unsubstantiated rumours of attempts to crown three-year-old Peter instead of him underline the potential difficulties of Peter and his mother. The Miloslavskys had been pushed into the background when their kinswoman Tsaritsa Maria died and Alexis married Natalia Naryshkina in 1671. The new tsaritsa's father Kirill attained full boyar status and younger clan members received prestigious appointments as chamberlains, while even some lesser relatives found themselves installed in provincial governorships. The Naryshkins' clients benefited accordingly. In 1676 it was the Miloslavskys' turn again. With Fedor's accession, their fortunes rose and the Naryshkins' declined; leading members of Natalia's clan were exiled, including Artamon Matveev. These gains were temporary, however. Fedor chose his own favourites, showing no preference for his maternal relatives, and there is no reason to believe that he entertained any personal animosity towards his young half-brother. Even so, twice in the six years following his father's death Peter narrowly escaped being pushed further down the ladder of succession. Fedor's first wife, Agafia Grushetskaia, and her newborn son Ilia died in July 1681. Early in 1682 he took a second wife, the noblewoman Martha Matveevna Apraksina. As long as Fedor remained childless, custom dictated that his younger brother Ivan was his heir, but custom was soon to be flouted.

The strel'tsy revolt of 1682

On 27 April 1682 Fedor, who had always been sickly, died and Peter, a month short of his tenth birthday, was declared tsar on the grounds that his mother was alive to act as regent and his elder half-brother Ivan was 'weak-minded', a decision which did not long remain unchallenged. To be sure, Ivan's afflictions precluded his taking the initiative in either civil or military affairs. Russia had no written law of succession to exclude the accession of a younger brother under these circumstances – observance of primogeniture was a matter of custom rather than constitution – and Peter had the support of Patriarch Joachim, who carried great authority. But the politics of kinship and popular notions of justice proved stronger than pragmatism.

With Peter proclaimed tsar, the Naryshkins and their clients could expect to wield some real power in his minority and to retain key posts when he came of age. One of the very first actions of the new regime, which had Tsaritsa Natalia as its figurehead, was to recall Artamon Matveev from exile. But the Naryshkins apparently had not reckoned on a lethal combination of unrest among Moscow's armed guard, the strel'tsy, and the fury of the affronted Miloslavskys, who found a spokeswoman in the spurned Tsarevich

Ivan's sister, twenty-five-year-old Sophia, that 'ambitious and power-hungry princess', as a contemporary described her.[7] By and large women's role in Muscovite power networks, as elsewhere, was confined to their usefulness as marriage partners and mothers (a clan could boost its fortunes by making good marriages) and in some cases, especially if they gained appointments as ladies-in-waiting in the royal household, to behind-the-scenes lobbying on behalf of male relatives. Widows with under-age sons and dependent male relatives, like Tsaritsa Natalia, could become even more powerful; but open political manoeuvring was hampered by the Muscovite custom of keeping élite women in semi-seclusion, with special conventions limiting contact with male non-relatives. Even so, these women still enjoyed considerable authority derived not simply from their royal blood, but from a religious view of political power which stressed the role of royal wives and daughters as champions of Orthodoxy and intercessors on behalf of their men folk and the realm. This view was underpinned by the use of analogies with female saints and strong women from the Bible and Byzantine history who in case of need acted independently. In Muscovy both male and female power, although wielded in separate spheres, were conceptualised and expressed in terms which interpreted piety not as restrictive and passive but empowering. Royal power was seen as collective, as evidenced, for example, by the inclusion of royal women in oaths of allegiance. Visible authority may usually have been exercised by men, but when Sophia found herself in a position to take over in the absence of mature male relatives, she had the sanction of a long-standing tradition. Any one of Tsarevich Ivan's other five sisters could have taken on the role, but evidently Sophia was the boldest and most outspoken.

It is possible that by this stage she had already taken as her lover or at least formed a strong attachment to one of the leading men in the boyar council, Prince Vasily Vasil'evich Golitsyn (1643–1714). Their relationship is said to have begun when Sophia was caring for the ailing Tsar Fedor, to whose bedchamber Golitsyn often reported. In 1681–82 he was a prime mover in the abolition of the code of precedence and in devising a new scheme for making military appointments. Much of the evidence of the couple's intimacy rests on hearsay and rumour, plus some coded letters dating from the later 1680s. What is beyond doubt is that once in power Sophia relied on Golitsyn to spearhead both her foreign and her domestic policy and showered him with rewards and honours. Over-reliance upon his skills as a military commander was to hasten the downfall of both of them.

Sophia's main aim was to get Ivan on the throne, but to achieve this she needed to find support beyond the circles of the boyar council, where few men, if any, were active supporters of Tsarevich Ivan. Luckily for her, at the time of Fedor's death the strel'tsy were ultra-sensitive to rumours of abuses and injustice in high places as a result of continual disputes over management, pay and conditions. After two weeks of negotiations, during which the new Naryshkin government handed over unpopular officers to strel'tsy mobs, a rumour that Tsarevich Ivan had been strangled by his 'ill-wishers' and that the same evil men were preparing to assault the strel'tsy brought mutinous regiments to the Kremlin. Here on 15–17 May the strel'tsy settled personal grudges by butchering some of their own commanding officers and unpopular government officials and also singled out members of the Naryshkin clan and their associates as 'traitors' to Ivan, possibly with the help of a list drawn up by Sophia. About forty persons fell victim to axe and pike, including Peter's uncle Ivan Naryshkin (who was accused of trying on the crown) and Artamon Matveev, who was hacked to pieces. Peter witnessed several of these brutal murders when he and Ivan were brought out onto a balcony in front of the palace to reassure the mutineers that they were both unharmed.

The mob's fury was not directed at Peter himself, who was sanctified by his royal descent, but at 'wicked advisers' whom they suspected of manipulating both boys for their own ends, but it is unlikely that the nine-year-old realised this. His experience – terror for his personal safety as he witnessed people close to him slaughtered (Matveev had been standing next to Peter and his mother seconds before he was thrown on to the soldiers' pikes in the square below) – must have been psychologically damaging. Later he recalled these violent incidents as a sort of metaphor for what he had to overcome: the wild beast face of Russia, which acted with brute force on the basis of rumour, superstition and prejudice rather than by exercising reason and brain power. It has been argued that this strel'tsy revolt and subsequent ones inculcated in Peter a basically pessimistic notion of human nature and ultimately the realisation that barbarism can only be overcome by its own methods in order to allow the rule of reason to flourish.

Sophia and the 'Khovanshchina'

The role of Tsarevna Sophia Alekseevna in these violent events has been widely debated. Although there is no direct evidence that she had the 'Machiavellian' tendencies attributed to her by some contemporaries (she left no personal writings which throw light on her motives), still less that she plotted to kill Peter and his mother, who remained unharmed throughout her regency, she vigorously championed the claim of her brother Ivan to be tsar. Once the strel'tsy had retreated from the Kremlin, reassured that Ivan was alive and well, in late May 1682 a compromise was found in the form of a joint tsardom, with Ivan as senior tsar and Peter as junior, with reference to Byzantine precedents and the rhetorical formula that Ivan would rule at home while Peter went to war against Russia's enemies. An oath of allegiance to Tsars Ivan and Peter was sworn on 26 May but there is no contemporary record of the formal establishment of a regency. The monk Silvester

Medvedev, a fervent supporter of Sophia, relates that the strel'tsy presented a petition that same day asking 'that the government of the Russian realm be administered by the pious wise Sovereign Lady, the tsarevna and great princess Sophia Alekseevna', and that she finally 'agreed to take upon herself that great labour',[8] but Medvedev may have doctored his account towards the end of the 1680s when he and others were trying to prepare the ground for Sophia to be crowned and were anxious to show that popular acclaim was the legal basis for her rule. Whatever the nature of the arrangement made in May 1682, in the course of the 1680s Sophia became ruler and from about 1686 began not only to add her name to those of her brothers in royal edicts but also to include *samoderzhitsa*, the feminine form of *samoderzhets* (autocrat) among her titles. But titles could not disguise the dilemma: was she to remain in power until Ivan's death, since his need for a regent was permanent, or would she step down when Peter came of age? It is significant that she never demanded that Peter, the fatal flaw in any scheme for the perpetuation of her power, be removed from the throne. Whether this demonstrates a lack of political acumen or a wise acknowledgement of real politics is difficult to say.

On Sunday, 25 June 1682 the Kremlin bells rang out for the coronation of Tsars Ivan and Peter in the fifteenth-century Cathedral of the Dormition in a double version of the modified Byzantine ritual first used for the coronation of Ivan IV in 1547. An additional set of regalia – the special fur-trimmed crown known as the Cap of Monomach, orb and sceptre, pectoral cross and shoulder mantle – had to be prepared for Peter and a two-seater throne was constructed. Peter's coronation robe of heavy Italian gold damask, incorporating flower and crown motifs and trimmed with gold lacework, survives to this day. Sophia did not attend the coronation in person for Muscovite tradition generally barred women from such occasions, but Prince Vasily Golitsyn was there as her substitute, summoning the tsars to the service, standing on the raised platform beside them and holding Tsar Ivan's sceptre. Ceremonial duties performed by other magnates – for example, Prince Boris Alekseevich Golitsyn, a Naryshkin supporter, acted as Peter's sceptre bearer – indicate that the Miloslavskys were by no means clearly in the ascendant. This was underlined by the list of promotions made a few days later on Peter's name day, 29 June, where men more allied to the Naryshkins than to the Miloslavskys received boyar ranks. From Sophia's point of view, what had been achieved was not the elimination or total humiliation of the Naryshkin network, an impossibility as long as Peter was tsar, but a restoration of the fortunes of the Miloslavsky clan and their clients with, no doubt she hoped, an edge over the Naryshkins now that Ivan was nominally 'senior' monarch. A compromise had to be reached in order not to disrupt the expectations of promotion of members of leading clans. Once the tsars were crowned the aim was harmony and consensus up above, in order better to deal with the discord which still threatened to get out of hand down below.

The withdrawal of the strel'tsy from the Kremlin on 17 May marked not the end but a new stage in the troubles. Anxious not to be branded as traitors, the strel'tsy demanded that Sophia's government, equally anxious to avoid further bloodshed, absolve them of all guilt and erect a column on Red Square to commemorate the services which they had rendered by eliminating 'wicked men' who had 'plotted all manner of evil' against the crown. The Sophia–Golitsyn government duly erected the column, issued a charter, exiled disgraced officers and redistributed their property. But these measures failed to prevent a new wave of unrest, this time initiated by religious dissidents among the strel'tsy who demanded to know 'why they [the government] hated the old service books and loved the new Latin-Roman faith'.[9] Their appeal for the restoration of the 'old belief' was encouraged by Prince Ivan Andreevich Khovansky, the man who had replaced the murdered Prince Iury Dolgoruky as head of the strel'tsy chancellery. Acting as the troops' self-styled 'father', Khovansky, a veteran of campaigns against Poland and Turkey with a long record of service as military governor, made a show of mediating between the strel'tsy and the Kremlin and organised a meeting between the patriarch and dissident priests to debate the issue of the faith on 5 July, an event which Sophia, two of her sisters, one of her aunts and Tsaritsa Natalia attended. When the dissidents' spokesman, the defrocked priest Nikita, assaulted an archbishop, Sophia threatened to leave Moscow 'in order to tell all the people about this insubordination and chaos', a threat which she later carried out to considerable effect.

Nikita was arrested and executed, but Khovansky remained too popular with the strel'tsy for the government to touch him. Instead they began to reduce the power of the Khovansky clan by reshuffling chancellery personnel, relying on the fact that Khovansky had few supporters among the boyars. The royal party then set off on tours of estates and monasteries, leaving Khovansky precariously in charge in Moscow and increasingly isolated. Sophia announced that the tsars had been forced to leave Moscow 'because we could not tolerate the many offences, unlawful and gross actions and violations committed by criminals and traitors'.[10] Khovansky's failure to obey several orders, for example to send the royal bodyguard of mounted strel'tsy to attend Tsar Ivan's name-day celebrations on 29 August, allowed Sophia to isolate him further. His fate was sealed by the discovery of an anonymous (probably fabricated) letter of denunciation. On 17 September, her own name day, Sophia succeeded in luring Ivan Khovansky and his son Ivan to the royal summer residence at Vozdvizhenskoe outside Moscow. The charges against them centred on their 'evil designs upon the health and authority of the great sovereigns' which involved no less than plotting to use the strel'tsy to kill the tsars, Tsaritsa Natalia, Sophia and the patriarch, then to raise rebellion all over Moscow and snatch the throne. The lesser charges included association with 'accursed schismatics', embezzlement, dereliction of military duty, and insulting the boyars. The charges were full of inconsistencies and illogicalities, but their sheer weight sealed the Khovanskys' fate and Prince Ivan and his son were beheaded on the spot. Despite reassurances that the quarrel was not with them, the strel'tsy looked set to barricade themselves into Moscow, but eventually they were reduced to begging Sophia and the tsars, now ensconced in the Trinity Monastery to the north of Moscow, to return. The strel'tsy were forced to swear an oath of loyalty based on a set of conditions, the final clause of which threatened death to anyone who 'speaks approvingly of the deeds of late, or boasts of committing murder or makes up phrases inciting rebellion as before, or stirs up people to commit criminal acts'.[11] The royal party returned to Moscow in early November 1682.

A portrait of Ivan and Peter

The names of the great sovereign tsars and great princes Ivan Alekseevich and Peter Alekseevich, autocrats of all Great and Little and White Russia, may have appeared on the numerous orders and edicts issued during the 'Khovanshchina', as the period of unrest came to be known, but it was the 'great sovereign lady, pious tsarevna and great princess' Sophia Alekseevna and her supporters who took the decisions. The tsars were closely supervised fig-ureheads, alternately kept out of sight or shown to selected audiences as a token of the withdrawal or conferral of favour. Being in charge of the tsars was Sophia's greatest asset and she cleverly exploited the special significance attached to the royal presence, especially among the strel'tsy, whose muddled quarrel had always been with the 'wicked boyars'. Later in life Peter never gave Sophia and her supporters any credit for their shrewd handling of the Khovansky affair. Perhaps he was scarcely aware of the intricate manoeuvres which took place during the summer and autumn of 1682, except for the fact that he and his brother were moved back and forth between various royal res-idences, as though they were on the run. In the absence of personal reminis-cences about that fateful year we can only deduce its disturbing impact from Peter's treatment of the strel'tsy in 1698 and his determination to eradicate the corps.

Despite their senior–junior designation, the few depictions of the two tsars together show them as equals and more or less interchangeable, for example in the illustrations by unknown Russian artists of Peter and Ivan in their coro-nation robes for the large bound collection of manuscript portraits of Russian and foreign princes known as the Book of Titled Heads (*Tituliarnik*), a sort of heraldic and dynastic reference work compiled in the Kremlin Armoury workshops over several decades. Supplements contained pictures of all Tsar Alexis's sons, including a drawing of Peter dating from 1678. All the Russian images in the book were stereotypical, with the twelfth-century Kievan prince

Vladimir Monomach scarcely distinguishable from Tsar Alexis. The attributes of power and icon-like features suggest a fixed quality that looked to past traditions rather than the future. This manuscript portrait of Peter may have been the model for an anonymous and undated oil painting, which bears little resemblance to later authenticated portraits of him as a young man. The two tsars also featured in allegorical prints, embellished with a characteristic baroque mix of Christian and classical imagery. The earliest, an engraving by the Ukrainian artist Ivan Shchirsky for a theological work published in 1683, illustrates the text: 'It is good and seemly when two brothers rule jointly.' The two tsars in full regalia hover above a canopy containing a double eagle. Christ floats between them and above him is a winged maiden, the Divine Wisdom (Sophia), who influences and protects the two tsars in the heavenly sphere, just as their sister does on earth.[12] A somewhat later print by Shchirsky, illustrating the programme for a debate in the Kiev Academy, shows the tsars enthroned and immobile beneath a huge double eagle. In such compositions the tsars are mere effigies, inhabiting an invented sacred landscape, always dressed as though for a coronation, without any distinguishing features.

Foreign artists devised exotic images of their own, for example engraved half-length portraits of Ivan and Peter by L'Armessin of Paris and F. Jollain's study of *Les Frères Czars* in fur hats and stoles and holding sabres, produced to mark a Russian embassy (a disastrous one as it turned out) to France in 1686–87. The artists seem to be saying: the tsars of Muscovy are exotic, the 'other' and cannot be depicted using the same conventions as those used for Western rulers. Their sphere of activity was in the East. Similar imagery was used in the West for the Turkish sultan or the emperor of China. Muscovy was barely included among the Christian 'political' nations.

None of these early images or, indeed, anything from Russian official written sources, gives much hint of what Peter was really like. For a glimpse of his personality we must turn (with all due caution) to foreigners' accounts. The German scientist and traveller Englebert Kämpfer saw both tsars at a diplomatic reception in July 1683. Ivan sat 'motionless with downcast eyes' and had to be helped by an attendant to acknowledge the ambassadors, whom he greeted with a sort of 'babbling noise'. Peter, in contrast, 'his face held upright and open, made such an impression with his wonderful beauty and pleasant gestures ... that if the bystanders had beheld a young maid and not a royal personage before them, they would certainly have fallen in love with him'. Unlike the passive Ivan, Peter was so eager to ask questions that he had to be restrained. This restless curiosity never left him and often proved annoying to his companions and hosts. Kämpfer took him to be sixteen, rather than eleven.[13] Dr Laurent Rinhuber formed a similar impression during an audience in June 1684. Sophia's kinsman Ivan Miloslavsky assisted Tsar Ivan, explaining that he had poor eyesight. Peter, on the other hand, 'with his mouth half formed into a laugh gave us a friendly and gracious glance and scarcely had he seen me than he held out his hand of his own accord. An exceedingly handsome gentleman on whom nature has amply bestowed her powers.'[14]

It seems almost indecent to rub in any further the striking contrast between dull Ivan, who had severe visual impairment and perhaps mental handicaps (opinion differs as to the nature and extent of his disabilities), and bright Peter. As the Austrian envoy Johann Eberhardt Hövel remarked, 'such a feeble-minded and sickly man [as Ivan] was by nature unfit to rule'.[15] The only surviving image, much reproduced, of the mature Ivan painted in the Western manner shows no obvious signs of the 'imbecility' which less tactful observers mentioned, but there is no evidence that it is a true likeness. From today's viewpoint, Peter was clearly the better candidate for the job, especially if, with the wisdom of hindsight, one approves of his later reforms. Yet from the political-religious perspective of Russia in the 1680s Ivan remained the senior tsar by God's will, perfectly capable of fulfilling the symbolic functions of rulership as the motionless centre around which court ceremonial revolved. Piety, dignity and restraint in public, the ability to sit through receptions or stand through interminable church services, were important elements in the Muscovite idealised image of a good tsar. Peter's quick intelligence and impatience, on the other hand, which the educated foreigners Kämpfer and Rinhuber observed with approval, and his inability to sit or stand still, may actually have appeared unseemly and inappropriate to Russian contemporaries. And perhaps not only to Russians. As described by the Frenchman Foy de la Neuville, who visited Russia in 1689, Peter's liveliness verges on menacing hyperactivity:

Tsar Peter is very tall and quite well proportioned, with a handsome face. His eyes are big but so wild that he is pitiful to look at. His head shakes continually. He is twenty years of age. He amuses himself by making his favourites play tug o' war with each other, and often they knock each other out in their efforts to pay court. In the winter he has large holes cut in the ice and makes the fattest lords pass over them in sleds. The weakness of the new ice often causes them to fall in and drown. He also likes having the great bell rung, but his dominant passion is to see houses burn, which is a very common occurrence in Moscow since no one bothers to put one out unless there are 400 or 500 alight.[16]

Even if, as seems likely, Neuville never actually saw Peter, this assessment is still valuable for we know that the Frenchman had a number of influential informants among Peter's circle, including Andrei Matveev (the murdered Artamon's son) and Prince Boris Golitsyn, the cousin of Sophia's favourite, Prince Vasily. The shaking head and other alarming twitches have been attributed to the horrors Peter endured in 1682. A Swiss traveller, who saw Peter in Holland in 1698, reported that he suffered from convulsions in his eyes, hands and whole body. 'Sometimes his eyes roll right back until only the whites are visible . . . . He even has a twitch of the legs and can't stand in the same place for long.'[17] The dominant motifs in accounts of the 1680s are Peter's impetuousness and restlessness and his need for constant physical diversions, often trivial, sometimes cruel. The account by Prince Boris Kurakin (later ambassador in Holland) of how young Peter and his friends played at *sviatki*, a sort of Yuletide charade, is instructive, even if it was written long after the events described. Kurakin tells disapprovingly of how fat men were dragged through chairs, people's clothes were torn off and they were made to sit on ice with bare bottoms; they had to suffer candles being shoved up their backsides and air blown up them with bellows, resulting in at least one death.[18] Even when he was a grown man, Peter continued to enjoy inflicting similarly humiliating physical violence on his friends as a joke and they had little choice but to grin and bear it.

The regency

Once the dangers were past, the peculiar circumstances of the dual monarchy allowed Peter to indulge himself. On occasion he was still required to put in an appearance at ambassadorial receptions or important family anniversaries, but by and large he was relieved of ceremonial duties, which Sophia was happy to see performed by Ivan alone, who thus assumed a prominent and active role in the public eye as the Orthodox figurehead. She herself also took part in rituals, which emphasised her own role as pious protector of the realm. It was said that Sophia 'stifled Peter's natural light',[19] but the opposite was true. There was no question of Peter being either banished or persecuted; living away from the Kremlin suited him as much as it did Sophia. This 'sabbatical' from the routine burdens of rulership allowed him to pursue his own interests, which increasingly focused on military games and sailing, and to build up a circle of friends and assistants at a distance from traditional clan networks. Men from the boyar élite still predominated in Peter's entourage, but they were joined by foreigners and commoners. The company he kept in the 1680s–90s set the tone for Peter's personal circle for the rest of his reign, when he could variously be found in the company of army orderlies, foreign soldiers, doctors and shipwrights, dwarfs, giants, 'blackamoors', his personal choirmaster and chaplain, and fools and jesters of various types.

Peter played no direct role in either the domestic or foreign policy of Sophia's regency, even though his name appeared with Ivan's on all edicts and treaties. No doubt he would have endorsed the nineteenth-century historian Nikolai Ustrialov's dismissal of the Sophia–Golitsyn regime as one which produced 'nothing of any significance either for the benefit of the state or for the growth of the nation's industrial sources or for its education' and rejected Prince Kurakin's accolade that 'never was there such a wise regime in the Russian realm', which reached 'a pinnacle of prosperity'.[20] The truth lay somewhere in between. In many areas, Sophia's regime continued the policies of Alexis and Fedor to maximise the fulfilment of service requirements and the payment of tax liabilities (which involved updating land surveys and pursuing and returning fugitives), speeding up trials and maintaining law and order, especially with respect to the safety of the sovereigns, their treasury and the church. Rumours, recorded only in Neuville's memoir, that Prince Vasily Golitsyn wished to liberate the serfs, find no confirmation in the published legislation of the period, but may well reflect Golitsyn's concern with the linked issues of the peasant question and gentry service and with balancing a prosperous peasantry against the needs of national defence.

The regime's mildness in some areas, for example banning the cruel practice of burying alive women who murdered their husbands, was offset by its savage penalties for religious dissidents, who were pursued mercilessly by the state as well as the church. In 1685 a decree prescribed the use of the knout, torture and execution: those who 'incite the common people, their wives and children to burn themselves to death [as religious protest] will themselves be burned'. At the same time, developments in foreign policy forced the regime to relax restrictions on non-Orthodox residents; for this Golitsyn, who was unusual for a Russian in knowing Latin and Polish, became known as the 'friend of foreigners'. Catholic priests were granted entry to cater for Moscow's small community of foreign Catholics. With Prussian backing, Russia offered sanctuary to French Protestants fleeing from the 'sundry cruelties' of the king of France and made concessions to foreign merchants and industrialists to encourage them to set up businesses. In 1689 Russia signed commercial treaties with Prussia, laying the foundations for future Russo-Prussian co-operation during the 1710s. Russia's first institute of higher education, the Slavonic-Greek-Latin academy, founded in 1687 on the model of the Kiev academy, also relied on foreign teachers. Its first directors were the Greek monks Ioanniky and Sofrony Likhud (Lichoedes).

In its own eyes, the Sophia–Golitsyn regime's crowning achievement was the 1686 treaty with Poland, which ratified Russia's possession of Kiev and its immediate hinterland in return for Russia's agreement to sever relations with Turkey and Crimea 'on account of the many wrongs committed by the Muslims, in the name of Christianity and to save many Christians held in servitude' and wage war on Crimea.[21] This treaty of 'eternal peace', which drew Russia into the Holy League, was a landmark in Russia's relations with the Polish Commonwealth, a stepping stone towards the ascendancy achieved later in Peter's reign. In the shorter term, however, problems in fulfilling its clauses were to supply the pretext for Sophia and Golitsyn's opponents to overthrow them.

War and naval games. Preobrazhenskoe

While serious international business was going on, Peter, it seems, was amusing himself. The story goes that he discovered about 300 men idle at a former royal hunting lodge (he himself never much enjoyed hunting) and signed them up to play military games, then requisitioned others from regular units. Young nobles who would normally serve in junior court posts were recruited alongside local lads from a variety of backgrounds. The resulting 'play' (*poteshnye*) troops were formed into two regiments which took their names from the adjacent royal villages at Preobrazhenskoe and Semenovskoe to the north of Moscow. The troops' organisation – foreign ranks, training methods and uniforms – was modelled on the new formation infantry regiments first introduced in the 1630s. By 1684–85 the embryonic guards had their own barracks and a scaled-down wooden fortress which Peter named Presburg. A moat was dug and towers and gates erected, along with a church and an administrative block, all built of wood. Peter had his own modest billet, which he used for years to come. 'When at Mosco,' observed the future English ambassador Charles Whitworth, 'he never lodges in the palace, but in a little wooden house built for him in the suburbs [at Preobrazhenskoe] as Colonel of his guards.'[22] The fact that Peter did not have a regular palace is significant, for he lived and served at Preobrazhenskoe not as tsar but as a trainee. In deference to foreign expertise, all Russians, including the tsar himself, served in the ranks or as non-commissioned officers. Royal ceremonial functions were performed by a 'mock' tsar known as Prince-Caesar and there was also a mock patriarch. In the 1680s–90s Peter came to regard Preobrazhenskoe rather than Moscow as his capital. In other words, Moscow was symbolically deprived of its capital status some time before St Petersburg took over the function, evidence that psychologically Peter had broken with the Kremlin at quite an early stage in his career and had begun to replicate the established hierarchy with a weird version of his own.

The official history of the Russian fleet also begins in the 1680s with the discovery at another royal village, Izmailovo, of a sailing boat, which Peter himself later elevated to the symbolic status of 'grandfather' of his navy. Built in the 1640s, almost certainly of English-type construction, it is preserved in the Maritime Museum in St Petersburg. For Archbishop Feofan Prokopovich, who edited Peter's preface to the 1720 Naval Statute, where its story was first told in print, the little boat provided a striking emblem to illustrate the aphorism that 'great oaks from little acorns grow', for 'this Monarch was so particularly remarkable in all he did, that the very Pastimes of his Childhood are esteem'd, as Transactions momentous and weighty, and appear worthy to be recorded in History'.[23] The little boat was not, in fact, the first Russian royal ship. As Peter acknowledged in the Naval Statute, his father commissioned Dutchmen to build the three-masted *Eagle* in 1667–68, but it was burned by

Stenka Razin's rebels at Astrakhan in 1670 before it could put to sea. One of the ship's gunners, Carsten Brandt, was still in Russia when Peter advertised for a shipwright to repair the Izmailovo boat, thus providing a direct link with Tsar Alexis's initiative. The Dutchman Franz Timmermann taught him to sail. As far as we know, Tsar Alexis had little personal attachment to ships and the sea, but for Peter, they were to become a dominating passion.

Marriage

Peter did his best to avoid official engagements in the Kremlin, but there was at least one which he failed to escape. On 27 January 1689 he was married off to twenty-year-old Evdokia Lopukhina, daughter of a state servitor of middling rank. Like all Muscovite royal marriages, Peter's was determined primarily by dynastic calculations, in this case additionally to emphasise the fact that he was now a man who did not need a regent and in the hope of getting a male heir before Ivan did. Ivan had been married to Praskovia Saltykova (1664–1723) in 1684, but the marriage remained without issue until 1689, and then produced five daughters in quick succession: Maria (1689–92), Feodosia (1690–91), Ekaterina (1692–1733), Anna (1693–1740, empress 1730–40) and Praskovia (1694–1731). (There were rumours that this rich crop of girls was not Ivan's.) As was the custom, the tsars' brides were selected from clans well down the pecking order of the boyar élite, thereby (it was hoped) minimising rivalries among more prominent families. The new tsaritsas' male relatives and their clientele would add weight to the Miloslavsky and Naryshkin camps respectively without expecting rewards above their station.

In Peter's case, we know little about the preliminaries of the choice, just the bare fact that the couple were married in one of the palace chapels in a simple ceremony. The event was marked by the production of a manuscript book in a single copy entitled *The Token of Love in Holy Matrimony*, the frontispiece to which is a religious allegory featuring a notional likeness of the tsar and his bride in traditional brocade robes and crowns. Floating above them on a cloud, Christ and the Mother of God and Saints Peter and Evdokia bless the union, while scrolls with appropriate biblical texts ('There was a marriage in Cana of Galilee ...', 'And God created man in his image, male and female created he them', and so on) link the earthly and heavenly planes. The book contains verses by the court poet Karion Istomin in fashionable Polish syllabic metre, reflecting on the nature of royal marriage and the role of the body and the senses in human life and divine worship. This was a traditional marriage with traditional expectations, as emphasised by Evdokia's pose. The only known portrait of Peter's first wife in later life painted in the Western manner, of which numerous copies exist, is distinctly unflattering, showing her as a nun, a flabby-faced woman in a voluminous fur-trimmed robe of dark fabric, her hair concealed from view in a dark head-dress which blends into an even murkier background. In her youth, however, Evdokia was regarded as a beauty. Prince Boris Kurakin, who was married to her sister, wrote that the new tsaritsa was 'fair of face, but of mediocre intellect and no match for her husband in character'.[24] Her conventional upbringing is reflected in a handful of surviving letters which she wrote to Peter in her own hand in the early years of their marriage, formulaic texts dotted with standard terms of endearment and expressed in the submissive tone required of a royal bride: 'Your wretched little wife Dunka greets you . . .. Be so good as to write to me, my light, about your health, so that wretched me may be happy in my sadness . . .. You have not written a single line about your royal health.'[25] We do not know whether Peter, preoccupied with drilling troops and sailing, was ever 'so good' as to write to her: no letters survive from him to Evdokia. But Peter performed his marital duty in one respect at least: a few months after the wedding Evdokia was already pregnant.

The Crimean campaigns. Sophia and Golitsyn overthrown

The year of Peter's marriage, 1689, was to prove crucial in more ways than one. As part of Russia's commitments to the Holy League against the Turks, in spring 1687 Prince Vasily Golitsyn led a vast army south towards the Crimea. Weighed down with heavy supply wagons, for there was little chance of forage in the unpopulated steppes, the troops made painfully slow progress over difficult terrain, only to discover when they were still almost 200 miles away from the Crimea that the grasslands on which they were relying for horse fodder had been burned. Official reports variously blamed the Cossacks and the Tatars for starting the blaze. As men fell ill from drinking contaminated water, Golitsyn took the decision to turn back. Official reports later claimed that the khan and his Tatars 'were seized with fear and terror . . . and plunged into the depths of despair'[26] by the approach of the Russian army, but in fact the outcome was decided by logistics rather than battles. A campaign in which the enemy's non-appearance allowed little scope for military exploits thus acquired an exaggeratedly heroic colouring.

In February 1689 Golitsyn, reluctantly by all accounts, again set off for the Crimea. On this second campaign, he reached the fort of Perekop at the entrance to the Crimean isthmus. There were several engagements with the Tatars at which 'their majesties' men-at-arms courageously and boldly repelled the infidel in a bloody battle and drove them from the battlefield', as Golitsyn wrote in a dispatch.[27] But yet again, logistical problems, particularly an absence of fresh water, forced the Russian armies to withdraw after suing for peace, this time with even greater losses than previously as men and horses perished from thirst and sickness. Prominent among the charges later made against Golitsyn was the one that at Perekop he 'failed to carry out military operations and withdrew from that place and by [his] lack of enterprise great losses were inflicted on the royal treasury, ruin on the state and oppression on the people'.[28] There were no grounds for the accusations of dereliction of duty, still less that Golitsyn was bought off with Tatar gold, but the growing influence of Peter's supporters at court left Golitsyn more vulnerable than ever to rumour and innuendo.

Although Golitsyn was once again fêted as a hero on Sophia's instructions when he returned to Moscow in July 1689, this second failure gave his opponents the opportunity to undermine both him and Sophia, whose 'unseemly' appearances in public, especially in church parades, Peter had begun to criticise. Peter made a point of absenting himself from the welcoming party for the 'victorious' Golitsyn on 19 July and initially refused to give his consent to rewards for the other campaign commanders, which led, in the words of the Scottish general Patrick Gordon, to 'an open eruption or breach which was like to turn to animosityes' and caused 'passions and humors increasing lyke to breake out with a Poroxismus'.[29] Gordon (1635–99), a veteran of the Crimean campaigns who had entered Russian service in 1661, was soon to become a member of Peter's inner circle.

By the summer of 1689 Peter had good reason to assert himself: he was well into his majority (Fedor Alekseevich, it will be recalled, became tsar without a regent at the age of fourteen); his wife was pregnant; he had his 'play' regiments and foreign officers at his disposal and the support of the patriarch. Meanwhile, Sophia's side, led by Fedor Shaklovity, the so-called 'second favourite', a clever man of humble origins who had made his career in the chancellery administration, spread rumours about Peter's 'impious' behaviour and lack of respect for his ancestors, hinting that his ambitious uncle, Lev Naryshkin, was planning to flog the strel'tsy. The 'open eruption' predicted by Gordon came on 7 August 1689, when Peter was woken up in the night at Preobrazhenskoe with news that the strel'tsy were coming to kill him. A suspiciously large unit of strel'tsy had indeed gathered near the Kremlin, although later Shaklovity claimed that this was just a bodyguard to accompany Sophia to the Donskoy convent, where she went every year for the feast of the icon of Our Lady of the Don. This crisis may have been engineered by Peter's own supporters in order to force a confrontation between Peter and Sophia, which they knew she was unlikely to win given public dissatisfaction with the Crimean campaigns. Peter fled north to the Trinity-St Sergius monastery, where, in Gordon's words, 'he immediately threw himself upon a bed and fell a weeping bitterly'. Thus began a stand-off between Sophia's fast-dwindling forces in the Kremlin and Peter's supporters massed at Trinity. In mid-August Peter ordered the strel'tsy and infantry regiments to attend him there, but Sophia in an 'eloquent oration' (observed by Gordon, who was still in two minds whether to join Peter) managed to persuade them to remain. A few days later the patriarch left for Trinity and Sophia attempted to go in person to speak with her brother, but Peter turned her away, demanding instead that she hand over the 'blatant criminal' Shaklovity, now named as the author of a plot to kill Peter and his family. On 5 September the departure of foreign officers for Trinity, among them Gordon, proved a turning point. Shaklovity was arrested and subsequently executed along with other conspirators for plotting regicide, while Vasily Golitsyn, probably with the help of his cousin Boris, got off with the lesser charges of condoning Sophia's attempts to assume sovereign powers and of negligence during the Crimean campaigns. He was exiled in the north of Russia, where he died in 1714, a waste of a remarkable talent which, in different circumstances, Peter would have been glad to use.

As for Sophia, for the rest of his life Peter associated her with the dark forces of opposition, even if he blamed most of the active wickedness on her male supporters. The perpetrators of the so-called Tsykler plot against Peter in 1696–97 were executed over the exhumed coffin of Ivan Miloslavsky, a relative of Sophia who was identified by several contemporaries as the mastermind behind the 1682 rebellion. 'The seed of Ivan Miloslavsky is sprouting,' wrote Peter when he came back to Russia to deal with another strel'tsy revolt in 1698.[30] He recognised Sophia's 'great intelligence' but thought it was outweighed by her malice and cunning.[31] In a letter to Tsar Ivan, probably ghost-written by a Naryshkin adviser between 8 and 12 September 1689, Peter declared: 'And now, brother sovereign, the time has come for us to rule the realm entrusted to us by God, since we are of age and we must not allow that third shameful personage, our sister the Tsarevna S. A., to share the titles and government with us two male persons.'[32] Sophia was locked up without any charge in the Moscow Novodevichy convent, many of the modern buildings of which she had commissioned, under the supervision of a unit of the Preobrazhensky guards. From 7 September all references to her disappeared from official documents, as if the regency had never been.

II
Prelude to Greatness
1689–97

In the autumn we were engaged in martial games at Kozhukhovo. They weren't
intended to be anything more than games. But that play was the herald of the real
business. (Peter to Fedor Apraksin, April 1695)[1]

The Naryshkins

The departure of Sophia and Golitsyn was not a signal for the start of Peter's
personal rule, either constitutionally (he was crowned in 1682) or in practical
terms. The regent and some of her clients were removed and the hierarchy at
court adjusted itself accordingly, but the relationship between Tsar Ivan,
making stately progress in his heavy brocade robes, and Tsar Peter, now clad
in German dress, dashing from sailing expedition to military parade,
remained the same, despite efforts by Peter's relatives to push him into performing more ceremonial duties. Peter showed little inclination to 'rule the
realm', still less to reform it.

Members of the Naryshkin clan, who towards the end of Sophia's
regency had recovered some of the ground lost in May 1682, came bounc-
ing back into executive positions. A host of them were awarded boyar rank.
The most prominent was Peter's uncle Lev Kirillovich (1664–1705), whom
Boris Kurakin dismissed as 'a man of very mediocre brain and an inveter-
ate drunkard'.[2] The clan's most enduring legacy consisted of the many
sumptuous churches they commissioned from 1689 onwards in an ornate
style which later became known as 'Naryshkin baroque'. One of the finest
examples, the Church of the Intercession at Fili, built for Lev Naryshkin in
1690–93, with its soaring tower of receding octagons, gold cupolas and
intricately carved limestone decoration based on the classical orders, bears
witness to both the Naryshkins' wealth and their Westernised tastes. Inside,
the choice of icons followed the fashion for reflecting family history, in this
case with references to the clan's royal connections in images of SS Peter
and Paul, John the Baptist (Tsar Ivan's patron saint) and Alexis Man of
God. The icon of St Stephen bears a striking resemblance to the young
Peter, who often visited the church. All the icons were painted in an
'Italianate' style.

Notwithstanding their taste for the latest fashions in art and architecture, the Naryshkins were easily persuaded to take a conservative line on 'Latins and Lutherans'. The new regime cancelled several concessions made to foreigners during Sophia's regency and adopted closer supervision of aliens in general in order to stem the infiltration of heresy. On 2 October 1689 the Jesuit fathers Georgius David and Tobias Tichavsky were expelled from Moscow. Two priests were still allowed to serve the foreign Catholic community, but precautions were taken to ensure that they did not try to convert Russians or visit them in their homes. In October 1689 the Protestant mystic Quirinus Kuhlman was burned on Red Square together with his works. The governor of Novgorod was warned to take care that 'no more such criminals enter the country and that foreigners who in future arrive from abroad from various countries ... and claim that they have come to enter service or to visit relatives or for some other business in Moscow, should be questioned at the border and in Novgorod and detained and not allowed to proceed to Moscow until you receive our royal instructions'.[3] The atmosphere for a few months after Sophia's overthrow was so oppressive that Patrick Gordon, by now Peter's friend and adviser, contemplated leaving Russia, especially after the patriarch barred foreign guests from attending a royal banquet in February 1690.

Patriarch Joachim's Testament (he died in March 1690) sought to consolidate this anti-foreign policy. 'May our sovereigns never allow any Orthodox Christians in their realm to entertain any close friendly relations with heretics and dissenters,' he wrote, 'with the Latins, Lutherans, Calvinists and godless Tatars (whom our Lord abominates and the church of God damns for their God-abhorred guile); but let them be avoided as enemies of God and defamers of the church.'[4] Joachim's successor Adrian, consecrated in August 1690, held similar views. The religious life at court, with Tsar Ivan at its centre, continued unabated, the court records meticulously detailing the order of ceremonies and the colour and cloth of the participants' costumes. For a time, Peter also found himself forced to put in regular appearances to underline the ascendancy of his mother's party. On Easter Sunday in April 1690 we find the two tsars processing into the Dormition cathedral for matins past ranks of servitors clad in robes of gold thread (anyone not clad in gold was barred from entry by armed strel'tsy), walking round the church behind the icons and crosses, then proceeding to pray first at the tombs of their ancestors in the cathedral of the Archangel Michael, then in the cathedral of the Annunciation, after which they attended mass in a private chapel.

Two months earlier the Kremlin had witnessed celebrations which even Peter could not wriggle out of. On the morning of 19 February 1690 Peter and Ivan went to the Dormition cathedral 'to join in prayers and give thankful praise to the Lord God, our blessed protectress the Mother of God and the Moscow miracle workers and all saints, asking them to grant the sovereigns many years of health and to grant many years of health also to the newborn, pious Sovereign Tsarevich and Great Prince Alexis Petrovich of all Great and Little and White Russia.'[5] After the service the tsars treated members of the boyar council to goblets of wine and lesser ranks to vodka. At the same time a number of promotions were announced, including Peter's uncle Martem'ian Kirillovich Naryshkin and his wife's uncle Peter Abramovich Lopukhin the Younger to the rank of boyar.

Peter put his own mark on the occasion: the birth of his first child was celebrated not just with the customary church services and peals of bells but with cannon fire and drumbeats. Foreign-led infantry regiments were drawn up in the Kremlin, where their colonels delivered congratulatory speeches and in turn were presented with gifts and vodka and ordered to fire off rounds of shot. Alexis was baptised by the patriarch on 23 February in the Kremlin Monastery of Miracles, where Peter and his mother also attended mass. Over the next few days there were firework displays and banquets, where more promotions were announced. The Naryshkins and Lopukhins had good reason to celebrate, for nothing was more important to a clan than male heirs. Despite Peter's apparent indifference to Evdokia, in October 1691 another son, Alexander, was born. Sadly, Alexander died the following May, and was laid to rest beside Tsarevich Ilia, the infant son of Tsar Fedor. Peter did not attend the funeral as he was otherwise engaged. Some authors mention a third son, Paul, said to have died in 1693, but neither his birth nor his death is recorded in the admittedly incomplete palace records and there is no marked tomb. By the middle of the 1690s Peter was estranged from Evdokia and the son whose birth they celebrated so enthusiastically in 1690 was to provide one of the most harrowing chapters in his life.

Foreign friends

Peter, meantime, deaf to the church's dire warnings about the dangers of defilement, was spending more time than ever in the company of 'heretics', often as a guest in their homes in the Foreign Quarter. The first foreign home which Peter is said to have visited – on 30 April 1690 – was that of Patrick Gordon, who had become his adviser not only on military matters, but also on politics and fireworks, the latter another of Peter's lifelong enthusiasms. Gordon was one of the Foreign Quarter's leading Catholics, but this did not deter Peter. Peter became even closer to the Swiss mercenary Franz Lefort (born 1655/6), who came to Moscow in 1676 and fought in the Crimean campaigns. Assessments of his talents vary. Boris Kurakin, who took a dim view of most of the younger Peter's friends, complained that Lefort 'spent day and night in pleasure, dinners, balls and banquets', encouraging Peter to indulge in debauchery and excessive drinking.[6] He was also knowledgeable about trade and diplomacy, but the key thing is that Peter admired and trusted the

older man. On receiving news of his friend's death at the age of forty-two in
1699 (from drink, according to Kurakin) Peter allegedly complained that he
was now left 'without one trustworthy man'.[7]

Peter got to know other foreign soldiers and merchants, attending their
banquets, weddings, baptisms and funerals. Lefort's palace in the Foreign
Quarter, with a splendidly appointed ballroom added, was turned into a
semi-official residence for holding receptions, which according to Kurakin
featured 'debauchery and drunkenness so great that it is impossible to
describe it'.[8] In October 1691 Peter attended a party in the Foreign Quarter at
the home of the tavern keeper Johann Georg Mons, which is probably when
he first met his future mistress Anna, Johann's daughter. Peter picked up other
skills from his foreign friends, starting to learn Dutch (from Andrei Vinius, a
government official of Dutch descent), as well as taking lessons in dancing,
fencing and riding. There is little evidence that he undertook any formal education or serious reading, however.

Nowhere is the spirit of Peter's activities, poised between the old and the
new, better illustrated than in an entry in the palace record for 27 April 1690
(April was traditionally the start of the royal pilgrimage season), when 'the
Great Sovereign Peter Alekseevich deigned to visit Kolomenskoe'. For this
trip a rowing boat was got up to look like a sailing ship; boyars followed in
two boats and strel'tsy went in front in seven, and 'as they sailed along the
water there was firing from cannon and hand guns'. The play regiments sailed
in smaller craft. Tsar Ivan travelled by land.[9] Thus we see two tsars, one firmly
rooted in old Russia, the other encouraging novelty. Peter did not neglect his
religious duties entirely – in May 1690, for example, he made a tour of
monasteries, as his father and brother had done before him – but more often
than not Ivan carried out such duties alone. Contemporaries noticed this turn
of events. Boris Kurakin records: 'First the ceremonial processions to the
cathedral were abandoned and Tsar Ivan Alekseevich started to go alone; also
the royal robes were abandoned and Peter wore simple dress. Public audiences
were mostly abandoned (such as were given to visiting prelates and envoys
from the hetman [the Cossack commander], for which there were public processions); now there were simple receptions.'[10] This apparent simplification of
court ritual in fact involved both the elaboration of a new court calendar,
from which old feasts were dropped and to which new ones were added, and
the introduction of 'mock' rituals alongside real ones.

Many of Peter's unofficial activities are recorded in Patrick Gordon's diary.
In 1690 he spent his birthday at Preobrazhenskoe enjoying gun salutes and
target practice. On 19 January 1691 he visited the boyar P. V. Sheremetev and
the next day Gordon had such a dreadful hangover that he could not get out
of bed until the evening, a condition which he experienced on many occasions. A dinner at Boris Golitsyn's on 16 May led to similar consequences.
And so on. Royal account books for 1690–91 show numerous entries for

orders for 'German dress' for Peter and members of his play regiments, for example a purchase of 'good English cloth, dark grey', for which the chamberlain Gavrila Ivanovich Golovkin (1660–1734), Peter's future chancellor, passed a payment of 75 roubles.[11] Among foreign goods shipped to Archangel in 1692 for Peter's use were mathematical instruments, two globes, a large organ, four large clocks, five barrels of Rhine wine and a barrel of olive oil.[12] Arguably, in making such purchases Peter was merely continuing trends encouraged by his father and brother, but the cumulative effect of the things he bought and the company he kept created a more Westernised environment than they had known.

Prince-Pope and Prince-Caesar

Throughout his life Peter remained as much attached to objects as to ideas, more at ease with the concrete than the abstract, although he was capable of appreciating the symbolic and the emblematic. He also had a crude sense of humour. This is worth bearing in mind when examining the origins of one of Peter's most controversial creations, the All-Drunken, All-Jesting Assembly, a group of people close to the tsar who engaged in parodic religious ceremonies, presided over by a 'Prince-Pope' (*kniaz'-papa*) and other mock churchmen. Peter may well have gleaned inspiration from the real election and installation of Adrian as patriarch in August 1690. Not only was Peter obliged to attend, wearing the heavy robes and regalia which he so disliked, but he had to sit through a speech in which the new patriarch appealed to God for deliverance 'from Latinism, Lutheranism and Calvinism and all other heresies'.[13] It is probably no coincidence that Peter and his friends elected their own mock 'arch-pastor' not long after this ceremony. According to tradition, the first mock prelate was Matvei F. Naryshkin (whom Kurakin, scathing as ever, described as 'stupid, old and drunk'),[14] but the best-known incumbent was Peter's former tutor Nikita Zotov, referred to in some sources as 'Patriarch Bacchus', one of the attendants of the real patriarch at the enthronement in 1690 and holder of the post of Prince-Pope until his death in 1717.

One formulation of the Prince-Pope's titles was 'patriarch of all Iauza and Kukui', the latter a vulgar name for the Foreign Quarter, which underlined the undoubted influence of Peter's foreign friends, in whose homes and taverns he joined in drunken rituals and bawdy drinking songs addressed to Bacchus. The British specialised in this brand of humour; later the 'British Monastery' or Bung-College in St Petersburg, had its own Father Superior and included among its activities punishments supervised by 'the staff surgeon and pinkle smith or prick farrier'. At about the same time Peter began to construct a mock court, presided over by His Majesty Prince-Caesar (*kniaz'-kezar*), who often appeared with the Prince-Pope on festive occasions in a parody of the Byzantine symphony of tsardom and priesthood. For more than twenty years the mock throne was occupied by Prince Fedor Romodanovsky (1640–1717), who was succeeded by his son Tsarevich Ivan. As Prince-Caesar, Romodanovsky had his own residence and church at Preobrazhenskoe, all built of wood, and as director of the chancellery of the Preobrazhensky regiment and the tribunal attached to it he also held real power. An early recorded example of the combined antics of the mock court and church assembly was the wedding in January 1695 of Iakov Turgenev, a secretary in the Preobrazhensky regimental office, in which the bride and groom rode in the tsar's 'best carriage' with a retinue of boyars and courtiers in fancy dress decorated with animals' tails and pulled by bullocks, goats, pigs and dogs.[15] A new cultural topography was being constructed which paralleled the traditional 'sacred landscape' in which Tsar Ivan and Patriarch Adrian continued to function. Peter's part in his new invented world was variously as the humble subject (trainee bombardier or trainee shipbuilder) of Prince-Caesar and deacon in attendance on Prince-Pope. It demonstrated his ability to set the rules and choose his own roles.

The death of Natalia Naryshkina

Change was in the air, much to the consternation of traditionally minded courtiers. Then in November 1692 Peter fell ill and for ten days was at death's door. There were rumours that many of his supporters were preparing to flee for fear of reprisals from Tsar Ivan's camp if Peter died. In fact he recovered, with more zest for life than ever, and in July 1693 set off for Archangel to see the sea, an important landmark in his life. This historic journey had much in common with royal outings of old to country estates and monasteries – the accompanying retinue was listed according to rank, from boyars to secretaries, and Peter travelled with a priest, eight choristers, two dwarfs and forty strel'tsy – but more and more the lifestyle of the two courts diverged. Peter celebrated the Russian New Year on 1 September 1693 in Archangel to the sound of gun salutes from both foreign and Russian ships in the harbour, while back in Moscow Tsar Ivan, clad in robes of red velvet, 'deigned to go from his royal chambers to the cathedral' to hear the patriarch celebrate the liturgy 'according to the usual rites'.[16]

Peter did not entirely neglect his religious duties. Just before departing for Archangel he visited his father's favourite place of pilgrimage, the St Sabbas monastery at Zvenigorod, but this was not enough to allay his mother's fears that her son was falling into bad ways and would face mortal danger at Archangel. In letters she urged him to return and Peter found excuses to stay. Natalia's final letter reads:

As a favour to me, my light, come home without delay. I'm so very sad that I can't see you, my light and joy. You wrote that you intend to await the arrival of all the ships, but you have seen the ones that have arrived already, so why do you have to wait for the rest to come in? Don't scorn my request. You write in your letter that you have been to sea even though you promised me that you wouldn't.[17]

Peter returned to Moscow and resumed some of his ceremonial duties, perhaps to make amends for ignoring his mother's wishes. (There were no ships to see in Archangel once the sea froze over, anyway.) On 5 January 1694, the eve of Epiphany, he attended mass in the palace chapel of SS Peter and Paul, while Ivan alone, dressed in a white robe, attended a ceremony of blessing the water and prayers for the royal family in the cathedral. The next morning both tsars appeared in full ceremonial regalia and crowns to participate in a lavish procession of icons and crosses from the cathedral to 'Jordan', a place marked in the ice on the Moscow river just below the Kremlin, where the patriarch dipped a cross into the water and sprinkled the tsars, then the crowds, with consecrated water. This ceremony had long been a major event in the court calendar and was one of the few Muscovite customs to survive into the eighteenth century, perhaps because it could be adapted to include a strong military presence, in this case both strel'tsy and guards, carrying standards and weapons. It is significant that Peter failed to put in an appearance in the cathedral for services for the feast of Metropolitan Philip of Moscow on 8 and 9 January, one of several feasts of leading Moscow churchmen which Patriarchs Joachim and Adrian promoted. The scribes specifically noted his absence, as they did on 12 January, the feast of St Tat'iana, when only Ivan attended the celebrations of his aunt Tat'iana's name day.[18]

The official ceremonies for women's name days continued to be all-male affairs. In general, royal women were mentioned in the court circulars only with reference to births, deaths, weddings and prayers for their long life, so the records for the first half of January 1694 gave no hint that Tsaritsa Natalia was ill. Then on Thursday the 25th, the feast of St Gregory the Theologian, they note her death. The following day her open coffin was placed on a sledge draped in black velvet and taken the short distance from the palace to the Kremlin Ascension convent, to the sound of a funeral knell tolled in the bell tower of St John 'in the ancient manner, with a muffled peal'. Patriarch Adrian walked beside the coffin and behind him Tsar Ivan, preceded by members of the boyar council, courtiers, officials and chief merchants. In the convent chapel Natalia was laid to rest next to her predecessor Maria Miloslavskaia. Peter had been with his mother on the day before she died, but, as the scribes noted, 'the great sovereign tsar and great prince Peter Alekseevich, autocrat of all Great and Little and White Russia, did not process behind the body of the pious sovereign tsaritsa and did not attend the burial'.[19] He visited her tomb on the day after the funeral and again on 1 and 13 February, but mainly it was left to Ivan alone to attend the requiem masses for Natalia's soul.

Peter revealed his true feelings in a letter to the future admiral Fedor Apraksin (1661–1728), brother-in-law of the late Tsar Fedor and one of Peter's most loyal friends: 'It is hard for me to tell you how bereft and sad I feel; my hand is incapable of describing it fully or my heart of expressing it. So, like Noah, a little rested from my misfortune and leaving behind what cannot be restored, I write of what is alive.'[20] In 1706, consoling Gavrila Golovkin on the death of his mother, Peter wrote that if his own mother had lived to such a great old age as Golovkin's he would have been grateful to God.[21] There was real affection between mother and son, who had weathered many crises together, but Peter's restless nature apparently prevented him from waiting at his mother's deathbed or wasting too much time grieving when he had so much to do. The only surviving portraits of Natalia show her as a widow, her hair hidden and her face framed by a severe black head-dress in old Muscovite style, with little hint remaining of the young woman who allegedly relaxed the rules of the female seclusion in the 1670s and enjoyed attending her husband's theatre. She was the person who had provided what security and continuity Peter had known. With her death, many links with the past were broken and lip-service to the old ways could be abandoned more easily.

The Kozhukhovo manoeuvres

In the months following his mother's death, Peter returned to his favourite pursuits. In the summer of 1694 he abandoned Moscow and the court during the pilgrimage season to return to Archangel and pursue his passion for shipbuilding and seafaring. Yet he did not omit to visit the relics of saints on the Solovki islands, where he founded a chapel and erected a cross to commemorate his visit. Much of his attention was focused on preparing for what became known as the 'Kozhukhovo manoeuvres', a mock campaign staged in September 1694 with a force of 30,000 guardsmen and strel'tsy. Tsaritsa Natalia's death deprived those leading men of the Naryshkin camp who lacked close ties with Peter himself of a useful figurehead and threatened a new configuration of forces which might have worked to Peter's disadvantage. Now for the first time Muscovites were presented with a demonstration of the real strength of Peter's 'play' troops, as armies commanded by Prince-Caesar Fedor Romodanovsky, the 'King of Presburg' and Ivan Buturlin, as the 'King of Poland' (in some sources also described as the 'tsars' of Preobrazhenskoe and Semenovskoe), paraded through the city. The staged battle, which featured an assault with explosives on a specially constructed fortress, left twenty-four dead and fifteen injured. Peter placed members of both the

Lopukhin and Naryshkin clans on the losing side, perhaps to make the point that he did not intend to be beholden to *any* of his relatives unless they proved their personal worth. He himself posed as 'King' Fedor's loyal subject, participating in the action as an ordinary bombardier. This was among the first of many such demonstrations of royal authority operating in the guise of assumed humility. No wonder people were confused.

Menshikov

Peter's neglect of the old hierarchies and proprieties was also demonstrated in his choice of companions, not just foreigners but also Russians, of whom the closest was Alexander Danilovich Menshikov (1673–1729). Menshikov's origins were obscure. Later he deliberately kicked over his own traces, acquiring a genealogy which traced his ancestors back to the ninth-century warrior band of Prince Riurik the Viking and a whole portfolio of titles and orders. Some early sources refer to him as 'gentleman' (*dvorianin*), but it was widely believed at the time that Aleksasha or Aleksashenka, as Peter called him, was 'of low birth, lower than the gentry'.[22] Certainly, he had no close links with any of the families of the Muscovite élite. His was a 'rags to riches' tale, a poor boy raised above boyars and princes of ancient lineage eventually to become the most titled man in the realm after the tsar himself.

The circumstances of Menshikov's first meeting with Peter are a matter of conjecture. Thomas Consett, later British chaplain in St Petersburg, tells a story about Alexander being arrested in 1691 for challenging the tsar while on sentry duty, then being rewarded for his vigilance.[23] A favourite version was that his father was a stable lad turned pastry cook and that young Alexander met the tsar while peddling his wares. This story features in anecdotes in which Peter reminds Menshikov many years later that he has the power to return him to his pie-selling origins whenever he wishes ('Alexander! Don't you forget who you were and how I made you what you are now') and Menshikov appears with a tray of pies as a joke.[24] In fact, Menshikov's father served as a non-commissioned officer in the Semenovsky guards regiment and may have been brought to Russia as a prisoner of war from Lithuania and converted to Orthodoxy. In 1693 Alexander's name appears in the second rank of bombardiers of the Preobrazhensky regiment, an indication that he was already close to 'bombardier Piter'. (By this time Peter had taken to writing his name Dutch-style in Latin letters.) They were together at Azov in 1695–96, sharing a tent. By the time of the Grand Embassy in 1697 Peter and Alexander were inseparable.

Menshikov was in some ways on odd choice of companion. Boris Kurakin, who knew French as well as Russian, accused him of being illiterate. His biographer N. I. Pavlenko confirms that, in contrast to the volumes of paper which survive covered with Peter's scrawl, not one letter, or even a corrected draft, has ever been found in Menshikov's hand, although he did learn to form a clear signature. Recent investigations suggest that he could read, but not write. Why was Peter, who valued learning, so lenient with Menshikov in this respect? Charles Whitworth may have come close to the truth when he wrote '[Menshikov's] parts are not extraordinary, his education low, for the Czar would never let him learn to read and write, and his advancement too quick to give him time for observation or experience.'[25] Peter laid so many responsibilities on Menshikov's shoulders that he had no time for systematic study. It is not inconceivable, either, that it suited Peter to have a semi-literate favourite, just as later it pleased him to crown an illiterate foreign peasant woman as his empress and to surround himself with jesters and fools. The key to advancement within the inner circle lay more in 'personal chemistry' than in formal qualifications. Menshikov had a number of qualities which recommended him to Peter. He was versatile, energetic, loyal, but capable of acting on his own initiative. He shared the tsar's sense of humour and capacity for alcohol. Not that Peter was blind to Menshikov's shortcomings, of which ambition was one; throughout the 'honeymoon' of their friendship in the 1690s, Peter stopped short of awarding his friend officer's rank, which he earned only after the battle of Narva in November 1700, and then only the lowest rank of ensign.

It has been hinted, in both foreign memoirs and Russian sources, that there was an additional element to the friendship. Rumours survive in the records of the Preobrazhensky chancellery (where the perpetrators were tortured) that Peter and Menshikov 'lived in sin'. More specifically, a merchant Gavrila Nikitin was arrested in August 1698 for blurting out while drunk that Peter took Menshikov to his bed 'like a whore'.[26] It has also been pointed out (with no evidence) that in the seventeenth century Russian homosexuals shaved, in an attempt to give a new slant to Peter's preference for being clean-shaven, which was later enshrined in a ban on beards. The correspondence between the two men in their youth certainly demonstrated warm feelings. The first extant letter from Peter to Menshikov, dated February 1700, begins 'Mein gertsenkin' (from German: 'child of my heart'). Variations in other letters include 'child of my soul', and 'my heart', as well as the more neutral 'my dearest comrade' and 'my best friend', always expressed in misspelt German-Dutch.[27] Menshikov usually addressed Peter more formally, but occasionally a 'dear heart' crept into the letters which he dictated, too, as in one dated October 1704 addressed to 'mein gerts kaptein'.[28] A letter from Peter in 1703 captures the tone of their friendship more than a decade after they met: 'Be here tomorrow by midday; I really need to see you, and I need to see you here, and tomorrow is a day off [Sunday]. So I ask you to be here tomorrow without fail. I write again, for God's sake, don't put off coming because you think it's unhealthy here. It's really healthy, and I only want to see you.'[29] Life without Aleksasha was 'like food without salt'.[30]

We should beware of reading modern nuances into letters written in Russian three hundred years ago or accepting rumours at face value. Peter's relationship with Menshikov was a complex one, which changed with the years, through both men's subsequent marriages and shared successes and disappointments. It also had its violent side. The Austrian envoy Johannes Korb, in Russia in 1698–99, witnessed several occasions on which Menshikov felt the tsar's fists, including one when Peter knocked him out, 'so that he lay stretched at full length, quite like a dying man at the feet of irate Majesty'.[31] Menshikov may have become rich and powerful, building up his own clientele networks over the years, but he was ultimately Peter's creation. They could never be equals.

The Azov campaigns

Soon the two young men were to have the opportunity to see real military action. In the wake of the disastrous Crimean campaigns of 1687 and 1689, which attracted little allied support, Russia began to lose confidence in the Holy League, fearing to be excluded from any future peace negotiations with the Turks. In an attempt to recover Russia's prestige, gain a stronger bargaining position with the allies and ward off Turkish attacks on Ukraine, in 1695 Peter reopened hostilities in a campaign against the Turkish coastal fort of Azov at the mouth of the River Don. He dispatched two armies, the joint force of Boris Petrovich Sheremetev and the Ukrainian hetman Ivan Mazepa to the Dnieper to deflect the Tatars from the mouth of the Don and a smaller unit consisting of the Preobrazhensky and Semenovsky guards and strel'tsy on river craft down the Don to Azov itself.

In this, as in some subsequent campaigns, Peter ceded nominal authority to others. The commander-in-chief was Aleksei Semenovich Shein while the tsar marched as a bombardier in the Preobrazhensky regiment. The first Azov campaign was a failure, which Peter blamed on multiple command, tactical errors and technical deficiencies. In particular, the Turks were able to replenish supplies from the sea with no Russian ships to hinder them. He hired foreign engineering specialists for the next campaign in an effort to avoid such fiascos as an incident in which mines planted on ramparts far away from the enemy blew up 130 Russians without doing any damage to the Turks.

On 29 January 1696 Tsar Ivan died and on the following day was buried. The funeral ceremony observed a time-honoured pattern: the coffin was borne out of the palace and into the Cathedral of the Archangel Michael to the solemn toll of a funeral bell. The patriarch officiated, walking in front of the coffin at the rear of a long procession of priests; behind came secular

persons, headed by Peter and prominent boyars, followed by Ivan's widow
Praskovia and various female members of her household (but not, according
to official records, Ivan's sisters). In the cathedral, mass was celebrated, then
the funeral service was sung over the open coffin, after which Peter took leave
of his brother, followed by courtiers, who went up to kiss the dead man's hand
'with floods of tears and wailing'.[32] Finally Ivan was laid to rest in the cathedral next to his brother Tsar Fedor. Throughout the following forty-day
period courtiers kept a twenty-four-hour vigil in groups of ten. This ceremony, so fitting in its simple dignity for a tsar whose role had been almost
purely ceremonial, was the last of the old-style royal funerals. Peter's departure from this world almost exactly twenty-nine years later was to be marked
in a different place and a different manner. Ivan's death robbed him of a
brother whom he had always held in affection, and of a figurehead. From now
on Peter was free to elaborate his alternative scenarios and the traditionalist
camp found themselves without a tsar.

Both the failure at Azov and the death of Ivan forced Peter to take stock.
Early in 1696 he implemented a number of measures, characterised by what
was to become the typically 'Petrine' use of speed, technology, mass recruitment and command from above. The prime example was the preparation of
galleys at Voronezh on the Don for a renewed campaign in 1696, a huge effort
in which thousands of the tsar's subjects were expected to do their bit, from
the leading churchmen and merchants who reluctantly supplied the cash to
the hapless labourers drafted in to hack ships out of green wood. At the end
of May 1696 Peter's land and water-borne forces – 46,000 Russian troops,
15,000 Ukrainian Cossacks, 5,000 Don Cossacks and 3,000 Kalmyks – laid
siege to Azov. By early June a Russian flotilla was able to take to the sea and
cut off the Turks' access to reinforcements. Russia's success was also aided by
General Gordon's plan of a 'rolling rampart' and the services of Austrian engi-
neers. On 18 July the fortress surrendered.

Peter's first military victory prompted some striking cultural manifes-
tations. There were services of thanksgiving, to be sure – in Russia as in every
other European country victory and defeat were inextricably linked with
God's will – and prayers for the souls of the dead, but from now on religious
processions were supplemented by secular parades bristling with 'pagan' symbols, imperial Roman references and imagery. Triumphal gates of classical
design were erected, bearing Julius Caesar's words: 'I came. I saw. I conquered.' There were references to Christian Rome, too, and stock comparisons of Peter with the Emperor Constantine the Great. Peter marched in the
parade wearing Western dress behind the official heroes Admiral Lefort and
General Shein, while the religious authority was parodied by Prince-Pope
Nikita Zotov in a carriage. This was the first major public display of the new
manners, which until now had by and large been confined to semi-private
indulgence at Preobrazhenskoe or in the Foreign Quarter.

Ivan's death removed the main *raison-d'être* of the old-style Muscovite court, for which Peter had no use, except sometimes to mock it. Many formal rituals now had to be enacted without any tsar at the centre, while Peter's own circle was presided over by Prince-Caesar Fedor Romodanovsky. Such developments did not go unremarked. At some time in 1696–97 Father Avraamy of St Andrew's monastery in Moscow handed Peter a missive. Avraamy had heard rumours about Peter's bad behaviour and decided to give the young tsar some good advice before it was too late, beginning his tract with the story of the Creation and the warning that 'good tsars give right judgement, bad ones forget the fear of God'. He appealed to Peter to resume the straight and narrow path, to heed the advice of churchmen rather than laymen. Good men had hoped that after Peter's marriage he would abandon childish games, but Peter still indulged in 'jests and japes' and activities unpleasant to God. War games and sailing were distracting him from his duties, which he had left in the hands of intriguers and embezzlers, 'wicked' power-seeking boyars. Avraamy ended up in a monastery in Kolomna (a mild punishment), where he continued to write to the tsar.[33] Other critics wrote anonymous letters, a time-honoured way of getting a message to the tsar. A typical example, left in a church in Moscow, warned that Peter had been 'seduced by Germans and German women into the Latin faith' and was even being poisoned by them. The author lamented the lowering of moral standards and the prevalence of smoking and advised the tsar to attend church services to avert a Turkish attack. Another letter described Peter's entourage as 'a swarm of demons'.[34]

Peter paid little attention to such protests by 'fanatics', but he was disturbed by the so-called Ivan Tsykler affair, an alleged plot against him masterminded by a group of state servitors from leading families. The participants, who included Fedor Pushkin and Aleksei Sokovnin, voiced dark fears about Peter's decision to take a trip abroad, due to begin in spring 1697. Sokovnin was horrified by the inclusion of two of his own sons in the list of young nobles to be sent abroad to study. According to Patrick Gordon, 'they all confessed that they had an intention to have murdered his Majesty and to that purpose had tryed to draw the streltsees to their party'.[35] Mention of the strel'tsy and of bringing back Golitsyn and Sophia led Peter to order the exhumation of the corpse of Ivan Miloslavsky, who had died in his bed in 1685 and whom Peter had always regarded as one of Sophia's major associates. The open coffin was brought to the executioner's block on a sledge drawn by pigs, and the blood of the executed Tsykler and his accomplices was 'sprinkled on the dead carkass which in some places was rotten & consumed'.[36] All the corpses were then left on view on Red Square until the summer. This gruesome spectacle (similar displays were common in Western countries) occurred just a few days before Peter set off for the West, a grim confirmation that he had no intention of being diverted from his plans to travel abroad.

III

The Grand Embassy
1697–99

I am a student and I seek teachers. (Inscription on Peter's seal)

Peter Mikhailov

In March 1697 Peter left Russia for the first time, bound for Western Europe. One of the stated aims of this so-called Grand or Great Embassy was to publicise Russia's recent success at Azov in the hope of obtaining further aid for the alliance against the Turks, while paying courtesy calls on friendly European rulers 'for the confirmation of ancient friendship and love, and the weakening of the Turkish sultan, the Crimean khan and all their Muslim hordes, the enemies of the Cross of Our Lord'.[1] For Peter this also was to be a personal voyage of discovery in his quest for practical knowledge, ideas and inspiration; he carried a seal with the inscription: 'I am a student and I seek teachers.' He was to see with his own eyes the extent to which Russia differed from the countries which he visited in its social, economic, technological and cultural development and to find confirmation of what he already must have sensed in Moscow's Foreign Quarter, which offered an intriguing glimpse of many aspects of Western urban life, but without the historical setting and cultural and social diversity of the real towns – Amsterdam, London, Berlin, Dresden, Vienna – that Peter saw during his travels. Not the least of the problems he had to confront was Europe's negative image of Russia, and indeed of himself as the exotic ruler of a 'rude and barbarous kingdom' who attracted more curiosity than respect.

The irony is that Peter tantalised the curious public even more by attempting to conceal his true identity under a commoner's disguise. The 250-strong contingent which left Moscow in March 1697 with a thousand sledges was headed not by the tsar but by a trio of plenipotentiaries: Franz Lefort, Fedor Golovin and the Foreign Office official Prokopy Voznitsyn. 'Never has there been such a big embassy,' Lefort wrote to his brother Jacob. 'I have six pages, four dwarfs, about twenty liveried servants, who will all be splendidly dressed, five trumpeters, musicians, a pastor, surgeons, physicians and a company of

well-equipped soldiers.'[2] Although grand in scale, the delegation was traditional in its composition and in the exhaustive instructions (running to
thirty-three volumes) issued to it by the Foreign Office in the tsar's name. But
it was augmented by a decidedly non-standard component: thirty-five
Russian 'volunteers' bound for the Dutch Republic to study shipbuilding and
navigation, among them Peter Mikhailov, a decurion (*desiatnik*) or officer in
charge of a unit of ten men, and his best friend, Alexander Menshikov.

Peter's decision to travel incognito has usually been attributed to his
loathing of diplomatic protocol and his desire to retain the freedom to work
and observe without getting bogged down in official duties. It was a signal to
his hosts that the usual formalities should be suspended, rather than a sus-
tained attempt to conceal his identity, which would have been doomed to
failure. As an excited correspondent of the London *Post Boy* informed its
readers in August 1697, 'The Prince is said to be 7 foot high!'[3] (By now he had
in fact reached the height of 6 feet 7 inches.) Peter dropped his disguise when
it seemed important, notably in Vienna in June–July 1698 when he took part
in key negotiations about the future of the anti-Turkish alliance. The sub-
terfuge may also have been an attempt to hide for as long as possible the fact
that the tsar had left Russia (an unprecedented event in peacetime), to dupe
not only the Turks, who might stage an attack in his absence, but also the
tsar's subjects, who were not accustomed to their sovereigns subjecting themselves to the hazards of the heretical West. Muscovite politics was an intensely
personal affair, revolving around the ruler's physical presence, and an absent
tsar left an uncomfortable vacuum in the seat of power. Edicts issued in
Moscow during the Embassy maintained such familiar formulae as 'the great
sovereign decreed', giving no hint that Peter was missing. There is also a less
easily definable aspect to Peter's incognito, which we shall encounter again
and again: a love of play-acting and 'pretendership' which verged on a desire
actually to be someone else. The Embassy charade was a natural extension of
the play regiments and the mock court, a provocative challenge to Peter's
companions, who were forced to collude and even assume different identities
themselves. Probably only a crowned autocrat with Peter's forceful personality
could get away with it.

Peter's disguise attracted rather than deflected attention. Peter Lefort,
Franz's nephew, writing to relatives in Switzerland in the middle of August
1697, found it impossible to keep the secret: 'I want to tell you, without subjecting myself to the risk of actually writing it, that the person whom you
mentioned is with us. And everyone knows. We did all we could to hide the
fact but it was impossible .... The rumour is so wide-spread that people run
after every Muscovite thinking that it's His Majesty.' In early September he
wrote: 'We are no longer hiding the fact of the tsar's presence as it would be
pointless.'[4] Peter's semi-incognito was to produce some awkward incidents,
one of which had very serious repercussions.

The insult at Riga. Prussia

In Riga in Swedish Livonia, which the Embassy reached on 31 March 1697, Peter tried to inspect ships in the harbour and to sketch a plan of the fortifications, which understandably aroused the suspicions of the Swedish governor, who at the same time made no special arrangement to receive or honour Mr Mikhailov. Peter was asked to move along by armed guards. Apparently insulted that he had *not* been treated like a tsar and outraged by the high price of accommodation and transport (the onset of spring forced the Embassy to exchange their sleds for wheeled vehicles), he left Riga on 8 April, three days before the main party. Bad memories of the city were stored up for future reference. Turning the East–West rhetoric of 'them and us' on its head, he later referred to his reception as 'barbaric and Tatar-like'.[5] The Swedes claimed, on the contrary, that they had treated Peter's delegation with all possible civility, greeted them with ceremonial gun salutes and given them the best lodgings. They pointed out that it was not usual for diplomatic personnel to look around forts with telescopes and make sketches of fortifications. For the time being, though, relations with Sweden remained officially cordial. In December 1697 Peter congratulated the sixteen-year-old King Charles XII on his accession and promised to keep the established treaties in perpetuity.

Peter had a better time in Mitau at the court of the duke of Courland, who arranged a programme of feasts and entertainments, at which Peter behaved like a 'second Bacchus'. On 20 April he set off for Libau, where on 2 May he embarked on the ship *Saint George*, docking three days later at Pilau in Brandenburg. On 9 May, well ahead of the main Embassy, which was welcomed with splendid parades on 18 May, he had his first meeting with Frederick, the elector of Brandenburg, who respected the 'high personage's' disguise by putting on a splendid firework display which included an illuminated screen with the words 'Vivat Tsar and Great Prince Peter Alekseevich', allegedly addressed to the tsar back in Moscow. In Königsberg Peter Mikhailov took lessons in the 'bombardier's art' from Peter von Sternfeld, who awarded him a proficiency certificate. In June Lefort signed treaties with the Prussians on friendship, trade and training opportunities for Russians, although assurances of mutual aid in the case of enemy attack were only expressed orally. Peter spent several weeks in Pilau awaiting the latest news from Poland, where a contest for the throne was in progress, and was pleased to hear of the victory of Frederick Augustus, elector of Saxony, the candidate favoured by Russia and Denmark, over the French-backed Prince de Conti. On 30 June he set off for the Dutch Republic.

In Koppenbrügge near Hanover Peter met Sophia-Charlotte, the wife of the elector of Brandenburg, and her mother, Sophia, electress of Hanover, who invited him to dinner and dancing. In letters the two women later remarked on the tsar's 'rustic' table manners, his shyness and lack of gallantry.

He seemed more at ease with the dwarfs in his party, whom every now and then he kissed, than dancing with the German ladies; their whalebone corsets puzzled the 'Muscovites', who had little experience of socialising in mixed company. Even so, the electresses were charmed by Peter's 'natural manner and informality'. If he had a better education, they thought, he would be a splendid person, because he had 'much merit and much native wit'.[6] Such social encounters were an essential part of Peter's Western education and contributed to his vision of civilising Russia, which included ending the traditional segregation of men and women.

The little house at Zaandam

When Peter met the electresses he was dressed like a Dutch sailor, in anticipation of his arrival on 8 August in the Amsterdam suburb of Zaandam, where he rented a room at the back of a blacksmith's house. The house was tiny, with a box-like guest room only slightly longer than the height of an average person, but it suited Peter, who preferred confined spaces to grand palaces. In fact, he spent only about a week in his cramped lodgings. On 15 August, uttering the words 'Too many people!', he was forced to quit by curious crowds, who even clambered on to neighbouring roofs to catch a glimpse of the tsar of Muscovy. Zaandam residents handed down many tales about Peter, for example how he was partial to a glass (or two) of gin and liked to converse in Dutch. Several anecdotes centre on the themes of modesty and mistaken identity, such as the story of Peter's conversation with a shipwright's wife: 'Your husband's a skilled worker,' says Peter. 'I know him well because I built a ship with him.' She asks: 'Are you a carpenter too, then?' and Peter replies: 'Yes, I'm a carpenter too.'[7] In reality, few people were taken in by Peter's disguise, although many deemed it sensible to play along with it.

Peter chose the Zaandam cottage for practical reasons – it was on a canal about five minutes from the quay where he was planning to work – but the little house also formed part of the stage set for his play-acting, in this case in the role of ship's carpenter Peter Mikhailov. It also provided material for subsequent myth-making about the Carpenter Tsar, both in the later imperial and in the Soviet eras. Not everyone approved of such 'affectations' of modesty. When Napoleon visited Zaandam in 1811 he expressed disapproval of Peter's inappropriate sailor habits and the 'absurdity' of the by then half-ruined little house. But Napoleon, we recall, rose to be emperor and to rule half of Europe from humble beginnings, unlike the hereditary tsar Peter, who chose to simulate humility. In 1865 Prince Henry of the Netherlands commissioned a wooden structure to protect Peter's cottage and in 1886 William III gave it as a gift to Alexander III, who sponsored a major rescue operation, during which the whole building was lifted on to a stone foundation and

wooden and iron supports were built. In 1895 a stone casing was added, which
survives to the present, as does an inscription by Alexander I: 'Nothing is too
small for a great man.'

The Dutch Republic

Peter transferred to the centre of Amsterdam where he was looked after by the
burgomaster Nicolaes Witsen, who had visited Russia and shared Peter's
interest in ships and collecting curiosities. On 17 August he toured the city
and on subsequent days enjoyed firework displays, one of which featured four
columns supporting a globe with 'nautical wonders' at the corners, and inside
a double eagle with the Latin inscription VIVAT TSAR PETER ALEKSEEVICH,
flanked by figures of Mars and Hercules. The Dutch East India Company
agreed to admit 'the distinguished personage living incognito' together with
ten of his companions to work in their yards under instruction from the
master shipwright Claas Paul. (The Russian team saw the launch of their first
frigate, the *Peter and Paul*, on 9 November.) On 1 September in Utrecht Peter
had his first (secret) meeting with the Dutch stadtholder William of Orange,
since 1688 also king of England. The details of their conversation were not
officially recorded, although various texts survive which emphasise Peter's
admiration for William ('the most brave and most generous Hero of the
Age'), his distrust of France and his desire to promote trade.[8] A week later the
king staged a sumptuous dinner for his guest. On 22 September the whole
Embassy was received by the Estates General in the Hague, a reception which
took some time to organise as a result of different opinions of protocol. Their
hosts explained to the Russians that the deputies were not the servants of a
monarch but held high office in their own right and merited appropriate
respect. This proved an inopportune moment to request money from the
Dutch, who pleaded poverty as a result of the Nine Years' War with France,
just ended by the peace of Ryswick (autumn 1697), not to mention the fact
that France, with whom they had just concluded peace, was the Turkish
sultan's protector.

Peter spent four and a half months in the Dutch Republic, much of it
devoted to studying shipbuilding, punctuated by sailing and naval displays
and visits to windmills, engravers' workshops, hospitals, botanical gardens
and other sights. He was particularly fascinated by the curiosities and rarities,
assembled from all corners of the globe, in which the Republic abounded. He
visited Jacob de Wilde's gemstone collection and the museums of Levinus
Vincent and Frederick Ruysch, highlights of which were about '50 small
bodies, undecayed, preserved in alcohol', some of which later ended up in
Peter's own chamber of curiosities in St Petersburg, where they can be seen to
this day. Peter also attended some of Professor Ruysch's gruesomely illustrated

public lectures at the Amsterdam Anatomical Theatre, one of the places where he acquired a taste for performing dissections and autopsies. What may seem a macabre interest to modern readers was not so unusual in Peter's time; Samuel Pepys, for example, describes a similar theatre in seventeenth-century London where audiences regularly watched dissections while eating their lunch. Peter took away from this part of northern Europe the impression of a well-ordered state, well-planned towns with clean streets and solid houses, thriving commerce and crafts, and a people in control of their environment. Many years later he advised the trainee architect Ivan Korobov to 'learn the manner of Dutch architecture, especially foundations which are needed here for we have the same conditions with regard to the lowness of the land and also the thinness of the walls; also learn how to measure the proportions of gardens and to decorate them with trees and figures, which nowhere in the world are so fine as in Holland.'⁹ No major Dutch architects are known to have worked in St Petersburg, but the Dutch principles which Peter admired – the intersection of the city by canals, the construction of embankments, the formal layout of gardens, and the use of brick and tiles, including blue and white Delft tiles for interiors – were later reflected in his new city of Sankt-Piter-Burkh, which came to be known, among other things as 'New Amsterdam'.

England

On 9 January 1698 Peter left the Embassy proper in the Dutch Republic and sailed across the Channel with his team of trainees to England in Vice-Admiral Sir David Mitchell's ship, the *Yorke*. As it was later recounted in the preface to the Naval Statute (1720), having acquired practical experience in Holland, Peter turned to England (not on his original itinerary) to acquire theoretical knowledge 'in the Mathematical way'.¹⁰ In fact, most of Peter's time in England, too, was devoted to practical activity and visiting the sights rather than to theoretical studies, for which he had little patience. There were ample opportunities for acquiring a range of naval expertise, from a better understanding of the role of a navy in a modern state to getting hands-on experience of building ships in the Royal Naval Dockyards at Deptford.

English motives for welcoming this strange guest were chiefly commercial. The Russia Company, the descendant of the trading company formed by the first English merchants in Moscow in the 1550s, was pursuing a long-term policy of recovering commercial privileges lost in 1649, when Tsar Alexis's government had protested about the execution of Charles I. In the end, the winner of a contract to sell tobacco to Russia, signed in April 1698, was not the Company but Peregrine Osborne, marquis of Carmarthen, who was able to tempt the tsar to visit England in the first place with the gift of the frigate

Royal Transport, the most modern vessel of its kind afloat. As far as political
alliances were concerned, the English still regarded Russia's role in the world
as marginal. Russia was not in competition for colonies overseas. It had no
navy to speak of. They acknowledged Russia's success at Azov, but the port's
location further encouraged the view that Russian foreign policy was distinctly eastern-oriented. A contemporary poem portrayed Peter and William
as 'the Twins of Fate', each illustrious in his own sphere:

> [Peter's] Glist'ning Sabre on proud *Asia* Gleams,
> Dazling the Frighted *Tarters* by its Beams;
> Its Conquering Steel shall to the *East* give Law,
> Whilst NASSAW's Scepter keeps the *West* in Awe.[11]

Over the next two decades Britain was to watch the growth of Russian sea
power in the Baltic with growing anxiety, but for the time being relations
were cordial and no restrictions were imposed on Peter's own shipbuilding
studies or on his hiring British naval experts for use in his 'eastern' campaigns.

Kneller

We have no clear idea of what Peter looked like before he embarked on the
Grand Embassy. The few surviving early 'portraits', as we saw earlier, are
either stylised effigies or imaginative reconstructions by foreigners. In 1698
the twenty-five-year-old tsar finally comes to life in the famous full-length
portrait painted in London by Sir Godfrey Kneller and now hanging in
Kensington Palace in London. Even if Kneller's was not the first true likeness
of Peter painted from life (there is a reference to a sitting in Königsberg in
1697, for example) it was certainly the most successful of the early images. Sir
Godfrey (1646–1723), court painter to a series of English monarchs, was a
busy man. He probably painted only the face (the Austrian resident minister
Hofmann recorded a sitting in early February), which meant that Peter did
not pose in the setting of the completed painting, which would have been
added by Kneller's assistants. The master repeated the same set formulae –
column and crown to our left, warship in the background to the right, the
tsar in royal ermine and armour – as he used in his portrait of James II
(1683–84, National Portrait Gallery, London), which itself was a variation on
a fairly hackneyed theme. It was lucky that the warship motif from James's
portrait (James was high admiral of the fleet) was so appropriate for the sea-
loving tsar, while the emblematic armour, of a kind which was no longer
worn in battle, and a marshal's baton, honoured Peter as a military leader. But
the very fact that in West European terms Kneller's portrait is conventional
and unremarkable, albeit apparently a good likeness, immediately recognised

by contemporaries who saw it, makes it something of a landmark in the history of Western perceptions of Russian rulers. All traces of Russian exoticism and barbarism were expunged, to produce an unambiguously Western royal image in the grand register. For perhaps the first time a Russian ruler was depicted as 'one of us' as opposed to 'one of them'.

To the wider British public in 1698, of course, Russia was still 'as remote as China ... the land of ice, of barbarism and of ignorance'.[12] That a Muscovite monarch should come to the West to receive education and culture and take them back home with him instead of waiting passively for them to arrive or (more likely) resisting them was regarded as remarkable. Peter's aim, British observers agreed, was 'to see countries more civilised than his own, and especially nations who have developed a Navy, which is his master passion' and 'to take patterns for civilising his own rude people'.[13] It seemed natural, then, to honour Peter as a token European ruler in the making, as Kneller did in his portrait, the features of which soon reached a wider public through the medium of prints (notably by the famous engraver John Smith) and miniatures on enamel, and also spawned numerous copies on canvas.

There are other portraits of Peter from this period, however, which remind us that the break with Old Russia was far from complete and that artists abroad still catered for a public which expected its Muscovite monarchs to look exotic. A painting by the Dutch artist Pieter van de Werff (1665–1718) shows Peter dressed in a more native style, which at least one commentator thought was more like Peter than the 'idealised' portrait by Kneller, who was too used to 'flattering lords and ladies'.[14] A print by the British engraver William Faithorne, based on Kneller's likeness, also presents a more Muscovite Peter in a fur hat, while a medal made by the Saxon engraver Christian Wermuth to commemorate the Grand Embassy presents a sort of composite Western–Eastern Peter in laurels and armour but wearing a fur-trimmed robe, inscribed CZAR ET AUTOCRATOR ... CULTIORES EVROPAE REGIONES INVISIT (he visited the most educated regions of Europe). Similar contrasts may be observed in two experimental half-roubles minted in Moscow in 1699, the first showing Peter full face as in icons, wearing the Cap of Monomach, the second as a Roman emperor in profile, with laurel wreath and mantle. After 1700 the Muscovite Peter was more or less to disappear from view.

Impressions of foggy Albion

Peter made the most of his three months in England. In London he visited the Royal Observatory, the Mint (in the Tower), the Arsenal, and the Royal Society. He went to Portsmouth and on the way back visited Windsor Castle, where an Order of the Garter ceremony may have given him some ideas for his own Order of St Andrew, which he instituted in 1699, and also spent a night in Christ Church College, Oxford. Sometimes he just wandered round the streets. On 9 March, writes the compiler of his journal, 'a female giant came to see us for lunch. She stretched out her arm and without bending the decurion walked under the arm.'[15] He enjoyed 'the choicest Secrets and Experiments' conducted for him by the physician Moses Stringer, which included dissolving and separating metals.[16] and some trips to the theatre, where he saw, among other things, *The Rival Queens, or the Death of Alexander the Great* by Nathanial Lee. He also had a fling with the famous actress Laetitia Cross.

Peter appreciated the British first and foremost as seafarers, as encapsulated in a statement, recorded by the British engineer John Perry and in other sources, 'that he thinks it a much happier Life to be an Admiral in England, than Czar in Russia'.[17] If he really did say that he found the British Isles 'the best, most beautiful and happiest place on earth', he surely had the seas, rivers and ships of 'foggy Albion' in mind.[18] For Peter the highlights of his visit included sailing on the Thames, inspecting ships and attending a naval review at Portsmouth. But notwithstanding William III's view that Peter was 'interested only in ships and navigation and is quite indifferent to the beauties of nature, to splendid buildings and parks',[19] he did take an interest in non-naval matters. Some architectural historians may have found William III's architecture over-plain and lacking in grandeur, but this was probably a positive virtue to a young monarch with modest resources and a taste for small buildings. Peter visited Kensington Palace, which William bought in 1689 and had restored and altered by Sir Christopher Wren (1632–1723), and Wren's new wing at Hampton Court. Wren's majestic Royal Naval Hospital at Greenwich, with splendid views across the Thames, was begun in 1694, but was still mostly a building site when Peter saw it. Just behind it he would have seen Inigo Jones's Queen's House (1616), the first classical building in England and beyond it Greenwich Park, recently laid out in formal style by the French garden designer André Le Nôtre (1613–1700), creator of the gardens at Versailles, who also designed the formal gardens at Hampton Court. Later albums of prints of British mansions and parks were to provide Peter with ideas for his own projects.

In walks around the City of London where, the journal of his visit records, 'he climbed the column commemorating the Great Fire of London called the Monument' Peter saw Wren's numerous parish churches, some with spires and towers reminiscent of his own later Peter-Paul Cathedral. St Paul's Cathedral, founded in 1675, did not get its dome until 1702 and was declared complete only in 1711, but its imposing scale may have reminded Peter that even in a country like Britain, where the church was firmly subordinated to the crown, grand ecclesiastical architecture remained a prominent feature in the capital city and glorified the monarch as well as God. The Anglican church interested Peter greatly. He visited the archbishop of Canterbury at Lambeth Palace, where he saw an ordination and a service. One of the churchmen whom Peter met was Bishop Gilbert Burnet (1679–1715), who wrote that Peter was most attentive when he explained the authority that Christian emperors assumed in matters of religion, and the supremacy of the English kings. They discussed icons, the saints and the formulation of the Trinity. At the same time, Burnet found Peter 'a man of very hot temper, soon inflamed and very brutal in his passion'.[20]

Peter was curious about the British system of government and several stories survive on this theme. In order to see the king in parliament, for example, he was 'placed in a gutter upon the house-top, to peep in at a window, where he made so ridiculous a figure that neither king nor people could forbear laughing, which obliged him to retire sooner than he intended'. This gave the Austrian ambassador occasion to report 'the rarest of things: a king on the throne and an emperor on the roof'.[21] The official journal fixes the date of this visit as 2 April, when Peter attended a joint session of the Lords and Commons. The entry for this day describes how he heard 'various orators and the reading of law suits, bills and addresses', which, according to an anecdote, prompted the response: 'It's fun to listen to the sons of the fatherland telling the king the blunt truth. We ought to learn from the English in this respect.'[22] This remark should not be interpreted as a statement in favour of parliamentary government, however. It was the Lords whom Peter observed speaking 'truthfully', who in their capacity as advisers physically surrounding the king may have struck him as not much different from his own boyar council, even though the lords did not prostrate themselves before the king or refer to themselves as his 'slaves', practices which Peter was trying to eliminate at home. He probably regarded the king as an absolute monarch much like himself.

In fact, although on paper Britain was a strong monarchy – the king could declare war and make peace, call and dissolve parliament, issue pardons, appoint cabinet ministers and officers – the royal finances were limited (money was granted by parliament) and the monarchy was not protected from public opinion. Not surprisingly, Peter was struck by the contradictory messages about British royal power which the Tower of London provided. On the one hand, he learned that the Tower housed state prisoners, sent there by rulers with powers much like his own; on the other hand, the axes which cut off the heads of Mary Stuart and Charles I were displayed, but hidden from Peter in case he threw them into the Thames to express his disapproval.[23] Peter rejected the accusations made by foreigners that he ruled his subjects like 'slaves'. He was adamant that 'English freedom is not appropriate here [in Russia] .... You have to know your people to know how to govern them. I am happy to hear anything useful from the lowest of my subjects; their hands, legs and tongues aren't fettered.'[24] This anecdote represents the relationship between tsar and subjects in traditional, patrimonial terms. In Russia people were free to appeal or speak to the *tsar* (although in law direct petitions were discouraged), but not to channel their appeals through institutionalised bodies. The independent judiciary, parliament and corporate bodies, which in Britain regulated relations between ruler and ruled, were absent.

In London Peter and his companions were confronted with a bewildering choice of products – trade and commerce were the foundation of Britain's wealth – and what he bought, both for personal and public use, tells us much about his priorities. His largest purchase was tobacco, a commodity which Peter regarded not only as a source of profit but also as a signifier of cultural reform. (Russian conservatives denounced the evils of smoking for religious, not health reasons.) He bought mathematical and navigational instruments, watches and clocks, clothes, wigs, books, boxes, swords, and a coffin as a model for Russian coffin-makers. An intriguing purchase were some lawyers' gowns in black cloth. Their fate is unknown, but it is possible that they were intended for the use of the Drunken Assembly. He also bought several black slaves, at £30 for a female, £20 for a boy.[25] Although serfdom had died out in Britain long ago, slavery was still a flourishing business in the empire, even though comparatively few black slaves went to owners in England. These live purchases remind us that Peter shared the taste of many contemporary European rulers for human 'exotica', as 'blackamoors' were regarded, and for freaks of nature ('monsters') such as dwarfs and giants, which were collected with the same enthusiasm as rare shells, plants and animals.

Peter left vivid impressions in England, where from the start he confounded expectations of how a monarch should behave. When he first arrived in London, repeating his Dutch experience he rented a small house near the Strand with just two rooms on each storey, which gave him easy access to the Thames. When the prince of Denmark (husband of the future Queen Anne) paid a visit he was surprised to find the tsar still in bed and three or four other persons crammed into the tiny room. They had to open all the windows to clear the terrible stench.[26] Even more notorious is the story of the damage which Peter and his friends inflicted on the famous diarist John Evelyn's house and garden (regarded as a horticultural marvel) at Sayes Court, their lodgings in Deptford, which resulted in a bill for £350 9s. 6d. damages.[27] The story about Peter pushing his companions in wheelbarrows through the famous holly hedge (described by Evelyn as 'impregnable') is anecdotal, but there are records of paving being ripped up and trees and plants destroyed. Evelyn himself was away at the time, but his servant referred to the Russian guests as 'right nasty'. Despite such bad behaviour, however, Peter generally aroused admiration rather than condemnation. The uncouth and untutored nosiness of a 'giant-genius' determined to reform both himself and his people, to overcome prejudice, superstition and ignorance by learning from others, formed part of a potent image which allowed Russia to be viewed simultaneously as 'Oriental' and alien, but also potentially 'one of us', albeit a junior, trainee version. If imitation is the best form of flattery, the British had every reason to approve Peter's good sense and forgive his naughty behaviour.

The strel'tsy revolt of 1698

In April 1698 Peter returned briefly to the Dutch Republic before heading south-east towards Vienna for his next major engagement. A correspondent in London sent Emperor Leopold of Austria, a stickler for etiquette who had ruled his country since 1658, a sneak preview:

> While he was here he went around all the time dressed as a shipwright, so who knows what sort of dress he will assume when he is in Your Imperial Majesty's court. He did not see much of the king as he refused to change his life style and had his lunch at 11 a.m. and his supper at 7 p.m., then went straight to bed and got up at four in the morning, which was very trying for the Englishmen who had to attend him.[28]

In early May Peter had news from Prince-Caesar in Moscow about a mutiny of the strel'tsy, which apparently had been successfully quelled, although Peter was not convinced that the culprits had been treated with suitable severity. Later in May he spent two weeks in Dresden, where he visited the chamber of curiosities, the arsenal and foundry and the castle at Fürstenberg, where he was treated to a shooting display and a tasting in some famous wine cellars. (For the rest of his life Peter did not stint himself when it came to good wines, which he purchased abroad in large consignments.) On 16 June the Embassy arrived in Vienna, where it enjoyed a lavish welcome. Peter was on his best behaviour at his first meeting with Emperor Leopold, unusually attentive to the emperor and his family, despite initially committing a *faux pas* by galloping into the audience chamber and overstepping the spot in the centre of the room where the two were supposed to meet. Highlights of Peter's stay in Vienna were two costumed balls, one given for his name day on 29 June (9 July) and another on 11 (21) July, which Peter attended dressed as a Friesian peasant, whom Emperor Leopold, getting into the spirit of things, toasted with the words: 'I know that you are acquainted with the great Russian monarch, so let us drink to his health.'[29] There was more show than substance to the formal negotiations, for the Austrians were on the point of making a separate peace. Their decisive victory over the Turks at Zenta (11 September 1697 NS) allowed them to press for peace on the basis of *uti possidetis* and to sign the Treaty of Carlowitz late in 1698.

Peter had already said his farewells to the emperor and was on the point of leaving for Venice, a watery paradise where a grand reception awaited him, when another letter arrived from Prince-Caesar reporting that the strel'tsy had mutinied again. Alarmed, he decided to cancel the next stage of his journey and return to Moscow without seeing Italy. (This is the official story. A Russian historian has argued that Peter did in fact visit Venice incognito on 19–20 July, the only gap in the verifiable schedule. If the visit did take place, there would have been little time for more than a fleeting impression.[30]) Leaving Voznitsyn in Vienna to continue talks, which had reached a dead end, and accompanied by Lefort, Golovin and Menshikov, Peter made rapid progress. News that the revolt had been suppressed did not persuade him to resume his planned itinerary. No doubt he had little confidence, given their assurances about the first outbreak, in the ability of his associates in Moscow to act firmly.

On his homeward journey, passing through Rawa in Galicia, Peter met Augustus, the new king of Poland, one of the most colourful characters of his era, who pursued titles, wealth and women with equal energy, even if the number of his illegitimate offspring has been exaggerated. The tsar and the king discussed their common interests and Peter expressed his wish to avenge the 'insult' suffered in Riga. Peter learned that Augustus had designs on Swedish Livonia, which offered his new Polish kingdom outlets to the sea. He also knew that Denmark was eager to reduce Sweden's possessions in north Germany and to discourage the ties of their neighbours the dukes of Holstein-Gottorp with the Swedish crown. Thus the outline of an alliance against Sweden was taking shape. Peter was captivated by the self-confident Augustus, an enthusiastic drinker and sportsman ten years his senior, and when he returned to Moscow he swaggered around in a tunic and sword presented to him by his new friend. A decade later, as we shall see, the senior–junior roles were to be reversed.

In terms of its stated diplomatic aims, the Grand Embassy was a failure, indeed was rendered redundant while it was still in progress, but it produced many practical results, notably the hiring of shipwrights, sailors, apothecaries, architects and other experts, as well as arrangements for training Russians abroad. In Britain Peter hired the engineer John Perry, the shipwrights Joseph Noye and Richard Cozens, and the mathematician Henry Farquarson, among others, while over the next few decades young Russians undertook apprenticeships in England as boat builders, anchorsmiths, joiners, locksmiths, furniture makers, metal workers and in other trades. Perhaps the main lesson that Peter learned in diplomacy was the importance of 'lateral thinking' on the question of coalitions for the pursuit of Russia's goals. The bad experience at Riga, cordial relations with Sweden's rival Prussia, personal friendship with King Augustus of Poland, the realisation that immediate further gains in the south were unlikely in view of the collapse of the Holy League, all pointed to a new phase in Russia's foreign programme. As far as Peter's personal development was concerned, the influence of the Embassy is incalculable. He came back not just a changed man but also a man more convinced than ever that Russia must change.

Wielding the razor

The Embassy crystallised Peter's image of Europeans, not in any profound historical or philosophical context (there is little evidence that he did much in the way of serious reading either before or during his travels) but in the immediate, concrete sense of what they looked like and how they behaved in their surroundings. And what in the first instance divided Russians and Western Europeans (of both sexes) into 'us' and 'them' were clothes and hair-styles. Peter made his initial onslaught on his subjects' appearance on 26 August 1698, the day after he returned to Moscow, when the Austrian envoy Johannes Korb was on the spot to record the scene:

> The report of the Czar's arrival had spread through the city. The Boyars and principal Muscovites flocked in numbers at an early hour to the place where it had become known he had spent the night, to pay their court . . .. Those who, according to the fashion of that country, would cast themselves upon the ground to worship majesty, he lifted up graciously from their grovelling posture, and embraced with a kiss, such as is only due among private friends. If the razor, that plied promiscuously among the beards of those present can be forgiven the injury it did, the Muscovites may truly reckon that day among the happiest of their lives.[31]

As the tsar hacked away at the long beards, the first to be shorn was General Aleksei Shein; next came Prince-Caesar Fedor Romodanovsky, then 'all the rest had to conform to the guise of foreign nations, and the razor eliminated the ancient fashion'.[32] Apart from the patriarch (exempted by 'superstitious awe for his office'), only a couple of boyars were let off on account of extreme old age or special links with the royal family. The campaign continued on 1 September, Muscovite New Year, when a court jester circulated among the guests at a banquet shaving anyone who still had a beard. 'It was of evil omen to make show of reluctance as the razor approached the chin,' writes Korb, 'and was to be forthwith punished with a boxing on the ears. In this way, between mirth and the wine cup, many were admonished by this insane ridicule to abandon the olden guise.'[33] Forced shaving was combined with another offence to tradition, when Peter failed to observe the usual New Year ceremonies over which tsar and patriarch usually presided jointly. Instead, 'common sailors' were allowed to mix with guests and gun salvoes accompanied the toasts. The attack on beards was thus part of a wider package of cultural reform, which, as Korb detected, Peter pursued by using ridicule to attack people's dignity, with an underlying hint of menace in the shape of razors held to throats.

Members of Peter's immediate entourage had already adopted a Westernised appearance – participants in the Grand Embassy swapped their Muscovite clothes for European in Holland in 1697, although on occasions they still wore high fur hats and brocade robes at grand receptions – while the wider court circle at home had little choice but to comply. Further afield, however, the measures aroused bitter protests. The British engineer John Perry attributed the opposition to the fact that 'the holy Men of old had worn their Beards according to the Model of the Picture of their Saints', and recounts the tale of an old Russian carpenter at Voronezh who hid his shaved-off beard under his shirt with the intention of taking it with him to the grave,[34] while Charles Whitworth spoke of the difficulty with which the nation 'submitted to the Razor ... their fore fathers lived unshaven, their priests saints and martyrs were venerable for their beards, then they were bid to imitate'.[35]

Dress reform followed. In February 1699, as Korb recorded, Peter demonstrated his dislike of traditional fashion by cutting off the long sleeves of some of his officers and ordering returning envoys to wear 'German dress'.[36] Peter's own sartorial habits were influenced early on by his friends in the Foreign Quarter, although in the 1690s Russian dress was still *de rigueur* for ceremonial occasions. Items of Russian clothing from this period survive in Peter's wardrobe in the Hermitage in St Petersburg, but there is no evidence that he wore Russian garments after 1698. Peter's own clean-shaven visage and 'German' attire and his imposition of the same on others were frequently cited as evidence of his ungodliness. An artisan interrogated in 1704 protested that Peter was destroying the Christian faith by forcing people to shave their beards, wear German dress and smoke tobacco.[37] This view was shared by the church. In the words of Patriarch Adrian, 'Latin Jesuits, Dominicans, Bernadines and others not only shave their beards but also their moustaches and look like apes or monkeys.'[38] One treatise warned: 'Look often at the icon of the Second Coming of Christ, and observe the righteous standing at the right side of Christ, all with beards. At the left stand the Muselmen and heretics, Lutherans and Poles and other shavers of their ilk, with just whiskers, such as cats and dogs have. Take heed whom to imitate and which side you will be on.'[39] In fact, the rule that laymen must be bearded has no basis in scripture and it was not long before pro-reform churchmen composed their own treatises to explain why the wearing of a beard was not essential for salvation.

Punishing the strel'tsy

It was no accident that Peter's assault on beards and traditional dress occurred soon after his premature recall to Russia to do battle with a group of men whom he had come to regard as symbols of Old Russian 'barbarism'. The strel'tsy had plenty to complain about. After the banishment of Sophia and Golitsyn, they were relegated to the losing side in Peter's mock battles, then subjected to hardships during the two Azov campaigns, which were followed not by rewards or even respite but by new postings away from their base in Moscow to the Polish border, with little hope of returning permanently to the capital. In June 1698 four regiments mutinied, as Peter learned in Vienna, but their revolt was quashed not far from the New Jerusalem monastery at Istra by troops under the command of Patrick Gordon. The rebels' petitions to the authorities confirmed Peter's worst fears: vows to kill the 'Germans' who were 'destroying Orthodoxy' mingled with threats to wipe out the new infantry regiments, their perceived rivals. During interrogations it became clear that the strel'tsy harboured vague notions of driving out 'traitors' and foreigners, establishing leaders sympathetic to them and restoring the 'old order' under which they, the strel'tsy, had enjoyed a privileged position.

Peter was dissatisfied by the investigation and the penalties imposed on the rebels before his return. A new round of trials, which began on 17 September 1698 and ended only in February 1700, aimed not to establish their guilt (which was regarded as proven), but to elicit information on 'accomplices' and motives. In particular, Peter suspected the involvement of Sophia, who since 1689 had been residing in a fair degree of comfort in the Novodevichy convent just a few miles from the Kremlin. Several testimonies mentioned a plan to restore her to power ('their hopes were pinned upon Tsarevna Sophia Alekseevna, for she had ruled the government previously') and evidence emerged of secret letters passing between the convent and the strel'tsy through the mediation of Sophia's sisters and some mysterious beggar women and strel'tsy wives. Johannes Korb recorded the rumour that 'she promised to put herself at the head of a new conspiracy of the Streliz [strel'tsy], and communicated her advice to them, suggesting the manner and the frauds by which the Strelitz might bring their dark and malignant designs into effect'.

On 27 September Peter went in person to the convent to question Sophia, the first recorded meeting between them for nine years. In Korb's view, Peter had in mind that 'Mary of Scotland was led forth from prison to the block by command of her sister Elizabeth, Queen of England', but there was to be no execution for Sophia, who denied any knowledge of letters or any attempt to communicate with the strel'tsy. In the end Peter made do with inflicting a symbolic death on his troublesome half-sister, who was forced to take the veil under the name Suzanna and to live under a stricter regime. To rub it in, a few corpses of executed strel'tsy were strung up just outside the windows of her living quarters and left there to rot. As Korb wrote, one held a petition in his hand, 'perhaps in order that remorse for the past may gnaw Sophia with perpetual grief'.⁴⁰ For the rest of his life Peter retained a deep suspicion of convents and monasteries as refuges for subversives and dissidents.

As for the strel'tsy, their past record was enough to ensure harsh sentences as a warning to others: 1,182 strel'tsy were executed and 601 flogged and banished. Men were broken on the wheel, heads were displayed on poles, corpses strung up. The execution of the strel'tsy, some beheaded by Peter himself, became one of the symbols of the tsar's ruthless determination to root out opposition. It is no coincidence that he prepared to deal with the strel'tsy by cutting off the boyars' long beards, the symbol of antiquity. The Russian artist Vasily Surikov's famous painting *The Morning of the Strel'tsy Execution* (1881) makes the point graphically, contrasting the traditional clothing of the bearded strel'tsy and their families, clutching candles and icons, with the Western uniforms of the clean-shaven guardsmen and the tsar himself in the plain green tunic of the Preobrazhensky guards. The largely symbolic, although still painful, cut of the razor about the faces of the elite was soon followed by the lethal stroke of the axe on the necks of the strel'tsy. Peter in person wielded both razors and axes, if only as a token gesture. The bulk of the cutting work was done by his associates. The message was not lost on the élite, who remained by and large obedient and subservient, but cruel retribution was not enough to suppress strel'tsy disaffection. If anything it made it worse, especially when after 1698 many were exiled from Moscow only to form pockets of discontent in other part of the empire.

In what was left of the seventeenth century Peter had one more symbol of the past to deal with. In 1697 he had written from abroad to close associates proposing that his unloved wife Evdokia take the veil, a wish which no doubt became even stronger as a result of his encounters with Western women during his travels. The Danish commercial agent Georg Grund recounts an interesting tale, not found in any other source, about a blazing row which erupted after Peter tried to appease his wife with gifts of trinkets bought from merchants in the Foreign Quarter, after he had just spent the night there with his mistress Anna Mons. Evdokia flung them to the floor and trampled on them, cursing 'that German whore'. Peter thereupon vowed to have nothing more to do with his wife.⁴¹ After his return to Moscow in August 1698 (when he immediately visited Anna) Peter tried to persuade Evdokia to retire voluntarily, but the 'pious tsaritsa' turned out to have a will of her own. She refused and so was unceremoniously dispatched to the Intercession convent in Suzdal', where she lived under armed guard. In May 1699 Peter sent an agent to Suzdal' to oversee a ceremony in which Evdokia was forced to take the veil under the name Elena. So secret and irregular was this ritual that not long afterwards Evdokia abandoned her nun's habit and resumed a secular life, entertaining visitors, travelling around the district in some style and taking a young army officer as a lover. There was more than a hint of irony when some years later Peter informed the Danish commercial agent Just Juel that he had divorced Evdokia in order to allow her 'to live a life of piety'.[42] His real motive was to obtain a divorce, but the failure to put the case through a church court and Evdokia's refusal to comply undermined the legality of the separation. When members of Evdokia's circle were interrogated many years later, much hinged on the question of whether or not she had been 'shorn' (i.e. taken the veil) in 1698–99. We shall return to this later when we consider the fate of her only surviving son, Alexis.

IV

War with Sweden
1700–8

We were avenging the insult dealt to us and our ambassadors in Riga . . . and also seeking the restoration of the provinces of Ingria and Karelia, which belonged to our ancestors, the great sovereigns of Russia, for many centuries, but which the Swedish crown in truth treacherously snatched by dishonest military means. (Peter on the reasons for the Swedish war (3 February 1709))

Ring out the old, ring in the new

A few years after Sir Godfrey Kneller painted his memorable likeness of Peter, the Dutch artist Godfried Schalken borrowed the face for his own portrait of the tsar, now in the State History Museum, Moscow, to which he added a long, extravagantly curled French wig in a style which Peter almost certainly never wore in real life, preferring to grab a wig off someone else's head when he felt cold. A print by the Dutch etcher Adriaan Schoenebeck from about the same period (1703–5) shows Peter in a similar wig topped by a hat and dressed in a foppish French tunic, rather than in the plain coat which he usually wore. Both portraits, Schalken's and Schoenebeck's, testify to the further Westernisation of Peter's image in the early years of the eighteenth century. The exotic 'Tatar-like' Muscovite has disappeared, to be replaced by another Peter of the artists' imagining, Westernised beyond probability.

Russia, too, was to enter the eighteenth century in slightly ill-fitting Western clothes and in step with at least some of its Western neighbours. In the late 1690s most Muscovites were not anticipating a new century at all, since Muscovy counted its years from the notional creation of the world (the birth of Adam) and began each new year on 1 September, on which date in 1699 they marked the start of the year 7208. The Muscovite New Year was a strictly religious occasion, when tsar and patriarch walked in a procession of crosses and icons through the Kremlin. But, like a number of traditional festivals, in the 1690s the New Year was celebrated with increasingly less pomp, especially during Peter's absences. In November 1699, the year after he returned from Europe, where he had celebrated 1 January 1698 in Amsterdam, Peter made his views clear in a brief personal decree: 'The year is to be written from the birth of Christ in all business matters.' More detailed edicts dated 19–20 December 1699, evidently anticipating protests from religious traditionalists, noted that not only many European Christian nations but also

Orthodox Slavic people followed the new calendar.[1] Peter did not go all the way to modernity, however, by numbering the day of the month according to the more scientifically accurate calendar introduced by Pope Gregory XIII in 1582. Instead, he stuck to the Julian system already in use in Russia and in most Protestant countries, including Britain, which by the eighteenth century had fallen eleven days behind the Gregorian calendar.

Peter's prescription for the celebration of this 'goodly undertaking and the new century' provides an early example of enjoyment by decree, which specified the details, right down to the type of festive greenery to be set up in public places. A firework display on Red Square on 1 January 1700 was to be augmented by better-off citizens setting off rockets and firing celebratory rounds from muskets, while poorer residents were told to pool their resources and provide a few flares and beacons. Protests from traditionalists that the Almighty created the world in autumn when there was an abundance of produce for Adam and Eve to eat were brushed aside.

Conservative feathers were soon ruffled some more. On 4 January 1700 an order was issued to Moscow nobles and to men of 'all ranks of service and chancellery and trading people, and boyars' bond slaves, in Moscow and in the provinces' to wear 'Hungarian' coats reaching just below the knee over breeches with a shorter under-coat or vest. Those who could were asked to appear in such garments by Epiphany, just two days away, the rest by Shrovetide. This decree must have elicited a poor response, since Peter extended the deadline to 1 December 1700 for men and 1 January 1701 for women to acquire their new wardrobes.[2] Mannequins wearing examples of 'French and Hungarian' dress were displayed at Moscow city gates, a 'show and tell' method which Peter frequently employed to ensure that people 'would not excuse themselves by pleading ignorance' (a phrase which appears in many of his edicts). In 1701 a further decree specified that all people, even peasants living and working in Moscow, with the exception only of priests and peasants working on the land, must wear German dress, including boots, shoes and hats, and ride on German saddles. Women of all urban classes, even the wives of priests and their children, had to comply. Tailors and cobblers who made or sold banned items faced stiff penalties.

Whether the average Russian town dweller appreciated the nuances of the latest fashions is doubtful. Even foreigners were in two minds about what was required. John Perry believed that Peter ordered Russians 'to equip themselves with handsome Cloaths made after the English Fashion' while the Dutch artist Cornelius de Bruyn mentions 'Polish' coats.[3] But the general contours of what Peter required were clear: for men a topcoat, long under-vest (waistcoat) and breeches, in other words the three-piece suit which West European urban dwellers had been wearing since the 1670s. For women the fashion was full skirts and tight bodices, often low-cut, forming a nipped waist outline.

The new dress codes caught on quickly at court, where it was difficult to evade the tsar's eagle eye, and in Moscow generally, where inspectors went around collecting fines and chopping off the hems of robes which exceeded the required length. Gone were the tall-hatted bearded boyars in flowing robes and women in high-necked waistless garments with hair-concealing head-dresses. As for beards, the only ones tolerated at court were on priests or false ones for masquerades and theatricals. Away from Moscow, however, there was opposition to the new fashions. In the town of Belev an official attempted to close shops selling Russian clothes, but they were open again the next day. He reported that even the governor and officials were all bearded and dressed in Russian style. In 1708 an informer reported that when the tsar was in Moscow everyone wore German dress but in his absence the wives of some of the tsar's leading officials wore old-fashioned gowns to church, even though they put skirts over them, 'cursing the sovereign's decree'.[4] The harsh climate, the high cost and a shortage of suitable tailors, as well as resistance to change *per se*, continued to hamper the spread of the new fashions in the provinces. The new dress codes, it should be stressed, did not apply to the mass of the peasants, most of whom had little contact with these alien beings in 'German' clothes.

Peter's army

At the same time as Peter did battle with his subjects' appearance, he was also preparing for more action on the military front as one war ended and another began. On 3 July 1700 Russia signed a thirty-year truce with Turkey, which ratified Russian possession of Azov and Taganrog, but did not grant control over Kerch (on the strait between the sea of Azov and the Black Sea) or allow free navigation of the Black Sea and the Straits, as Russia had unrealistically demanded. The news was announced in Moscow on 18 August with a splendid firework display and the next day Peter declared war on the Swedes, citing the Swedish crown's failure to give satisfaction for the insult inflicted on the tsar at Riga in 1697 and its 'illegal' occupation of the Russian provinces of Ingria and Karelia, which the Swedish crown snatched during the Time of Troubles'.[5] Later the war was also presented as a defensive one, on the basis of rumours that Sweden had plans to seize Novgorod, Pskov, Olonets, Kargopol and Archangel, 'thereby entirely to cut off the Russians from the Commerce with Foreigners'.[6] Opportunism played a part. The accession of the teenage Charles XII to the throne of Sweden in April 1697 and the aspirations of nobles in Livonia, led by Johann von Patkul, to break free of Swedish rule, promised (misleadingly) to ease Peter's task, while diplomacy followed its own momentum in the wake of the Grand Embassy. In July 1699 Russia formally joined an anti-Swedish coalition with Christian V of Denmark and in October with Augustus II of Poland. Both monarchs regarded Peter as a junior partner.

The allies promised more than they delivered. Augustus invaded Livonia in February 1700 but in the absence of the anticipated support from the Livonian nobles he failed to take Riga. He got no help from Poland, of which he was the elected king, but where he had no personal power base, which remained neutral at the beginning of the war in the hope of pressurising Russia into revising the terms of the 1686 Treaty of Moscow. Frederick IV of Denmark, who succeeded his father Christian V in September 1699, was forced to make peace by a Swedish attack on Copenhagen at a time when most of the Danish army was in Holstein. He signed the Treaty of Travendal with the Swedes on the same day as Peter declared war against them.

Peter was taking on a more formidable enemy than he imagined. Far from being a walk-over, Sweden's 'boy king' proved to be even more single-mindedly devoted to war than Peter himself, even simpler in his tastes and more indifferent to discomfort. Indeed, from 1700 to his death in 1718 he barely returned to the Swedish mainland. Not for him the relaxation of overseeing the construction of new gardens, planning masquerades, turning a snuffbox on a lathe or the dozens of other jobs which Peter managed to squeeze in while running the war. In comparison with Charles's bleak existence with his troops (he never married), Peter's troubled family life was to seem almost idyllic. Charles's great love, some would say his obsession, was his army, which was regarded as the best in the world, its soldiers credited with almost superhuman qualities. In the words of a clergyman who accompanied the Swedish troops later in the war:

> The whole world is witness to the fact that nowhere on earth could you see soldiers more easily bearing heat and cold, strain and hunger, who carried out orders with greater ardour, went into battle more readily at the signal, and were more prepared for death.[7]

The Muscovite army, on the other hand, had a poor reputation in the West, which the remote Azov campaign had done little to salvage. 'None but the Tartars fear the armies of the Czar,' remarked Johannes Korb in 1699. 'It is an easy matter for them to call out several thousand men against the enemy; but they are a mere uncouth mob, which, overcome by its own size, loses the victory it had but just gained.'[8]

Dismissing the Russian army as 'uncouth' and 'Tatar-like' was part of a broader Western discourse about Muscovy. In fact, the general trend in the Muscovite military since the sixteenth century had been modernisation and change. Peter regarded Ivan IV (the Terrible), who took Kazan' in 1552 with 150,000 troops and 150 pieces of artillery, as his 'forerunner and example'.[9] In the 1630s part of the Russian army was reorganised into 'new formation' regiments, comprising infantry, lancers and dragoon units trained and commanded by foreign officers. These forces were consolidated under Tsar Alexis, as Peter acknowledged: 'Everyone is well aware of the manner in which our father ... in 1650 began to use regular troops and how a Military Statute was issued; and thus the army was established in such good order that glorious deeds were accomplished in Poland [in the war of 1654–67] ... and at the same time war was waged against the Swedes.'[10] But during Peter's youth the Russian army suffered some resounding defeats, notably at Chigirin in 1676–78 and on the Crimean campaigns of 1687 and 1689, both of which, significantly, involved steppe warfare against the Tatars in thinly populated terrain, where 'modern' Western-style methods of warfare and logistics had little relevance. The war with Sweden, which saw Russian troops deployed in all sorts of situations and in all sorts of terrain, including naval battles and sieges, over a twenty-year period, was to require the utmost versatility and adaptability.

The élite core of a new army was already in place in Peter's two 'play' regiments, the Preobrazhensky and Semenovsky guards, members of which initially were distinguished by personal ties and loyalty to Peter and by the requirement to start from the lowest commissioned rank regardless of status. But as their ranks were replenished and other regiments were added to the army (over forty by the end of Peter's reign) Peter could hardly hand-pick every recruit. A system was needed. At the same time, he was dissatisfied with the old recruitment system based upon landowners reporting for duty as cavalrymen with their complement of armed retainers when a campaign was announced. In November 1699 he issued an appeal for volunteers 'from all free men' to sign up in the office of the Preobrazhensky regiment for a wage of 11 roubles per year. The annual salary was intended to allow regular troops to be full-time soldiers without having to supplement their income through trade and craft, as the strel'tsy had done. A decree of 1 February 1700 appealed to masters who wished to free their slaves and serfs to issue them with warrants of manumission so that they could be considered for enlistment as infantrymen.[11] Given the shortage of eligible free or freed men, however, a volunteer force could not meet Peter's requirements. Army life, anyway, was scarcely an attractive option. Soldiers perceived it as a condition 'close to the position of the serfs'. There was a saying that 'it is better to belong to the boyars; if you belong to the sovereign you live worse'.[12] In December 1699 Peter launched a conscription drive on the basis of the supply of one equipped and provisioned recruit from every fifty peasant households owned by landowners already on active service and one from every thirty households belonging to persons not on active military service or a payment of 11 roubles (that is, the yearly salary for one volunteer).[13] Conscripts and volunteers yielded twenty-nine infantry regiments and two dragoons, a total of 32,000 men. The commanding officers were all foreigners, with junior officers drawn from Moscow nobles of non-boyar rank, although the ratio of Russians to foreigners was to increase as the war progressed.

Narva 1700

There was little time to train the new troops. In November 1700 a Russian army of about 40,000, with a weak artillery, inexperienced and quarrelling commanders, unreliable supply lines and no prospect of allied aid, faced a Swedish force of less than 9, 000 men at Sweden's Baltic port of Narva (which Peter regarded as a Russian town), where the Russians had arrived in September already exhausted and maintained a month-long siege, during which munitions and supplies ran out. In late October King Charles landed at Pernau in the Gulf of Riga, reaching Narva on 19 (30) November, shortly after Peter left his camp to fetch reinforcements from Novgorod. The fact that the Russian troops were thinly stretched out over a great distance in their camp made it easy for the Swedes to break through their ranks. Many Russians, in poor physical and psychological shape, fled. Only the Preobrazhensky and Semenovsky guards stood firm. Eight to ten thousand Russians were killed, and thousands captured. Peter's disappearance from the scene was interpreted as cowardice. The Swedes issued a medal: on one side Peter stood near his cannon from which cannon balls were flying towards Narva, with the biblical quotation: PETER STOOD AND WARMED HIMSELF. The reverse showed Russians fleeing from Narva with Peter at their head, his crown askew and the inscription : HE WENT OUT AND WEPT BITTERLY.[14]

The 'rebirth' of the Russian armed forces after Narva was one of several legendary turning points in Peter's reign. The loss of some 150 Russian cannon precipitated a major production effort, including initially the symbolic melting down of church bells to provide metal. The death of Patriarch Adrian on 16 October 1700 was fortuitous in view of his mistrust of foreign officers and Peter's desire to divert some of the wealth of the church into state hands to help fund the war effort. Peter chose his own man, the recently consecrated metropolitan of Riazan', Stefan Iavorsky, a Ukrainian, as a stand-in and used the war with Sweden as an excuse to delay filling the vacant post, which was not formally abolished until 1721. There is an anecdote that Peter, tired of being pestered with requests to fill the vacancy, beat his breast and yelled (according to another version, flinging a dagger on the table): 'Here's your patriarch.'[15]

In January 1701 Peter revived the Monastery department, first established by his father, to supervise ecclesiastical courts and run the church's lands under the direction of a secular official, the tsar's close friend and relation (probably his illegitimate half-brother), Ivan Musin-Pushkin. In the past, a decree noted, monks were 'industrious and made their bread by their own labour and fed many beggars by their own labour, but the present-day monks not only do not feed beggars with their labours but themselves live off the work of others'.[16] Some historians have argued that in 1701 a complete secularisation of church lands and property was achieved. In fact, Peter stopped short of secularisation (which was started by his daughter Empress Elizabeth, continued by Peter III and implemented by Catherine II in 1764) and subsequently restored some of the church's property rights. Legislation issued in 1700–1 also regulated such matters as when and where monks could write (openly, not secretly in their cells). Only monks and nuns were to live in monasteries, to deter 'shirkers' from finding refuge; building work was restricted; staffing in bigger establishments was reduced; and the minimum age for women to take the veil was set at forty. Peter continued to observe the necessary religious rites like the good Orthodox Christian that he was and remained, but he was determined that church politics and finances would be conducted on *his* terms.

As far as the army was concerned, Peter did not achieve a miraculous transformation. The most marked improvement was in the artillery, which from 1704 served under the master of ordnance James Bruce (or Iakov Brius), a second-generation Scottish émigré who had accompanied Peter on the Grand Embassy. Korb's remark that the Muscovites were 'not skilled in the proper management of artillery' (1699) gave way to Charles Whitworth's report (25 March 1705) that the Russian artillery was 'extremely well served'. His informant, the British general George Ogilvie, 'never saw any Nation go better to work with their cannon and mortars, than the Russians did last year at [the second battle of] Narva'. But Ogilvie, in conversation with Whitworth at Grodno in September 1705, complained that Russians were still 'unskilled in the general motions of army' and suffered from a 'great want of experienced officers'. He admired the guards, but was less enthusiastic about the newer infantry, who were 'but indifferently provided with habits and firearms, nor can they be looked upon otherwise than as new levies'. The cavalry he thought not equal to the Swedes in pitched battle.[17] Ogilvie's opinions are corroborated in other sources, including Russian ones, which testify to chronic problems with recruitment, discipline, uniforms and supplies. Peter's army was not an overnight success.

Russia's achievements in the first few years of the war had much to do with the fact that it did not have to meet Charles's main army in pitched battle. The ignominy of Peter's defeat at Narva may have persuaded Charles that there was not much more to do in Russia, encouraging his decision to move against Augustus in Poland and Saxony. In July 1701 the Swedes occupied Courland. The following July Charles defeated an army of Saxons and Poles and occupied Cracow. While Swedish attention was focused elsewhere, Russia scored a first victory in the Baltic when Boris Sheremetev's army beat General Schlippenbach's forces at Erestfer in Livonia on 30 December, 1701, securing a further victory at Hummelshof in July 1702. There were more Russian successes in August at Marienburg and on 11 October at the fortress of Nöteborg on Lake Ladoga, captured after a two-week siege with the aid of naval support. Peter renamed it Schlüsselburg, the 'key' to the Neva. The outbreak of the long anticipated War of the Spanish Succession in the West in May 1702 lessened the likelihood of intervention by other powers. Peter wrote to Apraksin: 'Long may it last, God willing.'[18]

Of marriages and mathematics

The demands of war did not deflect Peter from his campaign to create new Russian men and women. In January 1702 Moscow witnessed the wedding of one of Peter's jesters, Filat Shansky. The festivities, held in the mansion of the late Franz Lefort, lasted three days, of which the first two were celebrated in Old Russian style, men and women dressed 'after the ancient manner of the country' in two separate rooms, one presided over by Prince-Caesar Fedor Romodanovsky and Ivan Buturlin, the 'junior' tsar, the other by Prince-Pope Nikita Zotov and 'Tsaritsa' Buturlina. Adriaan Schoenebeck engraved three scenes, which were inscribed with captions identifying the guests. John Perry described it: 'The Victuals and the way of serving it to the Table, was, on purpose for Mirth made irregular and disagreeable...their Liquor also was as unacceptable, the best of which (as in the Days of old) was made of Brandy and Honey.'[19] On the third day they all changed into 'German' dress, and the men and the women sat at table together, 'and there was dancing and skipping about, after the entertainment, to the great satisfaction of the Czar himself, as all his guests'.[20] Here was an acting out of transformation, a symbolic discarding of the old ways, dress and manners, presided over by the mock tsars and the mock patriarch, themselves figureheads of the rejected past.

In addition to its general cultural symbolism, Shansky's wedding feast also formed a prelude to a new law on marriage. Russian marriage contracts were made on behalf of the bride and groom, who usually did not set eyes upon each other until the contract had been sealed. In élite society such secrecy could be maintained only under a regime in which young unmarried men and women led separate lives. Once mixed social gatherings started to bring the sexes together before marriage, reform was inevitable, especially as the tsar believed that marriage based on choice rather than force would be conducive to higher birth rates. The new law of 1702 stipulated a six-week period of betrothal before the wedding during which the couple could meet and the betrothal be broken at the request of either party, although in practice parental choice continued to predominate.[21]

Peter pursued both cultural change and technical progress through educational reforms. In 1700–2 he founded the Moscow School of Mathematics and Navigation, modelled on the Royal Mathematical School at Christ's Hospital in London, hiring teachers Henry Farquharson (*c.* 1675–1739) from Aberdeen and Stephen Gwyn and Richard Grice, both Christ's Hospital graduates. Leonty Magnitsky, a graduate of the Moscow Academy, was appointed to work with the British teachers and to produce a book on mathematics, geometry and navigation in Russian. The Sukharev tower, a modern building erected in the 1690s, was appropriately equipped and teachers and pupils (volunteers and conscripts) were dressed in 'French outfits'.[22] By 1702 the school had 200 students, divided between the preparatory department and the naval division. Senior pupils studied an impressive curriculum of arithmetic, geometry, trigonometry, plane navigation, Mercatorian navigation, diurnals (astrolabe), spherics, celestial navigation, naval cartography and Great Circle navigation. Despite suffering from shortages of basic equipment in the early years, the Mathematical school and its successor, the St Petersburg Naval Academy (founded 1715), had a profound influence on Russian intellectual life, not only by producing the first generation of Russian explorers, surveyors, cartographers, astronomers and the like but also in the area of secondary education. Peter later called on its graduates to staff his new elementary schools.

Reformed printing houses began to cater for a public which Peter expected to be increasingly literate. In 1701 the Monastery department took over the Moscow Printing House and placed all publishing under civil control. Under the direction of F. P. Polikarpov the press began to produce such materials as logarithmic tables and lexicons, as well as government edicts. The Moscow Printing House was also initially responsible for producing Russia's first newspaper, *The News (Vedomosti)*, which was created on 16 December 1702 to carry reports 'about military and other affairs, which need to be made known to the people of the Muscovite realm and neighbouring states'.[23] The first issue was dated 2 January 1703, and carried news from the Northern War. *Vedomosti* remained a government organ with a limited circulation. Controls from above and lack of initiative and expertise from below meant that a Russian free press was still in the distant future.

The founding of St Petersburg

In spring 1703 Russian troops made their way from Schlüsselburg down the Neva river towards the Finnish gulf. In May they captured the Swedish fortress of Nyenkans (Nienschantz) on the Okhta river. The story continues in an official history of Peter's reign, compiled some years later:

After the capture of Nyenkans a council of war was sent to determine whether to fortify this spot or to find a more convenient place (since this one was small, far from the sea and not well fortified by nature), and it was decided to look for somewhere else and after a few days' search they found a convenient island, called Lust Eland, where on 16 May (Trinity Day) the foundations of a fortress were laid and named Saint Petersburg.[24]

There were more elaborate, allegorical versions of the founding story. One recounts how Peter walked to the centre of the island (the present Peter-Paul fortress) and saw an eagle hovering overhead. He grabbed a bayonet, cut two strips of turf, laid one on top of the other in the shape of a cross, then made a cross from some wood, which he erected on the turf, with the words: 'In the name of Christ Jesus on this place shall be a church in the names of the apostles Peter and Paul.' The story goes on to recount how later two birch tree trunks were driven into the ground to suggest gates, on one of which the eagle, first mentioned hovering over the island, landed, then hopped on to Peter's arm. The writer records the legends that Constantine the Great was led to Byzantium by an eagle and that the apostle St Andrew, *en route* from Kiev and Novgorod, planted his staff in a spot not far from St Petersburg and blessed the region. Peter's city was placed firmly in the context of Christian world history.[25]

In fact, no contemporary first-hand account survives of the founding of St Petersburg – in 1703 it was still just a fort, not a city – and Peter was not even on the spot on the legendary date of its foundation. His first recorded reference to it appears in a letter dated 1 July 1703, reporting that the Russian flag had been planted by the ex-Swedish fortress.[26] The dedication of the fortress church took place on 29 June, Peter's name day, and the fortress itself was consecrated on 1 October, the feast of the Protecting Veil of the Mother of God and also the date of the capture of Kazan' by Ivan IV in 1552. The notion that the future city was built on 'empty' land is also mistaken, but was used for rhetorical effect by Peter's publicists and soon became part of Petrine mythology, most powerfully in the opening lines of Pushkin's poem *The Bronze Horseman*, which pictures the tsar looking out over a wilderness punctuated by an occasional fisherman's hut. In fact, in addition to the fort of Nyenkans, there were populated settlements in the area, including the fairly substantial residences of Swedish officials. The old fort itself was not destroyed until 1709, in a symbolic detonation to mark the victory at Poltava. The rubble was used in the fast-growing new city.

Did Peter in 1703 regard the 'city' as anything more than a hastily erected earthwork fortification? It appears that he did, even if we cannot know precisely how his ideas were formulated. Our anonymous chronicler, recording the construction between 24 and 27 May 1703 of Peter's first wooden cabin in St Petersburg, hints at a symbolic as well as a practical agenda. When Menshikov suggested that it would be easier to obtain ready-cut timber by dismantling a house from the nearby fort, Peter refused, saying: 'I want wood to be felled on the spot and a palace to be built from it in order to remind people what a wilderness this island was.' The said 'palace' was sprinkled with holy water and an icon of the Trinity was placed in it.[27] One of the first engravings of the town (by Peter Picart, 1704) features an expanse of water with ships in the middle ground and spires of the fortress and adjoining land in the far distance, a reflection of Peter's priorities. Another early print bears the legend 'Petropolis 1703'; a few years earlier Peter used the same name to refer to Azov.[28] Soon Peter was comparing his own city of St Peter with both Rome and Paradise, to which St Peter holds the keys. In a letter to Menshikov dated 28 September 1704 he wrote: 'If God grants, we expect to be in the capital (Piterburkh) in three or four days', and on 7 April 1706 he called it 'Paradise', a notion which he was to repeat many times.[29]

Martha Skavronska

At about this time Peter met the woman who was to become not only his wife but also his successor – the future empress Catherine I. In the summer of 1702 a young woman named Martha Skavronska fell into Russian hands when Field Marshal Sheremetev took the Livonian town of Marienburg, where she was working as a servant in the family of the Lutheran pastor Ernst Glück. Sheremetev is said to have passed her on to Menshikov and Menshikov to Peter, probably at the end of 1703 (when Peter split up with Anna Mons) or the beginning of 1704. In a letter written in 1717 Catherine, as she became known, hinted at 1 March as the anniversary of their first meeting. Menshikov no doubt had his own reasons for giving the tsar such a 'gift' and he and Martha/Catherine, both outsiders, were to remain firm allies. In the early period of their relationship Peter addressed her with the rather crude and virtually untranslatable 'matka' (old girl) or 'Muder'. A note dated October 1704 in which Peter sent regards to Menshikov on her behalf, together with greetings from his dog Lizetka and Iakim the dwarf, hints at her status in Peter's odd extended household.[30] Towards the end of 1704 she bore Peter a son, the 'little Peter' (Petrushka) mentioned by Peter in a letter from Poland to Daria, Menshikov's future wife, and Varvara Arsen'eva, who were looking after the child and its mother.[31] Another son was born the following year. In October 1705 the women sent Peter congratulations on the capture of Mitau castle in Courland 'as a result of your labours', adding, 'and we too have been amusing ourselves thanks to your labours, and we thank you most graciously for your favour, which we hope to enjoy again, and congratulate you on this newborn boy ... Peter and Paul beg your blessing and greet you.'[32] Menshikov also congratulated the women on the 'new arrival' in a letter dated 27 October 1705 from Lithuania. These boys must have died in infancy. Neither was included in the list of members of the imperial family later buried in the Cathedral of SS Peter and Paul in St Petersburg.[33] The first of the couple's offspring to be officially acknowledged was born on 27 December 1706. In a letter dated 29 December 'Mr Colonel' was informed of the arrival in St Petersburg of the 'newborn girl Catherine', and asked not to grieve at the birth of a daughter.[34] Young Catherine died from unspecified causes in July

1708, another melancholy statistic in the unhappy history of the couple's estimated ten offspring, of whom only two girls, Anna and Elizabeth, survived to maturity.

The background, nationality and original religious affiliation of Peter's second wife are still subject to debate. Whether she was the illegitimate daughter of a serf or the orphaned daughter of a Swedish officer, her 'lowly' origins were notorious. The snobbish Princess Wilhelmina of Bayreuth, who saw her in 1719, remarked that 'you only had to take one look at her to see that she was low-born. . . . From her clothes you could have mistaken her for some German strolling player.'[35] By 1704–5 she was an established part of Peter's life, but lacked official status and recognition, to the extent that foreign observers, who often discussed the rest of Peter's family, including his banished first wife, did not mention Catherine at all. Catherine and Peter between them had to invent an identity and place for her. This included conversion to Orthodoxy and the new name – Catherine (Ekaterina) Alekseevna – which went with it. The cult of her patron saint, St Catherine of Alexandria, was established at court and in 1714 Peter founded the Order of St Catherine in his wife's honour. Unlike Muscovite royal brides, she lacked an established kinship network (no doubt not having to contend with ambitious, interfering in-laws was an advantage in Peter's eyes) and had to forge alliances of her own, notably with Menshikov, another of Peter's 'creations'. With the years Catherine acquired a household of her own, but her greatest ally was Peter himself. She travelled with him round the battlefields of Poland and Lithuania, to Poltava in 1709, to the Pruth in 1711 and Persia in 1722, and accompanied him on his journeys to Western Europe.

The first known portraits of her, dating from the 1710s, depict a full-figured, attractive woman, of whom a foreign observer wrote: 'She has a pleasing plumpness; the colour of her face is very white with traces of natural, quite high colour, her eyes are dark and small, her hair the same colour, long and thick, fine neck and hands, a mild and very pleasant expression.'[36] In temperament and tastes Catherine was a match for Peter, over whom she exerted a calming influence. She was strong (a visitor records how she lifted up a heavy mace with one hand after Peter's orderly had failed to budge it) and unshockable, sharing Peter's vulgar sense of humour and his fondness for practical jokes and heavy drinking. Apparently, she was illiterate. That the all-powerful tsar of Russia should choose such a woman as his wife and in 1724 crown her as his empress was no odder than the fact that his best friend was reputed to be the son of a pie seller and that Peter liked to be known as Mr Mikhailov.

Makarov and the Cabinet

In 1704 another of Peter's closest associates enters the scene, when Aleksei Vasil'evich Makarov (1674/5?–1750) was appointed secretary to the tsar's Cabinet office. Rumour has it that Peter first spotted the promising young scribe in 1693 on a visit to Vologda, where Aleksei's father was also a clerk. Makarov became Peter's right-hand man, his virtual 'shadow', accompanying him on his campaigns and travels abroad, but always aware of his lowly station. He was the perfect complement to the illiterate Menshikov. The Cabinet functioned wherever Peter happened to be and all sorts of business came under its control in addition to the co-ordination of the domestic and foreign policy which passed through Peter's hands. It administered Russians training abroad and foreign specialists in Russia; the St Petersburg Chancellery of Building; some mines and works; Peter's chamber of curiosities (the Kunstkamera); and his gardening office, which also ran the royal aviaries and menagerie. Cabinet staff kept the tsar's journals (both appointments diaries and records of activities) and supervised the writing of the official 'History of the Swedish War'. Trials of special interest to the tsar, denunciations involving treason, attempts on the sovereign's life and crimes against the treasury were reported to the Cabinet, as were petitions, anonymous letters and new inventions, which Peter liked to investigate personally. It handled items of petty expenditure, such as wages and clothes for palace servants, goods purchased by agents abroad for Peter and his family, the costs of Peter's lathes and personal boats, and tips and gifts from the royal purse, such as 'rewards for the declaration of monsters, for mothers and midwives at the birth of children and various other such items'. The Cabinet also paid Peter his military service and labourer's salaries in his various ranks as captain, colonel and ship's carpenter.

Makarov ran the Cabinet with unusual efficiency. His 'Rules on Procedures for Cabinet Business' (1721) noted that 'except in the above-described manner, business cannot be conducted without confusion, therefore these procedures must be observed correctly in all particulars and abided by'.[37] He handled much of Peter's correspondence, even on matters of prime importance. Unlike Peter, he had beautiful handwriting and an excellent grasp of spelling and grammar. In their turn, correspondents often applied to Makarov rather than the tsar. One petitioner wrote: 'Makarov speaks and writes only on behalf of the sovereign, but his influence is felt by everyone.'[38] People seeking preferment for a relative, intervention in a lawsuit or a decision on a landed estate relied on him to find the right moment to put their request to the tsar, who was notoriously changeable in his moods. For all his power, Makarov never forgot his modest origins and addressed the magnates with whom he corresponded as 'your humble servant'. He never enjoyed the same easy familiarity with Peter as did Menshikov, nor did he amass anything like the latter's wealth and titles. His annual salary of 400 roubles compared poorly with the salaries of top army officers and foreign architects and his two grants of landed estates amounted to no more than 130 peasant households. He was, in a word, precisely the sort of honest, efficient specialist which Peter despaired of finding more of to man his expanding administrative machine.

War in Poland and the Baltic. The Astrakhan revolt

In January 1704 Augustus II was deposed by the Swedes and Charles's protégé, Stanislas Leszczynski, was elected king of Poland. The Swedes agreed to help the Poles to regain territory lost to Russia by the treaties of 1667 and 1686. This was a serious blow for Peter, especially now that he faced the prospect of Turkey joining an anti-Russian league. He did not abandon Augustus, however, because he was desperate to keep Poland in the war and he still had some support there. In August 1704 a Russo-Polish treaty recognised Augustus as the rightful king and promised him Livonia. The Baltic campaign continued to go well for Russia. In July 1704 the Russians took Dorpat (Tartu), on 9 August Narva (revenge for 1700) and on 16 August the neighbouring town of Ivangorod.

Throughout 1705–6 Russian units under the commanders Boris Sheremetev, Carl Rönne, George Ogilvie, Nikita Repnin and Fedor Golovin raced all over Lithuania and Courland. Peter himself was constantly on the move. February–April 1705 found him in Voronezh, where he celebrated Easter and launched a ship called *The Old Oak*, but complained because Menshikov could not join him. 'Everything here is fine, thank God, there's only one thing that grieves me, as you yourself are aware, especially as I was never apart from you for this holiday before.'[39] Arriving back in Moscow at the end of April, he fell ill with a fever. He wrote: 'This illness has increased the pain of separation from you, which I have suffered many times, but now I can bear it no longer. Come and see me as soon as you can, to cheer me up.' Menshikov, arriving in Moscow in mid-May, was able to report that 'through the mercy of Almighty God the tsar has been cured of his sickness'.[40] On 30 May Peter celebrated his birthday at Preobrazhenskoe and the following day left Moscow for Smolensk *en route* for Polotsk, where he arrived in early June. Reports came that a Swedish fleet, consisting of twenty-two warships and auxiliary vessels, had attacked Kotlin (Kronstadt) island off St Petersburg, but had been headed off by a much smaller Russian squadron under the command of Vice-Admiral Cruys, causing many Swedish losses. At the same time 10,000 Swedes under Major-General Mengden approached St Petersburg but were forced to retreat. During this war the Swedes were not to get so close to Peter's capital again.

Peter held his name-day party in Polotsk and a few days later departed for Vilna, arriving on 8 July with the main army. Here he remained until early August, then moved on to Mitau in Courland. In mid-September he was back in Poland, in Grodno, where he stayed until 7 December when he left for Moscow. In early September 1705 news had reached Peter of serious disturbances in Astrakhan, where on 30 July strel'tsy, in collusion with rebellious townspeople, ambushed the town guards and began a massacre of officers and government officials. Letters from the rebels to the Don Cossacks and other potential allies declared:

> We stood up in Astrakhan for the Christian faith and against shaving and German dress and tobacco and because we and our wives and children were not admitted into God's church in old Russian dress. And those who went to church, of both male and female sex, had their garments chopped up and were pushed out of God's churches and sent packing and the governors and officers hurled all manner of abuse at us, our wives and children, and they, the governors and officers, bowed down to pagan idols and forced us to bow down too ... and they, the governors and officers, tried to take away the guns of the servicemen on guard and tried to beat us to death.[41]

The fact that the 'pagan idols' (which the rebels confiscated as proof of ungodly practices) were in fact wig blocks indicates the cultural gulf between the handful of semi-Westernised officials and the mass of the population. Peter's assault on beards had recently intensified. On 16 January 1705, men 'of all ranks', including merchants and artisans (but not priests, deacons and peasants), were ordered to shave. Anyone who wished to keep his beard and whiskers had to pay a fine on a sliding scale according to status: 60 roubles for nobles, military officers and chancellery officials, 100 roubles for merchants of the first guild, and so on. Permits took the form of a beard token disc obtainable from the Police Office. Bearded peasants had to pay a kopeck each time they entered the city gates.[42] It seems likely that this degree was implemented only patchily outside St Petersburg and Moscow – the revenues raised from the beard tax were insignificant – but Peter's 'ungodly' assault on beards, first aimed at the élite in 1698, remained an important element in the traditionalists' case against him.

All sorts of stories circulated. A gunner claimed under interrogation that he had heard rumours in Moscow that the real tsar had gone missing and that the current one was a fake. In other letters the rebels mentioned the antics of the Drunken Assembly, 'instead of God-respecting carol singing they use masquerades and games, in which one of his courtiers, a jester, was given the title of patriarch and other archbishops'.[43] The Astrakhan rebels' plan of action echoed those of the strel'tsy in 1682 and 1698: to go to Moscow and kill any German, male or female, they chanced upon, to find the sovereign and appeal for the old belief to be restored and for permission not to have to wear German dress or to shave. A refusal would mean that Peter was not the real tsar and could be killed.[44] The rebels had no truck with direct anti-tsarist sentiments, however. Royal letters received in Astrakhan in October were treated with respect and prayers were sung for the tsar's health. Another story claimed that Peter was a prisoner in Sweden, that the boyars had taken over Moscow and that the rebels must march against them for the sake of the Christian faith and the tsar. Others claimed that the tsar was dead.

In the words of Charles Whitworth, 'the sudden change of Cloathes and Customes added new fuel to their discontent. But the specious pretence for all, was here as in other Countreys the zeal for their Religion.'[45] But as Whitworth realised, people were also protesting against heavy taxation and monopolies on salt and fish. Astrakhan had long been a place of exile for unreliable elements. Vagrants and fugitives flocked into town to seek work in the fisheries and saltpetre works. Trade duties and indirect taxes and labour burdens had recently been raised and food allowances to servicemen reduced. Cultural changes were symbols of wider discontent

Peter regarded the revolt as a resurgence of strel'tsy intransigence. He wrote to Fedor Apraksin, now Secretary of the Admiralty, on 21 September: 'I deduce that the all-gracious Lord has not yet finished pouring out his wrath and for twenty-five years now it has pleased him to give those destructive curs their way and solace in innocent blood.'[46] The spread of the rebellion beyond Astrakhan (the rebels tried but failed to capture Tsaritsyn) forced Peter to transfer Boris Sheremetev from Courland with two squadrons of dragoons and a battalion of infantry. Even so, he hoped that the threat of retaliation and the promise of a pardon would calm the situation and ordered Sheremetev to attack only in the last resort. Sheremetev took the town on 13 March 1706. Trials continued for the next two years. Eventually six men were broken on the wheel, 42 beheaded, 30 executed in Red Square, 242 in other parts of Moscow, and 45 died during interrogation. Peter was determined to root out the evil which had haunted him ever since he witnessed the strel'tsy massacring his relatives in May 1682. In the meantime, he consoled himself in the company of his friends. A letter sent to Menshikov from St Petersburg in March 1706 was signed by Peter's 'drunken' companions, the dog Lizetka, who affixed her paw, and the royal dwarf Iakim Volkov, who added that he had been given permission to be drunk for three days. The tsar signed himself 'Archdeacon Peter'.[47]

Waiting for Charles

In the West things were going worse than ever for Augustus II. In August 1706 the Swedes took Dresden and Leipzig. Under the terms of the Peace of

Altranstädt (28 September) Augustus renounced the Polish crown in favour
of Leszczynski and broke his alliance with Russia. The Swedes looked poised
to turn on Russia, but even now there were signs that Charles's advance might
be checked. On 18 October 1706 a joint force of Russian and Saxon troops
caused heavy Swedish losses at Kalisz, near Poland's western border. The hero
of the hour was Menshikov. Peter's earlier reluctance to make his friend into
a public figure evaporated and Alexander was richly rewarded: Peter presented
him with a diamond- and emerald-studded cane and verses were composed
in his honour, likening him to the faithful servant of Alexander the Great.

Late in 1706, in the town of Žolkiev near Cracow, Peter held a crucial
council of war. Orders issued in January 1707 prescribed guerrilla tactics and
a scorched earth policy in order to halt the Swedes' eastward march. Peter
wished to avoid a pitched battle for as long as possible. He was willing to cede
Dorpat, and if the Swedes were still not satisfied, to offer them cash in compensation for Narva or even to cede Narva; but St Petersburg must not be
relinquished under any circumstances. Charles, equally stubborn, declared
himself ready to fight to the last Swede rather than leave St Petersburg in
Russian hands. The king of Prussia's envoy in Altranstädt reported that the
Swedes expected 'to dethrone the Czar, compelling him to discharge all his
foreign officers and troops, and to pay several millions as an indemnifica-
tion'.[48] This may not have been a true reflection of Swedish policy, but such
rumours caused alarm in Moscow. Peter sought mediators, for example, the
duke of Marlborough, Britain's negotiator, but the duke politely declined the
incentives offered, which included the pick of titles to the principalities of
Kiev, Vladimir or Siberia and one of the biggest rubies in Europe.

The spring and summer of 1707 brought renewed fears of a Swedish attack.
In March 1707 Peter wrote to Fedor Apraksin from Poland: 'I can't tell you
anything more about what's going on, as all Polish affairs here are fermenting
like young ale. The Swedes are advancing, committing unspeakable atrocities
in Saxony.'[49] In the summer Moscow was put on the alert and a decree
ordered border areas to prepare for invasion: 'This war is now directed against
us alone,' Peter wrote.[50] At the end of 1707 news reached Peter, who spent
Christmas and New Year in Moscow, that a Swedish army of 45,000 had
crossed the Vistula. He set off for Grodno, departing again in late January in
the direction of Vilna just a few hours before Charles entered the town. It was
anyone's guess which way Charles would go next: into Livonia or towards
Novgorod (threatening St Petersburg); towards Smolensk (thence to
Moscow); or into Ukraine. At first he left Grodno in a north-easterly direction, which suggested that Pskov and Novgorod were his destination, but
then he moved south-east.

Peter was anxious but he did not succumb to defeatism. He wrote to his
son Alexis on 22 January 1708: 'Give greetings to my sister [Natalia] and the
others from me, and tell them not to grieve, for war is war and with God's

help all our men are eager to march and ready to fight. Instead of grieving let them pray, which will be more help to us.' A letter to the acting patriarch Stefan Iavorsky written on the same day stated that they were ready to lay down their lives for the church and the fatherland. Peter asked Stefan to pray for the assistance of the heavenly host who aided St Peter; if a saint needed such help, how much more did mere sinners require it![51] As always, Peter remained firmly convinced of divine intervention in human affairs while believing that God operated primarily through the agency of men. On 27 January, Catherine gave birth to another daughter, Anna, in Moscow. Tsarevich Alexis and Peter's sister Natalia acted as godparents for the 'new arrival'.[52] Peter was to become close to this particular daughter, but it seems unlikely that at the time he regarded the birth of another girl as a good omen.

On 29 January Peter issued a decree on a new typescript, the draft of which was covered with his own amendments, accompanied by a handwritten instruction to publish books in the new print. The so-called Civil script (*grazhdanskii shrift*), devised in 1707 and developed by a team of printers from Amsterdam, comprised 33 letters in upper, middle and lower case, based upon modern designs for Latin letters, with 'redundant' ones from Church script excluded. A new alphabet primer was prepared for press and the first book in the new type (a work on geometry by A-G. Burckhard von Pürkenstein, translated from the German) appeared in March 1708, but Peter was dissatisifed, adding more letters and amending others.[53] Civil script did not replace the older, more ornate Church script (*kirillitsa*). In fact, a third of the titles printed in the old script during Peter's reign were actually secular in content, for example laws and manifestoes, which were often read out in church. Ecclesiastical printing not only continued, notably for the production of liturgical and devotional works, but also considerably increased its output. Religious literature accounted for some 40 per cent of books published and sold more copies than secular works. At the same time, the introduction of the new script underlined the growth of the secular sphere, in the eyes of the state if not the reading public, who were reluctant to spend their money on technical books on fortification, siege warfare and geometry, but were not offered any entertainment in the form of fiction, plays or poetry, which accounted for just 0.2 per cent of titles published.

As for Peter, he took an interest in all aspects of publishing, from checking translations to specifying the size of books and the quality of the binding. His own library was an eclectic mix of almost 2,000 titles, the working section of which covered such topics as fortification, artillery, hydraulics, architecture, geography and history. Books on shipbuilding and navigation (including eighteen copies of 'General Signals' for the galley and seagoing fleets) accounted for about 12 per cent of the collection, politics, law and economics less than 3 per cent. Up to 50 per cent of the titles were foreign, but Peter also owned a large number of religious books (about 28 per cent of the collection),

ranging from standard liturgical texts in multiple copies to modern theological works by Orthodox clerics.

Peter arrived back in St Petersburg from Poland in March 1708, only to fall
seriously ill. On 6 April he wrote to Gavrila Golovkin:

> There is a saying that where God builds a church the Devil will find an
> altar: I was always healthy here in this heavenly place, but now I seem
> somehow to have brought a fever with me from Poland even though I took
> good care of myself . . . . I was plagued with it all Holy Week and missed the
> feast day services apart from the beginning of matins and the gospel read-
> ing. Now, thank God, I am returning to health but I haven't left the house.

On 8 April, he wrote again to Golovkin: 'I beg you to get on with whatever
you can in my absence. When I was well, I neglected nothing, but God alone
knows what a state I'm in after this illness, which turned even this place into
Poland, and if I don't get better and manage to have a rest, God knows what
will happen.'[54] He had hit a low point. 'You know that I have never written
like this before,' he wrote to Menshikov, 'but God sees when you have no
strength because without health and strength it's impossible to do your duty.'
He hoped that he would not have to report for duty straight away, but if he
did, he asked Menshikov to have transport arranged. The doctors' treatment,
which included doses of mercury, had left him as 'weak as a baby'.[55]
Clearly, Peter's associations of sickness with Poland (hell) and health with St
Petersburg (heaven) had symbolic and psychological connotations. Still not
knowing what Charles's plans were, he gave orders for his 'Paradise' to be fortified. Government bodies did not move to the new capital permanently until
1712–13, but Peter expected his family to spend more and more time there. In
1708 his sister Natalia supervised a visit by the royal women, who at Peter's
insistence travelled the last section of their journey in a huge convoy by ship
from Schlüsselburg. An anecdote recounts that Peter wished to 'accustom his
family to water so that they were not afraid of the sea and got to like the situation of St Petersburg, adding that "anyone who wishes to live with me must
often be on the sea".'[56]

Bulavin

Ill health struck while Peter was facing the most serious internal disorders
of his reign: the revolt led by the Don Cossack commander Kondraty
Afanas'evich Bulavin (*c.* 1660–1708). The rebellion, which had flared up in
autumn 1707, was a classic case of friction between ruling centre and Cossack
fringe. A census of the Don region in May 1703 specified that fugitives who
had arrived there since 1695 must be returned to their former places of resi-

dence, an order which posed a challenge to the traditional Cossack welcome for such renegades. The Don Cossacks also resented encroachment by outsiders upon their enterprises. It was the seizure of the Bakhmut salt works by Cossacks on government service in 1704 which first provoked Bulavin to protest. Rumours that the authorities intended to cut off beards, a special affront to Cossack dignity, also caused outrage. The catalyst came in July 1707 when Peter sent Prince Iury Dolgoruky to the Don to enforce the new rules on fugitives. In October Dolgoruky was ambushed and slaughtered by Bulavin, who, defeated in his turn by the Don Cossack commander Lukian Maksimov, escaped to Zaporozhie on the Dnieper, from where he sent out letters appealing for the defence of 'the True Faith', reassuring 'all top officials, good men and all common people who also stand firm with them ... we cannot be silent on account of the evil deeds of wicked men and princes and boyars and profit makers and Germans and cannot let them off for leading everyone into the Hellenistic pagan faith and diverting them from the true Christian faith with their signs and cunning tricks'.[57] Bulavin made common cause with workers in the Voronezh shipyards and labourers in Azov and Taganrog, with Nogai, Kalmyk and Tatar nomads, with peasants and religious dissidents, thereby provoking separate outbreaks of protest all over the region. This was a 'virtual replica' of the Stenka Razin rebellion of 1670–71 and a foretaste of the 1773–75 Pugachev revolt, with the difference that Bulavin did not put forward a pretender. In April 1708 Bulavin defeated Maksimov and on 1 May Don Cossack sympathisers admitted his army to their capital Cherkassk and elected him as their commander.

Early in April 1708 Peter had ordered eighteen-year-old Tsarevich Alexis, who had recently been entrusted with a series of grown-up tasks, to 'quench the fire [of rebellion] as quickly as possible'.[58] Fedor Apraksin he instructed to execute Bulavin's 'thieves' in Voronezh and 'hang them along the roads closer to the towns where they lived and thieved', as a warning to others.[59] Prince Vasily Dolgoruky, the murdered Prince Iury's brother, was dispatched with a force of 32,000 men and on 7 July Bulavin was killed after a failed attempt at taking Azov. Peter's response was jubilant. 'So this affair, thank God, had ended happily....Here, thank God, all is going well and today there was a celebration (*triumfovanie*) of this good event.'[60] Even though pockets of resistance continued into 1709, he was able to recall some 15,000 men to the Lithuanian front, where Charles was still poised, according to rumours, to 'march on Moscow, dethrone the tsar, divide his country into petty princedoms, summon the boyars and divide the realm between them into provinces'.[61]

On 3 July 1708 the Swedes won a victory over A. I. Repnin's troops at Holowczyn and proceeded to Mogilev. But as summer drew on into autumn, the tables were beginning to turn. 'The land is not so well tilled,' wrote Whitworth about the region through which the Swedes were passing, 'the villages few, their wooden houses of little value, and the furniture almost nothing, so that whenever an enemy approaches, the people are warned away with what they can save, and the cozacks set fire to the rest, as they have several times already done in sight of the Swedish army, who find all desolate before them, and as they advance will run further into want and cold.'[62] To make the terrain even less hospitable in August Peter spelled out his 'scorched earth' policy. If the enemy entered Ukraine, troops were to burn all provisions and fodder and corn in the fields and in grain stores or threshing floors in villages (although not in towns) which was superfluous to their own needs, Polish and Russian, not sparing buildings in the vicinity; bridges were to be destroyed, forests cut down. All mills must be burned and all the inhabitants sent out into the fields with their possessions and livestock. No millstones were to be left behind: they were either to be taken away or smashed. If anyone resisted going into the forest, their villages would be burned. This policy was to be broadcast in advance, with the warning: 'If anyone brings the enemy food, even for cash, that person shall be hanged; also anyone who knows [of such activities] but says nothing [will be executed]. Also those villages from which the food is given will be burned.'[63] A desperate situation required desperate measures.

But Peter also found room for the smaller things in life. On 17 August he sent the corpse of his dog Lizetka to Dr Nicholas Bidloo in Moscow, with a note asking the doctor to embalm her, using dry balsam 'so that she doesn't rot' (Peter took a keen interest in embalming) and begging the doctor 'to put his best effort into it'.[64] (Many years later the stuffed Lizetka was to be displayed alongside Peter's waxwork in the chamber of curiosities.) Lizetka had been Peter's constant companion, often signing or 'affixing her paw to' letters and sometimes delivering them. There is an anecdote about how Peter pardoned a man after Catherine attached a petition written in Lizetka's name to the dog's collar.[65] Food and equipment such as collars and chains for Peter's dogs are often mentioned in account books. Stuck in Vilna in the autumn of the previous year after a tiring and inconclusive campaign, Peter found solace in jotting down classical names for the puppies of another favourite bitch: Pirois, Eois, Aeton, Flegon for the dogs and Pallas, Nymph and Venus for the bitches, which he arranged to have trained to do tricks, such as taking off a hat, jumping over a stick, sitting and begging. In November 1708 he had Pirois and Eois sent to him in Ukraine, together with a list of the skills they had acquired.[66] Menshikov seems to have shared this passion. In March 1705 he sent Peter a puppy ('wonderful looking, with a wide jaw, and very stupid') to replace one which had been killed and compared him with a dog called Tyrant, 'the main difference between them being that Tyrant runs away from shooting but this one rushes towards the person who is firing'.[67] No doubt Peter's love for animals, as well as his dislike of hunting, will weigh more heavily on the balance sheet of his good and bad deeds with some readers than with others. Some of history's greatest villains have been dog-lovers. If anything, his relationship with his dogs provides a further illustration of the complexity of Peter's personality, his ability to mix work and play and to switch between the 'weighty' and the 'trivial' more or less at will.

Charles turns south. Mazepa

In late August Charles moved his troops to Mstislavl' in the Grand Duchy of Lithuania. It was anticipated that he would next make for Moscow or even St Petersburg. But in mid-September, discouraged from crossing the Russian border by reports of shortages of food and fodder all the way to Smolensk, some 60 miles away, the main Swedish army turned south. This proved to be a serious miscalculation, especially since almost immediately one of the supports on which Charles was relying was eliminated. On 28 September in an engagement near Lesnaia (about 30 miles south-east of Mogilev) General Löwenhaupt, travelling from Riga with 12,500 troops and a baggage train of equipment and provisions consisting of several thousand carts, was cut off from the main army and attacked by Peter's *corps-volant*. Löwenhaupt escaped to join Charles with only six or seven thousand of his men and had to abandon his wagons. Peter later referred to this as the 'first day of our good fortune'.[68] Lesnaia became one of the 'victory days' in the new court calendar.

What made Charles turn into Ukraine, rather than continuing eastwards? The main attraction was that he believed the region to be populous, rich in food supplies and lacking in strong garrisons. Moreover, Charles had made a secret agreement with Ivan Mazepa, hetman of Left Bank Ukraine, who pledged to supply the Swedes with 20,000 Cossacks, military bases and provisions. He was also counting on the assistance of Devlet Girei, khan of Crimea. Mazepa's notorious decision to 'betray' Peter is unremarkable in the context of Muscovite–Ukrainian relations during the period in question. He suffered the same dilemma as previous commanders of the Little Russian Cossack Host, who wavered between accepting the 'protection' of the fellow Orthodox tsar and being forced into service or pledging allegiance to non-Orthodox sovereigns, Polish, Turkish or Swedish, none of whom could be relied upon to observe traditional Cossack liberties. Since his investiture as hetman in 1687 Mazepa, despite governing like a ruling monarch, had remained loyal to Moscow, but now he believed that his obligations to the tsar were at an end: 'We, having voluntarily acquiesced to the authority of his Tsarist Majesty for the sake of the unified Eastern Faith, now, being a free people, we wish to withdraw, with expressions of our gratitude for the Tsar's protection and not wishing to raise our hands in the shedding of Christian blood.'[69] In his view, Cossacks had suffered enough deprivations fighting for Russia in the Northern War.

In October 1708 Mazepa fled to Charles's side. On 31 October Menshikov stormed and burned the hetman's headquarters at Baturin, killing, according to one estimate, some 6,000 persons 'without distinction of age or sex'.[70] This drastic action proved crucial, for it deprived the Swedes of men and supplies. Peter regarded the defection of his 'loyal subject' as a personal insult. He wrote to Menshikov: 'We received your letter about the totally unexpected wicked event of the hetman's treachery with great amazement.'[71] Mazepa was 'a new Judas', for whom Peter even created a mock Order of Judas, a parodic inversion of the Order of St Andrew which Mazepa had received in February 1700. After the hetman's death the medal was presented to Peter's jester, Prince Iury Fedorovich Shakhovskoy.

After Mazepa's defection and escape from Poltava in June 1709, Peter sent countless letters to individuals and groups in Ukraine which emphasised Mazepa's betrayal of Orthodoxy. The Ukrainian people learned how Charles had desecrated Orthodox churches in Lithuania, turning them into Protestant chapels, entered them with dogs, hurled the sacrament on the ground and other such violations, all commonplace elements in descriptions of religious abuse. Mazepa was excommunicated and an effigy of him was stripped of the Order of St Andrew and hanged. The anathematisation was read out in churches in Ukraine on the first Sunday of Lent until 1869. The new hetman, Ivan Skoropadsky, was assured that Cossack rights would be respected, except 'in cases of conflict with affairs of the state, such as treason'.[72] In fact, Peter had reason to be grateful for Mazepa's 'treachery' insofar as it helped to lure Charles into Ukraine, where, in the words of Captain James Jefferyes, the English envoy at Swedish field headquarters, the Swedes anticipated coming into a country 'plentifull of all necessaryes' and 'flowing with milk and honey'.[73] In the event, this turned out to be a mirage. Far from greeting the Swedes with open arms, Ukrainians generally offered passive resistance in the form of guerrilla warfare. The prospect of a restoration of Polish Catholic rule, via Charles's puppet Leszczynski, was no more appealing than the continuation of rule from Moscow.

Russia was now virtually under martial law. A decree of December 1708 announced the formation of eight provinces or *gubernii* (increased to nine in February 1709), each to be administered by a governor (*gubernator*) with extensive powers: Prince-Caesar F. Iu. Romodanovsky in Moscow, Menshikov in St Petersburg, D. M. Golitsyn in Kiev; P. S. Saltykov in Smolensk; P. A. Golitsyn in Archangel, P. M. Apraksin in Kazan'; I. A. Tolstoy in Azov, M. P. Gagarin in Siberia and F. M. Apraksin in Voronezh. Designated provinces were to support designated military units, by collecting money and supplies for the army within their own areas. Peter himself spent the final months of 1708 and New Year 1709 far from home, travelling from town to town in Ukraine, one of his least favourite places. He viewed these 'borderlands', far from the sea, as the antithesis of St Petersburg, his watery, Western paradise.

As he once wrote to Menshikov from near Grodno, a messenger had arrived from his 'Paradise', 'and brought much consolation', while from Dubrovna in 1706 he wrote to Fedor Golovin as though from 'hell, where I have not just enough but, alas, more troubles than I can cope with'.[74] Ukraine was soon to provide the setting of one of the decisive encounters of the war, which, in Peter's words, would lay the final foundation stone of the new capital.

V

From Poltava to Pruth
1709–11

Now with God's help the final stone has been laid in the foundation of St Petersburg. (Peter to Fedor Apraksin after the battle of Poltava, 27 June 1709)

Poltava

Peter remained far from confident of victory. In December 1708 he wrote to Apraksin: 'I don't expect this winter to pass without a pitched battle (since to wait until spring is not without danger), but this game is in God's hands, and who knows who fortune will smile on?'[1] There was no battle that winter, one of the severest in living memory. In early January 1709 hundreds of Swedes froze to death outside the Ukrainian town of Hadyach, where Charles made his winter quarters. The Lutheran pastor Daniel Krman, travelling with the Swedish army, describes how surgeons cut off frost-bitten fingers and toes. 'We experienced such cold as I shall never forget. The spittle from people's mouths turned to ice before hitting the ground, sparrows fell frozen from the roofs to the ground. You could see men without hands, others without hands and feet, some who had lost their fingers, faces, ears and noses, others crawling about on all fours.'[2]

Peter himself spent the first half of 1709 well away from the battle zone. In February he was in Voronezh and April and May found him in Azov and Taganrog for the first time in ten years, taking a course of strong medicine which left him feeling once again 'as weak as a child'.[3] He remained proud of his southern conquests, writing to Menshikov from Trinity fortress at Taganrog in May: 'In this place, where ten years ago we saw just open country, with God's help now we find a fine town with a harbour, and although when the master has been away for a long time not everything is in order, still there is something worth looking at.'[4] Charles, meanwhile, saw potential reinforcements falling away. On 14 May 1709 Russian troops stormed the camp of the Zaporozhian Cossacks on the Dnieper (a 'nest of traitors', in Peter's view) with the aim of averting an alliance between the Zaporozhians and the Tatars, both of whose support Charles was counting on. Swedish auxiliaries and supplies from the north also failed to materialise.

To gain time, in May the Swedes began to besiege the small Ukrainian town of Poltava on the River Vorskla. Peter moved north into Ukraine. On 31 May he wrote to Menshikov from Kharkov: 'I have just arrived here and shall try to get to you as quickly as I can. But we cannot afford to lose even an hour in this vital business, so if something has to be done, don't wait for me but, with God's help, do it.'[5] A few days later he joined up with the army and on 27 June went into battle with the Swedes outside Poltava, beforehand, according to legend, encouraging his troops with a famous speech:

> Let the Russian troops know that the hour has come which has placed the fate of all the fatherland in their hands, to decide whether Russia will be lost or will be reborn and improve its situation. Do not think of yourselves as armed and drawn up to fight for Peter but for the state which has been entrusted to Peter, for your kin and for the people of all Russia, which has until now been your defence and now awaits the final decision of fortune. Do not be confused by the enemy's reputation for invincibility which they have shown to be unfounded on many occasions. Keep before your eyes in this action that God and truth are fighting with us, which the Lord strong in battle has already demonstrated by his aid in many military actions; think of this alone. Of Peter know only that he sets no value on his own life if only Russia and Russian piety, glory and well-being may live.[6]

No original text or eyewitness testimonies survive, but the speech, first published in 1773, has often been quoted as a morale-booster for both the Imperial and Soviet armies.

By the time Peter met Charles in pitched battle for the first and last time, the odds were in his favour. The legendary resilience of the Swedish troops had been severely tested by two years on the move in alien terrain, by the bitter cold of winter and intense summer heat, skirmishes and shortages of food and fodder. Their numbers were depleted: Charles was left with an estimated 22,000 men to Peter's 40,000 and 5,000 irregulars. Still, in the past the Swedes had won battles when the odds were more stacked against them and the Russian troops feared them. This time, though, weakness in numbers was exacerbated by bad luck and miscalculations. They decided not to deploy their artillery, anticipating a quick breakthrough with cavalry, then had to face fire from seventy guns from the Russian camp, which cut through the already thinned Swedish ranks 'as grass before a scythe', as an eyewitness expressed it.[7] Even when the Swedes managed to fire a volley, the poor quality of their powder made most bullets fall short. Charles himself had a wounded foot and his already overburdened staff feared for his safety. His experienced bodyguards were among the first to be killed. The two Swedish generals Rehnsköld and Löwenhaupt were at loggerheads, with the result that the former failed to communicate the battle plan to the latter, who made a

fatal error in detaching his troops from the main army. General Roos sacrificed men by a prolonged attack on a useless redoubt in the initial stages of
battle. Calculations that the Russians would remain passive or could be cut
off from a difficult escape route (on the assumption that they would flee)
proved unfounded. Swedish losses on the battlefield were 6,901 dead/
wounded and 2,760 taken prisoner. Official figures put Russian losses at 1,345
killed and 3,290 wounded.

To Catherine, who was in the baggage train at the village of Vladimirovka,
Peter wrote: 'Greetings, Matushka! I report that this day the All-Merciful God
has granted us an unprecedented victory over the enemy. In short, the whole
enemy army has been knocked out, about which you will hear later. PS.
Come and join us to congratulate me in person.'[8] On 30 June the exhausted
remnant of the Swedish army, 14,299 men with 34 cannon, surrendered at
Perevolochna on the Dnieper to Menshikov's contingent of 9,000 troops.
Charles made his escape across the Dnieper into Turkish territory with his
aides, a handful of Cossacks and a few hundred cavalrymen.

The battle of Poltava generated some powerful legends, nearly all centred
on Peter himself. As an official report put it:

> And so by the grace of the All-Highest this perfect victory (few precedents
> of which have ever been heard of) was won with little effort and little
> bloodshed against a proud foe by His Majesty the Tsar's glorious weaponry
> and personal brave and wise command and the valour of the officers and
> men. For His Majesty showed his own courage, greatness of spirit and mar-
> tial skill in the highest degree, ignoring all danger to his own person.[9]

The 'Tale of the Three Bullets' recounts how Peter narrowly escaped death at
several points in the battle. One bullet pierced his three-cornered hat, leaving
a hole the size of a walnut, allegedly the same hat now kept in the Hermitage's
'Peter the Great's Wardrobe' collection, along with Peter's Preobrazhensky
guards uniform, the latter now a faded dark blue, although the original green
can still be seen below the cuffs. No bullet hole is detectable in the hat (as a
result of shrinkage caused by age, according to the curator), but Peter's bronze
breastplate, also preserved, appears to bear traces of a missile. Among the
treasures on show in the Kremlin Dormition Cathedral in the nineteenth
century was a cross, allegedly once the property of the Byzantine Emperor
Constantine, which, legend has it, stopped another bullet from piercing
Peter's chest.

Painters did not have to witness the battle in order to capture the required
poses: the equestrian image of the victorious ruler or general against the background of a battle was an artistic cliché, which could be customised with local
details. In one of the best-known versions, J. G. Dannhauer's *Peter I crowned
by Victory at Poltava* (1710s or 1720s), the rider on the rearing bay horse hold-

ing the emblematic commander's baton in his right hand, looking over his left shoulder at the viewer, is recognisably Peter, wearing the uniform of the Preobrazhensky guards and the Order of St Andrew. An allegorical winged female figure representing Victory hands down a laurel wreath for his head. In the background Russians (to our left) pursue fleeing Swedes (to our right) amidst smoky confusion. The grandest of the painted canvases on this theme produced during Peter's lifetime was Louis Caravaque's Poltava panorama, 281 × 487 cm (State Hermitage, 1718), in which Peter, on a horse rearing up on a slight promontory, gestures with his sword towards the battle scene below (where Swedes can be seen fleeing pursued by Russians) as he looks over his left shoulder towards a group of mounted generals. The scene was captured in other media – in prints, enamels, medals and tapestries – and continued to be reproduced long after the battle in order to keep alive a defining moment in Peter's personal career. By the time an equestrian image was used on engravings celebrating the peace of Nystad and the new imperial titles in 1721, Peter had not fought the Swedes on horseback for a good many years, but the conventional motif served to remind viewers of the crucial victories which had brought about Russia's new international status. Later, under the chisel of Etienne Falconet and the pen of Alexander Pushkin, the horseman remained the most enduring of all Petrine images.

After Poltava Peter made his way to Kiev (where on 24 July he had a meeting with Feofan Prokopovich, rector of the Kiev Academy and soon to become his chief publicist) and from there to Poland, in late September reaching Warsaw, from where he wrote to Catherine that he soon hoped to join her and told her not to make jokes about him 'amusing himself' as he was 'too old' for such things. He recounted how one of his companions had got drunk ('consorted too much with John Barleycorn') and injured himself falling off a roof. The letter was accompanied by a gift of fresh lemons.[10] Stopping off for various diplomatic meetings, Peter slowly made his way back to St Petersburg via Mitau and Riga. He spent a couple of weeks in St Petersburg before setting off for Moscow to celebrate his victory. On 18 December a triumphal parade set out from Kolomenskoe for the centre of Moscow. (On the same day Peter's daughter Elizabeth was born, a happy coincidence much exploited by publicists during her own reign as empress in 1741–61.) The parade, commemorated in a print by Aleksei Zubov, was described by an eyewitness as 'undoubtedly the grandest and most magnificent triumphal procession in Europe since the time of the ancient Romans',[11] but it also featured Peter's own peculiar brand of disguise. Even after this key victory, Peter did not claim the ceremonial laurels, either as commander-in-chief or as sovereign. In the formal march-past on 21 December his role was, as on previous occasions, that of colonel of his regiment, the Preobrazhenskys, which was followed by a battalion of the Semenovsky guards escorting trophies and prisoners from the battle of Lesnaia. Between the two regiments drove a carriage drawn by reindeer bearing the fool Vimeni, one of several jesters in Peter's entourage. The next day Peter and fellow officers Boris Sheremetev and Alexander Menshikov submitted formal reports on the victories at Lesnaia and Poltava to His Imperial Majesty Fedor Romodanovsky, who was enthroned in state to receive the captured Swedes. A portrait set up outside Romodanovsky's Moscow residence was captioned 'The unconquerable and most fortunate Emperor', ostensibly a reference to Prince-Caesar rather than to Tsar Peter, although the true identity of the victor was hardly a secret. The celebrations continued until 1 January, when the new year was marked by a huge firework display, the centrepiece of which was a fiery Russian eagle shooting an arrow into the Swedish lion. The Danish agent Just Juel described 'beautiful blue and green lights, invented by the tsar himself, and also numerous fiery globes and rains, which turned night into daylight'.[12] After Poltava the discourse that Peter himself could turn darkness into light and non-existence into being gained currency.

Turk of the North

The Poltava victory was, as Peter wrote many years later, 'a divine miracle; for it reveals that all human minds are as nothing against the will of God'.[13] Foreign observers viewed the 'miracle' with some foreboding. Leibniz wrote to the Russian envoy in Vienna in August 1709: 'You can imagine how the great revolution in the north has astounded people. It is being said that the tsar will be formidable to the whole of Europe, that he will be a sort of Turk of the North.'[14]

Victory allowed Peter to renew and extend the northern alliance. Poland was freed from Swedish occupation and Augustus was restored to the Polish throne. A meeting between him and Peter in Torun produced a new treaty of alliance signed on 9 October 1709, allowing Russia to station troops in Poland. A secret clause recognised Augustus's claim to Livonia. Augustus for his part realised that he owed his crown to Russia. The Poltava victory determined Russia's programme of maintaining the Polish Commonwealth's territorial integrity and 'golden liberties' (which more or less guaranteed opportunities for foreign intervention as a result of the Poles' inability to agree among themselves) right up to the first partition of Poland in 1772. On 10 and 11 October Russia signed treaties with Prussia and Denmark. Britain expressed willingness to act as mediator between Russia and Sweden, while the French were prepared for Russia to mediate, together with Denmark and Poland, in the War of the Spanish Succession, which was going badly. Diplomatically, Russia had never been in a stronger position.

The maritime powers were anxious lest Russia become *too* powerful. Britain in particular insisted that Sweden must not be allowed to collapse completely and that a balance must be maintained in the north. Nor was Russia totally secure in the south. At the beginning of February 1710 the Danish envoy Just Juel received a negative response to his king's request for aid for his fleet:

> Now on account of the state of war and many expenses, also for fear of a sudden attack by the Turks, for which emergency preparations are being made, His Majesty [the tsar] cannot help, but will do what can be done in the future.... In the meantime His Majesty the king should himself act for the common good and arm his fleet at his own expense and go into action, which he is capable of doing as they have been at peace for a long time while we have been at war.[15]

On 6 February 1710, however, news reached Russia that the 1700 peace treaty with Turkey had been renewed. Peter was relieved: 'For this fine deed, praise be to the all-powerful Lord: now we can turn our eyes and thoughts in one direction.'[16] Sweden's Baltic ports were ready for the taking. In early February Elbing was captured. On 14 June 1710 Peter entered the fortress of Viborg, subdued with naval support, which he declared to be a 'firm bulwark' for the city of St Petersburg. The conquest was duly celebrated in the company of the Drunken Assembly and proclamations were sent to allies and to the mock sovereigns Romodanovsky and Buturlin. On 4 July the 'famed and strong town of Riga was taken from the enemy with little loss with God's help' after a long siege.[17] This victory gave particular satisfaction to Peter, who had never forgotten the 'insult' of 1697. (In November 1709 he had reported to Menshikov from outside the walls of the besieged city that he had thrown the first three grenades into the town with his own hands, 'for which I thank God for allowing me personally the honour of starting the vengeance against this accursed place'.[18]) Several Swedish garrisons, many laid low by the plague which was raging round the Baltic, now fell to the Russians in quick succession: in August Dünamünde and Pernau, and in September Kexholm (Korela), the island of Oesel, the fortress at Arensburg and the Estonian port of Reval (Tallinn). Peter wrote to Romodanovsky on 10 October:

> I beg to inform your majesty that the All-Highest has granted us success in this campaign almost comparable with the last, for the last town, Reval, has surrendered to Lieutenant-General Bauer. And so Livonia and Estonia are cleansed of the enemy. In a word, the enemy on the left side of this eastern sea not only has no towns but also no territory left. Now it only remains to ask the Lord God for a good peace.[19]

Peter first visited Reval in December 1711 to view the fortifications and in 1714 he bought a plot of land nearby where he ordered a small house in the Dutch

style to be built with a view of the sea. Orchards and trees were planted, some
of which were still there in the late eighteenth century. At the same time he
commissioned a grander palace called Ekaterinental with cascades and foundations from the architect Michetti, replicating the pattern of a grand residence for formal receptions and a modest house for private use which can be
found at Peterhof, Strel'na and other estates.

There was no more talk of handing over Livonia to Augustus. A medal
issued to mark Russian victories has Peter wearing a laurel wreath, armour
and mantle, and on the reverse Hercules bearing a globe with the towns
Narva, Reval, Dorpat, Pernau, Arensburg and Riga marked and the legend in
Latin I HAVE THE STRENGTH TO BEAR SUCH A BURDEN.[20] Russia's occupation
of the Baltic ports was consolidated by maintaining and in some cases restoring local privileges and laws, extending to inhabitants 'the full protection of
His Majesty the Tsar'. Peter later ratified Baltic privileges in his General
Regulation of 1720 and in the 1721 Treaty of Nystad. Estonian and Livonian
laws were used as models for new Russian legislation, for example statutes on
landed estates and laws on provision for orphans. But privileges were accompanied by watchfulness. Peter wrote to the governor of Riga in 1716 warning
him that Sweden still had many supporters in the Baltic towns and that he
should act with caution, taking regular censuses of the population. All new
arrivals must be questioned and arrested on the least suspicion, curfews were
imposed and a maximum of 300 people were allowed into the town each day.
Carts and cargoes were to be searched for weapons, and ships docking in
summer searched below decks.[21] Religious freedom was guaranteed in the
conquered provinces, but facilities for Orthodox worship were extended. In
Riga a wooden Lutheran church and a chapel in the citadel were turned into
Orthodox churches (one in the name of SS Peter and Paul) and a destroyed
Catholic church in the town was restored and reconsecrated as Orthodox in
the name of Alexis Man of God, in honour of Peter's father, who had narrowly failed to take Riga in the 1650s.

For the German-speaking merchants and gentry, swapping Swedish rule
for Russian was not such a bad deal if it meant peace and the return of landed
estates confiscated by the Swedish crown, while the mass of the population
probably hardly noticed the difference. For them the main effect of war was
general devastation. Friedrich Christian Weber from Hanover, in Riga in
1714, recorded that the land was 'so dispeopled, that not the fourth Part of it
is inhabited, and the vast Number of Ruins of Gentlemens Seats, and other
Houses, shew what Ravage the War has made there'.[22] It was to be many years
before the prosperity of the region was restored.

Paradise regained. The growth of St Petersburg

In 1709 Peter was able to spend only a couple of weeks in St Petersburg, but with military operations again focused on the Baltic he was there for much of 1710, when, in the words of an official history, 'he ordered houses of amusement to be built of stone of fine architectural design, to embellish gardens and speed the erection of fortifications, and also gave orders for more houses to be built for naval servitors and merchants, and the gentlemen ministers, generals and distinguished nobles were ordered to build stone mansions'.[23] In February 1710 he wrote to Menshikov: 'I only hope that the Lord God may settle your affairs as quickly as possible and that we will see you here, so that you too may see the beauty of this Paradise as a reward for the labours in which you participated together with us, which I wish with all my heart, for this place really is thriving like a fine infant.'[24]

The Summer and Winter Palaces (the latter replaced by another in 1725, which in turn made way for the existing building, completed in 1762) were begun in 1710, as were the mansions of Menshikov, Gavrila Golovkin and other magnates, the Alexander Nevsky monastery and the wooden church of St Isaac of Dalmatia, the saint whose feast fell on Peter's birthday. In 1711 a *perspektiva* or avenue (today's Nevsky Prospekt) was laid, leading from the Admiralty, one of the first sites to be constructed, to the monastery. In 1712 the construction of the stone cathedral of SS Peter and Paul in the fortress began, although not until after Peter's death did it eclipse the nearby Trinity Cathedral (demolished in 1927) as the city's main church. The chief architect of several of these projects was the Swiss-Italian Domenico Trezzini, who came to Russia in 1703 and died there in 1734. He was also in charge of a team of Russian trainee architects. All the major architects of Petrine St Petersburg were foreigners. They included the Germans Johann Friedrich Braunstein, Georg Johann Mattarnovi and Andreas Schlüter, the Austrian Nicholas Friedrich Härbel, the Frenchman Jean Baptiste Le Blond and Italians Gaetano Chiaveri and Niccolo Michetti. Peter's own contribution to the planning of St Petersburg was substantial, not one important building being built without his participation at some stage of construction. The resulting 'Paradise' was a sort of ribbon development of buildings immediately adjacent to the River Neva and its branches, with a few focal points, such as the Peter-Paul fortress, Trinity Square (with government offices and the main cathedral) and Admiralty Square. Buildings were mostly constructed of brick, stuccoed in bright colours and decorated with bands of flat white pilasters and window surrounds and the horizon was punctuated by bold spires and the masts of ships. Everywhere there were patches of greenery, most of it artificially cultivated. From 1710 a bureau, headed by Boris Neronov, ran the tsar's gardens. Apprentice gardeners were summoned from Moscow, together with plants and seeds, exotic flowering, medicinal and fruit-bearing species as well as native varieties. For Peter, the city's poor soils, short summers and long, dark winters were no deterrent to transforming it into heaven on earth.

Two weddings

After Poltava St Petersburg came to be regarded as the capital, although no decree was issued and the transfer of the court and government offices from Moscow was effected in stages. The autumn of 1710 marked St Petersburg's inauguration as Russia's ceremonial capital, when it witnessed a three-day victory celebration on 8–10 October, followed by the wedding of Peter's niece, seventeen-year-old Anna Ivanovna, to Frederick William, duke of Courland, also aged seventeen, described as 'handsome, well-brought up and charming'.[25] The marriage had the blessing of Peter's ally the king of Prussia, the duke's uncle. For his part, Peter gained a useful channel of influence in Courland, which was a nominal vassal of Poland-Lithuania. This was, needless to say, not a love match. At the outset of negotiations the envoys from Courland asked for portraits of all three of Tsar Ivan's surviving daughters, any one of whom would have been considered a suitable bride. The marriage contract, signed on 10 June 1710 in St Petersburg, fixed the dowry at 200,000 roubles, which would allow the duke to pay off his debts and redeem mortgaged estates. Anna was to retain her Orthodox faith.[26] Peter instructed his niece on her priorities: 'Preserve the faith and law in which you were born, to the end of your days unswervingly. Don't forget your own people, but love and respect them above all others. Love and respect your husband as the head [of the family] and obey him in all things except the aforementioned.'[27]

The wedding, which took place on 31 October 1710 in the chapel of Menshikov's newly built palace, was the first important royal rite of passage to be held in St Petersburg and set the tone for others to come, with a public procession headed by musicians, which travelled to the church by boat. Near the quay groups of workers in funny costumes waved rockets. During the ceremony Peter held the crown traditionally used at Orthodox weddings over the head of the groom and Menshikov over the bride, but Peter got bored and ordered the priest to get it over with quickly. Parts of the service were therefore omitted. Two days of feasting followed. Fireworks on rafts on the Neva illuminated crowns over the letters A and F and two palm trees with entwined tops with the inscription: LOVE UNITES. On another screen Cupid with his hammer and anvil welded together two hearts under the inscription: TWO JOINED TOGETHER AS ONE. Peter himself explained the meaning of each allegorical picture as it burned.

The entertainments did not end there. On 14 November St Petersburg witnessed the wedding of the royal dwarf Iakim Volkov and his dwarf bride, a striking example of how 'real' and 'mock' court life intermingled. The tsar in person held the wedding crown over the bride's head and hurried proceedings along, just as he had at Anna's wedding. Anna and Frederick were now guests at the dwarfs' wedding feast, which was held in the same room in Menshikov's palace as their own. In fact, Peter had planned both weddings simultaneously, evidently seeing the second as a sequel to the first. In August 1710, a day after he ordered a pair of diamond earrings as a gift for his niece, he had instructed Prince-Caesar Romodanovsky to round up all the dwarfs in Moscow and send them to St Petersburg. Their owners were told to provide smart outfits for the dwarfs in the latest Western fashion, with plenty of gold braid and periwigs. In St Petersburg they were allocated to the lords and ladies who were to dress them up and transport them to the nuptials. On the day about seventy dwarfs formed the retinue for the wedding ceremony, which was accompanied by the stifled giggles of the full-sized congregation and even the priest, a spectacle made all the funnier by the fact that most of the dwarfs were of peasant extraction with coarse manners. At the feast in the grand hall of Menshikov's palace the dwarfs sat at miniature tables in the centre of the room, while full-sized guests watched them from tables at the sides. They roared with laughter as dwarfs, especially the older, uglier ones whose hunchbacks, huge bellies and short crooked legs made it difficult for them to dance, fell down drunk or engaged in brawls. Miniature cannons were standing at the ready and the groom had made his own fireworks, but they were not set off as Menshikov's only son, Luke-Peter (born February 1709), was seriously ill, and, indeed, died the same evening. The occasion was immortalised in an engraving made by Aleksei Zubov in 1711, entitled *The wedding and merriment of His Majesty the Tsar's dwarfs in St Petersburg at which were gathered a great many dwarfs in the house of His Excellency Prince Alexander Danilovich Menshikov. November 14, 1710.*

On one level, the dwarf wedding was just an entertainment. Being amused by the vertically challenged may offend modern sensibilities, but dwarfs were a standard feature of early modern European courts and noble households. (The famous painting of Henrietta Maria, queen of Charles I of England, with her dwarf John Hudson is one of several on the theme.) The 6 foot 7 inch tsar loved his contingent of resident dwarfs, who were liable to surprise guests by leaping from pies (sometimes naked), dancing on tables or trotting in on miniature ponies, as well as performing domestic duties and running errands. Iakim, the bridegroom, was with Peter at Poltava and later accompanied him abroad as a miniature servant. But like all Peter's mock spectacles, the dwarf wedding also operated on a more symbolic level. Its juxtaposition with the wedding of Anna and the duke and its imitation of certain elements suggested that the full-sized guests were watching caricatures of themselves, miniature 'lords and ladies' clad, like them, in unfamiliar Western dress. Peter's courtiers, like his new city, still had a long way to go before they were fully fledged, 'grown-up' Europeans. The coarse 'peasant' behaviour and drunkenness which so amused them in the dwarfs actually bore an uncomfortable resemblance to the well-attested gross manners of fully grown Russian courtiers, one aspect of which was only too tragically illustrated not long after. At the beginning of 1711 the newly-wed duke and duchess set off for Courland, but when they were less than 50 miles from St Petersburg, Frederick died. Just Juel reported that the duke was already ill when he left St Petersburg from the effects of excessive drinking and 'unpleasantness' suffered at the hands of Menshikov.[28]

Anna returned to St Petersburg forthwith, collected her widow's pension and embarked upon the nomadic existence which was to last until she became empress of Russia in 1730. No doubt she would have preferred to remain at home, but the presence of a Russian retinue in Courland was too valuable to Peter for him to allow her to return permanently. Over the years she received proposals from various suitors, but nothing came of them. Anna's life alternated between Russia and Courland, where her household expenses were regulated by Peter down to the last detail. When she became empress herself she proved a good student of Peter's peculiar brand of humour. Her own court featured a nobleman 'fool' whose main duty was to pretend to be a chicken and whom she married off to a Kalmyk woman in a palace of ice, perhaps recalling her own brief marriage.

War with Turkey

Frederick's sudden death contributed to the gloom which now descended on St Petersburg. On 23 December 1710 Peter had received the news that the Ottoman Empire had declared war on Russia and that his ambassador Peter Tolstoy had been thrown into the Seven Towers in Constantinople. Just Juel wrote that the Russians were so depressed by the news that they wandered around listlessly, although he attributed at least some of their limpness to the fast which preceded Christmas.[29] Turkish and Crimean affairs were an important element in Peter's calculations throughout the Northern War, particularly when the theatre of operations shifted to Ukraine in 1708–9. The Ottoman Turks had stopped short of intervention at the time of Poltava, but now Charles XII's escape to Turkish territory and his efforts to persuade the Turks to declare war on Russia tipped the scales. The rabidly anti-Russian Crimean khan Devlet-Girei offered troops to escort Charles back north and succeeded in winning the sultan's ear. French diplomacy, British bankers' loans to Charles and the intervention of the sultan's doctor and mother, all influenced the Ottoman decision to go to war.

Initially Peter himself was not averse to the prospect of a short, victorious war in the south. Russian success would deprive Sweden of a potential ally. He might even expand into Ottoman lands under the pretext of liberating

Balkan Christians. He issued orders for a large-scale mobilisation but preparations went slowly. Peter wrote to Menshikov: 'Don't be upset because I don't write often; really there's indescribable confusion and depression on account of the mess things are in here.'[30] Routine peace proposals were made to the Swedes, in the hope of avoiding war on two fronts, but Charles refused to relinquish even one province to buy what he regarded as a shameful peace. On 22 February 1711 Peter declared war, denouncing the 'oath-breaking' sultan as the ally of Sweden and Leszczynski and accusing him of using followers of Mazepa and Bulavin against Augustus and all Christendom. The document set out the history of Russo-Turkish relations for the past thirty years or so, itemising offences committed by Turkish subjects against Russia during truces.

The Senate

A handwritten edict dated the same day listed the names of ten men 'to govern in our absence' under the title of the 'ruling Senate'. The senators' duties, specified in another laconic edict dated 2 March, were to act as judges, supervise state expenses and eliminate unnecessary ones; increase revenues ('since money is the artery of war'); replenish the officer corps and track down shirkers; regulate receipts for money and goods in government offices; inspect and certify goods held in franchises or chancelleries and provincial offices; sort out salt franchises, increase trade with China and Persia and attract more Armenian traders. A footnote mentioned the appointment of officials called fiscals, who were supposed to unmask embezzlement, bribe-taking and serious infringements of the law by other state officials.[31] Peter clearly intended the new Senate to wield real authority: everyone, churchmen and laymen, must obey it as they did the tsar himself, under threat of cruel punishment or death, depending on the crime. It could even issue its own edicts independently of the sovereign. As Peter wrote to Menshikov on 11 March: '. . . we have given [the ruling Senate] full powers. Therefore write to them with all your requests, and write to us only to keep us informed in order not to waste time.'[32] The senators, for their part, had to swear to serve the sovereign's and state's interests 'to the last drop of their strength'. All senators had an equal voice and their decisions had to be unanimous.

Peter created the Senate in response to the impending conflict with Turkey. There was no detailed consideration of foreign models or lengthy discussions and redrafting, as was to be the case with some later reforms. Peter had a limited pool of talent to draw on. His closest colleagues were already occupied with the Northern War, including its diplomatic ramifications, or would be needed for the Turkish campaign (military and foreign policy tasks were omitted from the Senate's brief) and there was no single individual to whom he could entrust the country's domestic affairs in his absence. So he revived the Muscovite practice of leaving the capital in charge of a group of boyars when the ruler was away, but gave it a name suggestive of the spirit if not the substance of ancient imperial institutions. The Senate was thus one of many pieces of Roman 'window-dressing' with which the new empire was embellished.

The senators faced an unenviable task, for which their talents and experience ill equipped them. One of the original ten, M. I. Dolgoruky, was probably illiterate. His fellow senator G. A. Plemiannikov (died in 1713) signed on his behalf. Prince P. A. Golitsyn (1682–1722), the youngest of the original senators by more than a decade, was a junior member of his clan. Prince G. I. Volkonsky and V. A. Apukhtin were arrested in 1714 and had their tongues burned for 'taking out contracts for provisioning under false names, taking a high price and thereby burdening the people'.[33] The oldest and the most obscure of the first senators was N. P. Mel'nitsky (born 1645), who survived to serve only a year. Only two had close personal ties with the tsar: the boyars Tikhon Nikitich Streshnev, who at sixty-two was too old to serve in the army, and Ivan Musin-Pushkin, who had done useful work in the Monastery department. The rest probably owed their promotion to influential connections.

At first Peter was greatly disappointed by this hastily created body. His letters bristle with frustration. 'We are amazed that since our departure [for the war] from Moscow we have had no word from you about what is happening there,' he wrote on 4 May 1711.[34] Two weeks later he reprimanded them for writing with excuses 'just like the old judges … or has the oath which you swore not long ago already escaped your memory?'[35] Peter's closer associates were reluctant to channel business through persons they regarded as their inferiors. Peter reprimanded Menshikov: 'Please write to them (the senators) on all matters, because in writing to us here and from here to the Senate in Moscow more time is wasted in writing than if you write direct to them.'[36] Things hardly improved over the next few years. Senators were behaving 'in the old stupid manner'.[37] They misunderstood Peter's instructions: 'You should have been able to work out from our letters to you in which we kept repeating that this is vital to the interests of our state,' he wrote, 'that you were supposed to increase and strengthen the corps in St Petersburg, not to diminish it.'[38] They were inefficient and procrastinating: 'We have been informed … that you have not resolved one major case but just keep putting everything off from one date to the next, forgetting God and your souls. Therefore I am writing for the last time to say that if at least five or six major cases are not resolved by 1 November and if you do not put criminals who damage state interests for their own benefit to death, showing mercy to no one … it will be the worse for you.'[39] This ongoing correspondence provides revealing illustrations of the frustration and impatience which Peter constantly felt and expressed when other people's failings undermined or delayed his schemes.

'The true and lawful sovereign lady'

Peter had good reason to be apprehensive about the coming war. On 24 February he chided the official Aleksei Kurbatov for complaining about his posting as vice-governor of Archangel, 'like some faint-hearted Jonah, without regard for the troubles and grief in which your leader finds himself'.[40] He also felt the need to put his personal affairs in order. On 6 March 1711, the day of his departure for the Turkish front, 'it was publicly announced that the sovereign lady Tsaritsa Ekaterina Alekseevna is the true and lawful sovereign lady'.[41] Peter later explained to Menshikov that he had taken this step 'on account of the hazardous journey'. Were his daughters to be left orphans, their position would be more secure, 'but if God brings this business [i.e. the war] to a happy conclusion,' he added, 'we shall complete the formalities in St Petersburg'.[42] Peter knew from experience how quickly alliances at court could change and had every reason to fear the reaction of friends and relatives of Tsarevich Alexis and his mother Tsaritsa Evdokia if Catherine were to be left alone. If the couple were married secretly in November 1707, as some sources suggest, Peter clearly did not regard the ceremony as sufficiently legal and binding to protect Catherine from being banished and his daughters declared illegitimate in the event of his death. Just Juel's diary provides further clarification. During a visit to Tsaritsa Praskovia's residence in Moscow on 10 March 1711 Juel learned from Peter's nieces that just before his departure Peter had summoned them and his sister Natalia to Preobrazhenskoe and told them that in the future they were to regard Catherine as his legal spouse and as tsaritsa. If he were to die in the forthcoming campaign before he managed to marry her, they were still to regard her as his wife.[43]

Peter was aware of public disapproval of his alliance with a foreign commoner. Traditionalists continued to regard Evdokia as Peter's real wife. According to strict Orthodox rules on consanguinity, Peter was even accused of marrying his own granddaughter and niece, on the grounds that his son Alexis and his sister Natalia were Catherine's godparents at her conversion to Orthodoxy. In 1720 the monk Aleksei was accused of making similar allegations. Catherine 'consorted with foreigners and there would be harm done to Christians because she was not of local origins'. He added that Peter and his assistants failed to keep the fasts, under the influence of the 'fallen Western church of Rome', that Menshikov had been seen smoking in church and Aleksei Petrovich Saltykov had taken out his tobacco pouch and lit up right in front of the altar during mass.[44] Peter was not amused by allegations that his relationship with Catherine was a sign of his ungodliness. He had the monk broken on the wheel.

Battle on the Pruth

In mid-March Peter crossed the Polish–Lithuanian border on his way to meet the Turks. Catherine travelled with him. One of his hopes was that Russian action would spark uprisings in the Ottoman empire to sap Turkish morale. In a message to 'Christian peoples subjugated to Turkey' Peter wrote: 'I am taking upon myself a heavy burden for the sake of the love of God, for which reason I have entered into war with the Turkish realm ... because the Turks have trampled on our faith, taken our churches and lands by cunning, pillaged and destroyed many of our churches and monasteries.'[45] An appeal was also issued further afield to Christians in Serbia, Macedonia and Herzegovina. Standards carried in the campaign bore the image of the cross and declaration of Constantine the Great: UNDER THIS SIGN WE CONQUER. In mid-April Peter reached Slutsk in the Grand Duchy of Lithuania, where a council of war outlined a plan for a forced march to the Danube to head off the Turks before they reached Moldavia and Poland. Boris Sheremetev protested that he could not cover the ground in the time required; he was short of supplies, weapons and men, but Peter insisted upon *speed*. It was vital to reach the Danube before the Turks and join forces with local Orthodox rulers. A treaty was signed with Hospodar Dmitry Cantemir of Moldavia in April 1711: in return for military support, Moldavia was to become an autonomous Russian protectorate. But Brancovan, the hospodar of Wallachia, was less willing to co-operate. Wallachian nobles were of the opinion that 'it is dangerous to declare for Russia until the tsar's army crosses the Danube. Who knows whether Wallachia in the power of the Russians will be happier than under the domination of the Turks?'[46] The Russian army was very much in need of local support. Poor harvests had created food shortages along the way. Clean water was scarce and intense heat burned the grass, causing fodder shortages reminiscent of those during Vasily Golitsyn's Crimean campaigns.

In the event, the Turks did get there first. Cantemir supplied only about 5,000 men, while any lingering hope of aid from the reluctant Brancovan was dashed when he turned over his supplies to the Turks. On 23 June Peter arrived on the River Pruth in Moldavia and on 30 June wrote to Menshikov:

> Our march was indescribably hard on account of the heat and thirst ... I expect things to be resolved by the middle of July as to whether there will be a battle or not. May God bestow his grace on the righteous in this affair. People are saying that the Turks are not very enthusiastic about this war, but God alone knows if this is so. They have strong artillery, five hundred cannons.[47]

In the battle which took place on 9 July 38,000 Russian troops found themselves facing a combined Turkish and Tatar force of 130,000. Despite their superior numbers, the Turks suffered heavy losses in their first encounter with Russian artillery, but the Russians remained unaware of the extent of the damage inflicted and Peter refused to counter-attack before he had dug in his supply train. The battle was thus inconclusive, but the Russians could not afford to wait for an outcome because of shortages of food and ammunition. Peter's dilemma was summed up in a letter to the Senate dated 10 July: they were surrounded and he himself was likely either to die or be taken prisoner. In the latter event the senators were instructed to cease to regard Peter as their sovereign until he returned in person. In the event of his death they were to choose 'the most worthy' of his successors.[48] The text may not be authentic, but gives a fair estimate of the danger in which Peter found himself. In the end, disaster was averted by the moderateness of Turkish demands, which were probably tempered by news of the Russian General Rönne's successful raid on the Danube at Brailov on 7 July. There were also rumours that a huge bribe, including Catherine's jewels, persuaded the grand vizier to allow the Russians to retreat, but these stories almost certainly originated in Ukraine and Sweden after the event. Anxious to concentrate on conquests in the Mediterranean, Turkey contented itself with formal tokens of Russian with-drawal from Poland and, much to Charles XII's disgust, refused to give any further guarantees to Sweden.

By the peace treaty of 12 July 1711 Russia agreed to surrender Azov and its district to Turkey and to destroy its southern fleet. The forts at Taganrog and Kamenny Zaton (on the Dnieper above the Zaporozhian Cossack camp) were to be razed. There were clauses on Polish affairs (Poland was to be a free state), trade and safe passage home for Charles. Peter tried to put a brave face on it. In a letter to Fedor Apraksin dated 15 July he wrote: 'It is a sad thing to lose those places in which so much effort and expense have been invested, but this loss means a strengthening for the other business [i.e. war with Sweden], which is an incomparable gain for us.'[49] He wrote in a similar vein to G. F. Dolgoruky: 'On the one hand, this peace represents a loss; on the other by this event we have entirely disengaged ourselves from the Turkish affair and are [better] able with all our strength and with God's help to fight the Swedes.'[50] Writing to Apraksin in September he continued to look on the bright side: 'Of course, it's very painful, but it's best to choose the lesser of two evils, for you yourself can judge which war is the more difficult to con-clude.'[51]

Still, Peter was devastated at the prospect of losing Azov, which he could not bring himself to mention by name in his hand-corrected draft of the July treaty. 'The Lord God drove me out of this place, like Adam out of Paradise,' he is alleged to have said, using an image more often associated with St Petersburg.[52] He attempted to delay the handover and the destruction of Taganrog fort until he received confirmation that Charles had left Turkey, specifying that the foundations of the forts should be retained, 'as in time

God might make things turn out differently'.[53] Early in 1712 the Turks responded to these prevarications by declaring war on Russia again. Conflict was averted and a second peace treaty (the Iusuf-Pasha pact) was signed on 5 April. Further delays by the Russians in withdrawing troops from Poland prompted yet another declaration of war by Turkey in October, this time with Swedish and French backing. On 13 June 1713 a more lasting peace was finally signed at Adrianople, the first clause of which obliged Russia to withdraw its troops from Poland within two months. In fact, few of the clauses of the Treaty of Adrianople had any lasting effect. Peter did not 'keep his hands off' Poland. In April 1714 the sultan recognised Augustus II's possession of Polish Ukraine, which in effect ratified Russian influence; the Russo-Turkish border remained fluid; Cossacks and Tatars took little notice of agreements between Moscow and Constantinople; Charles XII returned to Sweden in November 1714, avoiding Russian territory; and Russia regained Azov in 1739. But peace allowed Peter once again to concentrate his efforts in the north.

Alexis and Charlotte

After the initial truce with the Turks in July 1711 Peter did not return to Russia but travelled to Poland, reaching Warsaw in late August, and then on to Saxony, where he visited Dresden (9–11 September) and Carlsbad (13 September to 3 October); here he took the waters, which he found a tedious experience. He wrote to Catherine on 19 September: 'You write that I should-n't hurry back to join you on account of my cure, but I think it's because you have found someone taller than me. Please write and let me know if he is one of us or from Torun? I rather think it must be a man from Torun as you want to get your revenge for what I did two years ago. That's just the sort of thing you daughters of Eve do to us old men!'[54] On 13 October he himself arrived in Torun to attend the wedding of his son Alexis to Princess Charlotte-Christina-Sophia of Wolfenbüttel in the palace of the queen of Poland the following day. It was a foregone conclusion that Alexis would marry a foreign princess and Charlotte was a good catch. The Brunswick-Wolfenbüttels were related by marriage to many of the royal and princely families of Europe. Charlotte's grandfather was Duke Anton Ulrich of Holstein-Gottorp and her sister was married to the Habsburg Emperor Charles VI. In theory, Alexis could have refused the match. 'Why haven't you written to tell me what you thought of her and whether you are inclined to marry her?' wrote Peter in August 1710 after the couple first met.[55] In 1718 in his manifesto depriving Alexis of the throne, Peter insisted that Alexis had been allowed to choose his own bride (as long as she was a foreigner) and had even asked his father to arrange the marriage. In reality, the idea seems to have been Peter's. Under the terms of the contract signed in April 1711, Charlotte was allowed to retain her

Protestant faith, but any children were to be raised in the Orthodox faith. Peter promised gifts of cash, tableware and carriages. When his new in-laws enquired about the whereabouts of these gifts in September 1711 Peter replied sarcastically that, having arrived in Germany straight from the war, he could hardly have tableware and carriages about his person.[56]

Menshikov sent a water-melon as a gift. It is not clear whether this was intended as a rare delicacy, a fertility symbol or a joke. One is inclined to think the latter, given Peter's half-mocking attitude to the proceedings. He wrote to Catherine on 14 October: 'On this day the wedding of my son took place, at which many distinguished persons were present ... I beg you to notify the all-jesting Prince-Pope and the others of this and ask him to bless the newly-weds dressed in all his robes together with all those who are there with you.'[57] A few days after the wedding Peter informed Alexis that he must continue his studies and war work. His new duties included organising food supply depots and river transport for the troops going to Pomerania in Menshikov's regiment.

Thus began an unhappy and ill-fated union. Rumour has it that Alexis found his bride too thin and pockmarked and was influenced by his friends' disapproval of a foreign Protestant bride, who was said to be cold and stand-offish and always surrounded by her German entourage. Other sources suggest that Charlotte was the victim: being dragged off to Russia's half-built capital to live with a reluctant husband was hardly an attractive prospect. In the words of a Swedish observer Lars Erenmalm, in St Petersburg in the early 1710s, although the tsarevich had visited foreign countries and studied their languages 'in everything apart from outer clothing, he keeps to the old Russian customs and it seems the prince only outwardly follows foreign manners and is polite to foreigners more out of fear of his father than by his own inclinations and wishes'.[58] According to Weber, Alexis avoided Charlotte in public and they lived separate lives. In 1714 he formed a liaison with Afrosinia Fedorova, the serf of his tutor N. K. Viazemsky. Such an arrangement was barely enough to raise an eyebrow in other royal courts of the period and even followed a pattern already established by Peter himself. His marriage to Charlotte produced a daughter, Natalia, in 1714, and a son, Peter, in 1715. But, as we shall see, Peter had other reasons for being disappointed in his son.

The best-known portrait of Alexis dates from about this time. Painted by Johann Dannhauer, it shows a narrow-faced young man with a long nose and large brown eyes, a high forehead with a receding hairline, and long dark hair. Under a fashionable red collarless tunic with large buttons and a blue lining, he wears a breastplate, to denote a prince on active service. His features hint at ill health: by this time tuberculosis had been diagnosed, apparently exacerbated by 'corrupt Habits' and excessive drinking.[59] Although other, more flattering portraits exist, in some of which Alexis looks like a replica of his father (perhaps wishful thinking on the artists' part), Dannhauer's is almost invariably the image chosen to represent him. Dannhauer probably painted a companion portrait of Charlotte at the same time, of which only a copy survives. It shows a pleasant, narrow-faced young woman fashionably dressed, with piled-up blonde curls, indistinguishable from hundreds of other female images of the period.

As for Peter, who was soon to celebrate his fortieth birthday, artists drew a veil over his disgrace on the Pruth. In Carlsbad and Torun the Czech artist Jan Kupetsky painted two portraits, one of which, much reproduced in engravings, has an overload of martial imagery, including a wild animal skin and a turbulent sky. Peter must have approved, for in a letter to his son in January 1712, Peter ordered him to send the portraits 'immediately'.[60] One was reproduced for the *Book of Mars or Military Affairs*, a compilation of accounts of Russian victories in the Swedish war. On 31 December 1711 Peter arrived back in St Petersburg to put Pruth behind him and get on with the Swedish war.

VI

Peter in Europe
1712–17

I am well, thank God, only life is hard, for I can't use my left hand, so I am obliged to hold the sword and the pen in my right hand alone. And you know how few helpers I have. (Peter to Catherine, 2 August 1712)

Peter and Catherine wed

On 1 January 1712 Peter wrote to the Senate from St Petersburg: 'And so, praise God, because of this victory [of the Danes over the Swedes at Wismar on 1 December] the year began here with celebrations. I consider it a piece of good fortune that I am able to write these words in my first letter of the year. May God be so kind henceforth.' Prince-Caesar, addressed as usual as 'Sire', received a similar letter.[1] The allies' main objective now was to evict the Swedes from their territories in northern Germany, starting with Pomerania, and Peter was as desperate as ever to get down to business. The year began with a flurry of letters to military commanders and diplomats, including orders to place all Swedish prisoners of war in Moscow under armed guard following rumours of an escape plan. His impatience is even more palpable in a list of thirty-seven instructions to the Senate dated 16 January–28 February, some only one or two lines long, others more substantial, all written in Peter's own inelegant hand, on such diverse topics as collective responsibility for desertion and penalties for harbouring fugitives, producing weapons and uniforms, appointing a commissar to distribute wages (to reduce theft), branding recruits, strengthening Ukrainian garrisons, and establishing an engineering school, hospitals and stud farms.[2] Negotiations with Turkey over peace terms dragged on. On 23 January Peter wrote to V. L. Dolgoruky: 'From the Turkish side, praise God, there is no opposition, for this hour Azov is already handed over and, I believe, with God's help, this business will have a good resolution, and although nothing has been heard of the Swedish king or anything else, even so Field Marshal Sheremetev has been left in Kiev with troops for better security.'[3]

Amidst diplomatic correspondence – to the kings of Denmark, Poland and Prussia – and letters on provisions and ships, he continued to consider more mundane matters. On 27 January he wrote to the military commissar Pankraty Glebovsky:

I have sent you examples of regular tents and a pyramid tent, from which you should make 899 regular tents and 190 pyramids for both regiments . . .. The canvas for making them should be obtained from the Admiralty department for cash. And make absolutely certain that they are made precisely according to the samples. I want these tents to be sent to Riga this winter, to be exact, by the beginning of March so that they are ready for the troops by spring for we don't have a single tent.[4]

The tents were duly dispatched from Moscow. Peter also found time to write a few words of comfort to the widow of the British merchant and factory owner Andrew Styles, a friend since his visit to England, whose death in January 1712 he mourned 'like someone related to me by blood . . .. But we cannot reverse what is done. Therefore, do not give yourself up to excessive grief . . . but comfort yourself with the immortal glory which he had and will have.'[5]

Peter also had some personal business to attend to, although it is barely reflected in his voluminous correspondence for the first month and a half of 1712. On the morning of 19 February he dictated letters to King Augustus of Poland, complaining about violations of the Russo-Polish Treaty of 1686, and to King Frederick of Prussia, congratulating him on the birth of a grandson. Later that day he married Catherine and proceeded to the newly built Winter Palace for his wedding feast.

Judged by the standards of traditional Muscovite royal weddings, this was a strange occasion. There were no official announcements to foreign rulers, no sign of the coronation regalia and gold-spun robes which tsars and tsarevichi usually wore to get married. It is not clear where the marriage service was held. Some sources mention the church of St Isaac of Dalmatia, but Charles Whitworth, who was a guest, states clearly that the wedding was held in Menshikov's private chapel in his palace on Vasil'evsky Island. Indeed, some scholars have concluded that this was not a wedding ceremony at all, but a delayed celebration of a marriage contracted hastily in March 1711 on the eve of Peter's departure for the Turkish war. This would seem to be confirmed by Aleksei Makarov's entry in the court journal for 19 February – 'the marriage of their majesties was happily concluded'– and by Peter's remark in a letter to the shipwright G. A. Menshikov that 'yesterday we concluded our old wedding'.[6] All the same, 19 February was celebrated henceforth in the court calendar as their majesties' wedding anniversary.

Some witnesses detected an air of masquerade about the whole proceedings. Peter's choice of dress, the uniform of a rear-admiral of the fleet, emphasised a naval theme, which was reflected in his choice of attendants (so-called 'fathers', 'mothers', 'brothers' and 'sisters'), who included (according to an undated, handwritten list found among his papers) Vice-Admiral Cornelius Cruys and Rear-Admiral I. F. Botsis, Cruys's wife and Tsaritsa Praskovia, the shipwright F. M. Skliaev and chief surveyor of the fleet 'Baas' I. M. Golovin, the duchess of Courland and Daria Menshikova and the bride and groom's daughters Anna and Elizabeth as bridesmaids.[7] There were many foreign guests (who were excluded from Muscovite weddings), including Charles Whitworth and Just Juel, who both left accounts. Notable by his absence was Tsarevich Alexis, who apparently stormed off to his estate in Ingermanland on the day of the wedding in protest, perhaps disappointed that there were no special celebrations for his birthday on 18 February.

The banquet in the Winter Palace was captured in an engraving by that invaluable chronicler of early St Petersburg, Aleksei Zubov, who provided a view of the palace's great hall, its true perspective and dimensions distorted in order to accommodate the assembled guests. The scene is redolent of the new culture: bewigged and décolleté ladies and foppish gentlemen dine in a baroque setting. Members of the Drunken Assembly sit at their own table in the centre. (There was a table for women members in a separate room and other guests were also accommodated in side rooms, which the engraving cannot show.) It is also possible to see hanging from the ceiling a bone chandelier made by Peter in his turnery and installed for the wedding. Menshikov, with his diamond-studded cane, supervises proceedings. Peter is easily recognisable in the centre background, while in the foreground Catherine, no bashful, pious tsaritsa, casts an almost flirtatious glance towards the viewer over her shoulder. But tradition has not been banished entirely: icons hang in the upper corners of the room and men and women, including the bride and groom, sit on separate sides of the table. The best man was the only male allowed to sit at the women's table on the first day. Toasts and dancing were followed by a firework display, which culminated in tableaux forming the word VIVAT and two entwined columns with the couple's monograms. Peter was represented by Hymen, the god of marriage, with a torch and an eagle at his feet, and the firework bride carried a burning heart and kissing doves. Above was a crown with the device: UNITED IN YOUR LOVE.[8] The following day the guests reassembled for fruit and sweets and more dancing.

By 1712 the newly-weds were already like an old married couple, with two children living and three dead. The first fruit of their official union, Maria, appeared just over a year later, on 3 March 1713, and died in May 1715, an addition to the sad list of Peter's children who died in infancy. Peter joked in a letter to Menshikov that he had heard from his wife that she had given birth to a son (*sic*!) called Maria, but his letters do not elaborate on his disappointment at the birth of yet another girl.[9] As for Catherine, the inner circle had little choice but to accept her as Peter's consort. Her birthday (5 April) and name day (24 November) were included in the official court calendar; but the wedding did not protect her from hostile public opinion. Many refused to accept the legality of Peter's divorce from Evdokia, and Catherine's first husband Johann seems to have died only in 1718. By and large, protests surfaced when they were uttered under torture in the Preobrazhensky office or some other government department or picked up by foreigners. In Russia there were no legal outlets for the expression of public opinion about the tsar and his family.

German affairs

Peter spent the first part of 1712 in the vicinity of St Petersburg and the Baltic, awaiting the outcome of talks with his allies for their joint campaign in north Germany. As he wrote to Augustus, the enemy may have been cleared out of Poland thanks to the battle of Poltava, but the war with the king of Sweden was not over yet and Poland was still in danger from an attack launched from Pomerania, to which end Poland must provision Russian troops, 'not for our own interest but especially to protect you . . . and the Polish republic from enemy attack . . . as we have no claims on the enemy territory ourselves'.[10] The request for provisions was repeated many times, including an appeal to the Polish senators. Menshikov, now a field marshal, was duly dispatched to Pomerania, together with Tsarevich Alexis, while Peter held the fort in St Petersburg. In March 1712 he issued charters to Estonia, one to the town of Reval, the other to the nobility, 'confirming all their previous privileges, rights of legal proceedings, law codes and customs which they have enjoyed of old'.[11] Most of his letters were concerned with the war. He asked Menshikov and others to keep an eye on the Danes (were they seeking a separate peace?), wrote to the king of Prussia requesting safe conduct for Russian troops through his territories and to Augustus complaining about the unsatisfactory provisioning of Russian troops. Occasionally matters further afield claimed his attention; for example, he informed the Senate that a man from Ustiug had reported that he knew of a much quicker and more convenient route to get to China, and asked them to investigate further.[12] He sent to Prince Kurakin an order for lime trees, to be temporarily planted in sand and shipped to St Petersburg.[13] In April he sailed to Viborg to collect provisions.

In June Peter set off westwards again, towards Stettin in Pomerania which was under siege by allied troops. 1 July found him in Mitau, the end of the month in Gribswald, where he wrote to the king of Denmark to express his consternation that, having made a long and fatiguing journey for their common interests, 'not sparing my health', and despite having sent three times the number of troops agreed, he had found the men idle for lack of artillery, which awaited the king's orders, while Frederick was besieging Bremen.[14] He found time to write to Catherine on 14 August, telling her he missed her and joking about the difference in their ages: if only he could be twenty-seven again: but she probably has no wish to be forty-two. (He was actually forty at the time.) A few days later he urged her to hurry and join him, and to bring the Prince-Pope with her, thanking her for the beer she had sent.[15] He also corresponded with his shipwright friend Fedor Skliaev, sending sketches of small boats. 'You can work out how to build them from the sketch – it's not a job requiring much skill, but very necessary to get them made by spring.'[16] In general, after a good start, the military situation advanced little in 1712. Lack of Danish naval support prevented the capture of the island of Rügen opposite Stralsund ('What can you do when you have allies like these?' Peter wrote to Menshikov in August) and allied efforts to counter the incursion of Swedish troops into Mecklenburg resulted in a heavy defeat for a Saxon-Danish force at Gadenbusch.[17] At the end of September Peter set off for the mineral springs at Carlsbad, visiting the king of Prussia in Berlin on the way. On 2 October he sent Catherine some oysters, with an apology that he couldn't find more as there were import restrictions as a result of plague. A few days later he reported that he had bought the dress which she asked for, but no more oysters. From Carlsbad on 11 October he wrote that he had begun to drink the waters 'in this hole', told her not to expect any news from 'the back of beyond' and sent greetings on the anniversary of the capture of Schlüsselburg, the 'start of our good luck'.[18]

Peter was far from home, but news reached him from all over his troublesome empire. In January 1713 Aleksei Kurbatov, the vice-governor of Archangel, wrote to complain about problems in his province, including the fact that people of all ranks were wearing old-style dress and not shaving, and, 'as I hear, previous governors have not used compulsion ... and so the laws which are passed are not kept; and people who come to the markets from other provinces nearly all wear Russian dress and beards, even young people. Truly, lord, such boorishness much be stopped and these heathen customs of dress rooted out.' Peter advised Kurbatov to 'try to correct this problem by degrees'.[19] At times the goals he set himself must have seemed as far as ever from being attained.

Finland

At the beginning of 1713 Peter sent Menshikov and Boris Kurakin to attend a peace congress in Brunswick. Menshikov's instructions specified that the lands which Sweden had 'unlawfully' annexed in the last century (i.e. Ingria and Karelia) must under no circumstances be ceded; Estonia with Reval must be retained as compensation for loss of revenue from the aforementioned and part of Finland ceded to Russia for compensation for the present war. If Livonia, except for the Dorpat district, could not be secured, it was to go to the king of Poland, a concession which Peter later withdrew. In April the Russians launched a campaign in Finland. The galley fleet, with Peter as rear-admiral, landed with 16,000 troops at Helsingfors in early May and took the town without a battle. In July Peter wrote to Menshikov: 'With God's help we hope that all the Finnish lands will be in our hands by the end of this campaign.'[20] During the campaign Peter was promoted to the rank of full general, some eighteen years after he first saw active service at Azov. He wrote to congratulate Catherine on becoming a general's wife, adding, 'like the rank of rear-admiral, this one was also awarded under strange circumstances, for I was made a naval commander while I was on the steppe and a general while at sea'.[21] On 30 August he entered Abo (Turku) on the west coast of Finland and by late October, in numerous dispatches home, he was able to report that the Swedes had been driven out of Finland.

Menshikov was busy, too. In June 1713 he besieged the Swedish general Magnus Stenbock in Tönningen fortress in Jutland and forced him to surrender with all his men. On 13 September Stettin capitulated to Menshikov and was placed under Prussian control.[22] Menshikov's rise seemed inexorable. A laudatory ode, 'The Laurel or Crown of Immortal Glory' (1714), likened him to the sun and to Alexander the Great (no longer just to Alexander's loyal assistant) and Alexander Nevsky, referring to his 'noble' origins in the Grand Duchy of Lithuania and describing his father as 'a glorious warrior of the guards'.[23] Peter was aware of the dangers of Menshikov's growing power, but could not do without his friend, even if the old terms of endearment had disappeared from Peter's letters, which get straight down to business, usually without any intimate greeting to the 'child of my heart' or any accompanying gifts.

Through all the diplomatic ups and downs – in April 1713 the Peace of Utrecht ended the War of the Spanish Succession, thus giving Britain and France more leisure to interfere in northern affairs – Peter continued to hope for peace. But the Swedes still had the power to resist, particularly by deploying their fleet. Peter expressed sorrow that his 'good proposals' to end a destructive war had been unsuccessful and that Charles continued to 'demand the impossible'.[24] Consolidating the Russian navy seemed to be the key. In September 1713 Peter wrote to Kurakin in Holland: 'I ask you to make every effort to buy ships, for our whole war is now centred around them.'[25] Between 1712 and 1716, before the St Petersburg yards were in full production, Russia actively bought warships from the Dutch and the British, acquiring vessels with such names as *Lansdowne, Oxford, Randolph, Arundel, London* and *Britannia*, despite protests from the Swedes. By 1716 the British, too, were beginning to doubt the wisdom of allowing these purchases.

At home in Russia the strain of war manifested itself in numerous ways. In January 1714 Peter ordered the Senate immediately to carry out an interrogation of the provincial governors (one by one) and call them to account for arrears in payments for the army and navy. They must be forced to hand over any ready cash and give a clear account of any shortfalls. No 'vague excuses' were to be tolerated. Any governor who prevaricated was to be placed under arrest immediately and 'to be given no quarter'.[26] But Peter's world of make-believe continued to exist alongside the realities of waging war and raising revenues. At the beginning of 1714 Peter Mikhailov and a small group of fellow shipbuilders wrote to Ivan Golovin, the mock chief surveyor of the fleet:

Your Honour Mr Ba[a]s, our highly esteemed teacher!
We the below-mentioned could not omit to send Your Honour greetings for the beginning of this New Year, to congratulate you and to wish you every happiness and success in your most wise enterprise [i.e. shipbuilding], in the hope that by your great efforts it will increase and grow to your immortal glory, as its leader [initiator] in Russia or our second Noah by calling; and most of all we hope that you will be so good as not to forget us and that you will pay us a visit. . . .
The following greet you, Your Excellency's pupils and servants. Peter. Richard Browne. Richard Cozens, Joseph Noye. Fedor Saltykov.[27]

Various contemporary witnesses attest that Peter was very fond of Ivan Golovin, whom he sent to Venice to study shipbuilding and to learn about the construction of galleys. On his return,

the monarch, wishing to know what he had learned, accompanied him to the Admiralty, led him to the shipyard and the workshops and asked him various questions. The answers showed that Golovin knew nothing. Finally Peter asked: 'Did you at least learn some Italian?' Golovin admitted that he didn't know much of that, either. 'So, what *did* you do?' the tsar asked. 'Most gracious sovereign,' Golovin replied, 'I hardly ever left my house.' Hot-tempered though the tsar was, he was so pleased with this candid and honest confession, that he celebrated Golovin's laziness by conferring on him the title 'Prince Baas'. . . Peter loved him for his directness, his loyalty and his native talents. In conversations where the tsar was, there was Golovin, too, and among his friends he was jokingly known as a learned man and an expert on the art of shipbuilding, or [from the Dutch] Baas.[28]

All witnesses agree that Golovin was chief surveyor of the fleet precisely because he was no good at building ships. We can thus place him within a network of mock appointments, which were linked with Peter's own use of disguises and pseudonyms, in this case the name Peter Mikhailov, which he first used as a trainee shipbuilder during the Grand Embassy. He even introduced a new toast: 'For the health of the family (or sons) of Ivan Mikhailovich', i.e. the ships of the Russian fleet. All the mock post holders were absolutely loyal, all close to the tsar. This was essential, because Peter made himself vulnerable by posing as their humble subject or pupil and had to be confident that none of them would take advantage of his assumed 'weakness'. On the contrary, the mock post holders were expected to demonstrate their loyalty by enduring insults and indignities without a murmur. As for the fleet, Peter took it extremely seriously and it was soon to come into its own.

Victory at Hangö

In July 1714 an impressive demonstration of Russian naval power ended in a victory over the Swedish fleet off Cape Hangö in Finland, where Russian ships surrounded a Swedish squadron and boarded it with infantry. The Swedish seagoing fleet was superior, but less manoeuvrable in Finnish coastal waters. The Russians deployed shallow-draught galleys and the strategic landing of troops along the coast. Peter was immensely proud of this, Russia's first significant victory at sea, which he dubbed the 'naval Poltava'. He wrote to Prince Mikhail Golitsyn:

> We beg to report the manner in which the Almighty Lord God was pleased to glorify Russia. For, after granting us many victories on land, now we have been crowned with victory at sea, for on the 27th day of this month by Hangö near the harbour of Rilax-Figl we captured the Swedish rear-admiral Nilsson Ehrenskiöld with one frigate, six galleys and two sloops, after much fighting and very fierce gunfire. It is true that till now in this war, as with our allies in the war with France, many generals and even field marshals have been taken, but not one senior naval officer. And so we send our congratulations on this our unprecedented victory.[29]

He ordered Prince-Caesar Fedor Romodanovsky, always the first to receive news of victories, to go to St Petersburg and set up wooden triumphal gates, 'however small', on the main square in time for the return of the fleet.[30] In St Petersburg in September the victory celebrations revolved around an escort of captured Swedish ships from Kronstadt and a parade of prisoners through triumphal gates on the quay, all presided over by Romodanovsky. Engravings by Zubov and Picart commemorated the occasion. As Peter reported to Fedor Apraksin, his superior in the Admiralty: 'I arrived here with the captured ships on the 9th of this month and on the same day we were all received by His Majesty [Prince-Caesar], where I handed over your letter. His Majesty deigned to ask after your health and praised your loyal service, whereupon he awarded me the rank of vice-admiral, for which I thank your honour for recommending me. Peter.'[31] Friedrich Weber was there to witness how they 'unanimously declared [Peter] Vice-Admiral of Russia in consideration of the faithful Service he had done to his native Country, of which Proclamation being made, the whole Room resounded with Sdrastwi Vice-Admiral, Health to the Vice-Admiral (which is the Russian Vivat.)'.[32] Catherine missed most of the fun. On 8 September she gave birth to another daughter, Margarita, who died less than a year later.

The fleet had apparently justified the expense lavished upon it, as well as providing Peter with essential scenery and props for his favourite roles. In the 1710s court life was increasingingly embellished with symbols and ceremonies connected with the fleet, from references to Neptune in engravings and medals to naval festivals. There are few images of St Petersburg which do not include ships, often dwarfing everything else. In Aleksei Zubov's 1714 view of Vasil'evsky Island ships captured at Hangö occupy the foreground. In his city panorama of 1716 the buildings are confined to a narrow strip in the middle ground and the foreground is filled with ships. The complex imagery of the fleet included giving favourite ships family names (Natalia, Ekaterina and so on), the creation of ships' 'biographies' (starting with the anniversary of a ship's launch) and descriptions of the peculiarities of an individual ship's 'behaviour', thus turning each vessel almost into a living person. 'Naval baroque' was a vital element in Petrine culture, another phenomenon which gives the lie to the easy assumption that Peter's was a 'utilitarian' reign. His near obsession – even his favourite snuffbox was in the form of a ship – transformed the fleet into something greater than the sum of its parts. At the same time, abroad the fleet was regarded as a real threat to the balance of power in Europe. 'This savage, cruel, and barbrous people design to become masters of the Baltic,' wrote Count Gyllenborg, the Swedish ambassador in London, in 1714. 'The Tsar's fleet will soon outnumber the Swedish and the Danish put together ... and will be the master of the Baltick. We shall wonder then at our blindness that we did not suspect his great designs.'[33]

The Prince-Pope's wedding

Even official accounts of the battle of Hangö, for example, in *The Book of Mars*, maintained Peter's incognito, referring to him not as His Majesty but as 'Mr Rear-Admiral'. Peter himself underlined his 'commoner' credentials by his choice of companions for the Finnish campaign: they included the 'black-amoor' Abraham Hannibal, his chaplain Bitka (who doubled as his chess partner), Peter Buturlin of the Drunken Assembly and various orderlies. As always, the worlds of business, play and make-believe intertwined, for in the midst of the Hangö celebrations Vice-Admiral Peter was planning more bizarre rituals. In October 1713 he had warned Prince-Pope Nikita Zotov of his plans to marry him off to the widow Anna Pashkova, a woman many years his junior.[34] In January 1715 this scheme came to fruition. Guests were instructed to appear in groups of three in matching costumes and to register their choice of fancy dress in order to avoid duplication. Peter inspected the lists and made the final choice. Among the masks were Menshikov as a Hamburg burgher, Gavrila Golovkin as a Chinaman, Ivan Musin-Pushkin as a Venetian and Peter Tolstoy as a Turk. Each matching group was assigned musical instruments.

Witnesses describe the wedding, which took place in St Petersburg, as a 'world turned upside down'. The 'young' groom was in his seventies, invitations to guests were delivered by stammerers, the bridesmen were cripples, the runners were fat men with gout, the priest was allegedly almost a hundred years old. The mock-tsar Romodanovsky, impersonating King David, was carried in a sled drawn by bears.[35] This event has been seen as a variation on the Western charivari or shaming ceremonies, intended to show how the tsar had the power to transform his subjects' lives. Instead of being allowed the 'seemly' and traditional option of retiring to a monastery in old age, which he had requested in 1713, the Prince-Pope (whose real-life equivalents, popes and patriarchs, were celibate) found himself married off to a bride made even more unsuitable by the fact that her father was a well-known Old Believer. Furthermore, the ill-matched couple were to be joined together in Peter's 'New Jerusalem', St Petersburg, Prince-Caesar Romodanovsky's antics as King David mimicking David's 'prancing' and the jubilation of the Israelites during the transfer of the Ark of the Covenant to Jerusalem (II Samuel 6: 15–16, 20–23). It seemed appropriate that the wedding took place in the wake of the naval victories of 1713–14, which set the seal on the new, maritime capital, already recognised as such by the transfer there of government departments (notably the Senate) and parts of the royal household in 1712–13.

The intended recipients of this somewhat oblique message about the new political order were the élite, who were left in no doubt about Russia's new cultural orientation. The year 1714 saw several significant landmarks in the state's interference in the lives of the nobility or 'upper service class': for example, Peter ordered a thousand families to relocate to St Petersburg. In February nobles were notified that their sons would be assigned to regiments from the age of thirteen and when called up would have to serve in the ranks before being considered for a commission. (Peter had demonstrated this principle in his own promotions.) All nobles were required to receive some form of education before they entered the services. In a decree of 1714 Peter ordered that 'in all the provinces children of the nobility and chancellery rank, of secretaries and clerks . . . aged from ten to fifteen are to study numbers and some part of geometry'. After completing their studies they were to receive a diploma, without which they would not be allowed to marry or to give pledges of betrothal.[36] In fact, there were never enough teachers (graduates were drawn mainly from the Mathematical school) fully to implement this programme of so-called 'cipher' schools and the nobles themselves were hostile. Richer nobles prefered to educate their sons at home, while poorer ones either resorted to the village priest or failed to provide schooling altogether. By 1726

nobles accounted for less than 3 per cent of the 2,000 students in twelve surviving cipher schools.

Perhaps most unsettling for the Russian élite was Peter's Law on Single
Inheritance, issued on 23 March 1714, which outlawed the ancient custom of
partible inheritance (dividing landed estates among all sons), stipulating that
'immovable property' (real estate) was to be left to one heir only, normally the
first-born son, but a parent could nominate someone else if the eldest son was
deemed unworthy. In the absence of sons, daughters could inherit.
'Moveable' property – money, goods, livestock – could still be divided among
all the children.[37] The main aim of the measure was to avoid the wasteful fragmentation of estates (said to put an added burden on the peasants) and there
was also the hope that those who did not inherit would rely on state service
for their living. The futility of resistance to various unwelcome developments
was underlined by Zotov's wedding, at which the cream of Russian society
donned fancy dress and played joke instruments at the tsar's bidding. Peter's
subjects were left in no doubt that there would be no return to 'ancient barbaric customs', such as Muscovite arranged marriages, permanent residence in
Moscow and division of property among all the heirs. Instead, the tsar was
free to devise new barbaric customs of his own.

The birth of two Peters

Peter's relations with his son did not improve after Alexis's wedding or his
own, although Catherine did her best to reconcile her husband and her stepson. As far as Peter was concerned, his son's marriage was just one in a series
of duties for Alexis. In 1713 Alexis returned to Russia, where he was required
to undergo a test of the knowledge he had acquired abroad and deliberately
injured his hand in order to avoid an examination in drawing. He set up
home in a palace on the left bank of the Neva between the residences of his
aunt Natalia and Tsaritsa Martha. There are frequent references in Alexis's letters to his poor health, which was hardly helped by the St Petersburg climate,
a topic which aroused Peter's annoyance rather than sympathy. Even his
physical debility was to be used against him; later, in 1718, Peter compared his
son unfavourably with his brother Tsar Ivan, who could not manage a rough
horse and was hardly even able to mount one, but loved horses; in other
words, moral fibre could compensate for physical weakness. The implication
was that Alexis was deficient in both physical and moral strength. In 1714
Alexis went to Carlsbad to take the waters. According to Weber, Peter ordered
him to return to St Petersburg promptly: 'It was said, he shewed but little
Inclination upon the Receipt of the Letter, and in his Answer; and that he
resented his being still continued a Serjeant.' Weber, incidentally, contributed
to Alexis's bad reputation by alleging that through keeping 'vicious Company'

he contracted 'such corrupt Habits, as could not fail producing as Aversion to him in all honest Minds'.[38] The birth of Peter's first grandchild, Natalia, in July 1714 did nothing to repair the growing rift. The naval victory at Hangö may have put Peter in a good mood, but this did not extend to his son. In January 1715 Peter wrote to Alexis:

> Have you assisted [me] since you came to Maturity of Years in [my] Labours and Pains? No, certainly, the World knows you have not. On the other Hand you blame and abhor whatever Good I have been able to do, at the Expense of my Health, for the Love I have bore to my People, and for their Advantage; and I have all imaginable Reason to believe, that you will destroy it all, in case you should Survive me.[39]

What precipitated this outburst? Partly it was disapproval of Alexis's bad treatment of the wife whom Peter had provided for him. Not long after the birth of Natalia, Alexis installed his mistress Afrosinia in the palace. When Peter heard of 'irregularities' in his son's household, he responded by appointing Daria Rzhevskaia, 'abbess' of the Drunken Assembly, to supervise his daughter-in-law. But Alexis's relations with his wife were not entirely curtailed. In 1715 Charlotte was pregnant again, as was Catherine; both were due to give birth in the autumn.

On 11 October 1715, in what he referred to as a 'last testament', Peter wrote again to Alexis, setting out the enormous efforts he and 'other true sons of Russia' had expended since the outbreak of the war to overcome the disadvantages which had hampered Russia's progress. He was aggrieved when he saw his unworthy heir's indifference to military affairs, rejecting Alexis's excuses about ill health and despairing that all his efforts to reform his son had been in vain. He would cut him off 'like a gangrenous limb'. 'I have not spared and do not spare my own life for my country and my people, so why should I spare you who are so unworthy? Better a worthy stranger than my own unworthy son.'[40] Here again was the principle of inheritance by the fittest, as set out in the 1714 Law of Single Inheritance and in legislation on state service, transferred to the battleground of Peter's personal life.

The next few weeks saw a series of events of crucial significance for the dynasty. On 12 October Charlotte gave birth to a healthy son, who was named Peter. Nine days later she succumbed to postnatal complications and died, apparently unmourned by her husband. On 29 October, Peter's own son, also named Peter, was born. This sudden abundance of male heirs and his wife's death, provides the background for Alexis's reply, on 31 October, to his father's letter of 11 October. He expressed his willingness to relinquish his claim to the throne, in view of the fact that he was 'unqualified and unfit for the task', his memory was gone and his health undermined 'by many illnesses'.[41] This was clearly not the reply that Peter had hoped for. On the one hand, he seemed determined to exclude Alexis from the succession; on the other hand, it went against the grain to allow his son to escape lightly by retiring to a monastery. Peter, as we know, generally regarded the monastic life as 'shirking', an option only for the aged and disabled and a few high-flyers bound for posts in the church hierarchy. The matter remained unresolved. Some writers believe that a 'party' was forming around Alexis, a sort of moral opposition to Peter's despotism and the burdens imposed upon the people.

A new grand tour of Europe

In February 1716 Peter set off to attend the wedding of his niece Ekaterina Ivanovna to Duke Karl Leopold of Mecklenburg, which was scheduled for 8 April in Danzig. His departure from St Petersburg marked the beginning of a lengthy European tour, from which he was not to return until October 1717. The match between his favourite niece and the recently divorced duke, described as 'the coarse, uneducated, wilful and highly eccentric owner of a scrap of German soil',[42] was prompted by Peter's eagerness to acquire a base in north Germany and better security for Russian garrisons in the region. The marriage contract, which brought with it the right of Russian merchants to reside and trade in Mecklenburg, free passage to Russian troops and the tsar's pledge to support the duke against his enemies, was signed before the couple met for the first time in March 1716. It constituted a virtual Russian protectorate over Mecklenburg, which especially alarmed George of Hanover, who as George I of Great Britain had reason to be wary of Russia's growing naval power.

While he was in Germany Peter issued his Military Statute, one of the clearest expressions of the ethos of the Petrine armed services and the impulses behind his reforms. The text was a compilation of earlier edicts and manuals, drawing heavily on Swedish and Austrian codes. In the preface, Peter is more generous than some of his own biographers in giving credit to his predecessors. He notes his own father's publication of a military manual (*The Training and Art of Infantry*, a translation of Jacobi's *Kriegs-Kunst zu Fuss*, 1647) and praises his achievements in training regular troops and beating the Poles:

But thereafter [under Fedor and Sophia] this enterprise was not increased in the growing light of knowledge but was virtually abandoned. What ensued next is still fresh in the memory, how we were unable to withstand not only against nations with regular armies but even against barbarians (shameful to recall). We pass over in silence what happened at Chigirin [in 1676] and on the Crimean campaigns [of 1687 and 1689], not only then but much more recently against the Turks at Azov or at Narva at the start of this war.

But when (with the Almighty's help) the army was brought to order, then what great progress was made with the Almighty's help against glorious and regular nations. Anyone can see that this occurred for no other reason than the establishment of good order, for all disorderly barbarian practices are worthy of ridicule and no good can come of them.

On 10 April 1716 Peter sent an advance copy of the statute to the Senate from Danzig, with the handwritten instruction: 'Lord senators, I am sending you the book of the Military Statute (which was begun in St Petersburg and finished here), which I command you to have printed in a large number, no less than a thousand copies ... and although it lays down the basis for military men, it also applies to all civil administrators, as you will see when you read it. Therefore when it is printed send a quantity to all the corps of our army and also to the governors and chancelleries, so that no one can make the excuse that he was ignorant of it.'[43]

Peter regarded military order as a model for other reforms. In the Spiritual Regulation (1721) the section on schools begins: 'It is known to all the world how inadequate and weak was the Russian army when it did not have proper training and how incomparably its numbers increased and how it became great and formidable beyond expectation when Our Most Powerful Monarch, His Tsarist Majesty, Peter I, instructed it with most excellent regulations. The same is to be appreciated as regards architecture, medicine, political government and all other affairs.' In a later section students are described as proceeding to their lessons 'like soldiers upon a drumbeat'.[44] Even so, Peter was aware of the dangers of doing everything 'by the book'. A supplement to the statute issued in 1722 reminded officers to do their best for the soldiers under their command and not burden them with unnecessary ceremonial guard duties. They should not cling to the Military Statute, 'like a blind man clings to a wall'.[45]

In May 1716 Peter met the king of Prussia in Stettin and the king of Denmark in Altona. The decision was taken to move Russian troops in preparation for a landing in Sweden, and in the meantime Peter and his companions went to Piermont to take the waters. The doctors banned consumption of alcohol, which meant that Peter's birthday had to be celebrated without the usual banquet. They passed the time shopping (Peter bought a child's bagpipes and a little paintbox) and playing chess and lotto. Peter was greatly saddened to hear of the death, on 18 June, of his sister Natalia, to whom he had been close since childhood. Natalia was in many respects a model for Peter's 'new women', one of the first to relocate permanently to St Petersburg. The inventory of her possessions showed that her home was furnished in Western taste and her wardrobes stuffed with the latest Western fashions, together with costumes and properties from her private theatre. But on the walls icons outnumbered portraits and her personal library comprised devotional works and saints' lives. The traditional image of the pious tsarevma was not so easily abandoned.

Early August witnessed a highlight of Peter's naval career when he assumed command of four fleets – the Danish, Dutch, British and Russian – off Copenhagen, as the allies prepared for their invasion of Sweden. Peter enjoyed this event, which was commemorated on a medal featuring Neptune riding the waves on sea-horses, even though the landing in Sweden was abandoned as a result of Russo-Danish disagreements and the deflection of the Danish fleet by Charles XII's operations in Norway. In Copenhagen Peter was reminded of disagreeable business. On 26 August he sent an ultimatum to Alexis, summoning him to join him. Alexis panicked. He turned south at Danzig (sending a letter misleadingly postmarked Königsberg to put his father off the scent) and headed for Vienna, in the expectation of getting help from his late wife's brother-in-law, Emperor Charles VI. The emperor offered Alexis a refuge, but the Viennese court was reluctant to get too involved and hopes of further aid were dashed when in July 1717 Austria clashed with Spain over Sardinia, which, incidentally, meant that the maritime powers and also France would 'have their hands too tied to interfere in affairs in the north,' as Boris Kurakin wrote to Peter early in 1718.[46] Alexis's defection still caused embarrassment and complications for Peter, who was only too willing to believe in a plot spearheaded by his son with the backing of foreign aid.

In October 1716 Peter arrived in Amsterdam, where he spent most of the winter. The now famous victor of Poltava quickly reverted to his Dutch shipwright's identity as 'Pieter Baas'. One of many anecdotes from this period relates how Peter objected when some Dutch merchants addressed him as 'Your Majesty' during dinner. 'Come, brothers, let us converse like plain and honest ships-carpenters,' he asked and demanded the jug rather than a glass when a servant poured him some beer.[47] He revisited his old haunts in Zaandam, looking round the little house and even doing a spot of work with bellows and hammer in the blacksmith's shop. He also visited the home of the celebrated collector and illustrator Meri Sibilla Merian on the day she died and bought two volumes of illustrations of plants and insects.

On 2 January 1717, at Wesel in the Netherlands, Catherine, who was on her way to join Peter, gave birth to a boy, who was named Paul. Peter wrote to her on 4 January, rejoicing at the birth of 'another recruit' and the following day dispatched letters to foreign rulers, including the king of France and the emperor of Austria. To Prince Mikhail Golitsyn he wrote: 'I inform you that on the second day of this month in Wesel my good lady gave birth to little soldier Paul. . . . Please inform the officers and men. I recommend him to the officers to be under their command and to the men as their comrade. Give all of them regards from me and the newborn.'[48] To his daughters Anna and Elizabeth Peter wrote: 'Congratulations on the birth of a second brother; give the first one a kiss from me and his [new] brother',[49] and to his newly

married niece Ekaterina he boasted: 'You are probably envious that we old
folk are more productive than you young ones.'⁵⁰ (Ekaterina's daughter, Anna,
was born in December 1718. Anna's baby son was to occupy the Russian
throne for just a year in 1740–41 as Ivan VI.)

Sadly, as Peter was composing his celebratory letters his new son was
already dead. As Catherine wrote to Boris Kurakin on 8 January: 'It is with
deep sorrow that I inform you that Almighty God saw fit to transport our
newborn son Tsarevich Paul from this world four hours after his birth. Truly,
this sadness is very painful, but what's done is done and so we bow to the will
of God.' In a letter of 11 January Peter wrote of 'the sudden turn of events
which changed joy to sorrow, but all I can do is to respond like Job, that man
of many sorrows, that the Lord giveth and the Lord taketh away'.⁵¹ One can
imagine that the death of a newborn son when his eldest son had betrayed
him was especially painful, but Peter did not allow personal grief to intrude
for long. From Amsterdam he proceeded to The Hague, Leiden, Rotterdam,
Antwerp and Dunkirk. Easter 1717 found him in Calais, where a special
wooden chapel was built for him to celebrate the liturgy. On 26 April he
reached Paris, where he remained until the second week of June.

Paris

Relations between Russia and France had taken a turn for the better after
reaching a low point in the late 1680s, when Russian ambassadors had been
virtually expelled after a series of misunderstandings. France played little part
in the Northern War as long as the War of the Spanish Succession tied its
hands and Russian action was concentrated in the eastern Baltic. But France
was interested in what happened in north Germany and anxious to maintain
a Swedish presence there, as a counterweight to the Holy Roman Empire.
Peter, too, had an eye on the wider diplomatic picture. In January 1717 a triple
alliance was formed between Britain, France and the Dutch Republic (joined
in August 1718 by Austria). During his visit to Paris Peter sought a friendship
treaty with France in order to minimise the danger of this alliance interfering
in the Northern War. He hoped, more ambitiously, to detach France from its
traditional Swedish connection and to form an anti-Austrian alliance, but
France resisted Russian overtures and restricted itself to reducing its subsidy
to Sweden.

Peter presented an odd spectacle to Parisian eyes. As usual, he rejected the
splendidly appointed apartments which had been prepared for him in the
Louvre, a building of overwhelming size, and sampled only some bread and
radishes, six sorts of wine and two glasses of beer from the spread which was
laid out, then headed for a private house where he immediately went to bed
in a small room intended for the servants. Peter wrote to Menshikov on 2

May: 'I arrived here safely on 26 April. . . . Travelling along the road into Paris I saw quite a bit of poverty among the ordinary people. The king is a real grown up and quite old in years, to be precise, seven: he has visited me and I him.' The boy king Louis XV, who succeeded his father in 1715, had only just begun his education. On 29 April he visited Peter in his apartments, when Peter met him at his carriage, kissed him and carried him up the steps. The next day Peter visited the king in the Tuileries.[52]

In Paris Peter was taken round the places which catered for the magnificence of the French court – the tapestry manufactures of Gobelins, the studios and workshops of painters, sculptors and jewellers, the Mint (where a medal was cast in his honour). He attended an opera in the regent's box, and the regent served him with a glass of beer in person. By and large, Peter was not much impressed by the subtleties of French cuisine, although he amazed his hosts by the quantities of wine he could knock back. His cook apparently prepared enough food and drink each day for Peter alone to feed eight people. One of his French minders reported that he enjoyed sharp sauces, brown bread, green peas, and fruit (oranges, apples and pears) washed down with beer and wine. His companions in Paris included Pavel Iaguzhinsky, M. D. Olsuf'ev, his secretary Makarov, his physician Dr Robert Erskine and the priest Bitka. French commentators noted that Iaguzhinsky and Bitka were his regular drinking companions and that Bitka was a glutton, who could consume twelve to fifteen bottles of champagne at dinner and was finely dressed for a priest. Numerous references to purchases of clothing for him survive in Cabinet accounts. He also performed the role of purse keeper, paying the cab fare for Peter's visit to Versailles, for example.

In Paris Peter visited the Botanical Gardens, Tuileries, the Arsenal, Observatory, Academy of Sciences (which later made him a member), Les Invalides (where he served the old soldiers with bread and soup and drank to their health), and the Sorbonne. He observed an eye operation performed by the English surgeon Wallace. He was greatly impressed by the gardens at Saint-Cloud, with their huge fountains which shot 135 feet into the air, and at Versailles on 14 May he inspected the gardens and fountains on the first of several visits. He spent the night in Madam de Maintenon's rooms in the Trianon, where her old servant was horrified by the Russians' bad behaviour. On 30 May he was back at Versailles for his birthday, when fireworks and illuminations were organised at Marly and torches and lamps were brought from Paris to light up the Agrippina fountain, his favourite. These visits and twelve albums of engravings of Versailles which he received as a gift from the royal library provided ample material for extending his own palaces at Peterhof and Strel'na, which he visited with new enthusiasm after the trip to Paris.

The best-known image linked with Peter's visit to France is attributed to the renowned court painter Jean-Marc Nattier which now hangs in the Hermitage. The painter emphasised military symbols – Peter is clad in shining armour, with his right hand holding a baton and resting on a medieval helmet complete with extravagant red plume, his left lightly holding a sheathed sword. He wears the Order of St Andrew. Peter's pose, his head half turned to gaze somewhat soulfully at the viewer, is static, but the thick of battle is suggested in the far distance on the right of the canvas. Nattier painted Peter in Paris, but went to the Hague to do a companion piece of Catherine. Peter did not take her to France, for fear, apparently, that her lowly origins would not command respect. Nattier got the message. His Catherine is thoroughly regal. Wearing a fashionably low-cut jewel-studded gown in a gold-spun fabric with fine lace trimmings, an extravagant stole of royal ermine, an elegant hair decoration and the red ribbon of the Order of St Catherine, she is set against velvet draperies dotted with crowns and double eagles, a crown and sceptre on a ledge behind and a columned backdrop suggesting a royal palace. Here was a consort fit for a tsar.

Return to St Petersburg. The Colleges

The couple's return to St Petersburg in October 1717 was marked with special pomp and ceremony, orchestrated by Menshikov. Keen to be the first to greet the tsar, Menshikov spent the morning of 9 October looking through his telescope from the gallery of his grand palace on the Finnish gulf at Oranienbaum. When he saw the tsar's ship approaching he went out to meet it in a boat and he and Peter entered Kronstadt harbour together, to the sound of gun salutes, and celebrated at Menshikov's Kronstadt residence. The next day Menshikov set off for St Petersburg in advance of the tsar to co-ordinate a reception in the freshly decorated Winter Palace, where Peter would be reunited with his children (who had been in Menshikov's care), each of whom had a little party piece prepared. Two-year old Peter Petrovich, seated on a miniature horse, presented his father with a text ('ghost-written' by Feofan Prokopovich, who since 1716 had been resident in St Petersburg) expatiating on the theme of 'the common good of the whole state', and apologising that Nature 'has not yet had time to supply me with the corporal organs with which to voice my heartfelt enthusiasm'.[53] Menshikov's three-year-old son Alexander delivered a speech in French, a reference to Peter's recent travels which also demonstrated the accomplishments of the new generation at home in Russia. Prokopovich himself had composed a sermon extolling the mind-broadening virtues of foreign travel. After the speeches Peter went straight to the Admiralty to inspect work on ships. On 12 October he and Menshikov visited the Summer Gardens, where considerable landscaping had been completed. As governor of St Petersburg, Menshikov was anxious to show off how much had been achieved during Peter's absence.

There was also less welcome news. On 21 October Peter wrote to Ivan Fedorovich Romodanovsky: 'I received your letter of 21 September upon arrival in which you inform me of the death of your father, for which I offer deepest condolences that he did not lose his life as a result of old age but from an attack of gangrene, still there goes everyone one way or another by God's will, bear this in mind and don't give in to grief. And please don't imagine that I have abandoned you, or forgotten your father's good deeds.'[54] 'Tsarevich' Ivan replaced his father in his dual offices of Prince-Caesar ('Sire') and head of the Preobrazhensky office, but it is doubtful whether he ever replaced Fedor Iur'evich in Peter's affections. To quote Boris Kurakin, the elder Romodanovsky may have had 'the appearance of a monster and the character of a wicked tyrant' and have been 'the greatest of ill-wishers, drunk day in day out; but he was more faithful to His Majesty than anyone'.[55] Peter missed him.

Throughout 1717 Peter had received peace proposals and offers of mediation. In December 1717 the Swedes agreed to a peace congress, which was scheduled to open the following May. With hostilities now in a low key, Peter entered on a bout of domestic reforms, on 11 and 15 December 1717 issuing edicts on the establishment of new government departments or collegiate boards known as *kollegii*, the idea for which was first mentioned in a note to the Senate in March 1715. The nine colleges were Foreign Affairs; State Revenues; Justice; State Accounting; Military; Admiralty; Commerce; State Expenses; and Mines and Manufacture. Their Russian names – Kamer-Kollegiia, Revizion-Kollegiia and so on – were borrowed from the Swedish. They were to be run on the principle that decisions were reached by a board which operated 'collegiately' on a majority decision, supported by a hierarchy of professional officials, who in turn were serviced by a team of chancellery clerks and copyists, assorted domestics and doormen. Voting members consisted of a president and vice-president (initially the former was a Russian, the latter a foreigner), four or five councillors and four assessors.

The nuts and bolts of the new system were borrowed from Sweden, and Austrian, Danish, Prussian and British procedures were also consulted, but an order of 28 April 1718 warned against slavish imitation: 'Any points which are inconvenient in the Swedish statute or incompatible with the situation of this country are to be included only if appropriate.'[56] A systematic explanation of the function and duties of college staff was set out in the General Regulation of 1720. One of the principles behind the interlocking institutions of central and local government devised in 1717–20 was the notion that the new system should work like a well-oiled machine without any need for the intervention of its inventor. In the words of an anonymous memorandum, usually ascribed to Leibniz, 'God, as a God of order, rules everything wisely and in an orderly manner with his invisible hand. The Gods of this world, or the likenesses of God's power (I am thinking of the absolutist monarchs), have to establish their forms of government in accordance with this order if they wish to enjoy the sweet fruits of a flourishing state for their great efforts.'⁵⁷ But the notion that justice could be obtained only by bypassing officials and official bodies and reaching the great sovereign was difficult to eradicate. An edict issued by Peter in December 1718 reminded petitioners who 'pestered' the tsar 'what a multitude there is of them, whereas it is one person they petition, and he is surrounded by so much military business and other burdensome work . . . and even if he did not have such a lot of work, how would it be possible for one man to look after so many? In truth it is impossible either for a man or even for an angel. . . .'⁵⁸ Four years later petitioners were directed to the newly created 'maitre de requêtes' (*reketmeister*) instead of bothering the emperor, 'giving him no peace'.⁵⁹ In fact, Peter himself did little to alter old views about royal power. The proportion of legislation issued as a personal (*imennoi*) decree of the tsar, sometimes written by him alone, increased rather than diminished after the installation of the new machinery of government.

Peter's image underwent a number of changes in the decade after Poltava. If in 1709–10 pictures of a man of action, a warrior on horseback, dominated, by 1717 artists were beginning to take a more rounded view of Peter, now in his mid-forties, presenting him as statesman, patron of arts and sciences (a member of the French Academy, no less), even a philosopher. Peter's favourite portrait of himself is said to have been the half-length study attributed to the Dutch artist Karl (Carel) Moor for whom Peter posed in Amsterdam in 1717; it was much copied thereafter, notably in Antwerp (in 1724–25) by Andrei Matveev, one of several promising Russian artists whom Peter sent abroad to train. Portrayed against a darkish background of sky and trees, Peter, dressed in a tunic with the blue sash of the Order of St Andrew across his shoulder, stares calmly and thoughtfully at the viewer. A glimpse of cuirass at the neck suggests that the tsar is, nevertheless, ready for war. The overall impression is one of balance between soldier and statesman. In Jacobus Houbraken's famous engraving of the portrait, the military theme is more to the fore, with oval medallions depicting cannons and anchors at its base.

There was a side of Peter which remained unrecorded by painters of the era. In December 1717 Prince-Pope Nikita Zotov died, thus necessitating the election of a successor. In contrast to 1700, when Peter made no attempt to replace the late Patriarch Adrian, now he wasted no time in asking permission of the new Prince-Caesar to fill the post: 'Our All-Mad Assembly has been left without a head; therefore we beg Your Majesty to see to the election of a Bacchus-like father for the vacant throne.'⁶⁰ Peter himself devised the details of the ceremonies:

> Having gathered in the old court of the pope each archpriest is to begin to sing the song of Bacchus, then the Prince Great Orator will climb onto a high place and read a sermon exhorting them to appeal to Bacchus fervently and not to repent . . . but with zealous hearts to carry out their elec-

tion and then they are all to go to the stone house to the conclave in the order set out in the register.

The election involved a ballot using eggs. The new pontiff was the former 'Metropolitan of St Petersburg' Peter Ivanovich Buturlin (d. 1723), who was consecrated on 10 January 1718, 'by the will of the universal Prince-Caesar and the whole of the All-Jesting Assembly'.[61] Peter continued to play the modest role of deacon, although in reality he personally devised all the Assembly's activities.

VII

Father and Sons
1718–20

> Everyone is well aware of the wickedness, just like that of Absalom, with which our son Alexis was filled and of how his schemes were foiled not by repentence but by God's mercy towards our country. (The Law on the Succession, 5 February 1722).

Peter and Alexis

In 1871, in the first exhibition staged by the group of Russian artists known as the Wanderers, Nikolai Ge contributed what was to become one of the most famous of Russian historical paintings. Peter, dressed in the dark green, red-cuffed uniform of the Preobrazhensky guards, sits on a chair with his legs crossed and stares sternly at his son Alexis, who stands to his right, thin and pale, with head bowed, his black clothes hinting at impending death. Ge borrowed Alexis's visage from the portrait by Dannhauer described earlier. Sheets of paper (a confession awaiting Alexis's signature?) are strewn on a table and one has fallen to the floor. On the walls some of Peter's paintings acquired abroad (the Dutch maritime artist Adam Silo was his favourite) can be picked out in the gloom. Although the background is authentic and still recognisable today – Ge set the scene in the Monplaisir pavilion at Peterhof, which Peter preferred to the grand palace on the hill because it stood right on the sea shore – the subject is invented, for there is no record of Peter and Alexis meeting at Monplaisir in 1718. But psychologically it rings true. Critics still fail to agree whether Ge intended to condemn Peter as an unnatural father and evoke pity for Alexis, or to arouse sympathy for the reformer's dilemma in dealing with a recalcitrant son, who, like Russia (for which Alexis provides a metaphor in either version), had to be chastised for his own good. As in many paintings of the period, the exploration of a historical theme was intended to throw light on the present. The painting also has religious allusions. In later works, for example *What is Truth?*, Ge dealt with the arrest and interrogation of Christ. Whatever Ge's intentions, he captures the drama of one of the most disturbing episodes in Peter's career.

In 1717 Peter had written to inform Alexis that although he had acted 'like a traitor' in seeking refuge abroad and inflicted insult and grief upon his father and shame upon his native land, he would not be punished if he returned to Russia. But if he refused he would be eternally damned.[1] Armed with this letter, Peter's agents Aleksei Rumiantsev and Peter Tolstoy tracked Alexis down to his refuge near Naples and persuaded him of the weakness of Austrian promises and the inevitability of his being intercepted, possibly (a terrifying thought!) by Peter in person. Alexis agreed to return to Russia on condition that he be allowed to marry his pregnant mistress Afrosinia and live quietly away from the capital. He gave his consent in a letter to Peter dated 4 October 1717, which he signed 'your most humble and worthless slave, unworthy of the name of son'.[2]

At the end of January 1718 Alexis arrived back in Moscow, where he learned that there were conditions attached to the unconditional pardon promised earlier: firstly, he must renounce the throne, and secondly, name the 'accomplices' who helped him to flee Russia. Fulfilling the first requirement was relatively easy as Alexis had indicated his willingness earlier to abandon his claim to the throne. On 3 February Peter issued a manifesto setting out the reasons for removing Alexis from the succession, which is addressed to the tsar's 'loyal servitors', who are, he assumes, all well aware of the efforts he took as a good father to educate Alexis to become a 'worthy heir' and of his unfailing 'parental anxiety and concern', which Alexis repaid with the stubborn refusal to heed his tutors ('the seed of learning fell upon stony ground'), seeking bad company instead. He had lived in discord with his lawful wife and brought shame upon himself by taking up with 'an idle, common serving wench', driving Charlotte to her death. 'Loyal servitors' were left in no doubt that Peter was acting in the interests of Russia: 'We could not keep an heir who would lose everything that with God's help his father had obtained and who would overturn the glory and honour of the Russian people, for which I spent my health, in some cases not even sparing my life.' The manifesto set out in detail Peter's efforts to bring Alexis back to Russia. It declared two-year-old Peter Petrovich as the new heir, sternly condemning as a traitor anyone who continued to regard Alexis as the successor, although Peter unambiguously 'forgives him for his crime and frees him from all punishment'.[3] Alexis duly signed a letter acknowledging 'my transgression before you, as a parent and a sovereign'. He took the oath of renunciation and swore allegiance to his younger brother.[4]

Witch hunt

It was the second condition about revealing all accomplices ('if anything is hidden, you will lose your life') which proved impossible to fulfil, for it depended on Peter's being satisfied that nothing had been concealed. The intensity of the investigation which followed was occasioned by Peter's own deep suspicions about the existence of a plot against him – that Alexis had

asked the Austrian emperor to raise a military force against Peter and was con-
templating the 'repulsive act and crime' of patricide – and had the support of
some members of Peter's inner circle, not least Menshikov, who feared the
consequences if Peter were to die and Alexis become tsar. A witch hunt began.
On 4 February Alexis received a set of questions, his replies to which seriously
implicated Alexander Kikin, a former 'play' soldier and volunteer on the
Grand Embassy, later director of the St Petersburg wharf, whose career had
been briefly interrupted by charges of embezzlement and corruption. Kikin,
it was claimed, had advised Alexis to enter a monastery, for 'the monk's cap is
not nailed to your head', then helped him to flee abroad. Kikin gave a clue to
the reasons for his change of allegiance while he was being tortured later in
1718, when Peter asked: 'How could a clever man like you go against me?' and
Kikin replied: 'The mind needs space, but you restrict it.'[5]

These and other answers from interrogations indicated that Alexis enjoyed
the sympathy of many members of the old nobility and suggested rumblings
of discontent at the very heart of Peter's circle. Kikin's correspondents
included Fedor Apraksin and Boris Sheremetev, although nothing incriminating was found against them. During his trial Alexis recalled conversations
between himself and Pavel Iaguzhinsky, the future procurator-general and
Peter's protégé, and with Aleksei Makarov, Peter's secretary, who warned him
to take care lest Peter pass the throne to his younger brother.[6] Makarov's
advice, like Sheremetev's suggestion that Alexis ought to cultivate more
friends in Peter's court, was hardly subversive, but such was the atmosphere
that anyone could fall under suspicion. Other alleged remarks by leading
servitors came closer to home. In Stettin in 1713 Vasily Vladimirovich
Dolgoruky, suppressor of the Bulavin rebellion and godfather of Elizabeth
Petrovna, told Alexis: 'If it were not for the tsaritsa's influence on the sovereign's cruel character, our life would be impossible.'[7] Iakov Dolgoruky liked
Alexis and discussed 'the people's burdens' with him, although he was cautious about being seen with him. Prince Dmitry Mikhailovich Golitsyn, governor of Kiev, sent Alexis books and he counted Prince Dmitry's brother
Mikhail and their cousin Prince Peter Alekseevich Golitsyn among his
friends. And, as if in final confirmation of the justice of his position, he
insisted that 'many people have told me that the common folk love me'.[8]

Prior to Alexis's defection in 1716 leading men naturally thought it prudent
to maintain at least discreet good relations with the heir to the throne. But
many such men, by no means die-hard traditionalists, lived in fear of Peter
and were weary of the unrelieved burdens of the war, which looked set to drag
on for ever, with all the associated impositions of forced relocation to St
Petersburg, compulsory service for young nobles in the ranks and orders out
of the blue to go on errands. There is no evidence of a conspiracy to restore
Muscovite traditions; on the contrary, a few of Peter's associates may well have
wished to extend the process of Westernisation to the political sphere, while

reducing some of the pressures of war and reform. In this scenario, Alexis, so much less energetic and demanding than his father, begins to look like a suitable candidate as a constitutional monarch.

The prelude to Alexis's trial was the investigation of his mother Evdokia (now the nun Elena in the Intercession convent in Suzdal', it will be recalled) and her friends. Despite the lack of any hard evidence of links between Evdokia's 'party' and Alexis's 'plot', many of the ex-tsaritsa's people fell victim to flimsy charges only indirectly linked to Alexis's flight abroad. Evdokia herself was accused of abandoning her nun's habit and living a life of luxury and debauchery. In a public spectacle in March 1718 the guards officer Stepan Glebov was executed by impalement after prolonged torture sessions, having been convicted of committing adultery with Evdokia and writing suspicious coded letters (which were never shown to contain anything incriminating). Alexander Kikin was broken on the wheel, as was Bishop Dosifei of Rostov, who allegedly told Evdokia that she would be tsaritsa again and foretold Peter's death. The abbess of the Intercession convent and the nun Kaptelina, Evdokia's confidante, were knouted and banished. Evdokia's brother Avraamy Lopukhin was executed later in the year.

The investigation extended to Alexis's middle-aged aunts, the half-sisters whom Peter had never really trusted because of their closeness to Sophia. Tsarevna Martha Alekseevna was charged with querying Peter's choice of his younger son over the elder and Tsarevna Maria Alekseevna was locked up in Schlüsselburg fortress on the grounds that she acted as a go-between for Alexis and his mother, meeting Alexis in Germany in October 1716 and sending Evdokia news of Alexis's escape abroad. As for Evdokia, she was banished to an isolated convent near Lake Ladoga with just one female dwarf for company. She proved a tough nut to crack, however, outliving her husband and making a brief return to court in 1728 during the short reign of her grandson Peter II. She died in 1731.

Freaks and monsters

On 13 February 1718, as the investigation of Alexis got under way and fear and suspicion spread, Peter issued another famous manifesto: 'It is well known that in the human species, as in that of animals and birds, monsters are born, that is freaks [the original uses both the borrowed word *monstry* and the Russian *urody*], which are collected in all countries as objects of wonder.' Ignorant people regarded such freaks as works of the devil, the decree explained, whereas in fact they are products of nature. People were commanded to deliver specimens (preserved in spirits if dead, or, in case of necessity, in double-distilled wine) to commandants in towns for a scale of payments: for dead items, the reward was 10 roubles for humans, five for animals, and three for birds, and for live exhibits (the most sought-after) 100, 15 and seven roubles respectively. 'Very weird' freaks attracted a bonus payment, 'slightly deformed' ones a lesser reward. Anyone caught concealing specimens was to be fined and the sum given to informers.[9]

The impulse behind this decree was patriotic as well as scientific. Peter believed that the Russian empire could yield up exhibits just as curious as those which Western collectors went to the ends of the earth to find. In 1714 he had founded his own cabinet of curiosities, the Kunstkamera (borrowed from the German *Kunstkammer*), based on a collection started in 1697–98 in the Netherlands and Germany. It was to grow significantly after Peter's visit to Europe in 1716–17, when he purchased Dr Ruysch's anatomical cabinet, the zoological specimens of the apothecary Albert Seba and the cabinet of the physician Gottwald of Danzig, which included minerals, shells and rare stones. Peter's taste for the bizarre and exotic was in keeping with the spirit of the so-called age of the Baroque. No doubt he was also encouraged by Leibniz's recommendation 'Concerning the Museum and the cabinets and *Kunstkammern* ... [which] should serve not only as objects of general curiosity, but also as a means to the perfection of the arts and sciences.' The collector in his cabinet was a sort of icon of the age of reason, his specimens, scientific instruments, books, paintings and engravings all evidence of his enquiring mind and broad vision. Peter regarded collecting as a mark of civilisation in his own associates, several of whom, including Menshikov, James Bruce, Robert Erskine and Andrei Vinnius, amassed their own cabinets.

Peter did not intend to enjoy his specimens alone. His idea was to establish a public museum which Russians would visit to look and learn, lured in by free coffee, wine or vodka. In 1718–19, under the direction of Dr Lavrenty Blumentrost and the librarian Johann Schumacher, a new building (still known today as the Kunstkamera) was started on Vasil'evsky Island, according to legend on the spot where a misshapen pine tree grew.[10] Peter's appeal for home-grown 'monsters' produced, among other things, an eight-legged lamb, a three-legged baby, a two-headed baby, a baby with its eyes under its nose and ears below its neck, Siamese twins joined at the chest ('arms, legs and heads normal'), a baby with a fish's tail, two dogs born to a sixty-year-old virgin and a baby with two heads, four arms and three legs, although the response was not as good as Peter hoped.[11] A special attraction of Peter's museum was the inclusion of live freaks among the exhibits. In May 1722, for example, Peter ordered a payment of 30 roubles to one Semen Shikov, peasant of the village of Senikov, for declaring a live female monster by the name of Natalia Antonova, and to the peasant Mikhail Piskurin, 'from whom that monster was taken', 20 roubles.'[12] A catalogue of the Kunstkamera compiled in the 1740s included two (sadly non-extant) paintings of the bearded peasant woman Aksinia Ivanova, one of them in the nude. In 1724, however, Dr Blumentrost refused to accept another live monster on the grounds that 'in the Kunstkamera we keep only dead freaks', no doubt because of the expense involved in clothing and feeding living exhibits even though some earned their keep as cleaners and janitors.[13]

'I have ordered the governors to collect monsters and send them to you,' Peter is said to have told his British physician Robert Erskine. 'Have show-cases made. If I wished to send you humans who are monsters not on account of the deformity of their bodies but because of their freakish manners, you would not have space to put them all.'[14] Peter waged a battle both with Russians and with himself to overcome their 'freakish manners' and to trans-form them into 'modern, civilised' persons. In this sense, Alexis was a test of Peter's powers of transformation. His failure to turn his own son into a new model citizen, as he saw it, was particularly regrettable and in the end required nothing less than the destruction of the failed experimental material. The irony is that Peter himself, with his great height and facial tics, was a physical oddity, whose own waxwork and personal belongings joined the Kunstkamera collection after his death, to sit among the pickled babies in preserving jars and the stuffed effigies of his horse from Poltava and his favourite dogs.

Alexis's trial

Alexis was tried by a special tribunal known as the Chancellery for Secret Inquisitorial Affairs. It made its initial investigations in Moscow, then in June 1718 moved to St Petersburg, where Alexis was locked up in the Peter-Paul fortress. Peter intended this to be a show trial, conducted with every sem-blance of openness by the standards of the day. Both church and lay officials were consulted and accounts of the proceedings were published in Russia and later abroad. The main charge against Alexis was high treason: he had sought Austrian aid to overthrow and assassinate Peter, 'hoping for his father's death with expressions of joy', as he allegedly confided to his confessor Father Ignat'ev. Nearly all the evidence for a plot was based on confession and hearsay, on flimsy written evidence in two letters sent by Alexis to the Senate from Naples, and a report from the imperial envoy Otto von Pleyer of a plot to kill Peter and proclaim Alexis, without any indication, however, that Alexis was the instigator. Much attention during the investigation focused on Alexis's moral and physical failings – his laziness, drunkenness, shirking, attempts to escape the succession – while his motive for wishing to kill his father was said to be his antipathy towards Peter's reforms. 'I shall bring back the old people and choose myself new ones according to my will,' he said, according to his mistress Afrosinia's testimony. 'When I become sovereign I shall live in Moscow, and leave St Petersburg simply to be like any other town; I won't launch any ships; I shall maintain troops only for defence, and won't wage war against anyone; I shall be content with the old domains. In winter I shall live in Moscow, in summer in Iaroslavl'.[15] Afrosinia was later released for her co-operation. The fate of the child she was carrying is unknown. It emerged that Alexis loathed Peter's entertainments, hated watching the launching of ships, and disapproved of reforms relating to dress and church property. In short, by preferring Moscow, hating naval matters and wishing to limit Russia's military conquests Alexis as good as threatened to destroy everything that Peter held dear. Once Peter believed in these mental acts of treachery, proving that Alexis had planned his father's physical annihilation was a mere technicality.

Interrogation under torture (the standard Russian trial procedure) began on the morning of 19 June, when Alexis was questioned on twelve points, accompanied by twenty-five blows from the knout. The procedure was repeated that evening, this time in the presence of Father Ignat'ev, who also received twenty-five blows. A further torture session took place on 24 June, this time with only fifteen blows, probably because of Alexis's deteriorating condition. Usually sufficient time was allowed between sessions for prisoners' wounds to heal, the aim being to extract confessions rather than to cause death. Peter invited leading churchmen to give their opinion on the case. Even they denounced Alexis for confiding in people who loved the 'ancient customs' and for speaking with distaste of the novelties which his father had introduced, but they declined to reach a decision on the grounds that this was a civil case and subject to the tsar's absolute power. Although they were inclined towards punishment for an errant son (which they illustrated with copious biblical texts), they did not reject the option of mercy, for 'the heart of the tsar is in the hands of God'.[16] The 126 senators and civil officials who constituted the court duly delivered a guilty verdict and a sentence of death at noon on 24 June, but the interrogation by torture continued into the afternoon, for Peter was desperate to extract more information. The next day Alexis was confronted with letters found in his house. On the 26th he was tortured again. That same evening he was dead.

The death of Alexis

An entry in the record book of the Peter-Paul fortress garrison states:

> On June 26 [1718] at 8 a.m. there gathered in the garrison his majesty, the illustrious prince [Menshikov], Prince Iakov Fedorovich Dolgoruky, Gavrila Ivanovich Golovkin, Fedor Matveevich Apraksin, Ivan Alekseevich Musin-Pushkin, Tikhon Nikitich Streshnev, Peter Andreevich Tolstoy, Peter Shafirov and General Buturlin for a session in the torture chamber, after which, having been in the garrison until 11 am., they dispersed. On

the same day at six in the evening, being under guard in the Trubetskoy bastion of the garrison, Tsarevich Alexis Petrovich expired.[17]

In official reports Alexis's death was attributed to a seizure. As Weber recorded: 'The next Day ... early in the Morning the News was brought to the Czar, that the violent Passions of the Mind, and the Terrors of Death, had thrown the Czarewitz into an apoplectick Fit.'[18] Unofficial versions included death by poison and the rumour that Peter had strangled Alexis with his bare hands. A story attributed to Rumiantsev, one of Alexis's escorts back to Russia, dated a month after the tsarevich's death but thought to be a later forgery, claims that Alexis was suffocated in his sleep on Peter's instructions in order to avoid the shame of a public execution. The most likely cause of death is the most obvious: Alexis, already weakened by imprisonment and illness (tuberculosis), was subjected to a series of savage beatings, the final two sessions, on 24 and 26 June, following each other rather too closely. The authorities tried to quash rumours and speculation. A letter written by the Dutch ambassador Jacob de Bie containing gossip about Alexis's death was apprehended and the rumours traced to the mother-in-law of Van Boles, a Dutch engineer working on the steeple of the Peter-Paul Cathedral. He admitted that 'while working on the new tower in the fortress, on the eve of the tsarevich's death, I remained there for the night unobserved and in the evening saw from up there the heads of some people in the torture chamber.'[19] Even this vague sighting was sufficient to lead to the arrest of the builder and his family.

Peter's reaction to his son's death can only be guessed at. According to Weber, Peter had a tearful last meeting with Alexis on the morning of his death and forgave and blessed him, but this is not confirmed elsewhere. We know only that Peter was present from 8 a.m. to 11 a.m. for the last and fatal torture session. Peter's attendance at vespers in the Trinity Cathedral that same evening has been explained by his need to pray for forgiveness, but this, too, is speculation, as Peter routinely attended the evening service. At Alexis's funeral on 30 June guests reported that the tsar was 'bathed in tears'. The priest chose the text from David: 'O my son Absalom, my son, my son Absalom', a reference which later reappeared in the new Law of Succession in 1722.[20] The tsar's own choristers sang at the service. Three days before the funeral, however, Peter celebrated the anniversary of Poltava, one of the liveliest events in the court calendar, on 29 June held the usual party for his name day, and the day after the funeral he toasted the launch of a man-of-war in the company of his new Prince-Caesar, Ivan Romodanovsky, and some English shipwrights. No trace of personal heart-searching or grief is to be found in his letters, which deal with the usual routine matters of state and diplomacy.

Peter's relations with Alexis have provided dramatic inspiration for historians, novelists, playwrights and painters. In his novel *Peter and Alexis* (1905), one of the most powerful fictional treatments of the topic, Dmitry Merezhkovsky constantly returns to the impossibility of penetrating Peter's feelings and getting to the real man. 'You look and your eyes seem to deceive you, you can't tell the tsar from the jester. He surrounded himself with masks. Wasn't the "tsar carpenter" also a mask, just another "masquerade in the Dutch manner?"' Merezhkovsky presents Peter and Alexis not as irreconcilable opposites, but as two sides of the same person, Peter all purposeful energy and action, but also brute force and hyperactivity, Alexis thoughtful and spiritual, but also a hopeless dreamer.[21] Peter may have claimed that he was driven by 'fatherly affection', but his understanding of fatherhood was far from modern-day child-centred concepts and he echoed the beliefs of his day when he wrote that 'private parents and with much more reason those who are beside invested with a sovereign authority, as we are, have an unlimited power over their children, independently of any other judge'.[22] Peter was first and foremost a monarch, a father only second. And he was a monarch with a mission, which his son failed to support in the worst possible way: by defecting. There was a sort of dreadful consistency in Peter's treatment of Alexis, which flowed from his insistence that no one, not even a son, was entitled to privilege and preferment which he had not earned, and from the belief that those born to high office were under a special obligation to serve. Yet we know that Peter could be forgiving of all sorts of shortcomings and weaknesses in those he loved, for example, tolerating Menshikov's illiteracy and even his crimes, or making a joke of 'Baas' Ivan Golovin's failure to master the art of shipbuilding. Peter's affectionate and indulgent treatment of his daughters by Catherine, to whom he never failed to write when he was away, show that he could be a good father, too, although perhaps he found girls, of whom less was expected, easier to love than boys. Probably at the heart of the Alexis affair lay the fact that Peter had never loved the child of his unwanted first marriage and Alexis found it impossible to love the father who had banished his mother when he was only eight years old.

We can only speculate on the impact that the terrible events of 1718 had upon Peter's second family. In the later stages of Alexis's trial Catherine was heavily pregnant with their last daughter, another Natalia, who was born on 19/20 August. If she did try to mediate on Alexis's behalf (he was, after all, her godfather as well as her stepson), no records survive. The trial poisoned the atmosphere at court, where fears of being implicated as one of Alexis's 'accomplices' must have lingered for months if not years. The Chancellery for Secret Inquisitorial Affairs continued to function after Alexis's death. Between 1718 and 1725 it investigated 370 'grave matters', including expressions of sympathy for Alexis, complaints against Catherine and further revelations about Evdokia's 'scandalous' activities in Suzdal', which led to the arrest of over 150 people. Even so, memorial services for Alexis were conducted for a year after his death. Even a traitor was not cut off from prayers for the souls of the dead, which were a vital feature of Orthodoxy, although his tomb was hidden away beneath the staircase of the bell tower of the Peter-Paul Cathedral next to his wife Charlotte and Tsarevna Maria Alekseevna (died 1723), rather than in the main body of the cathedral. In 1906, almost two centuries later, cracks were discovered in the floor and the three tombs had to be reconstructed. Three horizontal slabs and three vertical slabs of white marble, with crosses and inscriptions, were set up. In 1911 the commandant of the fortress reported that no lamps were lit over the graves. Only recently has the door to the recess been opened to allow visitors to the cathedral access to the long-neglected tombs, which are now regularly decorated with flowers.

Assemblies and The Honourable Mirror of Youth

The Alexis affair overshadowed 1718, but the war carried on as usual, more bogged down than ever in diplomatic complexities. In May 1718 a Russo-Swedish peace congress opened in the Åland islands. The Russian ministers Peter Shafirov, James Bruce and Heinrich (Andrei) Osterman went armed with General Conditions for Peace, which stipulated that Ingria, Karelia, Estonia and Livonia, including Reval and Viborg, were to remain Russian in perpetuity but that Finland could be returned to Sweden. Various plans were discussed, including a Russo-Swedish alliance, but they failed to reach an agreement. Then on 30 November (11 December) Charles XII was killed at Frederiksten in Norway while campaigning against Denmark, officially the victim of a stray bullet, although there were rumours that he was murdered. Peter is said to have wept at the news, perhaps as much in the realisation that this could be a setback to peace as out of grief for his old adversary. While Western powers were making their own arrangements with the new Swedish regime and carving up territories and spheres of influence in north Germany, Russia found itself isolated. But Peter's programme to make Russia part of Europe continued.

On 26 November 1718, he issued a decree on assemblies, prompted by his further observations of polite society during his foreign tour the previous year. It explained that 'assembly (*assemblei*) is a French word, which cannot be expressed in Russian in one word, but means a free meeting or gathering in someone's house not only for amusement but also for business'.[23] The first party under the new regulations was held in the house of the reigning Prince-Pope Peter Buturlin in St Petersburg on 27 November , making a firm association with Peter's mock court, which was often required to act out new rituals. So 'free' were the social gatherings envisaged by Peter that not only were they open to decently (i.e. Western) clad persons of either sex from nobles to craftsmen (servants and peasants were excluded), but the host was not obliged to greet or entertain his guests, not even the tsar, or even to be at home, in marked contrast to traditional Russian hospitality which involved elaborate rituals of meeting and farewell. (In early eighteenth-century England, it is worth noting, any member of the 'respectable classes' could gain access to the public rooms of the royal palaces on assembly or 'drawing room' days.) In Russia assemblies were intended to transcend the barriers of service class and family circle and also endorsed the sexual desegregation which Peter had championed since the 1690s. A gentleman could invite any lady to dance, even the empress. Guests were positively encouraged to indulge in activities once denounced by the church (and still abhorred by traditionalists) as 'foreign devilishness' – smoking, dancing, cards, chess and draughts and instrumental music and games such as forfeits, 'questions and commands' and 'cross-purposes'.[24] Bergholz records a Moscow assembly at which 'in the room where the ladies sit and dancing is held people were smoking and playing draughts, which caused a stink and clatter which was inappropriate in the presence of ladies and music'.[25] Even the higher clergy held assemblies, the first of which took place in December 1723 in the Donskoy monastery in Moscow.

Despite their alleged 'freedom', Peter's assemblies involved a characteristic degree of compulsion, both in the manner of their introduction and in their subsequent supervision. The police visited homes to check that everything was in order (the 1718 edict was issued in the name of Anton Devier, the St Petersburg chief of police) and the authorities sometimes demanded lists of guests. The perceived need to spell out the details by edict underlined just how recent and weakly rooted was Russia's adopted Western-style etiquette. A year earlier Russia's first behaviour book or etiquette manual had been published, *The Honourable Mirror of Youth, or a Guide to Good Manners,* incorporating charts of the Cyrillic alphabet in old (Church) and new (Civic) typescripts, followed by moral teachings: 'Love God and the Tsar, and oppose neither one of them'; 'Honour priests, respect your elders' and so on. One section comprised advice for young men, beginning with the command that 'Before all else children must hold their father and mother in great respect.' There were warnings against nose picking and sneezing in people's faces and instructions on the treatment of servants, deportment, dancing, conversation and 'how a young man should behave when sitting in the company of others':

> Do not eat like pigs and do not blow into the bowl so it splashes everywhere. Do not be the first to drink; hold back and avoid drunkenness; drink and eat only as much as you need; be the last one to finish eating . . . when you drink, do not wipe your lips with your hand but use a napkin, and do not drink until you have swallowed your food. Do not lick your fingers and do not gnaw bones but rather take the meat off with a knife. Do not pick your teeth with a knife but use a toothpick and cover your mouth with one hand when picking.

This advice was not devised specifically with 'barbaric' Russians in mind, as some commentators have suggested. It derives from Erasmus's *De civilitate morum puerilium* (1530), which retained its popularity all over Europe right up to the end of the eighteenth century. Instruction in the use of napkins, cutlery and toothpicks was part of the civilising process to distinguish gentlemen from the lower orders, which had occurred in polite Western society a century or more earlier. For all his desire for informality, Peter's foreign travels had taught him much about the standards of public behaviour required to earn the reputation of being civilised, even if in many of the households he visited this civilisation was the thinnest of veneers, especially in some of the minor courts of northern Europe. Russia did not have a monopoly on drinking, carousing and lewdness, but Peter learned that such behaviour was more acceptable if indulged in by men and women wearing the latest French fashions and with the proper accoutrements. So Peter imported such refinements as table napkins, individual table settings of plates (in Muscovy even boyars tended to dip straight into communal bowls), proper cutlery (although he carried around a spoon in his pocket for personal use) and glasses rather than metal beakers. Many foreign words to do with food and cooking appeared in the Russian vocabulary: *kofe* (coffee), *desert, frukt* (fruit), *ananas* (pineapple), *sous* (sauce), *anchous* (anchovies) and so on. The basic Muscovite joint of roast meat was supplemented by cuts of *bifshteks, entrekot, file* and *shnitsel,* prepared by a *kukhmeister* hired from abroad.

What is not usually observed is that the last 41 pages of the *Mirror* are devoted to advice for young women, under the headings 'The Crown of Maidenly Honour and Virtue', 'Maidenly Chastity' and 'Maidenly Humility', the first of which lists and describes twenty virtues, of which about half are related to piety and religious observance. Far from displaying the supposed new open ideals of Peter's reformed society, as encouraged by the mixed-sex assemblies, the texts for young women reinforced older codes. The *Mirror* echoed the sixteenth-century Russian *Book of Household Management (Domostroi),* which was read in noble households well into the nineteenth century, in its admonition to women to 'avoid all inclinations to lack of decorum and all evil temptations such as wicked conversations, unclean habits and actions, rude language, casual and lascivious clothing, seductive letters, lecherous songs, rude fables, stories, songs, histories, riddles, silly proverbs and abusive jokes and pranks, for these are an abomination before God'.

Peter's 'democratic' assemblies did not last long after his death, when they were replaced by gatherings of the nobility with strictly limited access. As far as élite women were concerned, there was to be no return to the seclusion of the *terem,* but those who read the *Mirror* were warned that they must attempt to combine the new socialising with the old proprieties. Neither fathers nor husbands appreciated spoiled goods. Assemblies and the new etiquette are yet another example of Peter's insistence on intervening in areas where previously

the state did not venture much. In the words of a later Slavophile commentator, 'above all the apparent jollity and revelry of life there reigned the iron
will of the head pedagogue, which knew no bounds – everyone made merry
by decree and even to the sound of drumbeats, they got drunk and made
merry under compulsion'.[26] Nothing was left to chance.

The chief of police

St Petersburg was always in Peter's thoughts, especially now that he was able
to spend more time there. The focus on fine buildings to embellish the water-
fronts now widened to include measures to improve the environment. This
was the first Russian city to be under 'police' administration (*politsiia*), in the
eighteenth-century sense of provisions for order, cleanliness and welfare, as
well as crime prevention. Peter picked up some ideas in Paris, which had its
own lieutenant-general of police. St Petersburg's first chief of police was
Anton Devier (Antonio De Vieira), a man of Portuguese descent whom Peter
hired in Holland.

With admirable resourcefulness, Devier supplemented the small workforce
allocated to him with the efforts of the city population at large. On 20 March
1720, for example, St Petersburg inhabitants of all ranks who owned horses
were ordered to bring a cartload of manure from each horse to a designated
place on Vasil'evsky Island; 'if people fail to carry out this order they will be
fined the sum of one rouble for each [undelivered] cartload. Let this be
announced in St Petersburg to the beat of drums.'[27] In October 1721 Devier
received an order for the construction of abattoirs at the mouth of the Moika
'to be built to resemble residences with false windows, and to improve their
appearance painted with paints obtained from the State Revenues College,
since when His Majesty was travelling along that river past the paper mills he
had a good look at the abattoirs which the butchers have built and found them
to be very poor, scattered all over the place, and the surrounding area was
dirty.'[28] In April 1722 he received another order for distribution: 'Anyone who
has to construct wooden buildings should boil moss well in boiling water
before using it [for stuffing cracks], because cockroaches hatch out in raw moss,
which contains flies and other vermin and they will subsequently grow and
multiply.'[29] (Peter was terrified of cockroaches.) Other public hygiene measures
involved setting up model stalls made of canvas to replace the ramshackle
premises used by street food traders, 'for better appearance and cleanliness'.
Apparently, people had been making tents from dirty, smelly rags, 'disgusting
to the human sight'.[30] In April 1721 there was an attempt to set up a regular
refuse collection service with teams of horses and drivers and vagrants to collect rubbish from outside houses.[31] Live detritus was not allowed to clog up the
streets, either. Beggars were banned, especially any who were on the streets 'out

of laziness and young people who are not being employed in work and for hire, from whom no good can come, only robbery'. There was a five-rouble fine for anyone caught giving alms to beggars. They were advised to dispense charity by giving their money to the hospitals or other such institutions.[32]

Residents were expected to improve the environment at their own expense. An edict of 17 August 1721 states:

All St Petersburg residents who were required by edict to plant maples on the streets and have already planted some are ordered by the end of this month in order to protect them from passers-by and to guard them from cattle to fence them off with boxes of the type which has been made on Admiralty Island opposite the newly built stone market. Also, anyone who in the future plants maples along the streets must be sure to make boxes as described above. Anyone contravening this order will be fined, and a notice to this effect is to be published in St Petersburg.[33]

Residents with property on the river were required to build their own portion of embankment, but regular repetitions of the order indicate that the response was poor.[34] In general, exhortation was supplemented with a system of harsh penalties – knout, exile and hard labour – for offences such as polluting the waterways, selling rotten meat and building double walls between adjoining properties (a waste of brick!).[35] According to an anecdote, Devier himself felt the tsar's cudgel on his back when during an inspection tour of the city Peter noticed that planks were missing from a bridge across one of the canals.[36]

Weber wrote in 1719: 'The new Regulations of Police, a thing unheard-of in Russia before, has already produced a very good Effect, particularly as to the Safety of the publick Streets.'[37] Street lanterns were installed in the better parts of town, which along with swing-beam barriers to close off main streets at night were as much to do with law and order as aesthetics, to ensure that the life of citizens was constantly under the authorities' spotlight.[38] The laying of drainage pipes and street paving 'according to the prescribed models' was an attempt to prevent St Petersburg turning into the muddy quagmire which Moscow became each spring and autumn.[39]

The comparative ease with which Peter created his model capital (even if it too seemed little more than a façade at times) emphasised the terrible difficulties of creating a model Russia. In 1718–19 he attempted yet another reorganisation of local government. A project published in November 1718 instructed the Senate: 'In the provinces all personnel in all offices are to be appointed and given instructions and other procedures after the Swedish model.' The new system was to be implemented by 1720, with a pilot project in St Petersburg province. Peter appended a list of Swedish terms for various posts, such as *lantsgevding* (from Swedish *landshövding*) in his own hand to the original decree.[40] In January 1719 sets of instructions were issued to new provincial officials. The new-style *voevoda*'s job description, set out in 46 articles, for example, included unmasking spies, protecting Orthodoxy, overseeing judges, maintaining military installations and defences, supervising factories, rounding up vagrants and runaways, taking inventories, conducting censuses (in preparation for the poll tax), keeping order, promoting businesses and crafts, supervising tax collections and fiscal staff, and monitoring the inheritance of estates.[41] In May 1719 fifty provinces were created by dividing up the old provinces (*gubernii*) into sections.[42] As we shall see, much of this proposal remained on paper, as did Peter's scheme (also of 1719) for the separation of justice from administration by subordinating judicial districts to the Justice College. By and large, however hard he tried, in the provinces older arrangements based on local strong men, clientele networks, custom and common law resurfaced and the new decrees remained unread and unenforceable.

The death of Peter Petrovich

The New Year of 1719 began with the usual programme of fireworks and the Epiphany ceremony on 6 January.[43] Peter's positive mood is reflected in the plans which he devised in the first week of January to send an expedition to Kamchatka and beyond in order to 'describe those regions and to ascertain whether America is joined with Asia, which must be done with the greatest of care, not only south and north, but also east and west and all to be put on a map'.[44] Although much of his attention was still focused on the Baltic, he never lost sight of the wider opportunities offered by an expanding empire. Nearer to home, Peter was preparing for the planting season, assembling a team of workers to collect trees for his gardens and ordering the parks supervisor at Peterhof to get flower beds ready for planting in spring, one in the 'Italian manner', the other in the French.[45] In late January he and Catherine visited the Martsial'nye springs near Olonets and the Petrovskie ironworks, from where he wrote to Menshikov declaring that he had never seen such fine factories and congratulating him as their 'founder'. He raised a glass to the name-day girl, Menshikov's daughter Maria.[46] Later he reported to Golovkin that they would soon stop taking the waters as 'I can't drink any more because of the strength of them, twice as strong as the waters as Spa.' (In the same letter he asked Golovkin to send one or more spies into Sweden via Danzig in order to ascertain what the Swedes would be doing with their fleet that spring.[47]) Catherine wrote to her daughter Elizabeth, 'Your dear father has started to take the waters, which are doing His Majesty a lot of good.'[48]

Peter's faith in the Olonets springs, which were discovered in 1716 by the German inspector of mines Wilhelm Henning, was increased by a 'miracu-

lous event' which he reported to Menshikov a week later, after he learned that
Menshikov had been ill. One of his musicians had been suffering for a year
with a chest infection, coughing up blood. The doctors advised him against
drinking the strong mineral water, but he drank some secretly and the next
day he was better, and had since grown fat. The doctors 'were amazed'.[49] This
incident prompted a public announcement 'On the action of the waters'. The
illnesses reputedly cured included scurvy, jaundice, vomiting, diarrhoea and
constipation, gravel (the disease which probably eventually killed Peter) and
hypochondria.[50] Dr Blumentrost explained the water's curative properties by
a chemical analysis, providing a secular slant on the miracle cures attributed
by common folk to various 'holy' springs. Peter's new spa was modelled on
several which Peter had visited abroad – Baden in 1698 and 1708, Carlsbad in
1711–12, Bad Piermont in 1716, and Spa in 1717. After Peter's death the 'native'
spa of which he was so proud, far from St Petersburg and with no local
interest, more or less ceased to function, although memories lingered into the
nineteenth century in the shape of two old birches known locally as Peter and
Catherine. It was revived in Soviet times, as we shall see.

Back in St Petersburg in late March Peter dispatched a series of missives on
revenue collecting to provincial governors. By now he knew better than to put
his trust only in the written word. He instructed Peter Boriatinsky, a
Preobrazhensky guardsman, to deliver a letter to the governor of Moscow and
his assistants in person and then 'to pester him ceaselessly to make sure that
he carries out the instructions without delay'. If they failed to comply,
Boriatinsky was instructed to fetter them by the legs and neck, put them in
chains and not release them until they had done so.[51] On 1 April 1719 Peter
invited an audience to watch a performance by Samson the strongman, only
to dismiss them with an inscription let down from the scenery bearing the
words APRIL FOOL. The year before Peter had staged a mock fire and summoned the brigade, who were then rewarded with beer and brandy.[52]

A few weeks later the mood changed dramatically. Since the proclamation
of Peter Petrovich as Peter's heir, his development and upbringing had been
closely monitored. Catherine's letters to Peter offer glimpses of their pride and
concern. In July 1718 she wrote that their son had been ailing because of
teething, but now, with God's help, was in good health and had cut three
teeth. 'And please take care, Dad, because he has a bone to pick with you;
when I remind him that his Papa has gone away he doesn't like it; he likes it
much better and is pleased when you tell him that Papa is here.' In August
she reported that young Peter was always amusing himself drilling his soldiers
and firing toy cannon, just like his father.[53] The boy's likeness was captured
by various artists, for example, in a much-reproduced portrait by Peter's
French court artist Louis Caravaque of Peter as Cupid with his bow kneeling
on a cushion, which holds a crown and the Order of St Andrew, predicting a
glorious rule to come, or in Johann Dannhauer's 1719 miniature on the inside

lid of a gold snuffbox, in which the small boy in a plumed head-dress sits on a pile of velvet and points to Dannhauer's own profile portrait of his father to his left.

In view of all this tender concern and expectation, the laconic report of the boy's death, on 25 April 1719, in the daily journal kept in Alexander Menshikov's household, makes painful reading:

> His Excellency [Menshikov] visited the palace and spent about an hour in the apartments of His Royal Highness the tsarevich, then left for his home. At four in the afternoon General Apraksin sent an orderly with the news that the tsarevich had died, at which His Excellency left at once for the palace, went to the apartments and made the necessary arrangements for the funeral.

The scribe adds the information that at the time of his death Peter Petrovich was 3 feet 4 inches tall.[54] The loss was not entirely unexpected – it turns out that the boy had always been 'weak and puny', lagging far behind his cousin, Peter Alekseevich, just a couple of weeks his senior[55] – but this did not make it any easier to bear. Catherine was too distraught to attend the funeral and Peter is said to have locked himself in his room for several days.[56] But their letters for April and May do not mention their bereavement and reference to it is oddly missing from diplomatic correspondence, as though Peter was reluctant to advertise his loss too widely, for Peter Petrovich's death once again left him without any male issue except his grandson, whom most people, following the old dispensation, must now regard as the heir presumptive. There was no official declaration either to confirm or deny it. Tsar Peter was alive and well and for the time being the question of the succession remained dormant.

A passion for the fleet

There was little time for grieving. The navigation season was under way and as ever Peter found comfort in ships and sailing, especially now that real action was once again in store. In May the Russian fleet captured Swedish ships off the Oesel islands and in July bombarded the Swedish mainland. The journals for June and July are full of navigational entries – weather charts, signals, battle formations – as Peter sailed aboard the ship *Ingermanland* to Hangö. He took a personal interest in every new vessel. On 22 June he wrote to the English shipwright Richard Cozens:

> I am writing about the ships which you built. The *Neptune* is a very fine ship and so fast that it's probably the best in the fleet. The *Hangö* also goes

very well and is very obedient to the wheel, only for its height not terribly stable and as we so far have not had a strong wind for sailing and it bends from a lightest breeze more than the others, we'll let you know what happens when we have some better weather.[57]

The activities of shipbuilders like Cozens and his friends Noye and Browne in Russia were beginning to arouse the anxiety of the British authorities, who passed an Act of Parliament to prevent British craftsmen working 'in foreign parts'. But, as the British envoy in Russia James Jefferyes pointed out, men such as Cozens would be hard to tempt back to England, 'for they are the most carressed by the Czar and consequently by all the great men of the kingdom; they partake of his diversions, and on festival-days sit at his own table when persons of the best quality are bound to stand and wait ...'. Only the offer of a much bigger salary might entice them to return home. In the past few years the Russian fleet had grown by some twenty-seven or twenty-eight ships of the line, of which a considerable number were built in St Petersburg and were said 'to be ships as good and as well built as any Europe can afford', with ten more under construction in the yards. Russian seamen 'grow better every day' and 'the Czar's fondness for the fleet is his predominant and favourite passion, which doubtless will prompt and push him on to advance and bring it in as great a reputation as possibly he can'.[58] Britain had good cause for concern.

On 13 July Peter sent a number of identical letters, including one to 'Sire' Romodanovsky, to report that the galley and the deep-water fleet had arrived, but 'we have not seen the enemy either on the water or in the entrance to the skerries; may God grant a good ending, but the beginning has been very propitious'.[59] A week later the men on the ships heard gunfire in the distance, which turned out to be Colonel Lacy's troops attacking the ironworks at Lesta Bruck. As the war dragged on (in September the Åland congress broke up), so did the need to raise money resurface, centring on the question of how to provision the standing army inside Russia now that action abroad was sporadic. Censuses were conducted as a preliminary to the introduction of a poll or soul tax, which was imposed on each male head or 'soul' rather than on households, as in the past. Counts or *revisions* identified some 5.5 million male souls liable to pay the tax (women were not counted), which was collected for the first time in 1724 at a rate of 74 kopecks per head. It was reckoned that it took 47 peasants to maintain one infantryman at a cost of 28.5 roubles per year and 57 to maintain one cavalryman. Crown and state peasants paid an additional 40 kopecks in quitrent and urban taxpayers paid 1.2 roubles. The new tax had considerable administrative and social implications. It clarified or changed the status of certain groups by turning them into taxpayers, for example, the single householders *(odnodvortsy)*, who were once classified among the non-taxpaying servitors. Some old social groups such as slaves disappeared as distinct categories and became liable to the tax on the same basis as peasants. Poll tax produced an increase in government revenues but economic historians continue to argue about whether it increased the burden on the individual peasant. Its introduction coincided with famine years, the period of harsh winters sometimes referred to as the 'Little Ice Age' which affected Russia most drastically in 1721–24, and a temporary decline in money supply as a result of the payment of compensation to Sweden after peace was made in 1721. Sums were fixed regardless of ability to work or pay, with minors and the aged included among the taxpayers. Warnings of the 'ruin' of the peasantry were sounded after Peter's death and the basic tax was reduced to 70 kopecks, but the poll tax itself turned out to be one of Peter's most enduring legacies, abolished only in 1887.

In December 1719 the College of Mines and Manufacture was established (in 1722 a separate *manufaktur-kollegiia* was created) and its functions were set out in a charter, the *Berg-privilegii*, which includes some interesting reflections on Russian enterprise:

> Compared with many other lands, our Russian state is blessed with large quantities of useful metals and minerals, which have not till now been mined with much diligence; since they have not been exploited as they should have been, much benefit and many profits, which could have been obtained for us and our subjects, have been lost. We acknowledge that the main reason for this has been partly that our subjects have not understood mining and what can be done with it for the good of the state and the people and partly also they have been unwilling to take the risk and invest money and labour for fear that once these mining works are established and making good profits they will be taken away from their owners. . . . [Therefore] all are allowed and each and every one is permitted, whatever his rank or dignity, in all places, both on his own land and on that of others to excavate, smelt, found and refine all types of metals. . . .[60]

The charter made clear that mines belonged to the crown and that a tenth of the profits must come back to the state. It also underlined the weakness of landed property rights. Owners of land on which another person excavated ores had no redress if damage was caused, but could claim a share of the profits. Not surprisingly, there were frequent clashes between landowners and their stewards and prospectors. Exploiting the enormous potential of Russian mineral wealth was to remain on the agenda for Peter's successors.

Statutes and regulations

Peter spent the first two months of 1720 in St Petersburg in a frenetic round of Yuletide visitations and assemblies – Dolgoruky's on 14 January, Golitsyn's on the 19th, Tolstoy's on the 21st, the Prince-Pope's on the 24th, a party on board ship on the 27th. February, before the start of Lent, was the time for weddings. The tsar attended at least five between 5 and 21 February, and on the 22nd he was the chief guest at the wedding of the giant Nicolas Bourgeois (Nikolai Zhigant) and a Finnish giantess. Giants were in shorter supply than dwarfs and Peter gave his permission for the couple to marry only when the bride-to-be was pregnant, in the hope of obtaining additional tall recruits for his guards. Bourgeois, it seemed, had no duties apart from being on view as his obesity made him incapable of doing much else. For this he was paid the considerable salary of 300 roubles per year.[61] After his death from a stroke in 1724 a stuffed effigy in his skin went on show in the Kunstkamera, where it was painted by the Swiss artist Georg Gsell. The ample skeleton is still displayed there today. Other entertainments recorded in the court journal for February included rides on bulls, dogs, bears and goats and a procession of the Prince-Pope in a giant jug 'at the tavern'.

As always, Peter had no difficulty in combining work with play. He visited the Admiralty on several occasions to put the finishing touches to the Naval Statute, 'on all which pertains to the good organisation while the fleet is at sea ... selected from five maritime regulations [French, British, Danish, Swedish and Dutch], with a substantial part added'.[62] The introduction declared that 'a potentate who has only land forces has but a single arm; he who also has a fleet has two arms',[63] and explained that the word 'fleet' was French: 'By this word is meant a number of water-going vessels travelling along together, or standing, both military and merchant'. The work illustrates two of Peter's approaches to the edification of his subjects. On the one hand, he was adept, with a little help from Feofan Prokopovich, at making his own myths. The preface to the Statute relates the history of Russia's naval exploits, culminating in the uplifting tale of Peter's little boat, the 'grandfather' of the Russian navy. To underline the point, the 1720 edition had an engraving of a sailing ship without a steering wheel and a naked boy sitting in it to signify inexperienced Russia. The text is highly allusive, transforming Peter's search for ever greater expanses of water to sail his ships into a sort of pilgrimage. On the other hand, the main body of the Statute illustrates Peter's blunt, practical side, his mania for written rules and regulations to specify precisely what each person's duties were, 'from the first to the last'. Book 3, for example, includes among the tasks of the shipboard janitor the responsibility for ensuring that people relieve themselves in the authorised places.[64] There are templates for ships' logs, provisions allocation, complete lists of tackle, and several pages on flag and lantern signals.

The end of February saw the publication of one of the most important pieces of legislation of Peter's reign, the General Regulation (*General'nyi reglament*, both words of foreign origin) for the administration of the Colleges, which went through twelve separate drafts before it appeared in print. Following the example of other Christian monarchs, the decree explains, Peter had founded the Colleges,

> for the sake of the orderly running of . . . state affairs and the correct allo-
> cation and calculation of his revenues and the improvement of useful jus-
> tice (*iustitsiia*) and police (*politsiia*) . . . also for the sake of the utmost
> preservation of the safety of his loyal subjects and the maintenance of his
> naval and land forces in good condition as well as commerce, arts and
> manufacture and the good establishment of his sea and land taxes and for
> the increase and spread of mining works and other state needs.[65]

The Regulation's 56 clauses are imbued with concern for public accountabil-
ity and the good order of the collegiate offices. No detail was neglected.
Audience chambers were to be equipped with good-quality carpets and chairs
(but no throne was provided for the tsar), the collegiate table must be covered
with a decent cloth and draped with a canopy and there must be a good clock
on the wall, an essential feature for someone as obsessed with time-keeping as
Peter. In 1724 it was specified further that the General Regulation must be
adhered to strictly and read aloud to officials in the same way as the Military
Statute was read out to soldiers and sailors '. . . for the proper understanding
of soldierly duty'.[66] No one must be given an excuse to plead ignorance as a
justification for his mistakes.

Each college had its own regulation, based on appropriately adapted
Swedish models. The 1720 law was thus a 'regulation of regulations', the proliferation of which accorded with Peter's belief that the common good was
best served by a large body of well-drafted legislation.[67] But how to make officials implement the regulations and 'loyal subjects' obey them? As Peter had
written in the revised duties of the Senate in 1718: 'How can a state be governed when edicts are not implemented, for contempt for edicts is in no
respect different from treason?'[68] This is a problem which Peter never solved.

Pastimes

On 29 February 1720 Peter set off by way of Schlüsselburg for a return visit
to the Martsial'nye medicinal springs, where he stayed until the end of
March. The springs, too, had their regulations: here games such as chess,
spillikins *(biriulki)*, billiards and a kind of shove-ha'penny called *trukt-tafel*
were interspersed with taking the waters, working on the lathe and visits to
the ironworks, where on 3 March Peter cast a large iron bar. There were dinners (on 12 March sixty persons 'of all ranks' dined with the tsar) and regular
church services, during some of which Peter sang with the choristers. Back in
St Petersburg he started a round of visits to estates and settlements around the

1. Tsar Alexis, engraved portrait, Vienna, 1670s.

2. Portrait of Peter I, ca. 1678, drawing from the *Book of Titles*.

3. Tsars Ivan and Peter, *Les Frères Czars*, engraving by F. Jollain, Paris, 1687.

4. Tsarevna Sophia, nineteenth-century engraving based on contemporary oil painting.

3. Tsars Ivan and Peter, *Les Frères Czars*, engraving by F. Jollain, Paris, 1687.

4. Tsarevna Sophia, nineteenth-century engraving based on contemporary oil painting.

1. Tsar Alexis, engraved portrait, Vienna, 1670s.

2. Portrait of Peter I, ca. 1678, drawing from the *Book of Titles*.

5. Peter I, painting by Godfried Schalken, ca. 1703.

6. Peter I, engraving, 1724, by J. Houbraken, after a painting by
Karl (Carel) Moor, Amsterdam, 1717.

7. Peter I, round portrait, attributed to Ivan Nikitin, 1721?

8. Tsarevna Natalia Alekseevna, Peter's sister, painting by Ivan Nikitin, before 1716?

9. Catherine I, painting by Jean-Marc Nattier, Amsterdam/Paris, 1717.

10. Tsarevich Alexis, painting by J.-G. Dannhauer, before 1718.

11. Tsarevich Peter Petrovich, copy of painting by Louis Caravaque, ca. 1717.

12. Tsarevna Anna Petrovna, Peter's daughter, detail from painting by Louis Caravaque, 1717.

13. Alexander Menshikov, painting by unknown artist.

14. and 15. Peter-Paul Cathedral, Domenico Trezzini, 1712–33.

16. The Merchants' Rows and Neva Embankment, St Petersburg, contemporary print.

17. Summer Palace, Domenico Trezzini, 1710–14.

18. Menshikov's Palace on Vasilevsky Island, Gottfried Schädel *et al.*, 1710s–1720s, contemporary engraving.

19. Peterhof, J. Braunstein, J. B. LeBlond, B. Rastrelli *et al.*, 1714–52.

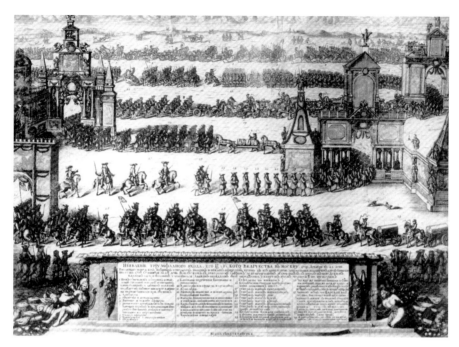

20. Poltava victory parade, Moscow, 1710, engraving by Aleksei Zubov.

21. The wedding of Peter and Catherine, 1712, detail from engraving by Aleksei Zubov.

22. Peter I, deathbed portrait by Ivan Nikitin, 1725.

23. Peter lying in state in the Winter Palace, print by A. I. Rostovtsev, 1725.

24. Wax model of Peter I in the Hermitage, Carlo Rastrelli, 1725.

25. Peter's little house in St Petersburg: (*above*) a modern view and a nineteenth-century print of the chapel.

26. 'Bronze Horseman' monument to Peter I, Etienne Falconet and Marie Collot, 1782.

27. Monument to the Tercentenary of the Russian Fleet, Moscow, Zurab Tsereteli, 1997.

28. (*above left*) Statue of Peter I, Peter-Paul Fortress, Mikhail Shemiakin, 1991.

29. (*above right*) Bust of Peter in the Moskovsky Station, St Petersburg, on plinth previously occupied by Lenin, 1990s.

30. Assorted Petrine memorabilia, including beaker and brass bust souvenirs from 1903.

gulf of Finland – Dubki and Kotlin on 29 March, Peterhof on the 30th. That day he also attended the funeral of Daria Gavrilovna Rzhevskaia: in 1717 she had been promoted to the office of 'Arch-Abbess' of the Drunken Assembly by the newly elected Prince-Pope Peter Buturlin, who wrote that he had lauded her 'exploits' (in drinking) before the Assembly, which had given its consent.[69] Her place was taken by Princess Anastasia Petrovna Golitsyna, who also performed the role of 'jester' in Tsaritsa Catherine's household. There followed a round of assemblies (Musin-Pushkin's on 31 March, Ivan Golovin's on 3 April), inspections of ships and visits to the Admiralty, Foreign Affairs and War colleges and the Senate. Easter week involved daily attendance at the liturgy and on Easter Sunday Peter took communion together with his daughters Anna and Elizabeth. On 16 April 1720 he attended mass, then had a walk around town and launched two boats. The following day after mass he visited Prince-Caesar and Golovin.

Throughout April, May and June the Polish ambassador was in St Petersburg and many of the court's excursions were for his benefit: for example, on 8 May there was a boat trip with sixteen barges and twenty-two skiffs. On 10 May they visited the Kunstkamera and the next day took a trip on a yacht. On 15 May they set off on a four-day trip which took them to Kronstadt, where they dined with the admiral and naval officers and visited the harbours and the fortress, then moved to Menshikov's palace at Oranienbaum. On 30 May they celebrated Peter's forty-eighth birthday (for some reason the journal keeper noted it as the start of his fiftieth year) with fireworks and two days later mourned the death of the Prince-Pope's wife at her funeral in the church of St Samson. On 9 June the Nevsky fleet set off on another expedition to Kronstadt, where the royal party inspected work on the harbour and canal. Peter and the Polish ambassador dined aboard the *Hangö* and visited the captured Swedish vessel *Wachtmeister*, thence to Oranienbaum on 13–14 June, where they 'walked in the grove by the ponds', then to Peterhof and Monplaisir, seven miles to the east, on the 15th. At nearby Strel'na they laid the foundations of a pavilion and at Peterhof drove in carriages along the avenues. Most days there were boat trips around the Finnish gulf, to Kotlin, Dubki, Sestraretsk. By now Peter must have known the gulf, which once seemed so vast, like the back of his hand. June the 25th saw the thirty-eighth anniversary of Peter's coronation, the funeral of Iakov Dolgoruky and the death of General Adam Weide, who was buried with full military honours at the Alexander Nevsky monastery on 30 June. Others who died that summer included Peter's chess partner, Father Bitka, and A. M. Golovin.

The journals for the summer of 1720 give the impression of a carefree, almost aimless existence – boat trips, launches of ships, garden walks, parties. On 30 July, having spent the last week or so cruising the gulf as far as Viborg, Peter sailed from Kotlin to Peterhof with Admiral Apraksin, Ivan Golovin and an assortment of naval officers and shipwrights. After Peter docked near

Monplaisir palace, Catherine, who had travelled by land from neighbouring Strel'na, joined him by the statue of Adam amidst fountains, where wine was served. (Eve stood at the opposite end of the park.) That evening the company took a turn round the gardens and dined in Monplaisir. The next day Peter acted as godfather at the christening of the son of Major Khotiantsov. After lunch they walked around in the garden again and towards evening, having crossed the canal by the new bridge which had just been finished, they drank wine and from there went to the groves, where they stacked newly-mown hay into ricks. 'At dusk His Majesty paid a visit to the major in his quarters. They spent the night at Monplaisir.' On 1 August they drove out to inspect the reservoir for the cascades and fountains and that evening 'made merry with various invented games'.[70]

Life was not quite so idyllic as these accounts of rural romps suggest. Peace remained elusive and in the latter half of 1720 Peter was occupied with naval operations. In one of the last major encounters of the war, on 27 July 1720 the Russian galley fleet under the command of Prince M. M. Golitsyn (the Younger) beat the Swedes off Grengham in the Åland islands, which had served as a useful base since the Russians snatched them from Sweden in 1714. The four Swedish frigates captured in the encounter were among the last trophies of the war. They were taken first to Kronstadt, then to St Petersburg, where Peter viewed them on 6 September. Aleksei Zubov commemorated the occasion in his engraving of a line of captured ships and Russian galleys sailing in front of Trinity Square with gun salutes from the fortress in the background.[71] On 8 September there was a triumphal ceremony with fireworks in the evening. Feofan Prokopovich used the occasion to muse on Peter's first boat: 'Who will not say that this small dinghy was to the fleet as the seed is to the tree?'[72] Training the future generation of naval men remained a priority. Ivan Nepliuev recorded one of Peter's most famous utterances in 1720 at an examination of naval trainees recently returned from abroad: 'You see, lad, even though I'm the tsar I have callouses on my hands, all in order to show you an example so that I may see fitting helpers and servants of the fatherland, even if I have to wait until I am old.'[73]

In autumn the fun resumed. Several entries in the journals contained the formula '*dovol'no veselilis*' (a good time was had by all), which was especially true for Peter when ships were involved. On 2 October the 66-gun ship *Astrakhan*, built by Joseph Noye, was launched; on 5 October it was the turn of Richard Cozens's ship *St Peter* and on 8–11 October the yacht fleet had an excursion to Schlüsselburg. Peter arrived in his yacht on the 10th, when he visited Menshikov's new residence and attended vespers in the fortress church before retiring for the night to his cabin. (Peter loved to sleep on board ship.) The next day – the sixteenth anniversary of the capture of Schlüsselburg – there was a procession of the cross for thanksgiving, followed by a dinner where, again, 'a good time was had by all' to the sound of a series of gun salutes.[74] Winter drew on. On 29 October the tsarevny and the grand duke and grand duchess transferred from their summer quarters to the Winter Palace and Peter travelled by sledge for the first time that autumn. After hearing vespers in the Summer Palace he played chess and spillikins all evening. The next day there was a trip on a wherry across to the Trinity Cathedral for the liturgy, then back to the Winter Palace. On 24 November, for Catherine's name day, the liturgy in the cathedral was followed by a grand dinner with ministers, fireworks and illuminations. The year ended with renewed hopes of peace.

VIII

The Year of Nystad
1721

He has brought us out of the darkness of ignorance onto the stage of glory before the eyes of the whole world and, as it were, transformed us from non-existence into being, bringing us into the society of political nations. (Gavrila Golovkin's speech conferring new imperial titles on Peter I at the celebration of the peace of Nystad, 22 October 1721.)

Yuletide visits

Peter celebrated the New Year of 1721 in good spirits in the company of his daughters, grandchildren, senators and ministers. The evening ended with 'a great number of rockets', the first of several spectacular firework displays in what turned out to be a year of victory. The customary Yuletide 'carol-singing' visitations with members of the Drunken Assembly followed. On 3 January Peter went to the homes of Peter Tolstoy, Mikhail Matiushkin, Ivan Golovin and Ivan Musin-Pushkin, on the 6th it was the turn of Admiralty colleagues Fedor Apraksin, Cornelius Cruys, Grigory Chernyshev and Fedor Skliaev and on the 8th A. M. Sheremetev, Anikita Repnin and Prince Trubetskoy.

Peter took great delight in devising bawdy rules and regulations for these occasions. A declaration to prospective hosts reads:

> Our intemperance means that we are sometimes so incapacitated that we cannot move from the spot and it may happen that we are unable to visit all the houses that we have promised to visit on a given day, and the hosts may be out of pocket as a result of the preparations they have made. Therefore we declare and firmly pronounce, on threat of punishment with the Great Eagle Cup, that nobody should prepare any food. And if we should deign to have a meal from someone, we shall communicate our orders in advance, and for confirmation we have signed this edict with our own hand and ordered it sealed with the great seal of Gabriel.

The rule about catering was apparently inconsistently applied, for another of Peter's memoranda states:

> Announcement of what each should have at home when we arrive: bread, salt, rolls, caviare, hams, dried chicken or hares, cheese if there is any,

butter, sausages, tongues, cucumbers, cabbage, eggs and tobacco. What we like best of all are wines, beer and mead. The more there is, the more pleased we shall be. . . .'[1]

Sometimes the revellers demanded money for their songs, in the manner of modern carol-singers. For the well-to-do people they visited (common folk were let off the hook), this was tantamount to having to pay a New Year tax. Peter did not invent the idea of Yuletide customs, although he put his own peculiar stamp on them. As Boris Kurakin wrote: 'There is an old custom among the Russian people before Christmas and after to play at *sviatki*, that is, friends gather together at someone's house in the evening and dress up in masquerade costume and the servants of distinguished people act out all sorts of funny stories. According to this custom His Majesty the tsar in his court also played at *sviatki* with his courtiers.'[2] For Peter such activities were rooted in personal relationships and private jokes and seemed more often than not to satisfy a need for letting off steam rather than to teach the Russian people a lesson about the evils of over-powerful organised religion. As Weber put it, 'the Czar among all the heavy Cares of Government knows how to set apart some Days for the Relaxation of his Mind, and how ingenious he is in the Contrivance of those Diversions.'[3] Peter, for example, was responsible for making a list of the Prince-Pope's 'servitors' in which all including Peter himself were given rude names based on the Russian for 'prick' (*khui*).[4] The iron hand of the autocrat was never very effectively disguised. The Prince-Pope was expected to discipline his subordinates. A document dated 23 April 1723 lists those members who had been 'disobedient' and were living 'in unruly fashion' in Moscow. The fact that it was drawn up and annotated by the tsar indicates that 'Archdeacon Peter' kept a firm hold on proceedings.

On 9 January Peter set off for a three-day trip which took him along the south shore of the gulf to Strel'na, Peterhof, Oranienbaum and Kronstadt. Then there were christenings, assemblies and weddings to attend, and he found time in between to work at his lathe, where on 28 January he made some small boxes, no doubt as gifts for friends. On 27 January Anna Petrovna celebrated her thirteenth birthday and on 3 February her name day, which was marked by the launch of the ship *Apostle Andrew* and a firework display at the Post Office. On 12 February Peter held a rehearsal with about fifty sleds for the forthcoming wedding of the recently widowed Prince Pope, Peter Buturlin, and on the 19th there was a ball at the Post Office to mark Peter and Catherine's ninth wedding anniversary, which from now on was included in the official court calendar. At the inevitable firework display a panel appeared lighting up the word VIVAT and the monogram of P. and C. in Latin letters under a crown.

The Holy Synod

The year began in a mood of celebration and relaxation; but the keeper of the appointments journal in the Cabinet office also recorded weightier business. On 14 February Peter attended mass in the Trinity Cathedral, where he heard an address from Archbishop Feofan Prokopovich on the creation of a new body called the Spiritual College, 'then the tsar went to the Spiritual College where all the hierarchs of the church and the ministers were gathered', and then went off for a spot of work on his lathe *en route* for assemblies at the homes of Aleksei Rumiantsev and the French minister Jean-Jacques Campredon. The new statute of the Russian Orthodox church, the Spiritual Regulation (*Dukhovnyi Reglament ili Ustav*), which was published on 25 January 1721, had been several years in the making. In November 1718 Peter had written: 'For better administration [of the church] henceforth I think it would be convenient to have a spiritual college. . . .'[5] Clearly, this remark was made with the new government colleges in mind and the new Synod board, like the colleges, comprised a president, two vice-presidents, four councillors, four assessors – all priests – plus one 'honest, right-thinking person of secular rank'. At its first session, however, the new body changed its name to 'Most Holy Governing Synod', echoing the title of the Senate. The Spiritual Regulation made clear that the Synod was interlocked with the state apparatus and, like it, subordinate to the tsar himself. Its members were 'individuals assembled for the general welfare by the command of the Autocrat and under his scrutiny, jointly with others' and they could not amend the Regulation without the tsar's consent. The president (Stefan Iavorsky, until his death in November 1722) was a mere chairman, with an equal voice with other members. Devout oppositionists were in no doubt that the tsar had usurped patriarchal authority, a view which seemed to be confirmed by, for example, the placing of a royal throne in the former patriarchal palace in Moscow. His was the decisive voice in the appointment of bishops and he interfered in church business as he saw fit. Long gone were the days when a Russian patriarch could assert, as had Nikon, that 'the tsar must be lower than the prelate and obedient to him'.[6]

A central concern of the Regulation and a supplement published in May 1722 was education: 'When the light of learning is extinguished there cannot be good order in the Church; there cannot be but disorder and superstitions deserving of much ridicule, in addition to dissension and most senseless heresies. . . . Learning is beneficial and basic for every good, as of the fatherland, so also of the Church, just like the root and the seed and the foundation.'[7] The Regulation envisaged a new academy in St Petersburg, which would offer a course of study based on grammar, geography and history, arithmetic and geometry, logic and dialectics, rhetoric and poetics, physics and metaphysics, the *Politia brevis* of Pufendorf and theology, with Latin as the language of instruction, for laymen alongside intending higher clergy. Students would go on excursions to places of interest, including the royal palaces, and would play games, sail and construct forts (all strongly reminiscent of Peter's own favourite pastimes as a youth), as well as engage in amateur drama and debates; accounts of the lives of great men and passages from history would be read aloud to them at mealtimes. This new academy did not open during Peter's lifetime, but several of the seminaries envisaged in the Regulation did, notably in the Alexander Nevsky monastery. Forty-five diocesan clerical schools also opened between 1721 and 1724, and after Peter's death these and other religious establishments prepared most of the staff and students for secular higher schools, including the Academy of Sciences gymnasium and university.

Monasteries also featured in the new legislation. There were now so many restrictions on taking monastic vows that it became almost impossible for a young, fit person to become a monk or a nun. Even older men retiring from public life were discouraged from taking vows. An anecdote pithily summarises Peter's attitude:

> Monasteries must use the revenue from their lands for deeds pleasing to God and for the good of the state, not for parasites. A monk needs to be fed and clothed and a prelate needs enough to maintain himself decently as befits his rank. But our monks have grown fat. The gates to heaven are faith, fasting and prayer. I'll clear them a path to paradise with bread and water, not with sturgeon and wine.[8]

The Spiritual Regulation was a key element in Peter's reforms. The official view was the one pronounced by Feofan Prokopovich at Peter's funeral in 1725 – that Peter strove 'to promote the improvement of the priesthood and true religion among the people'.[9] Jacob Stählin wrote: 'From his earliest years this sovereign had a sincere reverence of God, which he preserved inviolate throughout his life and expressed at every opportunity, especially by a deep reverence for the name of God and the divine laws and respect for the essentials of the Christian religion.'[10] Prokopovich and Stählin, of course, were among Peter's greatest admirers, whereas some of his critics doubted whether he was a Christian at all, a view encouraged by the blasphemous antics of the Drunken Assembly. Traditionalists denied that Peter was the Orthodox tsar. He consorted with foreigners, married one, looked like one (being beardless and dressed in foreign clothes), perhaps even *was* one. As early as 1700 the copyist Grigory Talitsky, who was later quartered for his crimes, denounced the behaviour of Peter and his circle and calculated that 'now is the last time come and the Antichrist has been born and by their reckoning Antichrist is the eighth tsar Peter Alekseevich'.[11] Later dissidents found the number of the Beast (666) in Peter's titles (computed from the numerical values of the letters in IMPERATOR, with the M removed) and in other Petrine words, such as senators (*senatri*) and Holstein. Portraits of Peter with Minerva were identi-fed as the icons of Antichrist, the 70 kopeck poll tax as the seven-headed ser-pent and Peter was said sometimes to take the shape of an animal, his German boots being identified with the 'cow's feet' of Antichrist. All this speculation was fully consistent with popular beliefs about the devil and demons, who were thought to be capable of changing their shape at will and appearing in various disguises.

By and large, even modern historians, while not accepting the Antichrist arguments, have tended to assume that Peter, the impious tsar, had no sym-pathy for traditional Orthodox piety. But there is evidence to the contrary. Peter imbibed his religious beliefs in childhood, through the Orthodox liturgy, prayers, catechism, Psalms and selected passages from the Bible, 'the wisest of all books', as he called it.[12] His personal library, like all Russian pri-vate collections at the time, contained a substantial number of religious texts. He went to church regularly, evensong on Saturday and mass on Sunday, usually in the Trinity Cathedral if he was in St Petersburg, and during Easter week he attended daily and took communion. He enjoyed singing in church and kept his own choir of church singers. Like his fellow Christian rulers, Peter never questioned the notion that Divine Providence played a part in determining human affairs. In July 1696 in letters to announce the surrender of Azov he wrote: 'Now with St Paul rejoice in the Lord, and again I say, rejoice! Now our joy has been fulfilled as the Lord God has rewarded our labours of these past two years and the blood that was spilt by bestowing his grace.'[13] Such sentiments did not diminish as he grew older. In July 1709 he wrote to the British merchant Andrew Styles, thanking him for his congratu-lations on the victory at Poltava but reminding him that 'to God alone belong the glory and honour (for this is a divine deed: he raises up the humble and subdues the mighty)'.[14] This view was reiterated in 1724 when Peter was plan-ning the anniversary celebrations. The Poltava victory was indeed 'a divine miracle; it reveals that all human minds are as nothing against the will of God'.[15] He believed that 'we have a path laid before us which is unknown to us but known only to God', and that all people wished to go to heaven, 'when our time comes'. (Peter was in no hurry to go.[16]) He saw divine purpose in nature. Looking through a microscope, for example, revealed 'a book of God's marvels . . . clearly showing the Creator's great wisdom'.[17] Examples could be multiplied: Peter's letters are peppered with references to 'God's grace' and 'the will of the Almighty', as were those of his fellow monarchs, Protestant, Catholic or Orthodox. Atheism was not an option.

Peter's army, navy and civil service all had a use for religion in its proper place, with chaplains appointed to all service units. The Naval Statute, for example, stipulated that chaplains were to conduct services on board ship on Sundays and feast days ('if bad weather does not prevent it'), preach sermons, administer to the sick and dying (to ensure that no one died 'without fulfilling his Christian duty') and generally supervise moral standards.[18] All state officials took an oath of loyalty on assuming office, in which they swore to serve the sovereign, his family and heirs by kissing the gospels and the cross.

At the same time, Peter was a bitter opponent of superstition and asceticism. His attitude towards icons is particularly instructive. Icons were part of his environment, as they were of every Orthodox Christian's. He venerated an image of the Saviour, which he carried with him on his campaigns and demanded on his sickbed shortly before his death. But he cracked down hard on hoaxes associated with icons, as in the case of a priest who tricked people out of their money with a 'miraculous' image, who was challenged to make the icon perform miracles in Peter's presence and defrocked when he confessed to fraud.[19] Naval chaplains were instructed to set up just two or three icons, not large folding iconostases, and not to light superfluous candles, 'in order to protect the ship from damage'. In general, they were not to do anything which might cause interruption and hindrance to the general ship's business.[20] True religion was supposed to make people more, not less, rational. When Peter admonished the Synod to do battle with the popular rituals associated with the pagan summer festival of Kupalo, he reminded them that in olden times people had still not totally accepted Christianity. Now, however, 'by God's grace the people shines in piety', so there was no excuse for tolerating rituals (people were drenched with water and thrown into rivers and ponds) which were 'repulsive to God' and which also (a characteristic touch of good sense) 'posed a threat to human life'.[21]

Although Peter appreciated the need for prayers – all his campaigns were preceded by prayers and victory parades accompanied by thanksgiving – he had little understanding of the contemplative life. Priests were needed to officiate at church services, baptise babies, bury the dead and perform other necessary duties, including many for the state, such as reading edicts in church, but he could not see the necessity for thousands of monks and nuns 'merely' to pray. Monks were supported by peasant labour, the fruits of which were thus diverted from more pressing public needs. The solution was to cut down on the precious resources used up by monks (by reducing the number of monks and/or their rations) and to increase the useful labour of the remaining monks (and other 'superfluous' church people), by diverting their efforts into aiding the sick and destitute, teaching and other useful occupations.

Peter trusted in empirical knowledge and humankind's ability to forge its own destiny and achieve happiness on earth in preparation for heaven within the general framework of God's laws and plans. 'Reasoning is the highest of all virtues,' he wrote, 'for any virtue without reason is hollow.'[22] Religious customs could be suspended if they conflicted with the common good, hence although Peter opposed work on Sundays in principle, the rule could be suspended 'in extreme emergencies', as could fasts. 'The inhabitants of St

Petersburg daily have cause to wonder when they compare the present time with the past,' wrote the Prussian minister Mardefeld in 1722.

> At the beginning of this reign fasts were observed so religiously that anyone breaking or rejecting them was burnt. Now they write and preach publicly that fasts are nothing more than rituals established by men. All those surrounding the emperor, wishing to distinguish themselves from the common folk, hardly keep any fasts, apart from a few stubborn old men who refuse to renounce the faith of their fathers.

He pointed out that even assemblies and balls carried on during fast periods.[23] Peter's religion was quite free of all ideas of the unquestioned superiority of Orthodoxy and the heresy of other faiths, although he seems to have been prejudiced against Jews and Jesuits. Even so, recognition of the validity of other Christian denominations, and willingness to borrow elements from them, did not shake his conviction that for historical reasons Orthodoxy was the proper faith of the Russian people and it was the Russian tsar's duty not only to defend and preserve Orthodoxy but also to reform and improve it, without touching its essential doctrines or basic rituals. The church was there to serve the state, not vice versa. As for Peter's own belief, it has been described as a 'simple soldier's faith',[24] although a 'simple sailor's' would be even more appropriate.

Celebrations and executions

As a settlement with Sweden drew nearer, there was a mood of celebratory anticipation in St Petersburg. On 5 March 1721 Campredon attended a banquet to celebrate the launch of the significantly named 86-gun vessel *Friedmacher* (Peacemaker). The tables set out in the cabins included one for the Prince-Pope and his cardinals, who indulged in prodigious drinking, singing and smoking. Guards prevented the guests from leaving early. Campredon commented that he had never had such a terrible experience, but at least he managed to snatch a conversation with the tsar, who was generally difficult to pin down.[25] (Foreign envoys frequently complained of the lack of a regular timetable of diplomatic reception days.) Campredon records many social horrors. At a party a week earlier Menshikov handed round enormous glasses of Hungarian wine 'without mercy' and commanded all to drink to the health of the fleet ('the tsar's principal delight'). The Frenchman, on the point of 'expiring', was saved by the start of the fireworks which allowed him to sneak away unobserved.[26]

Festivities were punctuated by more sombre occasions. In late February Peter wrote to Prince-Caesar Ivan Romodanovsky in Moscow regarding the execution of the commandant Volkhov, convicted of robbery. 'Have him executed, as a criminal … and do not bury his body in the ground but let it lie on top of the ground for all to see until the spring, as long as the weather is not too warm.' He instructed Romodanovsky to intensify his pursuit of all such thieves.[27] On 16 March Prince Matvei Petrovich Gagarin, the former governor of Siberia, was executed. Investigation showed that he had ruled Siberia as his own personal domain and had embezzled vast amounts of state funds. When his property was inventoried after his death, a search of his Italianate Moscow palace on Tverskaia Street, built in 1707 by the architect Giovanni Fontana, revealed not only the usual rich man's silver and gold dinner services and cutlery, rich carpets and icons studded with diamonds but also carriages with silver wheels and horses shod in gold and silver. The precious metals may well have been obtained from some of the 'gold and silver objects found in the earth' which Peter ordered Gagarin to collect in Siberia in 1717. Despite the extravagant scale of Gagarin's crimes, Peter was reluctant to execute him because of his family's close connections with the upper echelons of the court. One of his daughters was married to a son of Chancellor Gavrila Golovkin and his son to Peter Shafirov's daughter. Gagarin was held in prison for two years but refused to confess so in the end Peter had no choice. The gallows was set up in front of the Senate house and all officials were forced to attend (a grim warning!), then had to dine and drink with the tsar.

The extent of Gagarin's crimes demonstrates just how far Peter's Russia was from being a 'totalitarian' state, in the sense of everything being controlled efficiently from the centre according to a unified ideology. Siberia provides an instructive, if extreme, case study of lack of co-operation, and of resistance from the bottom to the top. It has been calculated, for example, that the population of Siberia was some 30–40 per cent higher than the figure indicated by Peter's censuses; in other words taxes were spectacularly underpaid. Cultural reform also met with resistance. In 1705–6 inhabitants of Siberia petitioned to be allowed to keep their old clothes and saddles because they could not afford the prescribed Western replacements, and the government had little choice but to withdraw its order.[28] There was no serfdom in Siberia, which was far from the main points where the armies were mobilised, hence few nobles. This was Russia's 'Wild East', where even a towering figure like Peter had little influence.

Anna and Karl

Peter did not let the execution of Gagarin put him off his favourite pastimes. The same day he launched the 66-gun *St Catherine* and the following morning left for Riga, where he spent all of April and the best part of May. The main purpose of this trip was to arrange the marriage of his eldest daughter Anna to Karl Frederick, duke of Holstein-Gottorp, who was invited to Riga to be inspected by his prospective parents-in-law, but not by his thirteen-year-old prospective bride, who remained in St Petersburg with her sisters. Anna Petrovna was regarded as beautiful and intelligent. The best-known image of her is a portrait painted in 1717 by Louis Caravaque, in which dark-haired Anna and her blonde younger sister Elizabeth appear as nymphs with sprigs and baskets of flowers, wafting draperies and a hint of breast, suggestive of fresh, fruitful marriageability, although they were aged just nine and eight when it was painted. Was a version of this painting shown to Duke Karl? Or was it something more conventional, along the lines of Ivan Nikitin's portrait which, although painted even earlier (1716), makes her look older, with grown-up décolleté and piled-up hair. Both the French envoy La Vie and Frederick Bergholz thought Anna the spitting image of her father, as did Duke Karl's secretary Bassewitz, who declared her to be a beauty, with regular features, a gracious smile, pink and white complexion and bright eyes.[29]

In the question of his children's marriages Peter, like his fellow European monarchs, was motivated more by reasons of state than by considerations of conjugal happiness. Karl Frederick's status as heir to the Swedish throne made him an eligible bachelor despite the fact that he was apparently short, plain, indifferent to all intellectual interests and a heavy drinker. Peter was opposed to forced marriages – Bassewitz noted on several occasions that Peter 'although he was [Anna's] father, deemed her consent essential'[30] – and he loved his daughter, but arranged marriages were the order of the day. Even the non-consent of a prospective spouse could be used as a bargaining counter in diplomatic negotiations and in general children were expected to put duty before personal desires, answering yes or no as their parents dictated.

The Riga journals and letters for March–May 1721 show that Peter was as much concerned with matters navigational as matrimonial. Even when he fell ill, he recovered resting on board ship, regarding the sea air and motion of the waves as beneficial. As always, he eagerly awaited the start of the navigation season, anticipating the first reports of the breaking up of the ice in the Finnish gulf. On 22 March Peter reminded Admiral Apraksin to dispatch ships to Reval as soon as the ice began to break, 'by the first wind, for you are well aware of [the conditions in] this channel [he uses the Dutch *farvater*], if you miss the wind then much is lost'. A letter to Menshikov written on the same day was all about the weather. Journal entries for late March to mid May in Peter's own hand were entirely devoted to the topic.[31] On 1 April he went out on the Dvina in a skiff and the next day reported to Apraksin that the ice on the Dvina had started breaking up. The weather was really spring-like, warm with showers and you could see whole expanses of earth in the fields. It was a good time to plant trees.[32] He told Menshikov that the ice had broken and ships were on the move and with the same letter sent some willow branches from Riga and asked his friend to send branches cut on Palm Sunday to find out which town, Riga or St Petersburg, had an earlier spring. A week or so later he asked Menshikov to send him buds and leaves from trees in the palaces at Peterhof and Dubki every week, marked with the date when they were picked.[33] Menshikov also sent him a parcel of St Petersburg vegetables.

Peter still found time to write to Anna, asking her to kiss Elizabeth (Lizetka) for him and the 'big noisy girl Natalia and my grandchildren'. He reported that he had had a visit from the duke, 'a nice-looking young chap', who especially asked to send Anna his regards. On 1 May he thanked his daughters for sending him some pencils in a case, 'which I needed as you can't get them here, for which God's grace be with you'. Perhaps he used them to sketch the ship which is mentioned in his notes.[34] (His agents, it seems, were seeking a match for eleven-year-old Elizabeth, as mentioned in several letters.[35]) There were further receptions and dinners for Tsaritsa Catherine, who arrived on 24 March to be greeted by a parade of townspeople, and for the duchess of Courland, Anna Ivanovna, who was temporarily resident in Riga. Easter fell in early April that year, which meant a week of daily attendance at church and communion on Sunday. Later in April there were boat trips almost daily. On 22 May Peter left for a change of scene on a visit to Reval, where he celebrated his forty-ninth birthday. (The journal gets it wrong again, recording his fiftieth.) Here, too, the highlight of the visit was sailing, aboard the ships *Elephant* and *Samson* (named for the battle of Poltava, which took place on the feast of St Samson), and a trip on the *Ingermanland* to Rogervik, before he returned to Reval to set off for home.[36]

Peter regarded his new acquisitions on the Baltic coast as extensions of St Petersburg, watery mini-Paradises where he could mess about in boats to his heart's content. They were also Russia's own little bit of the West, with a well-educated German-speaking élite and hard-working peasants, who could supply various kinds of expertise, from legal procedures to more efficient ways of tanning leather and harvesting grain. On 11 May 1722 Peter wrote to Prince D. M. Golitsyn, president of the College of State Revenues:

> Have scythes and rakes made on the model of the samples, as many as possible, and see to it that next summer everyone in the grain-growing regions harvests in this manner, for [and in a first rough draft Peter underlined the following words] *you yourself know that, even if a thing is good and necessary, if it is new our people will not do it unless they are forced to.*[37]

The edict combined example (actual scythes were sent to provincial governors) and compulsion. The governor of Riga was ordered to select and dispatch suitably trained peasants to Russian grain-growing regions, accompanied by armed guards. There is no evidence, however, that this measure made any impact on Russian farming practices.

Old statutes and privileges of the Baltic provinces were maintained or restored in order to encourage trade and enterprise on the basis of laws and structures which had proved effective in the past. But there was no ambiguity about who was in charge. In February 1720 the magistrates and councillors of Riga had been rebuked for failing to keep up with repairs of the fortifications and maintenance of the garrison and munitions stores and for irregularities in the election of magistrates and in court procedures. The visit of the tsar and some of his family in 1721 served the useful purpose of reminding the locals of political realities, a message which was underpinned by the celebration of Easter with full Orthodox rites. Peter marked out his territory further by measuring a plot for a garden and a palace in Riga.

Summer in St Petersburg

Peter arrived back in St Petersburg on 19 June where, as was usual when he returned from an extended journey or campaign, he reported to 'King' Ivan Romodanovsky. Thereafter there was a round of anniversaries in quick succession – coronation day on 25 June, followed by Poltava and then Peter's name day on the 29th, with the usual balls, fireworks and gun salutes. In the Summer Gardens on the 25th Frederick Bergholz, who was awaiting the arrival of his master the duke of Holstein from Riga, witnessed the entry of grenadier guardsmen with buckets of raw alcohol which they forced the guests, even ladies, to drink from wooden scoops. Informers were on hand to tell on anyone who tried to escape the 'bitter cup' and there were sentries at the gates to stop people leaving. Only around midnight when Peter, dressed in a simple sailor suit of green fabric, gave the signal were people allowed to go, crowding out through the one exit. On 3 July the royal party sailed to Peterhof on the yacht *Natalia*. Peter, as always, stayed in Monplaisir, but he held a banquet in the Grand Palace. On 8 July after dinner they started up a new fountain in the lower park. Throughout July the royal party travelled back and forth between various estates – Dubki, Ekaterinhof, Strel'na, Kotlin – where palaces were being built and gardens laid out or extended. This was a time of frenetic building activity and Peter's letters and papers are full of correspondence and notes about the finer points of his various projects.

As always, there was lots of drinking. On 27 July Bergholz and the duke went to the Admiralty for the launch of a ship named after St Panteleimon whose feast fell on that day, the anniversary of the naval victories at Hangö and Grengham, over which Peter presided in person, welcoming the guests on board where tables were laid with cold snacks. The duke brought his own wine in the hope of avoiding the rough vintage which Peter served, but Peter insisted that his wine was 'healthier' than the duke's. When Menshikov was caught with a glass of Rhine wine (Peter had ordered that only Hungarian would be drunk) he had to drink a penalty of two bottles of the strong wine, after which he collapsed in a drunken stupor and had to be carried home. Admiral Apraksin was so drunk he wept like a baby. As in the Summer Gardens, armed guards stopped the guests from leaving until Peter was ready to release them.[38] In early August there were fleet manoeuvres, which Peter attended on board the *Ingermanland.* On 8 August they let water into the Peterhof canal, a short channel linking the Grand Palace with the sea shore, and rowed along it. On 24 August the journals record a walk by the great fountain and cascade, strolls around the avenues and the ponds and dinners in the Grand Palace. The anticipated news of peace added to the holiday mood.

Nikitin's portrait

Throughout August Peter awaited news from the Finnish town of Nystad, where peace talks with Sweden, begun in April, were nearing a successful conclusion. On 29 August he asked Menshikov to make preparations for a public announcement (he had heard that some monarchs sent out cuirassiers with white sashes and trumpets to announce important treaties), but warned him to take care that news did not leak out prematurely 'to avoid any shame if peace is not signed'.[39] On 1 September Peter visited the hospital for sick soldiers and sailors on Kotlin Island, where, the court journal records, two days later 'the artist Ivan Nikitin painted his majesty's portrait (*persona*) and then His Majesty was pleased to attend mass'.[40] The fate of this portrait of Peter, painted on the eve of the most important celebrations of his career, is uncertain. There is documentary evidence that Nikitin, whom Peter had sent to study in Italy, painted Peter at least three times from life, in 1715, 1720 and – our reference – 1721, but not one painting of Peter with Nikitin's signature survives and it has proved impossible to match these references conclusively with canvases which have been attributed to the Russian artist. Traditionally, the Kotlin portrait is identified with the small head and shoulders study of Peter on a circular canvas which now hangs in the Russian Museum in St Petersburg. This portrait shows the older Peter and, unusually for contemporary studies, it eliminates nearly all extraneous details, such as regalia and orders, not to mention allegorical figures, and sets the subject against a dark, neutral background, thereby concentrating all attention on the face. The portrait's psychological depth, its portrayal of what one writer termed the 'tragic loneliness' of Peter's last years, led Soviet historians to attribute it to Nikitin, the only Western-trained Russian artist active at the time, on the grounds that no foreign painter could possibly have captured Peter's essence so successfully.

Even Nikitin's most recent biographer Androsov is reluctant to concede the round portrait to a foreigner's brush, because in his view it could only have been painted by someone who knew the tsar well and sympathised with him, in other words by a 'Russian person, patriot and citizen'. But he is doubtful whether this was the painting which Nikitin did on 3 September 1721, when Peter should have looked joyful and optimistic in response to the good news from Nystad, as opposed to weary and regretful, perhaps even sick. For that reason he hazards a guess that the round picture was painted six months later at Martsial'nye mineral springs, when Peter was again taking a cure.

The peace of Nystad

In fact, Peter had not yet received official confirmation of the peace when Nikitin painted him on 3 September. The news reached him while he was on his way from Kotlin to Dubki later that day, when two couriers overtook him hotfoot from the congress at Nystad. 'And with that news His Majesty took the two men with him and set off in all haste for St Petersburg.'[41] The twenty-four clauses of the Treaty of Nystad, signed on 30 August (10 September), established 'eternal peace' on land and sea. Sweden ceded Livonia, Estonia, Ingermanland, part of Karelia with Viborg and its district, with the towns of Riga, Dünamünde, Pernau, Reval, Dorpat, Narva, Kexholm, and the islands of Oesel, Dagö and Meno. Russia agreed to evacuate Finland and to pay Sweden two million reichsthaler as compensation. There were also clauses on trade, the rights of the former Swedish provinces, religion, landed estates, Russian troops, prisoners of war, ambassadors and envoys and extradition.[42] The treaty set the seal on Russia's new status as a European power.

On 4 September St Petersburg celebrated with a service in the Trinity Cathedral, followed by short speeches (Peter officially reported the peace to Prince-Caesar) and gun salutes from the fortress. Heralds with a white banner depicting an olive branch and a laurel wreath went round the streets and beer and wine were supplied for the public. More lavish plans were soon in hand. On the 9th Peter wrote to the governor of Riga:

> We wish to report that the all-merciful God has been pleased to bless this cruel and dangerous war of twenty-one years' duration with a good and desirable peace, which was concluded on 30 August at Nystad and with which we congratulate you. For such divine mercy we must give threefold thanks: the first as soon as this news is received, the second on 22 October, the third on 28 January, the latter two [celebrations] to be carried out simultaneously all over the realm. All three are to be marked with three rounds of cannon fire.[43]

The festive mood continued on 10 September when about a thousand masked revellers turned out to celebrate the Prince-Pope's wedding. If Zotov's wedding in 1715 was a 'rite of passage' to mark St Petersburg's ascendancy over Moscow, Buturlin's (his second marriage) celebrated St Petersburg's triumph over Stockholm. The tsar attended in his favourite disguise of a ship's drummer, as did Menshikov, with Catherine as a Friesian peasant. They mingled with Neptune, Bacchus in a tiger skin draped with vine leaves, giants dressed as babies and assorted Romans, Turks, Indians, abbots, monks and nuns, shepherdesses, nymphs and satyrs, artisans and peasants. The fattest, least mobile courtiers were chosen as runners to announce the wedding. Bears, dogs and pigs, trained to walk very obediently in harness, pulled carts.[44] The bride and groom drank toasts from cups shaped liked male and female genitalia (of a large size, according to Bergholz who witnessed the occasion) and after the feast they were led to Trinity Square to an improvised bedchamber inside a wooden pyramid, which had been set up in 1720 for the reception of captured Swedish ships, with holes drilled in the walls for prurient spectators. Day two of the wedding feast included a ceremonial crossing of the river by the Prince-Pope and his 'cardinals' on a bridge of linked barrels led by Neptune riding a sea monster. The Prince-Pope floated in a wooden bowl in a great vat of beer into which he was tipped when he reached the other side. The wedding feast combined well-tried elements of Peter's 'world turned upside down' with novel variations on 'shaming' ritual (comic voyeurism) and drunken revelry (the outsized beer barrel).

The ratification of the treaty on 23 September was followed by another masquerade on 3 October, this time with a naval flavour when the Nevsky fleet sailed to Kronstadt and back, with everyone in fancy dress. On 11 October there was a 21-gun salute to mark the anniversary of the capture of Schlüsselburg. As Peter had ordained, St Petersburg officially celebrated peace on 22 October (the anniversary of the liberation of Moscow from the Poles in 1612), starting with a service in the cathedral, followed by a sermon from Prokopovich and a speech from Chancellor Golovkin, who asked Peter to accept the imperial titles: Father of the Fatherland (Roman *pater patriae*), Emperor (*imperator*) of All Russia, Peter the Great (*Maximus*):

We thought it right ... in the manner of the ancients, especially the Roman and Greek people ... also as was the custom of the Roman Senate in recognition of their emperors' famous deeds to pronounce such titles publicly as a gift and to inscribe them on statues for the memory of posterity.[45]

This was not the first time that Peter had been equated with a Roman *imperator* or military commander, a commonplace motif in major European states at the time. (British readers may know the statue of King James II as Roman emperor which stands in front of the National Gallery in London.) In Russia Roman imagery was first seen at the Azov triumphs in 1696, and from 1700 the tsar's profile portrait on the new rouble coins was consistently Roman. The new titles outraged traditionalists, however, who believed (wrongly) that the term 'Father of the Fatherland' usurped the spiritual authority of the now defunct patriarch-father. Even the designation 'First', which Peter had used regularly long before 1721, reflected an alien tradition. Muscovite tsars were called by their name and patronymic (hence Aleksei Mikhailovich), never by a number. In fact, some regarded the title 'Great', in imitation of military commanders of antiquity, as less immodest than 'First'.

Such doubts were not reflected in the official accounts of the celebrations, which continue:

> Then from all the people both inside the church and outside there went up three great joyful cries of *Vivat*, accompanied by a simultaneous thunderous blast of noise from trumpets and cymbals and drums and a round of fire from numerous cannons and guns from the guards and a hundred and twenty five galleys and thirty-three field regiments.

Peter then made a speech, translations of which were distributed to foreign diplomats:

> (1) I very much desire that all our people should be fully aware what the Lord God has done for us in the past war and by making this peace. (2) We must give thanks to God with all our strength, but while hoping for peace we must not weaken our military efforts, in order to avoid suffering the same fate as the Greeks [i.e. Byzantines] and the Greek monarchy. (3) We must strive for the common good and profit, which God sets before our eyes both in internal and external affairs, which will bring relief to the nation.

There followed gun salutes and more prayers of thanksgiving, during which the tsar 'with great devotion and genuflections offered up prayers to the Almighty'.[46]

During a feast for a thousand people in the Senate house the tsar gave orders that no guest should leave while he retired to his yacht for a nap. Bassewitz regretted that he had forgotten to take some cards along to ease the tedium but Bergholz managed to escape to the Four Frigates coffee house for a breath of air. That evening the city was illuminated by candles in windows and braziers of tar and firewood on the streets. The centrepiece was a temple of Janus (the double-faced god who looks to the past and future), with open gates, revealing Janus illuminated in blue, with a laurel wreath in his right hand and an olive branch in his left. This marvellous edifice was designed by the Frenchman Nicholas Pineau (later the designer of Peter's funeral) and constructed by an Englishman for the sum of 570 roubles. Peter lit the illuminations by setting off an eagle motif which flew along a rope from the Senate building. Screens depicted Justice fighting two Furies, a boat coming into harbour and pyramids that gave out a bright white light. The doors of the temple were closed by two warriors representing Russia and Sweden, who joined hands in a sign of peace, then from the fortress and boats in the harbour about a thousand guns fired simultaneously, 'and from this great round of gunfire it seemed as if the whole fortress and the River Neva were covered in flame'. [47]

An even bigger Janus temple than the one in St Petersburg was erected for the Nystad celebrations held in Moscow at Yuletide 1721–22. Lavish triumphal gates were built for Peter's arrival on 18 December, when he was greeted by the president of the Holy Synod, Stefan Iavorsky, and by teachers from the Moscow Academy. The duke of Holstein, still in Russia, sent his musicians, and tables with food and drink were set up. Feofilakt Lopatinsky and Feofan Prokopovich delivered victory sermons in the Cathedral of the Dormition on 1 and 28 January 1722 respectively. Thereafter, Peter ordered that the peace be celebrated every year 'both in religious and civil manner' on 30 August, the anniversary of the signing, which coincided with the feast of St Alexander Nevsky.

The Russian Versailles

Moscow was not neglected – in 1722 it received its own chief of police – but St Petersburg commanded most of Peter's attention. Bergholz, who had visited Russia with his parents in 1709–14, found that by 1721 'the city has changed so much that I simply did not recognise it'. He was especially impressed by Nevsky Prospekt, which linked the Admiralty with the Alexander Nevsky monastery. 'Despite the fact that the trees planted on both sides in rows of three or four are still small,' he wrote, 'the street is unusually fine with its great length and the clean state in which it is kept ... It makes a splendid sight such as I have encountered nowhere else.' [48]

Peter did not complete his city, but his architectural legacy survives in the grid plan of the numbered 'line' streets on Vasil'evsky Island, the straight course of Nevsky Prospekt, the spires of the Peter-Paul Cathedral and Admiralty, in white classical pilasters and window surrounds against the coloured stuccoed walls of the Kunstkamera, Alexander Nevsky monastery, and the other few surviving early eighteenth-century buildings. The focus of many celebrations, as we have seen, was the Summer Palace, the chief attraction of which was its riverside site. The palace itself is comparatively small, just fourteen modest rooms. Only a few couples could have lined up in the

ballroom on the first floor, Catherine's territory and the most lavishly decorated part of the palace, while the ground floor, its entrance decorated with
Dutch tiles, housed Peter's quarters, including two kitchens. One room
accommodated his wind measuring instrument, with huge clock-faces and
allegorical designs referring to Russian naval power, made in Germany in
1714, another his lathes and tools. The ceiling of the nursery, on the first floor,
was decorated with a scene of 'Peace and Tranquillity', featuring flying
cherubs and horns of plenty. In the green room oval panels depicted allegorical studies of Europe, Asia, America and Africa and glass cabinets displayed
curiosities. Mirrors were hung high up on the walls as decorative items, along
with portraits of the tsar's family and associates and maritime subjects: the
whole décor of the palace reflected the interests of Peter and his family, but at
the same time indicated the international cultural context in which they now
operated. Well lit by large windows and easily visible from several vantage
points, the palace could not have been more different from the old royal
apartments in Moscow, with their religious frescos and linked chapels, hidden
behind the Kremlin walls.

The Summer Palace was not quite as modest as is looks today. A whole
complex of buildings once stood in the grounds, with stables, storerooms, servants' and guest quarters. There was a grotto, hothouses and glasshouses. The
gardens were splendid, the setting for Peter and Catherine's outdoor summer
parties. Zubov's 1717 engraving, taken as from an aerial view looking south
towards the gardens over the Neva, shows the river frontage, the palace itself
built right on the riverbank in the north-east corner, with a canal to one side
for direct access to boats to sail across the river to the fortress and Trinity
Square. The embankment walls are lined with galleries in the shape of triumphal arches; canals and trees in serried ranks like troops create the main
lines of an orderly and rational plan; garden plots are divided by diagonals
reminiscent of the St Andrew's cross; the gardens are dotted with fountains
and statues, including the famous 'Tauride' Venus, purchased in Italy, and
characters from Aesop's fables, each with a plaque bearing a short explanation
of the tale.

Menshikov's palace on Vasil'evsky Island, started in 1710, was much
grander than Peter's, with several wings and courtyards. To Weber the main
façade appeared to be 'after the Italian Manner',[49] stuccoed and painted in the
two-tone favoured in a climate more often gloomy than sunny and topped
with a steep Dutch roofline. Behind was a formal garden with trees in the
Dutch style. Inside the palace the blue and white Delft tiles which Peter liked
so much covered not only the walls of living apartments but also some of the
ceilings. The Menshikovs were *nouveaux riches* and the illustrious prince was
not too proud to flaunt his royal connections: the entwined letters P and M
(Peter and Menshikov) in the metal banisters of the main staircase, ceilings
decorated with the cross of St Andrew, the fresco of a warrior bearing the tsar's

features. The Grand Hall, which Peter often 'borrowed' for receptions, was decorated with mirrors, classical statues alluding to military victories and pilaster capitals bearing reliefs of Menshikov's knightly orders and coronets. These political touches contrast sharply with the homeliness of his sister-in-law Varvara's apartments, the wall tiles featuring cupids and household objects such as cups, brushes and chairs. The chapel of the Resurrection was a basilical design with spire, reminiscent of the Peter-Paul Cathedral. Like the Summer Palace, Menshikov's residence was built right on the water's edge, its main entrance immediately opposite a landing stage. In Zubov's engraving of 1717 it appears to float on the water.

Not far from the palace one of the grandest buildings in St Petersburg, the Twelve Colleges (now part of St Petersburg University), was at the planning stage. Begun in 1722, it consisted of twelve units housing the audience chamber, Senate, the Colleges and the Holy Synod. The building's design – a long façade with twelve individual but uniform entrances – reflected Peter's intention that the staff of each college should bear individual responsibility for their college's business whilst offering a unified façade to the public gaze. The architect Trezzini expressed anxiety that the colleges were to be built 'all in a row' but that construction was to be handled by individual offices, and warned of delays if each college was responsible for its own construction. Peter relented by allowing all the materials to come from one place, but insisted that the principle of individual administration of buildings be retained.[50]

Out of town, Peterhof was the main focus of Peter's attention in the remaining years of his life. Bergholz described it in August 1721:

> The main building consists of two storeys, of which the ground floor is only for servants, the first floor for the tsar's family. Down below there are splendid galleries with fine columns, upstairs a magnificent hall with a wonderful view of the sea. . . . From the main façade of the palace a splendid cascade flows down into the lower gardens over three terraces, which stretch the whole width of the palace, made from unhewn rock and decorated with iron and gilded relief figures on a green background. It is a splendid sight. The lower garden, through which there runs a wide stone-lined canal right opposite the palace, is full of flower beds and beautiful fountains.[51]

Peter took a personal interest in hydraulics and had a hand in designing a number of the fountains: both the grand palaces at Peterhof and Strel'na were built on bluffs and linked to natural water systems which allowed impressive complexes of fountains and cascades to be operated from the accumulated waters flowing downhill from a reservoir. The grounds were laid out by the German architect Johann Friedrich Braunstein (in Russia from 1714 to 1728) who also designed Monplaisir and the Marly (1721–23) and Hermitage (1721–24) pavilions. The whole complex was, as Bergholz later wrote, a 'new Versailles', which to some extent reflected Peter's intention. In France in 1717 he had acquired an album of views of the palace and gardens at Versailles which he always kept in his study.[52] Strel'na palace a few miles further east along the gulf was also intended to vie with Versailles. The garden would be 'of a vast Extent' and a 'noble and costly Palace' was to be built on the hill, but Peter's death brought work to an end and the site did not attract the support of his daughter Elizabeth as Peterhof did in the 1740s, when the famous architect Bartolommeo Rastrelli extended it.[53] Today the palace is still a virtual shell and hardly features in guidebooks, although plans for converting it into a presidential residence were reported in 2000.

After Nystad, the Petrine cult, centred on St Petersburg, grew inexorably. But the city, like Peter, had its detractors. In November 1721 a severe flood damaged many buildings, including the Temple of Janus built for the Nystad celebrations the previous month. 'If, without being superstitious, one can give any credence to a certain prophecy, this city is at risk of being destroyed by water one day,' wrote the French envoy La Vie, who saw the water level in his apartment rise to a height of three feet.[54] Despite all the positive evidence of new buildings, flourishing gardens and growing population, many people shared La Vie's view. There was still something façade-like, insubstantial about St Petersburg, not to mention (in the eyes of religious conservatives) something diabolical. Members of the 'God's people' cult, later known as flagellants, declared that the Antichrist was living in St Petersburg and that the city would be destroyed 'like Sodom and Gomorrah'.[55] Even the less fanatical wondered how long it would survive its founder, who had created it, like so much else, 'from nothing'.

IX

Ranks and Regulations
1722–23

Laws and decrees should be written clearly so that they cannot be reinterpreted. There is little justice in people but much perfidy. (Peter, from Nartov's *Anecdotes*)

The Table of Ranks

In the first weeks of January 1722 Peter worked on and off in his *laboratoriia,* as he called it, making and testing fireworks; on 21 January he went out visiting with the Drunken Assembly; and on the 24th he issued one of the most famous and influential edicts of his reign, the Table of Ranks – *Tabel' o rangakh* in the Germanised language which Peter favoured for naming his institutions. Even though some of the old Muscovite ranks were still in use – boyar, *okol'nichii, stol'nik* and so on – they were being superseded by newer titles which clearly differentiated military, civil and court offices and were based on foreign (often Swedish) originals. Peter now imposed a rational framework on a mainly pre-existing jumble of terms.

The Table divided the service elite into three columns – military, civil and court – its very layout reflecting Peter's passion for orderly, regulated legislation. The military column was further subdivided into four: infantry, guards, artillery and navy. The vertical columns were then divided horizontally into fourteen numbered grades (*klassy*), each containing a variable number of offices (*chiny*), in order to correlate status and identify seniority across the different branches of the services. There were marked variations of complexity. The guards column, set two grades higher than the rest, for example, had just eight classes, each containing only one office. The most crowded column was the civil service, with sometimes a dozen or more *chiny* packed into one *klass* in order to accommodate Peter's newly created central and provincial officials. Court grade 14 also contained numerous offices, including court librarian, head chef and barber. The chart was accompanied by nineteen explanatory points.

The decree was several years in the making. Peter's helpers, led by Andrei Osterman, consulted such foreign sources as Frederick I of Prussia's regulations and the statutes of Christian V of Denmark and Charles XI of

Sweden. Point 8 in the explanatory section, for example – the crucial rule that only service rank gives a person eminence in society, regardless of his origins – is found in the regulations of Sweden, Denmark and Prussia. English, French and Spanish ranking systems were also examined, but were regarded as less appropriate for Russian conditions. Peter edited the drafts, leaving only four clauses untouched, crossing out some offices, adding or re-grading others. The revised project was then presented to the Senate and Colleges for discussion.

Misconceptions persist about this most enduring of Peter's reforms, one of the most widespread being that it demonstrated a firm and consistent commitment to meritocracy to the detriment of lineage. Peter's own example is often quoted. 'By taking upon himself both a Post in his Navy, and in his Army, wherein he acted and took the gradual Steps of Preferment, like another Man,' wrote John Perry, '[Peter wished] to make his Lords see that he expects they shall not think themselves nor their Sons too good to serve their Countrey, and take their Steps gradually to Preferment.'[1] Peter even had his promotions confirmed by the mock sovereign, Prince-Caesar, in order to underline that he had earned his advancement. Certainly the Table was strict about qualifications for actual jobs. No office was supposed to be allocated to any candidate who was unqualified for the duties involved, which in practice meant serving for the period deemed necessary to gain experience and certificates. Neither grade nor office could be inherited or bought (which distinguished the Russian system from many others, for example, the French) and there were strict penalties for demanding deference or a position higher than one's position in the Table, although certain occasions – meetings of friends and informal assemblies – were declared 'rank-free'.

But birth and marriage continued to confer privilege, as they did in other countries. The first explanatory point confirmed the precedence of princes of the blood and royal sons-in-law (one of which Peter was about to acquire). Point 8 blended two principles: it conceded 'free access' to the court to sons of princes, counts, barons and the aristocracy 'before others of lowly office', but stressed that the emperor expected such people 'to distinguish themselves from others in all cases according to their merit'; they would not be awarded any rank until they had served the tsar and Fatherland. Newcomers from non-noble families who reached grade 8 in the civil service or grade 14 (the lowest) in the military officer lists became hereditary noblemen. But certain civil offices were designated as temporary, conferring rank on individuals only as long as they held them. All new nobles had the right to acquire coats of arms, while old coats of arms and patents of nobility were to be supervised by the chief herald.

The Table of Ranks was intended to encourage the service élite to perform more efficiently, while the concept of nobles as natural leaders of society was endorsed by the fact that high-flying commoners who reached the required grades were granted noble status, including its heritable aspects. Eminent people, whatever their origins, were expected to have clothing (Western, naturally), carriages and livery appropriate to their office and calling. The Holstein secretary Bassewitz grasped the point: 'What [Peter] had in mind was not the abasement of the noble estate. On the contrary, it all tended towards instilling in the nobility a desire to distinguish themselves from common folk by merit as well as by birth.'[2] As anyone who has read nineteenth-century Russian authors such as Gogol, Dostoevsky or Chekhov will know, the Table of Ranks left its mark upon Russian society for the rest of the imperial era.

The succession to the throne

Just two weeks after the Table of Ranks appeared, Peter issued a manifesto on the succession to the throne (5 February 1722), the opening clause of which referred to the 'Absalom-like wickedness' of the late Tsarevich Alexis. It concluded:

> We deem it good to issue this edict in order that it will always be subject to the will of the ruling monarch to appoint whom he wishes to the succession or to remove the one he has appointed in the case of unseemly behaviour, so that his children and descendants should not fall into such wicked ways as those described above, having this constraint upon them.

In the manifesto accidents of birth and custom are firmly subordinated to reason and the common good. Most telling is the reference to Peter's decree of 1714 'that immoveable property might be left to one son, leaving to the will of the parent which son he wishes to inherit, with regard to worthiness, even if it is the younger in preference to the elder.... How much more concern we need to show for the integrity of our whole realm, which with God's help is now more widespread than all can see.'[3]

Even in this very personally motivated piece of legislation Peter did not suggest that the monarch ought on principle to look beyond the imperial family and raise a commoner to the throne, any more than the Table of Ranks envisaged throwing open army commissions and top government posts to peasants. Still less is there any idea of trusting the choice of monarch to popular acclaim or corporate interests. In other words, the normal expectation was that those born in the palace should occupy the throne and dispose of it by their own will. The ideas behind the manifesto were more fully explained in the book *The Justice of the Monarch's Right to Choose the Heir to the Throne*, first published in August 1722 and generally attributed to Feofan Prokopovich. This work identifies the divine basis of monarchical power with reference to scripture, Byzantine and classical authors, but also uses a Western frame of reference to natural law, drawing on modern writers such as Grotius and Pufendorf. The author argues that 'the will of all the people' delegates power to rulers for the sake of the common good, constituting a 'contract' between people and ruler. Even if a monarch is (or becomes) evil, people cannot take back the power they have granted; a monarch may choose to adhere to man-made law but is not obliged to do so, since rulers are subject directly to God, not to intermediaries such as the church. The thrust of the argument was to show that there was no rational or divine justification for preferring primogeniture, a mere *custom* which could be set aside for a higher purpose, in this case to ensure the worthiness of the successor.

Peter's only male heir under the old dispensation was the late Alexis's six-year-old son Peter. But Alexis's trial poisoned Peter against his grandson as an heir, if not as a person, for he feared young Peter could provide a rallying point for opponents of reform. Peter Alekseevich was not ill-treated, but he was not given any special prominence. For example, his name days and birthdays were not included in the official court calendar. In December 1721 Peter's daughters received the title *tsesarevny*, but his grandson continued to be known simply as grand duke (*velikii kniaz'*), not *tsesarevich*, a term which only later came to refer to the male heir. In a terse letter to young Peter's German tutor on 17 May 1722 Peter wrote that 'the time has come to teach our grandson'.[4] Otherwise, he paid him little attention, reserving his affection for his daughters. As for designating an heir, as the manifesto required, Peter seemed to be in no hurry. People could only speculate on where his choice would fall.

The publication of the succession manifesto must have stirred up unhappy memories, but apparently did not prevent Peter from enjoying himself. The carnival parade in Moscow on 31 January 1722 (a continuation of the Nystad celebrations) took the form of floats in the shape of ships mounted on sledges. Peter's was a 36-gunner in full sail modelled on the *Peacemaker*, firing small cannons and manned by children dressed as cabin boys, who had to lower the sails for the ship to pass under the triumphal gates, and Catherine's was a gilded gondola. The Prince-Pope was drawn along on a throne with Bacchus at his feet on a barrel, followed by his 'cardinals' mounted on bulls or in sledges drawn by pigs, bears and dogs. There followed white-bearded Neptune in a giant shell and the mock abbess with her 'nuns'. Menshikov's ship contained 'abbots' and was followed by Prince-Caesar in a boat full of stuffed bears. There were more parades and parties on the following four days, at which Catherine appeared sometimes as a 'simple Dutchwoman', at others as an Amazon, a popular choice of costume at several carnivals. (An Amazon costume, apparently the only Russian masquerade outfit to survive from this period, can be seen in the Kremlin Armoury.) On the last day of the carnival Moscow ladies who had criticised St Petersburg ladies for drinking too much were forced to sit at a special table and drink as much as they were given.

More legislation

On 7 February Peter set off for Olonets on a route which took him through Pereiaslavl, Iaroslavl', Vologda, St Cyril's monastery and Beloozero. His destination once again was the Martsial'nye mineral springs. On 18 February he began to drink the waters and also attended the consecration of the church of SS Peter and Paul which he had built. As always, he brought a travelling lathe with him and various board games to pass the time. His health, it seems, was not strong, but back in Moscow at the beginning of April Peter launched into a veritable frenzy of legislation. On 5 April he issued the Admiralty Regulation and a supplement to the Naval Statute. On 6 April, he published an edict on the post of *reketmeister*, an office modelled on the *maître de requêtes* at the French court, to whom appeals could be addressed by individuals complaining about delays, red tape and abuses in hearings of cases in colleges and other bodies. Only the *reketmeister*, not the emperor (who 'never got any peace'), was to receive petitions. If for some reasons he would not or could not accept a petition, it was to be referred to the Senate. 'The sovereign is concerned for his subjects to ensure that each case will always receive fair and swift judgement,' Peter wrote, 'and that cases are resolved as His Majesty's edicts command, justly and in the stipulated time and that no one should be oppressed by unfair judges and red tape.'[5]

Peter constantly agonised over how to have effective government under autocracy without the need for the autocrat to intervene. To his way of thinking, orderliness (*reguliarnost'*) ought to result if you had good statutes, from short edicts to multi-claused regulations. Nothing was too trivial to be regulated and tidied up: in April 1722 he even launched a campaign against uneven tombstones in churchyards. Any slabs not flush with the ground were to be taken up and relaid, 'since stones which are untidily and improperly laid inflict ugliness on holy churches and get in people's way'. Ever thrifty, Peter ordered that pieces of stone chipped off during repairs should be used for church building.[6] In 1724 the Synod received the following order: 'Throughout the Russian state wax candles are to be made in such a fashion that every candle has a thickness at its base twice that of its top, and the upper thickness is half that of the lower. The length should be five times the thickness at the base.'[7] Did anyone take any notice of orders like these? The impulse behind the edict on candles with thick bases was presumably fire prevention, but Peter seems to have regarded edicts as an end in themselves, rather like the lists which he constantly drew up. Generally we know only that his orders were not being carried out when he (or his successors) had them reissued. So, for example, instructions were constantly repeated on building 'new-style' river and coastal boats with different-shaped hulls from the old ones (which Russian boat builders continued to favour) and on making fabric in wider sizes, which failed to take into account the peasant weavers' inability to buy wider looms or even to accommodate them in their homes.

Peter was especially proud of his many lengthy statutes. In a note written by hand in November 1722 for inclusion in the ongoing history of the Northern War he recalled that the Military Statute was started in St Petersburg in 1715 and finished in Danzig and the Naval Statute was started in 1720 and finished in 1722, and 'done all by hard work, not just by orders [to someone else] but by the sovereign's own labour, not only in the morning but in the evening, twice daily it was done at various times'.[8] Therein lies one of Peter's problems: the statutes which were supposed to bring about order, enterprise and initiative originated not in some representative or corporate body but from one man, albeit with some assistance from information gatherers. This 'do-it-yourself' philosophy sprang from a lack of faith in other people getting things done and, increasingly towards the end of his life, a fear of treachery and intrigue. Law must be unambiguous and there must be plenty of it, for wickedness was all-pervasive. As Peter stated in a famous edict to the Senate, issued on 17 April 1722:

Nothing is so vital to the administration of the state as the firm keeping of civil laws, for laws are written in vain if they are not adhered to or if they are played with like cards, one suit being picked up after another, something which was more common in this country than anywhere in the world and sometimes still happens when some people do their utmost to undermine the fortress of the law.[9]

This decree also contained strict warnings against individual interpretation of the laws and a firm reiteration that the tsar was the chief legislator and everything must have his approbation. Peter wanted it to be displayed on boards on a table 'like a mirror, before the eyes of judges in all places, starting with the Senate right down to the most minor courts'. In February 1723 Peter added other notices to these display boards, one setting out penalties for 'swearing, shouting and talking' and a warning that 'he is cursed who does God's work carelessly', the other to remind people of 'state laws and their importance, as the first and chief matter'.[10] An example of such a display case – known as a *zertsalo* (mirror) – survives in the commandant's house of the Peter-Paul fortress, a three-faceted stand on legs, pyramidal in shape, with glass panels behind which the royal decrees could be displayed, topped with an ornate crown and double eagle motifs.

State intervention in the economy was a particularly contentious issue. Peter made genuine efforts to promote the Russian entrepreneurial class and believed in the superior efficiency of free labour, but 'creating' a capitalist class was hampered by limited social mobility and the shortage of free workers. In 1715, for example, he tried to farm out cloth manufacture to individuals to end dependence on foreign sources, and warned 'if they won't do it willingly, then make them do it by force'.[11] This led to merchants being transferred by decree to Moscow. State peasants were routinely 'ascribed' to factories. Peter also had to juggle with the conflicting demands of serf owners and factory owners. A decree of 18 January 1721 had given factories the right to buy serfs, but comparatively few people took advantage of it, perhaps because the purchase of 'souls' required capital outlay for unskilled workers.[12] A decree of March 1722 banned the removal of 'fugitive' workers from industries in order not to impede production.[13] Peter promoted industry with subsidies and concessions (interest-free loans, exemptions from taxes and service requirements, guaranteed purchases by the state) and imported industrial technology and personnel. On to these old principles he grafted modern features, such as centralised fiscal departments and the Colleges of Commerce and Mines and Manufacture to promote national wealth, plus 'mercantilist' policies, such as standardising weights and measures, improving communications and introducing a protectionist tariff (1724) and a reformed decimal currency.

Peter's economy operated in a traditional framework, however: it was the war which created its momentum, autocracy and serfdom which allowed Peter to cope with military demands. 'This absolute master uses his subjects at his will, and their wealth in what share he pleases,' as Johannes Korb expressed it.[14] A subsistence economy generated just enough surplus for the state to take its share (which included debasing the currency, as required) without utterly ruining the population, who were also subjected to 'fleecing' by officials and local strong men lining their own pockets. Russians had little capital, no systems of insurance or quality control. The credits for foreign trade and ancillary services (insurance, shipping, brokerage) were supplied by foreigners. It is not surprising that merchants were unwilling to take risks.

The procurator-general

One of the most important edicts issued in April 1722 was a document on the duties of the procurator-general (*general-prokurator*), which was published simultaneously with a new formulation of the duties of the Senate. There are six drafts of the document on the procurator's duties, all with Peter's corrections. Ever since he created the Senate in 1711, Peter had felt the need to keep an eye on it, appointing first an inspector-general then a guards officer to ensure that senators 'on pain of death' got on with their work and refrained from quarrels and bad behaviour. The new procurator-general's job was spelled out in the usual numbered points. He was to see that the Senate 'does its duty and acts in all matters which are subject to the Senate's scrutiny and resolution truthfully, diligently and correctly, without wasting time and in accordance with the regulations and edicts' and that 'business is completed not only on paper but also put into action according to instructions ... '. If he discovered negligence or dishonesty, he must immediately bring the matter to the Senate's attention. He was to act as the 'tsar's eye'.[15] In 1724 the procurator-general's duties were extended to the Colleges, where he was expected to keep an eye on the office personnel, for, as Peter admitted, 'I am sure that behind our back there are many abuses.'[16] In the spring of 1722 the imminence of a new military campaign added urgency to the task of 'guarding the guardians'. As Peter announced to the Senate on the eve of his departure for war with Persia: 'Here is my eye, with which I shall see everything. He knows my intentions and wishes; what he deems necessary, that do; and even if you feel that he is acting against my interests and those of the state, even so, do what he says, inform me and await my orders.'[17]

The role of the tsar's 'eye' was an unenviable one, but Peter found an able candidate for the post in Pavel Ivanovich Iaguzhinsky (1683–1736). The young Iaguzhinsky (his father, from Lithuania, was the organist in the Lutheran church in Moscow) had served as an orderly in the Preobrazhensky guards, where he became close to the tsar. He won military honours at the battle of Pruth in 1711, when he was promoted to general adjutant. In 1716–17 he accompanied Peter to the Netherlands and France, travelling in the same carriage, and in 1719–21 he served on a series of diplomatic missions. Foreigners described him as talented and intelligent, an outsider who owed his rise to his relationship with the tsar.

Despite Peter's confidence in him and his experience (in 1718 he had already acted as the tsar's 'eye' by supervising the newly established Colleges), Iaguzhinsky doubted his ability to keep order amidst the passions of, as he put it, a Senate 'riven with discord'. Just a few days after Peter's departure for the war a quarrel flared up between Menshikov and Peter Shafirov, who complained about insulting references to him and his brother as people of 'Yiddish' origin whose father was a 'slave'. Iaguzhinsky's view was that 'when the sovereign's favour is conferred upon a person his former baseness and low birth are thereby concealed'.[18] In a letter to the tsar he proposed that the Senate ought on principle to be composed of men of 'middling rank' so that there should be fewer quarrels between strong personages. Iaguzhinsky apparently combined efficiency and honesty with hard drinking, as he 'despaired of achieving anything in the sea of perfidious and cunning men who will not forsake their own particular interests for the sake of the sovereign's'.[19] This did not stop him profiting from Shafirov's subsequent banishment, when he received an island which had previously belonged to the deposed vice-chancellor and some of his servants. Like all such newcomers, Iaguzhinsky had to feather his own nest as best he could and look to the future by making alliances at court.

Procurators, inquisitors and police chiefs

The package of legislation issued in 1722 implemented Peter's conception of the interlocking parts of the state apparatus, in which institutions were supervised by a hierarchy of individuals, with safety valves installed at various levels to allow the bypassing of the system by 'whistle blowers' unmasking wrong-doing from below and all-seeing 'eyes' peering in from above. The Admiralty Regulation, for example, contained a clause on the duties of the Admiralty procurator, who was to ensure that board members did their duty, wasted no time and observed the regulations. This post was to be 'the eye of the procu-rator-general in this college'.[20] The congruity of church and state organis-ations was further emphasised by the creation in May–June 1722 of the post of over-procurator of the Holy Synod: 'a good [lay]man who is bold and should be familiar with the administration of Synod affairs'. He, too, was the sovereign's eye, the assistant of the procurator-general and his deputy. A list of his duties issued in June 1722 mimicked the document on the procurator-general: the new official was to 'sit in the Synod and make quite sure that the Synod does its duty and acts in all matters which are subject to the Synod's scrutiny and resolution truthfully, diligently and correctly, without wasting time and in accordance with the regulations and edicts'. [21] The church already had additional spying mechanisms. In 1721 'inquisitors', an arch-inquisitor in Moscow and provincial ones in all bishoprics, were appointed to supervise churchmen, bishops in particular. The main task of the arch-inquisitor and his underlings was to initiate proceedings against insubordinate priests. Bishops, who in earlier times had ruled their dioceses more or less unchecked, became 'agents of the Synod'. Everybody, it seemed, was watching or being watched by someone else.

The instructions issued to the newly created Moscow chief of police in June 1722 provide a glimpse of attempts at extending urban regulation beyond St Petersburg. The chief's duties included supervision of building regulations and fire prevention (detailed rules were included for the use of stoves and the operation of bathhouses) and maintenance of pavements and bridges. For crime prevention, street barriers and night watchmen were intro-duced, as in St Petersburg. Guarding public morals involved closing down gambling dens and rounding up and finding useful work for loose women, drunks, vagrants and beggars. The police chief was also responsible for regis-tering all strangers in town. He was to supervise public health, garbage col-lection and handling of food in markets, prevent river pollution and report outbreaks of infectious diseases. Paper and rags were to be recycled. 'Shooting for entertainment' on the streets was outlawed, as was horse racing, a favourite pastime with cab drivers.[22] But the chain of command was unclear. In October the Moscow police chief was reprimanded for issuing some instructions on building regulations without seeking the Senate's permission. Yet again the tension between individual enterprise, strict regulations and existing pecking orders hampered efforts to get things done.

The section of the population which most easily evaded the tsar's eyes – his own and his surrogates' – was the peasantry, who by and large came under official scrutiny as individuals only if they went to towns. An edict of 6 April 1722 required peasants visiting towns on business to get permission from their landlords or village elders in the form of 'maintenance papers', a reiteration of a decree of October 1719 which declared it illegal for peasants to travel from town to town or village without a pass. Such measures were variations on much earlier attempts to minimise peasant flight in order to reduce the evasion of taxation and army service. Only occasionally did Peter try to extend his sense of urban orderliness to the village, and with poor results. In July 1722, for example, an edict was issued

> on [re]building burnt-out villages and hamlets in accordance with plans, and plans were sent out with the edicts, but now [in 1724] His Imperial Majesty has been made aware that in the *gubernii* and provinces, in villages and hamlets, peasants' houses on burnt-out sites are being rebuilt not in accordance with this specification but after the previous practice, without leaving any cottage gardens and hemp-fields between the houses. Therefore His Imperial Majesty has decreed that confirmatory edicts be sent out to all the *gubernii* and provinces stating that from now on peasants in the villages and hamlets must without fail build according to the specification .... Wherever a village or hamlet has burnt down or people want to resettle a site then the landlords themselves, or, in the absence of landlords, their bailiffs and elders, should immediately mark out the site according to the published edict and drawings and compel the peasants to build in accordance with the edict and ban absolutely the building of houses in the previous manner.[23]

There is no evidence that this decree had any impact on the layout of villages. By and large peasant life remained unregulated from above; in sharp contrast, a vast number of rules and regulations applied to state servitors, both in their office and in their private life, and increasingly to town dwellers. The bulk of state legislation which touched peasants was to do with counting them, taxing them, recruiting them into the army and trying to get them back if they ran away. Other matters were dealt with locally, usually by the peasants themselves. As long as they remained in their villages, there was no attempt to meddle in their dress, customs and lifestyle, or in agricultural practices.

The Persian campaign

Russia, established on the Caspian Sea since taking Astrakhan in 1556, had a long-standing interest in the region and what lay beyond, especially the lucrative silk routes. The belief persisted in the existence of a river route to India from the Caspian but Peter's government also had a realistic grasp of the troubles in Central Asia which made Russian influence over or domination of part of the region possible. In May 1714 Peter had dispatched a mission headed by Prince Aleksandr Bekovich-Cherkassky to Khiva by way of the eastern Caspian with instructions to investigate rumours of gold finds on the Amu-Dar'ia river and to survey and chart the east coast of the Caspian. In 1716 Cherkassky was sent back to the mouth of the Amu-Dar'ia with instructions to win the confidence of the ruler of Khiva, but on entering the city, most of the Russians were slaughtered. Cherkassky's head was sent as a gift to the emir of Bukhara and his body stuffed and put on display.

In 1721 the overthrow of the shah of Persia in an Afghan revolt and protests by Russian merchants about violations suffered in Daghestan, a protectorate of the shah, provided a pretext to return to the region. Peter's objectives were the Persian provinces on the western and southern shore of the Caspian, including the trading ports of Derbent and Baku. The alleged persecution of Transcaucasian Christians, Armenians and Georgians living under Muslim rule also provided a pretext for limiting Turkish expansion in the region. In July 1722 Peter assured Prince Vakhtang of Georgia: 'We hope with the help of God by the time that this messenger reaches you already to be on the Persian shores, therefore we hope that this news will be pleasing to you and that you will join us with your troops for the Christian cause in fervent fulfilment of your promise.'[24] In the end, however, Peter abandoned the plan to push southwards to the Georgian city of Tiflis when support failed to materialise.

Peter took almost boyish delight in this campaign, which gave him new opportunities for messing about in boats, both on the journey south along the Volga to Astrakhan and on the voyage to the 'Persian shores', when he kept navigation logs and issued orders on boat building and naval protocol. Catherine went with him, accompanied by her 'jester' Princess Anastasia Golitsyna. Peter's dogs also went along, including Prince, who got lost and was returned by a man who was rewarded with a rouble and 50 kopecks. An orderly was in charge of feeding the dogs and buying equipment such as beds and sheepskin coats to keep them warm on the road from Tsaritsyn to Moscow on the return journey.[25]

The tsar's party left Moscow in mid-May, reaching Nizhny Novgorod on the 26th. On inspecting the docks and discovering that ships were being built 'in the old manner' (a constant complaint), he issued reprimands. The royal party dined with members of the Stroganov merchant family, who virtually ruled the town, and visited their church. On 3 June Peter arrived in Kazan', 'where on his majesty's arrival they fired from cannon all over the town and he attended mass and dined with the metropolitan [Tikhon], whence to the convent [of Our Lady of Kazan], where there is a miracle-working icon of Our Lady of Kazan, then they visited the vice-governor [N. A.] Kudriavtsov'.

On subsequent days Peter inspected leatherworks and textile mills, then departed on 6 June for Astrakhan, which they reached on the 19th.

At this stage the campaign was not so dangerous or so arduous as to halt the usual June celebrations. On 25 June the fortieth anniversary of Peter's coronation was marked with gun salutes from ships and on Poltava day, 27 June, Peter appeared on parade with two companies of the Preobrazhensky guards who put on a display of volley fire. He sent a stream of orders home, on such diverse matters as fountains for his new residence in Reval, house building in St Petersburg, history writing, the publication of a book on Islam and additions to his cabinet of curiosities.

As usual, Prince-Caesar was left in charge at home, although Peter instructed him to deal only with urgent business. On 18 July the fleet set sail from Astrakhan and the next day Peter wrote to Romodanovsky:

Sire. I inform Your Majesty that this day we and *gospodin* general-admiral [Apraksin] left Astrakhan on your royal service with all the fleet and hope with God's help soon to reach the shores of Persia. Your Majesty's most humble servant, Peter.[26]

Another of Peter's 'mock' personnel, Chief Surveyor 'Baas' Ivan Golovin, was on board. An anecdote tells how Peter had a laugh at his expense by ordering his retinue to bathe in the Caspian Sea, which involved diving from a board. When the terrified Golovin hesitated, Peter forced him under with the little ditty: 'Down goes Baas, to drink Caspian kvas.'[27] (The water of the Caspian was particularly bitter-tasting from oil deposits.) Golovin, to whom Peter deferred when he was playing his shipwright's role, was often the butt of Peter's jokes. In November 1721 at the wedding of Golovin's daughter to Prince Trubetskoy, the tsar went up to Golovin, who was greedily tucking into a huge bowl of something in aspic, and stuffed more of the jelly down his throat, forcing his mouth open to get it in. 'Baas' apparently suffered such indignities uncomplainingly.

Peter withdrew to Astrakhan that autumn, leaving others to continue the campaign into the following year, having issued an order to Governor Volynsky to buy 2,000 camels and 500 pairs of oxen, at a calculation of 15 roubles per camel and 10 roubles per pair of oxen.[28] Peter wrote that compared with the 'difficult and bloody' Swedish war the present one was 'easy and profitable'.[29] In fact, the campaign proved costly in men, many of whom fell sick, and in ships and supplies, and only brought temporary gains.

Carnivals and a funeral

In December 1722 the Synod erected triumphal gates in Moscow to celebrate the capture of Derbent on the Caspian, which had fallen to the Russians on

25 September. Peter was greeted by a choir from the Latin school dressed in hired wigs and crowned with greenery. He and Catherine saw in the New Year in the old capital. The journal for 6 January (Epiphany) records that

> they went carol singing in the palace where Tsarevna Natalia Alekseevna of blessed memory once lived, then all the revellers awaited his majesty and then revelled in the town called Presburg [Preobrazhenskoe], which is on the River Iauza opposite that same palace, and in the evening they went revelling in his Majesty's house then at night in the Foreign Quarter in the house of the director of the Moscow Cloth factory Ivan Tames. Today His Majesty did not attend [the ceremony of blessing] on the Jordan and the troops were not lined up as the ice was very weak and in some places had not frozen over.[30]

The winter continued mild. For carnival 1723 they used the ship-sledges from the previous year, sixty-four of them, even though the snow had melted. The procession visited various sites, including the triumphal arches set up on Red Square for the peace celebration the previous December. The master of ceremonies was James Bruce. The third day of the carnival, 19 February, coincided with Peter and Catherine's wedding anniversary and on the final day there was a festive burning of 'the old house' at Preobrazhenskoe, which produced a 'splendid effect'. Peter made a speech: 'Together with this house, in which I worked out my first plans for war against Sweden, may there disappear any idea which might again make me take up arms against that state and may it be the most true ally of my empire.'[31] The empress and her ladies rode in a barge, all dressed as Amazons. There was also amusement to be had from the spoils of the Persian war. In 1722 four young Kalmyks were sent from Astrakhan to Moscow and fitted out in 'simple garb'. They were treated (and neglected) rather like household pets, abandoned in Preobrazhenskoe when the royal party departed for Moscow. Catherine arranged for them to be fed and given beer and kvas when she heard that 'they are dying of hunger and keep drinking water and are now all lying down'. A couple of days later a servant was warned to travel carefully with the Kalmyks and dogs.[32]

On 25 February Peter left Moscow for St Petersburg where he arrived on 5 March. Four days later Tsarevna Maria Alekseevna, Peter's last remaining half-sibling, died at the age of sixty-three. It was remarkable that she survived so long, given her association first with Sophia, then with Tsarevich Alexis. Somehow she, the only one of Tsar Alexis's daughters to travel abroad, managed to adapt to the new life while retaining traditional manners, as suggested by the scene at her deathbed, which was surrounded by priests, 'who in accordance with the ancient method of comforting the souls of the dying brought her food and drink and enquired in piteous tones whether she had a sufficiency of everything required for the maintenance of life in this world'.[33] Peter was apparently angered by this 'superstitious' display, but he observed the proper obsequies. As the journal notes, at the liturgy in the Trinity Cathedral on 10 March His Majesty and all dignitaries were dressed in black. On 12 March the tsarevna's coffin, drawn by a team of horses on a black-draped sleigh and with a canopy over it, was transported from her home on the Fontanka across the Neva, which was lined with men of the Preobrazhensky and Semenovsky guards holding candles, to the service in the Trinity Cathedral, thence to the unfinished Peter-Paul Cathedral.

The grandfather of the navy

On 22 March the ice melted near the fortress, three cannon were fired and a flag was raised to signal that the tsar had gone out on the river for the first time that season. Thereafter he spent as much time on board ship as possible, this year with the added excitement of the arrival of his first boat, 'grandfather of the Russian navy', from Moscow, an event which was celebrated with a special regatta for his birthday on 30 May. As Prokopovich had said in a sermon in praise of the Russian fleet, delivered in 1720, the boat was the seed which sprouted the tree of the fleet. 'From that seed there grew this great, marvellous, winged, weapon-bearing tree. O little boat, worthy of being clad in gold. Some seek the planks of Noah's ark on Mount Ararat; my advice would be to keep this boat and preserve it as an unforgettable memorial.'[34] Peter personally made elaborate arrangements for the boat to be brought from Moscow, where it had been on display in front of the Dormition Cathedral in the Kremlin. To receive it, as if to underline the theme first elaborated in the Naval Statute, a plinth was carved with the inscription THE AMUSEMENT OF THE CHILD BROUGHT THE TRIUMPH OF THE MAN. There were plans also to honour another of Peter's early boats, the yacht in which he made his first sea voyage in 1693. In 1723 Iaguzhinsky wrote to Archangel, 'if even a few remnants of the yacht are found, have them put in a convenient place and guarded'.[35] Thus were myths made in Peter's own lifetime.

Nearly all the anniversaries, both personal and national, which clustered in the summer months of 1723 were celebrated with boat trips and regattas known as 'marine assemblies' aboard the craft of the so-called 'Nevsky fleet' of civilian vessels. Sometimes religious feasts also featured a watery element, such as the blessing of the water for the feast of the True Cross at the Trinity Quay, on 1 August. For Russians less enthusiastic about the sea than Peter one of the new capital's most disagreeable features was the amount of time people were expected to spend in boats, for there were no permanent bridges over the Neva during Peter's reign. Dignitaries were required to maintain one yacht, one barge and two launches and to join the royal sailing parties to Strel'na, Peterhof, Kronstadt and beyond. The idea for the St Petersburg regattas came to Peter during his travels, especially in Holland and England, but it is doubtful whether Western regattas were accompanied by such a high degree of regulation and compulsion. Peter took personal offence at lack of enthusiasm for nautical jaunts and non-attendance was punished with the same sort of penalties as for dereliction of military duty. In June 1723, for example, nine people incurred a fine of 15 roubles for failing to turn up to greet the arrival of the 'grandfather' of the fleet.[36] On 30 July 1723 Peter issued an order to Devier:

> There has been constant disobedience about attending the marine assemblies, and today attendance was poor. . . . Therefore those who were not in their barges, except for legitimate reasons, are to be fined 50 roubles tomorrow, and not allowed until the next day to pay. If they say that they have no money then take goods instead and at the same time inform them in their homes that if they do the same again the fine will be doubled, and for a third offence they will be banished to the spinning mills.[37]

On 1 September 50-rouble fines were collected from Admiral Apraksin, James Bruce, Cornelius Cruys and Peter Apraksin, but Archbishop Feodosy of Novgorod had his 50 returned after his excuse was accepted.[38] As this incident indicates, even top men in the government and church were not let off. For some unlucky people the boat trips even proved fatal. On 13 June Peter's page Ivan Drevnin drowned while taking a trip on the 'grandfather'. His body was fished out of the river the following day. This incident and his funeral are laconically recorded in the journals, just part of the routine of court life in the summer of 1723.[39]

There were other deaths that summer. On 22 August Prince-Pope Peter Buturlin died. His funeral in the church of St Samson was attended by Peter and Catherine, generals and other dignitaries dressed in black. Archbishop Feodosy officiated. The coffin was carried under a black pall by under-officers from the home of privy councillor Zotov, son of an earlier mock prelate. On 30 August, Nystad day, a masquerade processed from the coffee house to Trinity Quay, where most people got into barges and boats to accompany Peter in the 'grandfather', which he sailed to the Nevsky gates of the fortress to the sound of gunfire.[40] The small craft, steered by Peter, rowed between the warships of the Russian navy, 'in order that the good grandfather could receive due honour from all his splendid grandsons',[41] as the navy fired guns in honour of the boat and the creator of the navy. The festivities finished with a service in the Alexander Nevsky monastery. After this the boat was replaced on its plinth in the Peter-Paul fortress, but in 1724 Peter ordered that it be brought out on the water and taken to the Alexander Nevsky monastery every year on 30 August.[42]

The Persian war ends

On 8 September 1723 Peter received the good news that Russian troops had taken the Caspian port of Baku. As he wrote: 'We had much [celebratory] bombardment on that evening when the news was received.'[43] The treaty signed with the new shah of Persia ceded Baku, Gilian and Derbent to Russia 'in perpetuity' in return for Russian aid against the shah's enemies.[44] The Persian war provides some valuable insights into the colonial policies of the expanding Russian empire. Peter instructed his commanders to treat non-Christian populations firmly but tactfully,

> on pain of death to cause no devastation or oppression to the local inhab-
> itants, but rather to reassure them to remain in their homes and to have no
> fear ... firstly because without this they will flee and we will be left with
> everything empty; secondly, because we shall distress everyone and thereby
> lose everything of which we have a common need, therefore it is better to
> work for what is permanent and solid rather than for a small temporary
> gain.[45]

He told another commander that resistance must be met with force. Even so, 'in all the measures that you employ try to avoid destroying this province. Also at times and as occasion demands you need to treat these peoples proudly and more severely because they aren't like people in Europe.'[46] In other words, Peter regarded his country as an expanding *European* Christian nation, which was bringing civilised values to the conquered. In the event, it proved impossible to maintain the Caspian coastal strip. The anticipated commercial profits failed to materialise and the costs of military occupation exceeded revenues. Most of the territories were returned to Persia in 1732.

In September 1723 there was a carnival in St Petersburg which lasted several days with almost a thousand masks, which included the duke of Holstein's party (now a permanent feature at court) dressed as Romans. For most of the time Peter wore his favourite sailor's costume, but one day he appeared dressed as a cardinal and proceeded to ordain four 'priests', then changed back into the sailor's outfit. Catherine was an Amazon one day, a grape seller the next. The carnival ended at the house of Prince-Caesar and was rounded off with a massive drinking session.[47] The Persian ambassador arrived in St Petersburg to ratify the treaty, which gave an excuse for another boat trip to Kotlin island on 2–3 October, one of the last of the season, but not before Peter had shown the no doubt bemused ambassador some of his lathes and presented him with two telescopes. Peter remained on Kotlin to inspect work on the fortifications and from there went to inspect canals.[48]

Death of Tsaritsa Praskovia

On 15 October Peter received the news that his sister-in-law Tsaritsa Praskovia had died. Tsar Ivan's widow was by all accounts a pious and uneducated woman, devoted to an assortment of orphans, holy fools and cripples who lived in her house. One might expect Peter to have had little time for such an unreformed character, but he frequently confounded expectations. He treated his sister-in-law with deference and affection and on one occasion even paid off a 2,000 rouble debt on her behalf. No doubt Praskovia's love of the bottle helped to bring the two together; she was a fringe member of the odd assortment of people who made up the Drunken Assembly. Her good relations with Peter may also have had something to do with the fact that she was sufficiently astute to make concessions to the new times. Her three surviving daughters (two others died in infancy) were raised as modern young women and provided Peter with useful marriage fodder, while Praskovia herself was happy to entertain foreign visitors and appear at court functions.

Peter helped to organise her funeral on 22 October, applying the same theatrical detail as he did to the organisation of masquerades and regattas. The catafalque was topped by a canopy in mauve velvet and a golden double eagle motif on ermine. Crowns, sceptre and orb and a royal standard were set out nearby. The coffin, placed at the top of several steps, was lined in white satin and Praskovia was dressed in a robe of the same satin, with a long veil cascading over the steps. The scene was illuminated by twelve large candles and dozens of candelabra, set off against black draperies and festoons. The room was also decorated with various unspecified 'allegories'. Twelve captains in black cloaks and with black cockades stood on guard.

The funeral parade from Praskovia's house on the embankment near the Winter Palace to the Alexander Nevsky monastery took two hours. Wailing and screaming, a standard feature of Muscovite funerals, were expressly forbidden. The coffin, set high up on an open black carriage and covered in black velvet, was accompanied by guardsmen and followed by a long procession of state officials, army and navy officers; Peter, Catherine and the dead woman's daughters Ekaterina and Praskovia, in full mourning with their heads dramatically covered in long veils, brought up the rear. Their sister Anna was at home in Courland and did not learn of her mother's death until some time later. Women rode in carriages, men went on foot. The whole procession was flanked by soldiers holding lighted torches. In church, a priest delivered a funeral oration (sadly nonextant) and a portrait of Praskovia's late husband was placed in her coffin. This occasion illustrates how funerals had become 'designer' occasions dominated by Western-inspired invention rather than tradition, intended to impress a much wider public than Muscovite ceremonies, which were confined within the Kremlin walls. The cost was borne by Peter's Cabinet office, which for months afterwards found itself dealing with appeals from Praskovia's many creditors.

Pulling uphill. Bribery, corruption and red tape

As the season for boat trips and excursions drew to a close, Peter turned to matters of state. High on his agenda was the issue of how to inculcate and develop honesty, responsibility and enterprise in the ruling élite and as usual he sought solutions in regulations and penalties. An edict of 25 October 1723 (published in February 1724) declares:

> Whosoever shall commit an injustice in a court or in any matter whatso-ever entrusted to him or which is a part of his duties and he commits that injustice for his own ends, knowingly and of his own volition, that man, as an infringer of the state laws and his own duty, shall be condemned to death, either physical (*naturalnoiu*) or political (*politicheskoiu*) according to the severity of the crime and deprived of all his property.[49]

In this decree Peter makes a clear distinction between crimes against the state and the existing order (including brigandage and religious dissent) and the much lesser matter (in his view) of 'particular' crimes against the person. In the latter case 'only' an individual was injured and the decision to prosecute could be left to the aggrieved party and/or in local hands. At the same time, Peter made efforts to reform legal procedures in order to facilitate the resolution of 'particular' cases. The decree 'On the form of trials' (5 November 1723) gathered together and tried to simplify legislation on the use of written evidence, bail, forms of petition and other procedures.[50] But the frequent repetition throughout the century of orders to speed up trials and reduce red tape underlines that even the most perfect procedures could not solve the problem. Bribes remained the most effective means of getting a settlement. This was not an exclusively Russian problem, as anyone who has read Dickens knows.

Peter was frustrated that his reforms were not working more quickly and that few people seemed to understand his most cherished ideas. In a manifesto on the encouragement of factories issued in November 1723 he wrote:

> It's true that there are few who are willing to participate, for our people are like children who, out of ignorance, will never get down to learning their alphabet unless the master forces them to do so. At first they find it tedious, but when they learn their lesson they are grateful. This is evident in the current state of affairs where everything has to be done by force, but already thanks can be heard and fruit has been produced. It is the same with manufacturing: it is not enough just to make proposals. This may happen in places where there is already a firm tradition, but here an enterprise is sometimes initiated but not implemented . . . it is necessary both to use compulsion and to provide aid in the form of manuals, machines and other items and thus be a good steward.[51]

Peter's concerns must be seen within the context of not just a personal schedule and private goals but also as a timetable for the reform of a whole nation. Only then can we begin to appreciate the dismay he must constantly have experienced when his goals were thwarted by individual and collective lethargy and resistance. Few state officials regarded bribery and misappropriation of state funds as crimes. The problem was expressed graphically by the peasant entrepreneur Ivan Pososhkov's famous image of Peter pulling uphill with the strength of ten men and millions pulling downhill. This is an exaggeration, of course. Peter did have some committed and energetic supporters. But in view of the number who apparently abused his trust, it seems unlikely that by 1723 he had complete faith in anyone. Several high-profile cases were fresh in his mind: in 1721 the execution of Gagarin, the former governor of Siberia and in 1722 the trial on corruption charges of Peter Shafirov, who was condemned to death by beheading, but was reprieved at the last moment as he lowered his head to the block. His Moscow house went to Peter Tolstoy, all his wine was sent to the palace and distributed to various officials, and money invested abroad was allocated to Russian students.[52] Peter was much struck by this example of 'treachery', for he had personally raised Shafirov, son of a converted Jew, to high office, making him a baron in 1710 and senator in 1717.

It was Menshikov, with whom Shafirov had a joint venture in fish oil production, who brought the charges against his partner, but Peter had no illusions about Menshikov's honesty, either. 'Aleksasha' had long been under a cloud of suspicion for illegally acquiring property in Ukraine, but managed to evade the serious charges of corruption brought against him by government officials in 1714. In 1718 he was brought before a tribunal on charges of embezzlement, involving estimated losses to the treasury (including 'insider dealing' on grain contracts for the army in the 1710s) of more than 1.5 million roubles. Friendship prevailed and Menshikov was restored to favour upon payment of a heavy fine. 'Menshikov will always remain Menshikov,' Peter allegedly remarked.[53] In the words of Pavel Iaguzhinsky, one of the few men to escape corruption charges in Peter's lifetime, it would be unwise to issue an order to execute anyone who stole as much as the price of a piece of rope, as Peter once proposed, 'unless Your Majesty wishes to be left alone without servitors or subjects. We all steal, only some more and more visibly than others.'[54]

The provinces were particularly impervious to Peter's reforming efforts. In October 1723 the inspector of mines Wilhelm Henning sent a memorandum from Siberia:

I am heartily sorry that you have not been here in person and do not know the state of affairs in Siberia in any detail. It's true, the governor here, Cherkassky, is a good man, but he lacks courage, and has few decent assistants, especially in the local courts and police department. As a result local affairs do not flourish and the people have to bear a heavy burden.

Henning urged Peter to give Cherkassky the support of more officials from central institutions:

> Terrible deeds are in evidence, the poor peasants suffer ruin at the hands of officials, and in the towns much oppression is caused by the officials sent from the local finance office and the merchantry has been so badly damaged that an artisan with any capital is scarcely to be found, which has led to a decline in revenues. Lord, do not begrudge the administrators here a decent salary, for no one here owns villages [i.e. serfs] and everyone has to eat and even if a man is good, if he has no means of livelihood he is forced to feed himself by illegal means; at first he will take enough to satisfy his needs, but then he will try to get rich. In this way you will suffer great loss and the people will be ruined.[55]

The old system of officials feeding off the local population by extracting 'gifts' in money and kind, ostensibly outlawed in the late sixteenth century, was alive and well. The weak were as vulnerable as ever.

The year looked set to end on a sombre note. On 17–18 October the Neva and the Little Neva froze over, an unusually early frost and an early end to the navigation season, which always put Peter in a bad mood. Official mourning for Tsaritsa Praskovia lasted until 24 November. There was much state business to deal with. Peter's papers include numerous drafts of the decree 'On the forms of trial' and on issues of trade and manufacture. Much correspondence was also devoted to unrest in Ukraine, from where a stream of complaints arrived against Cossack officers and officials reported fears of Cossack collusion with the Crimean Tatars. But Peter continued to maintain his precarious balancing act of dealing with the trivial alongside the weighty, slipping in and out of his alternative identities and pursuing his various hobbies. Papers for December 1723 include sheets and sheets of the tables of ships' parts (all measured in feet and inches) which he found so fascinating. He wrote several letters to 'Sire' Ivan Romodanovsky and every now and then he dropped into his shipwright's identity, writing to 'Baas' Ivan Golovin and signing the name Peter Mikhailov alongside the signatures of his fellow shipwrights Richard Cozens, Joseph Noye and Richard Browne in support of the petition of one Dmitry Dobrynin to be paid his wages and be awarded his master's certificate.[56] On 24 December he penned an order for 'three Friesian-style jackets made from the pattern sent to you on paper, one in black velvet, the other in cinnamon brown cloth, the third in cinnamon serge with a flannelette of the same colour'. He gave precise specifications for the buttons (the same colour as the buttonholes) and hems, and ordered three pairs of breeches in the same materials and colours. It is not clear whether these sailor outfits, ordered from Holland, were for masquerades or for everyday wear.[57]

The same eye for detail can be found in a handwritten note on a project for a garden in Moscow sent to the Dutch doctor Nicholas Bidloo in December 1723:

> On the big pond on the two islands and on the octagonal island you are to build summerhouses (*liust'gosy*, from German *Lusthaus*), also places for doves and small birds near the wood and other embellishments suitable for a garden, and across the canals bridges, little hump-backed ones, with railings on one side with just enough room for one person to cross (like they do in Holland); also send a drawing or ground plan of both residences and the garden.[58]

Peter was also beginning to plan an event which provided ample opportunities for enjoyable details: the coronation of Catherine as his consort. His handwritten draft on the topic survives, dated 15 November, in which he quotes Byzantine precedents for the crowning of consorts and praises his wife's personal courage, especially at the battle of Pruth, where she behaved 'in a manner more male than female'.[59] There were precursors for this accolade, for example in a speech to mark Catherine's name day in November 1717, when Feofan Prokopovich recalled her courage at the Pruth and her worthiness to be the first recipient of the Order of St Catherine.[60] On 24 December 1723, following Peter's instructions, Feofan ordered the Synod to prepare triumphal gates in Moscow for the coronation the following spring. He could hardly have guessed that less than two years later Catherine would be celebrating another coronation, but this time as empress in her own right.

X

A Coronation and a Funeral
1724–25

What are we doing? We are burying Peter the Great. Surely this must be a dream, an apparition? (Feofan Prokopovich's funeral sermon, 10 March 1725)

A year of peace

At 10 p.m. on 1 January 1724 fireworks celebrated the start of the only complete year of Peter's reign when Russia was not officially at war with a foreign power. There was 'the usual gunfire' from the Peter-Paul and Admiralty fortresses, after which Peter, Catherine, the duke of Holstein and other dignitaries dined in the Senate house. Several days of carousing followed, with visitations by the tsar's 'merry company' to the homes of leading officials. On 6 January after matins in St Isaac's Cathedral, the Preobrazhensky and Semenovsky guards (Bergholz estimated almost 10,000 troops) were drawn up and marched across the frozen Neva to Trinity Quay, with Peter at the head of the Preobrazhenskys in his colonel's uniform. Catherine watched from a window in the Winter Palace. As the journal records, after mass in the Trinity Cathedral, there was a procession of the Cross to a spot on the Neva in front of the Winter Palace chosen to represent the River Jordan. 'When the divine service at the Jordan was over the standards of all the battalions were taken to the Jordan and sprinkled with holy water and there was a gun salute from the fortress, then the soldiers fired a round of rifle shot.'[1] Peter was in a good mood. On 7 January he visited Strel'na, Peterhof and Oranienbaum on his way to Kronstadt. The weather was unusually mild. An entry in the journal recorded that from 3 to 18 January it was warm and rainy, that the roads were churned up and people drove in carriages rather than sledges. The holes and weak spots in the ice on the Neva made it dangerous to walk or ride on the river. On 9 January Peter wrote to Catherine: 'Another marvel to tell you: yesterday in Peterhof the fountain was working, which is something you wouldn't see even in France [at this time of year].' On the night of 13 January he attended and helped to extinguish a house fire, a favourite recreation since childhood. To Boris Kurakin and other ambassadors in Russian missions abroad he wrote: 'I think that now is a good time, seeing that there is no war anywhere ... to send tapestries by sea. . . . Our affairs in Persia, praise God, are going splendidly.'²

The Swedish, Turkish and Persian wars may have been behind him (in February Russia and Sweden signed a defensive alliance, heralding a new phase in their relations), but Peter had no intention of relaxing the pressure on his colleagues. An entry in the journal for 19 January 1724 reads: 'In the morning it froze over and there was a hard frost all day. In the morning His Majesty attended the Foreign College, then heard mass in the Trinity church, after which he was pleased to visit the coffee house, and those present who had not attended Prince Prozorovsky's funeral on the previous day were made to drink an eagle cup of wine as a penalty.'³ In February, when all courtiers and officials were required to take part in a masquerade, senators and government officials were ordered to remain in their costumes even during the morning session of the Senate and Colleges, which struck Bergholz as 'rather inappropriate, especially as many of them were fitted out in a manner most unbecoming to elderly men, judges and councillors; but in this case everything was done in accordance with the old Russian saying: may the tsar's will be done.'⁴ These and similar incidents confirm the impression that Peter's masquerades were not true carnival at all, in the sense of hierarchies being suspended and people being liberated from authority. On the contrary, they seemed to be motivated more by the need to impose and reinforce his own authority, at the same time allowing him to indulge his enthusiasm (not shared by all his associates) for organising and participating in parades and parties with a full supporting cast.

There was always a hint of menace in Peter's play. In January he had an exchange of correspondence with Prince-Caesar in Moscow. Romodanovsky wrote to complain that Major-General Chernyshev had conscripted some of his household servants into the army and navy. In his reply Peter maintained his usual mock-deferential mode of address, calling Romodanovsky 'Sire' and signing off 'With my most humble subject's respect I remain Your Majesty's servant, Peter.' Peter then informed Chernyshev that 'our sovereign' Prince-Caesar was very angry with him and ordered him to release the servants immediately. Neither man was left in any doubt about who the real monarch was.⁵

For some offenders Peter's disapproval went beyond mere banter and joke penalties. On 24 January 1724 Bergholz and Bassewitz witnessed a public execution, when the chief fiscal A. Ia. Nesterov was broken alive on the wheel for accepting bribes and robbing the treasury of 300,000 roubles, and a dozen or so lesser officials were beheaded or flogged with the knout and exiled to the galleys with their nostrils clipped. The system of fiscal officers, instituted in 1711 to root out bribery and corruption, had proven a failure, like so many of Peter's measures to improve the integrity of public servants. As we know, Peter was particularly unforgiving of crimes against the 'common good' and, as was usual on such occasions, all officials 'from presidents down to scribes' were obliged to attend the execution and take due warning.[6]

The Academy of Sciences

Capital and corporal punishment remained the norm even in those countries of Europe deemed most civilised, where cruel punishment was not thought incompatible with cultural refinement. On the contrary, those who offended against society's norms must expect stern retribution. In Peter's mind, too, there was no contradiction in inflicting harsh penalties on those who strayed at the same time as he encouraged the importation of Western arts and learning. In 1721 Peter sent his librarian J. D. Schumacher on a tour of Europe to recruit personnel for the creation of a 'society of sciences', like the ones he had seen in Paris, London, Berlin and other places. Late in January 1724 he published an edited version of the recommendations of Schumacher and Dr Lavrenty Blumentrost for a Russian Academy of Sciences, which opens with the words: 'For the spread of arts and sciences two types of establishment are generally used: the first type is called a university, the second an academy or society of arts and sciences.' Nine points followed. The Academy was to combine scholarship with teaching in a university (faculties of law, medicine and philosophy, but not theology) and a high school. The initial cost was estimated at 20,000 roubles, to be gathered from customs and licence fees in several Baltic towns.[7]

Peter saw practical reasons for founding an academy – existing schools had failed to produce civilian specialists in sufficient numbers – but by the end of his reign he had also come to appreciate the wider appeal of science and learning and to covet the acclaim enjoyed by their patrons. He was influenced by Leibniz's idea of Russia as a 'blank sheet' in terms of civilisation, ripe to be opened up for scientific research: first to geographical exploration, which in turn would stimulate the training of home-grown specialists. Peter expressed the idea of the national 'glory' to be won by scientific endeavour in a famous speech (recorded only by Weber) in which he imagined the 'transmigration of sciences' from ancient Greece, via England, France and Germany to Russia, which had the potential to 'put other civilised nations to the blush, and to carry the glory of the Russian name to the highest pitch'.[8] This sounds like a secular variation on the old theme that after the fall of Constantinople in 1453 Moscow had become the final destination of world (i.e. Christian) history, known loosely as the doctrine of 'Moscow the Third Rome'. In the eighteenth century, the baton of civilisation was to pass to a different Rome, the new city of St Peter, an ambitious notion given the low level of even the most elementary education in Russia. The Academy of Sciences did not open until after Peter's death, in August 1725, with an all-foreign faculty, mostly Germans, despite Peter's initial recommendation that at least two members should be from 'the Slav nation' in order to teach Russians. In fact, the Academy conducted all its proceedings in Latin and German. Not until Mikhail Lomonosov, who himself had received most of his higher education in Germany, joined it in 1741 did the Academy acquire its first Russian member. Even so, its significance for Russia's intellectual and scientific life was enormous and it proved to be one of Peter's most long-lasting institutions.

Taking the waters

Peter was a man of his time in combining scientific curiosity with love of the bizarre and exotic. The Kunstkamera collection continued to grow and Peter continued to take pleasure in entertainments which today would be regarded as being in dubious taste. The live 'exhibits' at his court included Kalmyks, Samoyeds from Siberia (in 1717 he placed an order for 'two young Samoyeds, between 15–18 years old, with the ugliest and funniest mugs you can find, dressed in their usual costume and ornaments'[9]) and, of course, dwarfs. The first day of February 1724 saw the funeral of the dwarf Frol Sidorov, to which all the male and female dwarfs resident in St Petersburg were summoned to follow the coffin in pairs all dressed in black, the smallest at the front, the tallest bringing up the rear. Six tiny horses pulled the coffin and the smallest priest in the city was enlisted to officiate. The procession included giants and the tallest guardsmen, among them the emperor himself, who paid for the wake.[10]

The funeral provided a suitable curtain-raiser for the carnival season. On 3 February Peter held an assembly for his daughter Anna's name day, culminating at 11 p.m. in fireworks forming the letter A. On 10–16 February the masquerade was held (on the 15th there was another funeral, this time for one of Peter's cooks) and on the 17th, the first day of Lent, Peter departed for some peace and quiet at the Martsial'nye springs, not forgetting to leave detailed handwritten instructions about 'what work to do on the ship while I am away'.[11] He arrived at Petrozavodsk on 19 February, the anniversary of his wedding to Catherine, who joined him there three days later. The next day Peter attended matins, then, without stopping for breakfast, set off for the spa, where the royal party began to take the waters on 24 February and continued until 7 March. There on the lathe which always accompanied him Peter worked on a model of Kronstadt and made a bone candelabra with five candle-holders for the church of SS Peter and Paul, inserting a scroll into the round central section inscribed: 'This object was brought here as a sign of gratitude to the Lord God for the healing waters and made there. 14 March 1724. Peter.'[12] In 1733 Empress Anna transferred the candelabra to the Peter-Paul Cathedral, where she opened the round compartment and read the slip of paper.

A document which Peter wrote during this visit shows how he liked to maintain an orderly regime even when on leave:

On the duties of the marshal while people are taking the waters
1. When the morning comes [the marshal] must immediately assemble the waking-up brigade in the reception room by the table and then go around the sleeping quarters with music.
2. When people start to drink the water everything must be in order and every ten minutes [the marshal will] give a shake of the rattle.
3. When two and a half or three hours have passed after the [first] drinking session, [he will] give another signal on the rattle that it's time to drink more water.
4. When another hour or one and a half hours have passed, then the marshal again will assemble the waking-up brigade and go to the kitchen and order them to bring the food, walking in front of it with the brigade.
5. While people are here taking the waters, the marshal must take care that the heating of the rooms, candles at night and other things are all in order, in the reception room and in the sleeping quarters.[13]

Peter's preoccupation with health matters is reflected in his correspondence. In a letter to his daughter Anna postmarked 'From the iron factories', he writes: 'Your mother has this minute arrived, thank God in good health, and you too travel safely, in the meantime we commend you to the protection of God.' On the same day he wrote to Fedor Apraksin, who had been ill: 'I heard that you intend to travel to Moscow. Of course you must not. You'll do yourself an injury. Your phlegm has been diluted by the medicine so when you go out in the wind you'll catch a sudden chill and will be worse off than you were before, and death will very likely soon follow as a result, so give yourself a rest and travel only when the doctor says it's quite safe.' Perhaps it was the tedious routine of drinking foul-tasting mineral water thick with iron deposits which reminded Peter to write to Boris Kurakin on 13 March and ask him to buy 200 bottles of good Hermitage wine and send them to St Petersburg that spring.[14] He also took the time to make arrangements for a local character: 'A peasant from these parts called Faddei is old and seems simple-minded, lives in the forest and comes into the village, where they regard him as a marvel. There are no reports of malice or dissidence, so in order to prevent any temptation, I have ordered him to be brought to the factory and fed there until his death.'[15] On 15 March he presented his candelabra to the church and on the 16th departed for Moscow. They stopped off at Vologda and on the 20th crossed the now thawing Volga at Iaroslavl', where they transferred from sledges to carriages. On the 22nd Peter called in at the Trinity monastery for matins, arriving in Moscow later that evening.

Catherine's coronation

Papers from Peter's time in Moscow reveal the usual eclectic mix of business: he reiterated the requirement that able-bodied officers and soldiers retired to monasteries must be made to work for their living; ordered architectural books from England; made arrangements for housing the library of the Holy Synod; visited the house of the late Fedor Golovin to inspect work on the new garden which Dr Bidloo was directing. On 25 March he attended matins in the Kremlin Annunciation Cathedral, perhaps as part of a preliminary reconnaissance visit for planning Catherine's coronation, which was held in the Cathedral of the Dormition on 7 May. Regimental music mingled with church bells as Peter and Catherine entered the cathedral, escorted by the newly formed cavalier guards and page boys in green velvet tunics, white wigs and hats with feathers. Catherine's gown, crimson velvet embroidered in silver with crown and floral devices, survives in the Kremlin Armoury museum, the only extant example of early eighteenth-century female dress. Her crown, made by a St Petersburg jeweller, differed from the traditional Cap of Monomach and other Muscovite crowns worn by male rulers, being more like an imperial crown in design and set with a ruby 'bigger than a pigeon's egg' and other gems. Peter was attended by Menshikov and Anikita Repnin, Catherine by Fedor Apraksin and Ivan Buturlin. Prince Dmitry Golitsyn and Andrei Osterman held her train, Prince Vasily Dolgoruky the orb, Ivan Musin-Pushkin the sceptre, James Bruce the crown and Peter Tolstoy the mace of state. The duke of Holstein, duchess of Mecklenburg and duchess of Courland, all seated on thrones for the ceremony, testified to Russia's expanding international connections.

Archbishops Feodosy and Feofan officiated during the ceremony, but it was Peter who placed the gem-encrusted state mantle on his wife's shoulders and the crown on her head and handed her the orb, after which she was anointed and received communion from the clergy. Feofan then delivered a sermon, describing Catherine as a heroine and comparing her with famous women of history and mythology. Links were made with the past in a second ceremony held in the Archangel Cathedral where the Muscovite princes and tsars were buried and which the Muscovite tsars used to visit after their coronation in order to emphasise dynastic continuity. Catherine honoured her female predecessors by paying a visit to the tombs of tsaritsy in the Kremlin convent of the Ascension.

The coronation was a public event, announced by heralds all over Moscow two days beforehand, although viewing of the ceremonies was restricted: guests required tickets to get into the cathedral, where they were seated in specially constructed stands. Crowds duly turned up outside to catch the gold and silver medals, traditional good luck tokens, scattered by Gavrila Golovkin, and to eat roast ox and drink the wine which flowed from two fountains, one spouting red the other white, pumped through pipes from the bell tower of Ivan the Great. They could also enjoy the magnificent firework display held on Tsaritsyn Meadow two days later. On 10 May an official edict ordered prayers of thanksgiving and three gun salutes to be fired 'as an announcement to the people' that Catherine had been crowned.[16] Despite the publicity, the people were passive onlookers at a thoroughly Westernised display of imperial power. The finer points of the ceremonies and decorations, detailed in descriptions of the coronation published in St Petersburg and Moscow, were intended for the élite, as was a print by the court engraver Ivan Zubov, which recorded the event with portraits of the emperor and empress based on true likenesses, dressed in the fashion of the period, mingling with antique gods and goddesses, including Neptune, Hercules and Pallas-Athene, allegorical figures of Glory, Truth, Piety and Foresight and putti in clouds. Peter points to a globe, as if to confirm Russia's new role in the world order. The inscriptions, in Russian and Latin, expatiated on the God-given joy of the occasion.[17]

On the face of it, a great deal of expense and effort was invested in a superfluous event. There was no precedent in Russia for the coronation of a tsaritsa, except the unwelcome one of False Dmitry's bride, the Catholic Pole Marina Mniszek, in 1606. Peter had declared Catherine his 'true and lawful sovereign lady' in 1711 and married her in 1712. She received the title empress (*imperatritsa*) by a decree of December 1721 which upgraded the titles of all the royal family in line with Peter's new ones. The main 'services' for which Catherine was commended in the manifesto of November 1723 and in Feofan's sermon occurred more than eleven years previously. So was Peter signalling his desire for Catherine to succeed him, as some historians believe? Bassewitz claims that Peter communicated this wish to a small group of people on the eve of the coronation, although no other records of this conversation survive and it seems possible that Bassewitz (whose master was soon to be officially betrothed to Anna Petrovna) included this detail retrospectively. In the absence of direct evidence of Peter's intentions on the succession in May 1724, the coronation should perhaps be taken at face value as what Peter said it was: a ceremony to honour Catherine. In terms of public recognition, it went hand in hand with Peter's creation of a Western-style court for his wife. It was a rebuke to those who muttered about Catherine's unsuitability as an empress and yet another demonstration of Peter's will.

Viewed from another angle, this crowning of a foreign peasant woman as empress was an example of Peter's upside-down world, the 'mock' universe of his own devising which he used to exert his authority and disorientate people. As Bergholz remarked, 'One could not help but marvel at Divine Providence which has raised the empress from the lowly station in which she was born and which she previously occupied to the pinnacle of human honours.'[18] Officials were required to demonstrate their loyalty to the empress by expressions of joy. They were uprooted from St Petersburg at considerable expense to attend the coronation, the exact date of which was a matter of speculation for weeks, then peremptorily ordered to return to the new capital in time for the tsar's name day on 29 June. Like other ceremonies of his own invention, it also gave Peter the chance to enjoy himself by drawing up guest lists, ordering costumes and working out details. There are many hand-written drafts among his papers from winter 1723. As events a few months later were soon to show, however, this time the joke may have been on Peter.

Family, sheep and other matters

While Peter and Catherine were in Moscow, an imperial presence in St Petersburg was maintained by Peter's two grandchildren and by his youngest daughter Natalia, whose attendance at church was recorded in the journals. On 30 May, for example, Peter Alekseevich attended a service in St Isaac's for his grandfather's birthday. Given that Peter was only eight years old and the two Natalias just nine and five respectively, their presence in church, supported by attendants, may be interpreted as a token of royal power in the absence of the main players. Peter was very fond of his youngest daughter, often referring to her in letters as 'our big girl' (*velikaia devitsa*). A portrait of her painted by Louis Caravaque at about this time shows her as a miniature adult dressed in the latest Western fashion, with an ermine trimmed train, dark-haired and dark-eyed like her sister Anna. In a note dated 10 May 1724 Peter asked 'Natal'iushka' to pass on his greetings to his grandchildren (her niece and nephew) and tells her about her mother's coronation, adding, 'God willing, we hope to be with you soon. PS. Today there will be fireworks.'[19]

Peter spent the rest of May in Moscow. On the 11th, thirty-four years after his first such excursion, he again travelled to Kolomenskoe along the river with a small flotilla. The interior of his father's old wooden palace had been preserved exactly as it was in the tsar's youth. There are hints of continuing ill health. On 18 May Peter had blood let from a vein in his left leg and in June he visited mineral springs near Kaluga, writing to Catherine that he was feeling better, thanks to the waters and God's help.[20] He also visited Miller's iron factories, where he did some work.

Peter allowed himself little respite. He was constantly monitoring his own legislation – checking on illegal trading out of Archangel, which was supposed to have ceded most of its business to St Petersburg; reminding members of the Synod to refer to him as 'emperor', not 'tsar'; moving people from one place to another and clamping down on attempts to evade resettlement. Nobles removed to St Petersburg, it seems, were breaking the rules by leaving their wives and children behind in Moscow. Officials' reaction to this breach of the regulations was over-zealous even by Peter's standards. In July he scolded the Moscow chief of police for forcing some very sick people and women who were about to give birth to pack up and leave. The police chief was ordered to give them time to recover before they left for St Petersburg, but not too much! [21]

New enterprises were on the agenda, such as sheep rearing in Ukraine. In orders dated 15 June 1724 Peter wrote: 'For the good of our whole state we have set up cloth factories … since God has blessed Little Russia with better air for the breeding of sheep than other regions of our state.' Sheep farmers were required (1) to build warm barns to keep the sheep warm even in summer at night; (2) to give them hay and water and salt in winter: 'And they should be given plenty of salt to make their wool grow better and keep the ewes healthy; and when there are wet snowstorms in winter and rains in summer, give them extra'; (3) to shear them twice a year, in March and September, and sell the wool to the state cloth factory; (4) to learn recipes for making medicines for sick sheep; (5) to keep black and grey sheep separate from the others; (6) to put the rams to the ewes on 26 October. [22] As usual, Peter's instructions left little to chance.

Peter arrived back in St Petersburg on 25 June, Coronation Day, where the festivities focused on the Summer Palace, which Peter sailed right up to in his yacht after attending mass in the Trinity Cathedral on the opposite bank of the river. The next day he wrote to Catherine, who had stayed on in Moscow, that all was well. The 'big lady in charge' (*bol'shaia khoziaka*), his daughter Natalia, was fit and growing up fast. But he was missing Catherine. 'When I go into the palace, I feel like running away – it's empty without you. If it weren't for the various holidays, I'd go to Kronstadt and Peterhof. PS. There are 100 foreign ships in port.' On 27 June, Poltava Day, writing to 'the friend of my heart', Peter sent a boat to meet her, laden with gifts of wine, beer, pomegranates, lemons and cucumbers. [23] The victory day festivities culminated in a party in the Summer Gardens which lasted until midnight, with cannon fire and fireworks on the river. His name day was marked with more cannon fire and entertainments until midnight. The next day he finally managed to get away to Peterhof. He welcomed Catherine back to St Petersburg on 8 July with a whole flotilla which sailed up the Neva to meet her yacht. The gunfire from various vantage points, church bells, religious services, partying and fireworks well into the small hours marked this out as an extraordinary reception to honour Peter's crowned consort.

Reflections

A note dated 16 August 1724 survives among Peter's papers, evidently intended as guidelines for a sermon for the forthcoming Nystad ceremonies. In it he comes closer than usual to reflecting on his reign:

In the first line you must mention the victories, then make the following points in the rest of the sermon:
(i) Our lack of knowledge in all matters. (ii) Especially at the start of the war which, not understanding the opposing forces and our own situation, we began like blind men. (iii) Mention how many domestic problems there were, also the affair of our son and the attack by the Turks. (iv) All other nations maintain the policy of keeping a balance of forces with their neighbour and were especially reluctant to admit us to the light of reason in all matters and especially military affairs, but they did not succeed in this. It is in truth a divine miracle that all human minds are nothing against the will of God and this must be emphasised.[24]

The tone of these jottings hints at the chip on Peter's shoulder: his resentment of other countries' marginalisation of Russia (keeping it from 'the light of reason'), a policy which Peter was not convinced had been ended by his victory over the Swedes. The same offended tone can be found in a message to the Synod dated 16 October 1724 for translators of books on economics: 'Since the Germans tend to fill their books with many useless stories, just in order to make them seem bigger, don't translate these passages but stick to the matter in hand.'[25]

Although he deplored Muscovite xenophobia and superstitious notions of 'contamination' from contacts with foreigners, Peter's own attitude remained ambivalent. Hired foreigners were obliged to train Russians, which they did with varying degrees of success. It was recognised that 'when the years of apprenticeship [of Russian pupils of tapestry weaving] are completed, it will be possible to send the foreigners back home and use His Majesty's subjects for this work, as a result of which this craft will remain in the Russian empire'.[26] Relations between foreign teachers and their pupils were often poor. Foreigners' inability to speak Russian could lead to misunderstandings, while their clothing, lifestyle and manners had more in common with those of Russian nobles than with the craftsman who worked under them. No doubt many of the latter shared the distrust of foreigners expressed by the peasant entrepreneur Ivan Pososhkov, who in the 1720s wrote that 'if any such foreigner wastes his time in idleness (as is the long-standing habit of foreigners), neglecting to teach his pupils – since he has come here merely to wheedle money out of us and then to make off home again – let him be sent home with dishonour . . .'[27]

Received wisdom notwithstanding, comparatively few non-Orthodox foreigners held positions of influence in civilian government. Indeed, it was Peter's policy to reduce their numbers still further on the grounds that foreign personnel were costly to employ and less effective than anticipated

in mentoring their Russian colleagues. Foreign personnel were more numerous in the army and dominated the upper echelons of the navy, although
here too Peter tried to restrict their numbers. The Naval Statute, for
example, specified that the skippers of Russian merchant ships should
recruit sailors 'of the Russian (*Rossiiskoi*) nation'. No more than a quarter of
the crew should be foreigners.[28] In the matter of shipbuilding, too, Peter
acknowledged Russia's growing expertise. In 1713 he wrote to Fedor Apraksin
criticising some of the new ships purchased in France, England and
Hamburg which he had just inspected in St Petersburg: 'They are truly
deserving of the name of foster children because they are as remote from our
ships as a foster father from a real one, for they are much smaller than ours,
and even though there are just as many guns, there is not so much space in
them.'[29]

Self-sufficiency was his stated aim. 'This paper was made here in a mill,'
states an edict of 1723, 'and we can make as much of it as we need in this
country and not only order it from France.'[30] An anecdote (much quoted in
Soviet works) makes the point less delicately: 'It's good to borrow sciences and
arts from the French, I would like to see all that in my own country; all the
same, Paris still stinks.'[31] On a similar note, the much-travelled Ivan Nepliuev
recorded a visit to a Russian carpenter's house where Peter urged him to
accept a slice of the carrot pie which the simple folk offered, because it was
'our own native food, not Italian'.[32] Peter was sensitive to outside opinion and
aware of the need to balance flattery through emulation against national pride
or even narrow-mindedness. The French minister in St Petersburg, Jacques de
Campredon, reported a visit to Peterhof in summer 1723 in a dispatch to
Louis XV:

> The tsar did me the honour of saying that as I had seen so many beautiful
> things in France he doubted whether I would find anything of much
> interest at Peterhof, adding that he hoped that Your Majesty had such a
> beautiful view at Versailles as here at Peterhof from where one has a view
> of the sea and of Kronstadt on one side and St Petersburg on the other. I
> told this Prince that I had good reason to admire the fact that during such
> a long war and in such a harsh climate he had been able to perfect these
> beautiful things and that I deemed them very worthy of Your Majesty's
> curiosity.[33]

Campredon's condescending tone (elsewhere he assured the king that
Peter's Marly pavilion at Peterhof was nothing like the original at
Versailles) was precisely the sort of attitude which Peter half expected and
hated.

Peter did not blindly adulate the more advanced (as he himself acknowledged) countries and was sensitive about Russia's image abroad and about

its acceptance as a full member of the 'political' nations, to which, in his view, its history entitled it. That Russia had not always been an underdog was illustrated by the life of Prince Alexander of Novgorod (1220–63), who beat the Swedes in 1240 on the Neva river and in 1242 defeated the Teutonic knights in the famous battle on the ice on Lake Peipus. Peter inaugurated the revival and enhancement of Alexander's cult in 1704 by planting wooden crosses at the spot not far from the Neva river where Alexander was supposed to have won his victory. (In fact, the battle took place farther off.) In July 1710 the Alexander Nevsky monastery was founded and Alexander's cult was encouraged as that of a local saint with strong links with Peter, his 'living reflection'. In a sermon delivered on 23 November 1718 (Alexander's feast day) Feofan Prokopovich described how the prince 'held firm the stern of his fatherland in those difficult times'. Russia was like 'a ship in distress', buffeted by Mongol storms on one side and Swedish on the other, its hull holed and cracked by Russia's dynastic struggles and disputes. But helmsman Alexander saved his ship and 'to this day the Neva is a Russian river'.[34]

To stress Alexander's association with Russia's recent victories, his main feast day was moved from 23 November (the date of his burial) to 30 August, the anniversary of the Treaty of Nystad. Peter had Alexander's relics transferred from the town of Vladimir and on 30 August 1724 took the gilded silver casket along the Neva in a barge to its new resting place in the monastery. The 'grandfather' of the navy was also brought out, flying the flag of St Andrew, a potent coming together of three of Peter's new or revived symbols of his St Petersburg-oriented empire. An estimated 6,000 spectators turned up to witness the procession and to enjoy bonfires, gun salutes and illuminations later that evening. The political motivation is clear; the analogies drawn between Alexander's and Peter's victories over the Swedes, the confirmation of the right to the land on the Neva which Peter's ancestors had fought to preserve, not to mention a reference to *translatio imperii* as St Petersburg received the baton from its illustrious predecessors were calculated to please churchmen as well as the lay public. Two hundred years later Alexander Nevsky was to prove equally acceptable to the political and ideological leaders of the USSR.

The William Mons affair

The festive atmosphere of summer and early autumn as recorded in the journals conceals a darker mood. The run of poor harvests which began in 1721 continued into 1724, bringing famine to some areas. Officials' salaries were reduced or left unpaid. The poll tax was collected for the first time, bringing protests. By 1724 so many people were defecting, especially into

Poland, that manned pickets were set up. Any fugitives apprehended were interrogated, flogged and sent home, or shot if they resisted arrest. Russia, it was said, was being emptied by illegal emigration. 'Everything is going wrong,' wrote the Saxon envoy in September 1724. 'Trade is coming to an end, there is neither navy nor paid troops, and everyone is dissatisfied and discontented.'[35]

Peter also had a run of ill health. According to the later testimony of one of his physicians, Dr Paulson, a disease of the urinary tract and bladder, which first came to light in the winter of 1723, recurred in summer 1724, when Drs Blumentrost, Bidloo and Horn performed an operation. Only a few hints of his indisposition can be gleaned from Peter's letters and papers. Writing to Menshikov on 29 August about the forthcoming Alexander Nevsky ceremony he mentioned being sick. In a letter to General Münnich, who was in charge of work on the Ladoga canal which he was planning to visit, Peter asked for water transport to be prepared as travelling overland 'will be somewhat difficult after my illness'.[36]

This did not deter him from setting off on a fairly gruelling journey, first to Schlüsselburg, where he celebrated the local 'victory day' on 11 October, then along the Ladoga canal to Staraia Russa. He returned to St Petersburg on 27 October. Around this time – on 2 November, for example, the journals record a visit to Dubki on the northern shore of the Finnish gulf – an incident is said to have occurred which came to be popularly associated with Peter's death some three months later. While visiting Lakhta on the gulf, the emperor ('that hero') waded into the sea to save the lives of a boatload of soldiers and sailors in peril in a storm, an event commemorated in histories, paintings, films and statues.[37] In fact, Stählin is the sole source for the incident, which is not mentioned in the court journals or by writers such as Prokopovich, who surely would not have wasted the chance to make the moral point that Peter refused to spare himself and ultimately sacrificed his life for the good of Russia, especially given the biblical associations of the incident. The lack of hard evidence may, of course, be due to Peter's modesty, which prevented him from publicising a brave act performed in the course of duty.

Whether he saved any soldiers or not, Peter returned to the capital fit enough to have an 'uncommonly good time' at the wedding of a German baker on 5 November. Then on Sunday, 8 November thirty-year-old William Mons, brother of Peter's former mistress Anna and Catherine's chamberlain and head of her estates office, was arrested, charged with abusing the empress's trust by taking bribes in cash and kind from petitioners and shielding wrongdoers from the law. His papers were confiscated and he and his associates were interrogated by torture. Rumours abounded that the real reason for Mons's arrest was that he had been having an affair with Catherine, which, according to some accounts, sent

Peter into a mad rage and convulsions and made him slam a door (or in other versions strike an expensive Venetian mirror) so hard that it broke.[38] The affair caused consternation in the palace, where many people, male and female, had connections with Mons. The unseasonably cold weather, signalling the end of the navigation season – on 14 November it snowed and the Neva began to freeze over – exacerbated the gloomy atmosphere.

On 16 November, another freezing day, Mons was executed. The court journal records: 'On this day there was an execution on Trinity Square of the following: the former chamberlain William Mons was beheaded, and the wife of Major-General Balk and the scribe Stoletov were flogged with the knout and the footman Balakirev was beaten with sticks.'[39] Matrena Balk, Mons's sister and Catherine's chief lady-in-waiting, who confessed to accepting a long list of bribes, which included not only money but also several sacks of coffee, twenty bales of hay and rolls of fabric and ribbons, was exiled to Siberia; Stoletov and Balakirev to hard labour in the Estonian port of Rogervik. Bergholz speaks of the calm with which his friend and fellow German Mons met his death and of his good qualities in general, although opinions differ about Mons's moral fibre. Five days after the execution, Bergholz notes, his body was still lying on the scaffold (standard practice in such cases).[40] Peter apparently had Mons's head preserved in a jar and presented to Catherine. Many years later Catherine the Great's friend Princess Catherine Dashkova discovered the jar together with another one containing the head of Mary Hamilton, a lady-in-waiting who was executed by Peter for infanticide, and whose dead lips he was reputed to have kissed, which confirmed Dashkova's view that Peter was a despot who treated people like slaves. She had them buried.[41]

Was Catherine Mons's mistress? The short time between Mons's arrest and execution fuelled rumours of an affair, as did Catherine's attempt to intercede on his behalf. The French minister Campredon remarked: 'Her relations with M. Mons were public knowledge and although she conceals her grief it is possible to see it painted on her face and in her behaviour.'[42] Other writers have thought it improbable that Catherine, who knew her husband's violent character, would take such a risk. It was one thing for her to joke about Peter's affairs (and for him to have them) and for him to joke about her 'meeting someone younger'; quite another for Catherine, who was dependent on Peter for everything, to take a lover. The fact that she did not bury Mons's head even after Peter's death, but apparently kept the jar, has also been taken as evidence that this was not a man she loved. Whatever the case, Catherine's household had been disrupted and she had no choice but to put on a brave face. The day after Mons's execution Peter ordered James Bruce to draw up a contract and a plan of ceremonies for the exchange of rings between their daughter Anna and the duke of Holstein, after a two-and-a-half-year courtship. On 22 November the court celebrated the betrothal with a grand ball, followed by a firework display featuring Venus in a carriage drawn by swans with the legend HAPPY CONCORD.[43] On 23 November the duke turned up at the Winter Palace with a band of musicians (that day people went out on the frozen river in sledges for the first time) and on the 24th Catherine's name day was celebrated in the usual manner.

As for Peter, he got back to work as his mind turned to practical matters – he drew up a long memorandum listing Russian fortresses, their functions and the state of their defences – and to the forthcoming Yuletide. Christmas and New Year were celebrated in St Petersburg (the usual services in the Trinity Cathedral) and on 6 January 1725 Peter led his Preobrazhensky guards in the Epiphany ceremony of the blessing of the waters of the Neva, just as he had done a year previously. On the 9th he and Catherine attended the wedding of Mishka, the manservant of Peter's orderly, Vasily Pospelov, to the musician Nastasia. In the days that followed the imperial couple attended assemblies at the homes of Peter Tolstoy, Cornelius Cruys and Ivan Siniavin and Peter also dealt with such routine matters as letters to army commanders and arrangements for winter billets. A letter to Fedor Saltykov dated 3 January shows that he was as impatient as ever to get things done: 'I've no idea whether you are alive or dead or have forsaken your duty and turned to crime, only since we left Moscow I have seen no reports from you. If you have not finished your business and arrived here by 10 February, you will be the cause of your own ruin.'[44]

Death

The threat was not to be carried out. Preparations were in hand for the forthcoming carnival, when, on 17 January, the keeper of the court journal recorded: 'His Imperial Majesty was ill and did not deign to go anywhere.' A week later he wrote: 'Since the 17th his Imperial Majesty has been ill and lying in his Winter residence in the upper apartment.'[45] Had Peter been superstitious he would have been wary of the last week of January. His mother died on 25 January and both his father and his half-brother Tsar Ivan on the 29th. This January was also to be Peter's last. The old bladder problem recurred – no doubt exacerbated by the customary Yuletide binges and the chilly ceremony on the ice on 6 January – and he suffered days of agony as a result of inability to pass urine, with brief periods of remission. Peter's foreign doctors, in the unenviable position of having a really sick emperor on their hands, had no idea what to do. On 25 January they drew off about a litre of putrid, foul-smelling urine, a procedure which precipitated another fever. On the same day they dispatched a letter to the king of Prussia, written as if by Peter in the first person but signed by Chancellor Gavrila Golovkin, asking the king to send his personal physician: 'Following a slight chill, I have been suffering from a severe indisposition.' A German translation accompanied it.[46] Infection set in. Non-medical remedies – an order for the release of prisoners 'for the sovereign's health' and round-the-clock prayers – proved as ineffective as medical ones. After enduring several more days of pain so agonising that it made him cry out and having received the last rites, Peter expired, according to Feofan Prokopovich's memorable account, in the sanctity of piety, between four and five in the morning of 28 January 1725 in his study, a room to one side of the Grand Hall on the first floor of the Winter Palace. He was, as official accounts meticulously recorded, fifty-two years, seven months and twenty-nine days old in the forty-second year, seventh month and third day of his reign.

Contemporary sources agree that Peter was killed by inflammation of the urinary tract which resulted in retention of urine, a condition sometimes known as gravel. The terms 'retention or blockage of water/urine' (*vodianoi zapor, uriny zapor*) and 'difficulty in passing water' (*trudnost' v nepriazhenii vody*) recur. The causes of this illness are unclear. A modern diagnosis might point to prostate trouble and Peter, with his insistence on operating on his own body, may have exacerbated the condition by using silver catheters to probe the urethra. Foreign observers tended to focus on the accumulated effects of half a century of tireless activity, both public and private. Campredon, for example, attributed the tsar's condition to 'the recurrence of an old case of venereal disease'.[47] Bassewitz writes: 'His activity allowed him no rest and he held in contempt all types of bad weather, and the sacrifices to Venus and Bacchus exhausted his strength and led to the development of gravel.'[48] Inevitably there were rumours of poisoning (at one point Peter apparently complained of a 'burning sensation' in his stomach), with Catherine and/or Menshikov as the main suspects, but the gravel mentioned by Bassewitz, a disease easily cured with today's treatments, seems the most likely. Even then the famous Professor Boerhaave in Leiden, whom Peter's doctors consulted, is said to have exclaimed that Peter could have been cured with medicine costing five kopecks if treatment had started in time. It is generally agreed that Peter hastened his own death by ignoring his symptoms and refusing to slow the pace of his activities.

'Leave all to ...'

Peter died leaving much business unfinished. Shortly before losing consciousness, he is said to have scrawled a note: 'Leave all to ...' and summoned his daughter Anna. Voltaire mentioned the incident in his *History of Peter the Great* and it was used in many later histories. In fact, the story appears in only one contemporary source, not Prokopovich, but the memoir of Bassewitz, whose aim may have been to persuade readers that Anna, his master's fiancée, was Peter's intended heir. Supposing the piece of paper really did exist, whose name did Peter want to write on it? Some historians believe that he could not seriously contemplate the possibility of dying, so failed to make a decision about his successor. His hand wavered even when he was so close to death because he did not know whom to choose. The principle behind the 1722 manifesto was that the ruling monarch should choose an heir 'with regard to worthiness' rather than with reference to seniority. But who was a worthy successor? Peter knew that traditionalists, still outraged by Alexis's death, backed his grandson Peter as the rightful heir, so he was reluctant to risk the reversal of his reforms by nominating him. The possibility of his ex-wife Evdokia acting as the boy's regent made this solution even more unpalatable. One of his three daughters, perhaps, as there was no restriction on gender? Anna was the eldest and the cleverest, but Peter may have preferred not to subject her to the burden of rulership. Some people believed that he was grooming Anna's fiancé the duke of Holstein as a candidate (as a German married to a Westernised Russian woman he could be trusted not to turn the clock back) and hoping that sons from the marriage would create a new male line. There is no reason to believe that Peter saw any advantages in female rule *per se*. If anything happened to Anna, Elizabeth could play out a similar scenario, although her marriage had not yet been arranged, and after her there was six-year-old Natalia (who in fact died a couple of weeks after Peter). Purely in terms of seniority and legitimacy, Peter's three nieces Ekaterina, Anna and Praskovia had a better claim than his own daughter, but none had a claim on grounds of merit. That left Catherine, in many ways an unlikely choice, but one favoured by a number of powerful men at court.

Deathbed portraits

The room in the old Winter Palace in which Peter died did not survive the many rebuildings on the site, but part of the ground floor immediately beneath it was preserved to form the basement of the Hermitage Theatre, built in the 1770s. A fragment of window surround and stucco from the old building can still be seen today if you look across to the eastern embankment of the Zimnaia Kanavka canal a few yards from where it enters the River Neva. Inside, a vestibule and a few rooms have been converted into a 'Peter I's Palace' museum, among the exhibits in which are a profile study of Peter on his deathbed, taken from the tsar's right side and attributed to the court painter, Johann Gottfried Dannhauer. A more famous head and shoulders portrait of the dead emperor, depicting him full-face from the left, hangs in the Russian Museum. Supposedly painted from nature, it shows Peter's features in repose, the slightly puffy, thickened visage familiar from the round portrait attributed to Ivan Nikitin. The impression of rest after a long battle perhaps provides a metaphor for Peter's lifelong struggle to drag Russia into the modern world. The ermine drape (surely not an accessory of the real sickbed) signifies the subject's regal status, while the lighting effects on the sheets suggest the flickering of the candles which must have surrounded the bed.

Although this is undoubtedly a modern painting, oil on canvas, from the hand of a Western-trained master, it has iconic features as an image of the last scene of an earthly life which was filled with secular feats of courage and, in a way, miracles. In modern art histories and catalogues the painting is usually attributed to Ivan Nikitin, on the grounds, as Soviet art historians insisted, that the portrait displayed a 'patriotic, purely Russian understanding of the image, a grief of loss which could be conveyed only by a Russian artist', while Dannhauer's lacked 'personal feeling' and was a cold, straightforward 'imitation of nature'.[49] Documentary confirmation of authorship is lacking, as is any official reference to painters coming to the palace in the hours after Peter's death. Differences in the clothing and pillows in the two paintings may suggest that Nikitin did his in the study right after Peter's death, Dannhauer after the transfer of body to the palace chapel. This debate illustrates the strong emotions which continue to be aroused by the whole question of cultural borrowing in eighteenth-century Russia.

There are no such doubts about the authorship of another striking relic of the dead Peter, which today sits in a glass cabinet in the basement of the old Winter Palace not far from Dannhauer's painting. Shortly after Peter's death the court sculptor Carlo Bartolomeo Rastrelli, a native of Florence, where wax effigies for funeral parades were a speciality, made death masks and casts of the emperor's hands and feet. These were then incorporated into the famous wax model, which had a wooden body made to the tsar's measurements and a wig made from his own hair cut during his Persian campaign. Stories about the model being fitted with a mechanism which allowed it to stand up to its full height have been discounted.

Peter may have seen similar effigies of French kings and queens in Saint-Denis in 1717, for example, the standing figure of Henri IV, complete with natural hair. Perhaps he also knew about the wooden facsimiles of English kings and queens, the faces based on death masks, which were displayed on top of their closed coffins during funeral parades, then stored in Westminster Abbey. Rastrelli himself referred to the figure (in a request for reimbursement of the cost of materials) as a 'model for the tomb',[50] which suggests that it may have been intended to be carried at Peter's funeral parade, perhaps even as an emergency substitute for the body, given the long period of lying in state. Apparently it was not used as such, either during the lying in state or during the funeral procession, or it would surely have been mentioned in accounts.

We know that churchmen later objected to some aspects of Peter's funeral (the Holy Synod refused permission for the publication of a detailed description of the decorations on the grounds that they were 'pagan') and the wax figure's uncanny imitation of life probably proved too much for Orthodox tradition.

Castrum doloris

In paying so much attention to the artistic activity around Peter's corpse in the last days of January 1725 we also touch upon important political issues, for these acts of visual commemoration sprang from the political and psychological needs of the people Peter had left behind. Peter had been in all senses a dominating and domineering presence. His family and favourites needed time to decide what to do. In the meantime, physical memorials of the tsar himself could bridge the gap between life with Peter and life without him. Dressing Rastrelli's wax model in the clothes he wore at Catherine's coronation provided a visible reminder of Peter's honouring of his spouse, who almost immediately emerged as the favoured candidate to succeed him. Piling up images of Peter's deeds underlined the need to preserve his heritage, to which there was much popular opposition. If the treatment of Peter's corpse could also appeal to Orthodox sentiments, for example, in a hint of saintliness as manifested in the incorruptibility of the body, so much the better. The fact that it was possible to record the dead tsar realistically in paint and wax owed much to his own clinical and unsqueamish attitude towards death and the human body, learned at dissecting tables in Amsterdam and Leiden. He often delayed funerals for autopsies to be performed, commissioned death masks, and had corpses embalmed, all in contravention of Orthodox custom. In France in 1717 Peter bought the Dutch anatomist Ruysch's secret recipe for preserving corpses, refusing to reveal it to French anatomists who were working on models of human organs. This was reflected in Prokopovich's *Short Account* of Peter's death: 'He was apprehensive of his approaching fate,' but noted 'philosophically' that from his own example 'you can see what a wretched creature is mortal man.' Such pronouncements were in keeping with Western accounts of 'good' or 'tame' deaths, but Peter's premonition of death has a modern update: he sensed the progress of his illness and despaired, 'for he was knowledgeable about anatomy'.[51]

And so Peter was not placed in his tomb, as were his Muscovite predecessors, within twenty-four hours or at most a couple of days of death in a ceremony attended only by the inner circle of courtiers and churchmen. This would have been, to put it crudely, a waste of a valuable asset. From early February to 10 March he lay on public display in a hall of mourning (referred to in contemporary accounts as *castrum doloris*) in the Winter Palace. The designer of this room was the French artist Nicholas Pineau, assisted by a team of mainly foreign artists and craftsmen. Beneath a canopy draped with the imperial mantle and skeleton devices, Peter's body lay clad in breeches and a shirt of silver brocade with lace cuffs and cravat, boots with spurs, a sword and his Order of St Andrew. The coffin was surrounded by nine tables holding Peter's regalia and other military and knightly orders and four 'bronze' statues (plaster with bronze paint effects) depicting Russia weeping, Europe, Mars and Hercules. Four pyramids of white marble on pedestals, draped with genies in mournful poses and allegorical representations of Death, Time, Glory and Victory, bore the legends SOLICITUDE FOR THE CHURCH, REFORM OF THE CITIZENRY, INSTRUCTION OF THE MILITARY and BUILDING OF THE FLEET, inscribed with verses extolling Peter's feats. A drape spread between the pyramids exhorted Russia 'to grieve and weep, your father PETER THE GREAT has left you'. Other pedestals bore statues of virtues: Wisdom, Bravery, Piety, Mercy, Peace, Love of the Fatherland and Justice. The whole room, illuminated by candles, was swathed in black, with festoons of black and white flowers and funereal drapes scattered with tears made out of silver satin. The spectacle was calculated to appeal both to the uneducated folk, who swarmed into the palace through a specially cut door from the Neva embankment, and to the more sophisticated public, including representatives of foreign courts, who would know how to interpret the Christian and classical imagery which extolled the monarch's feats in life, as well as grieving for his end.

Burial

By the day of the burial, 10 March 1725, the motionless tableau of Peter's body and its accoutrements had conveyed a number of important messages about the autocrat-reformer which could now be consolidated by a more dynamic spectacle. The sudden death of Peter's youngest daughter, six-year-old Natalia, on 4 March turned it into a double funeral, but few adjustments had to be made to accommodate her small casket. The length and route of the funeral procession were determined by the spatial configuration of St Petersburg. In Moscow the royal residence and the royal mausoleum (the Archangel Cathedral) were within a few dozen yards of each other within the walled space of the Kremlin, so that the transfer of the coffin from one to the other could be achieved in front of a selected audience and relatively quickly. In St Petersburg the Winter Palace and the Peter-Paul Cathedral, which Peter had built as a mausoleum, were on opposite sides of the wide frozen Neva river, and the path marked across the ice to link one to the other could be viewed from various vantage points on the embankments. Had Peter died when the river was ice-free, the transfer would have been accomplished by barge, which would arguably have been more in keeping with his tastes. We know about the parade in remarkable detail not only from published descriptions, but also from an image in watercolour and ink painted by an unknown artist on a scroll 10 metres long.[52] The parade was markedly military in character, with 10,638 troops from various regiments lining the route, but with ample provision for civilian and ecclesiastical participation. Cannon fire from the fortress at one-minute intervals mingled with church bells. The procession was led by drummers and trumpeters in black cloaks, merchants (including foreigners), deputies from the towns and the nobility of Estonia and Livonia. Thirty-two horses, among them Peter's favourite clad in black drapery and wearing plumes, carried the coats of arms of the Russian towns and provinces. Thus the empire, new and old, was represented. There was also a substantial priestly component, with choristers, deacons, priests, archimandrites and the members of the Holy Synod preceding the two coffins on their sledges. Peter's was draped in a black cloth and placed under a red velvet canopy topped with a large gilded crown. Peter's associates formed the centrepiece, some holding the ends of the coffin cloth, others, including the British ship's master Joseph Noye, holding the strings of the canopy, followed by Catherine supported by Menshikov, now the most powerful man in Russia, then Peter's daughters Anna and Elizabeth, Peter's nieces Ekaterina and Praskovia, his future son-in-law the duke of Holstein and his grandson Peter Alekseevich.

The arrangements clearly displayed the Petrine order of things in other respects, too. Inside the cathedral, men and women from the top six grades of the Table of Ranks were seated inside the temporary wooden chapel which had to be constructed for the occasion, with ranks 4–6 standing at a lower level, while ranks 7–8 stood outside in the main body of the church. There was, of course, no patriarch to officiate, as there had been in the seventeenth century. The cleric in the limelight was the man who delivered the funeral sermon, a relative novelty in the Russian Orthodox church. Feofan Prokopovich, archbishop of Pskov and Narva and vice-president of the Holy Synod, specialised in rhetorical compositions based on foreign prototypes, in this case very likely a Lutheran model, and drew on stock comparisons with biblical figures to laud the earthly achievements of the departed (his 'great talents, deeds, and actions'). He elaborated on the discourse that the dead monarch 'gave birth' to Russia and named him Samson (strong defender of the fatherland), Japhet (creator of the fleet), Moses (law-giver), Solomon (bringer of reason and wisdom) and David and Constantine (reformers of the Church). The gods of antiquity were tactfully omitted. The oration ended with a eulogy to Peter's successor and his creation, Catherine I, 'mother of all Russians', the embodiment of her husband's 'spirit'.

The last farewells before the coffin lid was closed were accompanied by 'indescribably sad wailing', especially from Catherine, who was mourning both a husband and a daughter. Thereafter there followed what amounted to a second forty-day vigil by the coffin. In fact, Peter was not actually buried (that is, lowered into a vault in the ground) at the time. His coffin stood in the centre of the church in the temporary structure for six years, where it was joined in May 1727 by Catherine's. The coffins stood together until May 1731 when both were lowered into the crypt on the order of Empress Anna. The *St Petersburg News* for 31 May reported that on Saturday in the eleventh hour of the morning, a service was conducted by Archimandrite Petr Smelich in the presence of members of the service élite and admiralty and many college officials. There was a 51-gun salute as the coffins were lowered.[53] An undecorated granite sarcophagus was placed over the spot with an inscription giving Peter's dates in the old and new styles: 'Autocrat of All Russia, Emperor Peter the Great, born in 1672, ascended the throne in 1682, left the earthly realm and migrated to the heavenly one in the year of the creation of the world 7233, the year of our Lord 1725, aged 52, in the forty-second year of his reign, on 28 January.'[54]

XI

Legacy

Akh, father bright moon!
Why don't you shine like you use to,
Like you used to, like before?
Why from evening till midnight,
Till midnight until the light of day,
Do you hide behind the clouds,
Conceal yourself in a dark cloud?
In Holy Rus,
In the glorious city of Petersburg,
In the Peter-Paul Cathedral
To the right by the choir stalls,
By the tomb of the sovereign
By the tomb of Peter the First
Peter the First the Great
A young sergeant prays to God.

And he weeps, like a river flows,
For the sudden death of the sovereign,
Of the sovereign Peter the First.
Amidst his sobbing, he says these words:
'Open up, damp mother earth,
On all four sides.
Open, tomb stone.
Lift up, gold satin drape.
Rise up, wake up, sovereign,
Wake up, little father Orthodox Tsar,
Look upon your dear troops,
Your dear and brave troops,
Who have been left orphans without you,
And orphaned have lost our strength.'

'Soldier's Lament by the Tomb of Peter the Great' (early eighteenth century)[1]

The emperor is dead. Long live the empress

The departure of a larger-than-life figure who had reigned in Russia since 1682 and ruled it for more than a quarter of a century, was bound to arouse strong feelings. From Moscow, where a requiem mass was held in the Dormition Cathedral, Senator Andrei Matveev, Peter's childhood friend, wrote to Aleksei Makarov that news of the 'tragedy' provoked such howls, cries and tearful wailing among men that women could scarcely have howled and sobbed more bitterly. 'I have never in my life seen or heard such horror among the populace as was heard in all the parishes and streets when the announcement was made.' Russian students in Amsterdam also 'wept inconsolably' at the news.[2] Ivan Nepliuev, who had been tested by Peter in person when he returned from naval training abroad a decade earlier, recalls that he was in a kind of 'delirium' for a whole day.[3] Judging by the admittedly problematical evidence of popular songs, written down long after the event, many common soldiers felt bereft, too. To what extent such reactions reflected ritualised responses is hard to say. One is reminded of 1953, when ordinary Soviet citizens wept on the streets at the news of Stalin's death.

The immediate response of Peter's sworn enemies is less easy to determine. Religious dissidents' delight at Peter's death, for example, has been linked with popular prints of 'The Mice Bury the Cat'. In fact, the subject, a carnivalesque 'world turned upside down', dates from the late seventeenth century and probably only some time after Peter's death were certain clues, such as the number of mourners and horses, used to link the print with his funeral cortège. It is easy to see why people made the connection, and also why the parody might be interpreted as a reference to the Drunken Assembly, which regularly featured pigs and bears harnessed to carts, as well as 'bestial' human behaviour, which traditionalists took as one of many clues that Peter was the Antichrist.

Abroad, Peter's death gave rise to fears of destabilisation. 'News we have had here of the late great Event in Muscovy by the Czar's death, which will undoubtedly have a considerable effect on most countrys in Europe,' a British commentator wrote.[4] In identical reports to their respective sovereigns the Prussian and the French ministers in St Petersburg wrote of 'the dread it has struck in the inhabitants who fear disturbances, above all as nothing has been settled concerning the succession'.[5] In fact, continuity was assured by the accession of Catherine. She apparently had no desire to rule and pressed the claim of Grand Duke Peter Alekseevich, but the powerful men who backed her – Menshikov, Pavel Iaguzhinsky, Aleksei Makarov, Andrei Osterman, Peter Tolstoy – were anxious to block the re-emergence of the late Tsarevich Alexis's party. Luckily for them, it was widely believed that Peter had indicated his wish for his wife to succeed him by crowning her as his consort. It was inconvenient that he had not named her publicly as his heir, but his supposed wishes proved sufficient to get the backing needed to clinch the succession with the support of the guards, also Peter's personal creation.

Catherine's short reign, which ended with her premature death in May 1727, provides an excellent illustration of how autocracy continued to operate successfully under a ruler who had little interest in or talent for ruling. Even Catherine's gender proved to be an advantage rather than a handicap. Her shaky qualifications for the job on the grounds of merit were offset by the rhetoric that not only would she rule in Peter's spirit but she had actually been 'created' by him, like gold in an alchemist's crucible. The last thing the men close to the throne actually wanted was another Peter – with all that implied about exhausting work schedules, the danger of being clouted with a cudgel or humiliated in some shaming ceremony. Compared with this, a woman ruler promised respite and some room for manoeuvre. Add the rhetoric of motherhood (Catherine was the all-caring Mother of Russia) and throw in some stock comparisons with classical rulers and goddesses, and the illiterate peasant woman was transformed into the ruling Empress of All Russia. She could enjoy the trappings of power, while the men who now ruled Russia, several of them also Peter's creations, could take stock and discreetly recommend suspending or discarding those parts of the Petrine heritage which were proving inconvenient and costly.

In a 'Memorandum on the needs of the state'[6] presented to Catherine in November 1726, the leading men of her government concluded that

> nearly all affairs – both spiritual and temporal – are in disarray and require speedy correction. ... Not only the peasantry, on whom the maintenance of the army is laid, are in dire need and are being reduced to complete and utter ruin by heavy taxation and continual punitive expeditions and other irregularities, but other areas such as commerce, justice and the mints are also in a state of decay.

They recommended that 'since the army is so vital that the state cannot prevail without it, therefore we must look to the welfare of the peasant, for the soldier is linked to the peasant like the soul to the body, and if there is no peasant there will be no soldier'. They called for concessions on the poll tax (which was reduced from 74 to 70 kopecks) and reorganisation in the countryside, where 'the peasant has a dozen or more commanders instead of one – military officers, fiscals, *voevodas*, forest supervisors and others, some of whom are not so much pastors as wolves attacking the flock'.

Menshikov and his colleagues proposed a partial demobilisation of the army, which would have the dual advantage of saving on wages and allowing some landlords to return to their villages to restore order. They hoped that 'the wretched peasantry, by which all the army and in part the fleet are maintained, may enjoy some respite and order and that many, when they hear of these concessions, will return from flight'. The authors of this memorandum had an agenda of their own, namely to redress the balance between the conflicting claims of the state and the landowners on the peasants' labour in favour of the landowners. It is no coincidence that the decades following Peter's death saw reductions both in the nobility's service requirements and in the poll tax. The memorandum also denounced several cherished reforms for destroying livelihoods, such as the diversion of the Archangel trade to St Petersburg and legislation on new looms, but nowhere did it criticise Peter himself, despite the fact that his policies had left many parts of Russia in ruins. The Memorandum of 1726 was for private consumption: official rhetoric told a different story.

The balance sheet of domestic reform

A medal issued in 1725 bears an image of Peter borne aloft by Eternity looking down at a seated woman personifying Russia, with attributes of the arts and sciences at her feet, and the legend: SEE WHAT A GOOD CONDITION I LEAVE YOU IN. A variation on the theme was the metaphor of Peter as sculptor. 'All Russia is your statue,' wrote Prokopovich in 1726, 'transformed by

you with skilful craftsmanship,'[7] like the Galatea-Russia fashioned by
Pygmalion-Peter's chisel depicted on Rastrelli's bronze bust. In his power to
transform, Peter was superhuman and death-defying. In a sermon delivered
on the first anniversary of Peter's death, Abbot Gavriil Buzhinsky, head chaplain to the fleet, declared: 'Peter the Great is alive: I am the resurrection and
the life ... and whosoever believeth in me shall have eternal life.'[8] Peter provided a stable reference point not only during the rapid turnover of emperors
and empresses which occurred in the years 1725–62, but also to the end of the
Romanov dynasty. The first principles firmly observed by Russia's eighteenth-
and nineteenth-century rulers were that Peter himself was beyond reproach
and that they ruled in his spirit.

Empress Anna (1730–40) shared her uncle's passion for jesters and masquerades, while mastering much of his rhetoric about the common good. His
daughter Elizabeth (1741–61), 'equally great, equally first/A goddess on earth
like Minerva', as the poet V. K. Trediakovsky enthused in 1756, exploited her
father's legacy shamelessly, while Catherine II (1762–96) cultivated the image
of Peter's 'spiritual daughter' in public, but privately deplored Peter's coarseness and brutality. As contemporaries declared, Peter gave Russians bodies but
Catherine gave them souls. In August 1770 in a splendid piece of political
theatre, she placed a Turkish naval standard captured at the battle of Chesme
on Peter's tomb, after which Metropolitan Platon delivered a sermon, which
began with the summons, delivered in a booming voice, 'Arise now, Great
Monarch, Father of our Fatherland. Arise and look upon your handiwork; it
has not decayed with time and its glory has not dimmed.'[9] In the congregation, Catherine's sixteen-year-old son Paul was terrified that his great-grandfather really was about to emerge from his tomb. As Paul I (1796–1801), he
emulated Peter by combining devotion to the common good with authoritarian rule, but neglected patriotism, to disastrous effect. Alexander I
(1801–25) was by all accounts less devoted to Peter's memory, but in 1814 even
he paid a visit to the little house in Zaandam, leaving a hand-written note:
'To Peter the Great from Alexander'. His brother Nicholas I (1825–55)
admired Peter to the point of veneration, contributing to his cult through
museums and monuments, while the bicentenary of Peter's birth in 1872 provided opportunities for a fellow reformer, Alexander II (1855–81), to cast some
of his own activities in the Petrine mould. His son, the bear-like Alexander
III (1881–94), admired Peter's qualities as a 'man of the people'. Perhaps only
the slightly-built Nicholas II (1894–1917) was uncomfortable with Peter as a
role model, preferring the more pious and cautious Moscow-rooted image of
the seventeenth-century Romanovs, although he did take advantage of the
Petrine anniversaries which fell within his reign.

So, some rulers admired Peter more than others, but officially his reputation was sacrosanct. The complete Petrine package of reform was another
matter, however. Central government by and large retained its Petrine out-

lines, the Senate and the procurator-general surviving until 1917 and the collegiate system until the early nineteenth century, but other administrative reforms quickly withered because they had never taken root. Among the first victims was much of the paraphernalia of provincial offices and posts with Germanic names. Peter's ambitious multi-tiered system of new courts and his attempt to separate the administrative and judicial systems also proved a failure, mainly as a result of the lack of qualified personnel and conflict with established local power bases. In 1727 the courts of appeal were closed and military governors resumed control in law as well as in fact. Peter may not have mastered the provinces and the periphery of his empire, but neither did his successors. They continued to experience both misconduct by local officials and widespread popular disobedience, at worst major outbreaks encompassing whole regions, of which the most devastating was the Pugachev revolt of 1773–74. Catherine II's response was the Statute on Provincial Administration (1775), which acknowledged that Russia's problem was not so much an overarching, all-powerful state as under-administration, which hampered both the government's ability to control the population and the people's access to redress and protection. This and other measures sought, with limited success, to harness the voluntary efforts of the nobility in the provinces, something which Peter tried to do but failed, mainly because his nobles were always on the move and under severe pressure.

Peter's belief that the best means of promoting the common good was to make laws, and plenty of them, proved illusory. In volume, Peter's edicts surpassed those of his Muscovite predecessors many times over, but his success in enforcing laws was patchy and his efforts to codify the laws came to nothing, so the vast body of old and new legal acts remained scattered in the archives of state departments. Often even the judges, who received no special training, did not know the laws. The Military and Naval Statutes, which at least existed in single published editions, were used for both civil and criminal cases well into the eighteenth century and Tsar Alexis's law code of 1649 continued to operate. Catherine II's attempt to codify the laws also failed, although she presented the exercise in a Petrine framework. A miniature portrait (1770–80) of Catherine writing her 1767 *Instruction to the Legislative Commission* features a marble bust of Peter on the desk beside her.[10] Codification was achieved only in the 1830s.

After Peter's death some of his own favourite legislation was repealed. This was the fate in 1731 of the Law on Single Inheritance of 1714, never popular with the land-owning service class. The 1722 law on the succession to the throne survived to determine the accession of six monarchs – Catherine I, Peter II, Anna, Ivan VI, Peter III and Paul – while two others (Elizabeth and Catherine II) used palace coups to establish their claims, then evoked Peter's spirit. The law was repealed in 1797 by Paul, who had lived in fear of his mother disinheriting him in favour of one of his sons. Thereafter for the rest of the Romanov era primogeniture was restored, which meant, among other things, no more women rulers.

It suited both the rulers and the elite to live with amended versions of some of Peter's civil reforms, for example the Table of Ranks, which survived to the end of imperial Russia. Peter did not intend to do away with a hereditary élite in principle, nor did he do so in practice. In 1730, for example, of the 179 officials in the top four classes of the Table, nine-tenths were descended from old Muscovite noble families and one-third from men who recently had been boyars. After Peter's death it became harder for outsiders to enter the Table. By the 1770s anyone liable to poll tax was excluded and it became harder to become a hereditary noble by being promoted within the civilian ranks. At the same time, it suited both the servitors and the state to reduce the period of compulsory service. In 1736 service was reduced to twenty-five years and in 1762 the requirement was abolished, although state service remained a way of life for most nobles.

Peter made an indelible impression on the church, which remained firmly subordinated to the state and without a patriarch until 1917, after which Russia's new Bolshevik masters reduced it even more brutally under a patriarch of their own choosing. For the rest of the imperial era the Holy Synod governed the church and the over-procurator watched over its personnel. There was no reversal of Peter's policy of reducing the church's financial independence and restricting entry into monasteries, principles which later in the century gained the seal of approval from the luminaries of the Enlightenment. Under Peter III and Catherine II peasants on monastery estates (about two million souls) were transferred from the church to the jurisdiction of the State College of Economy. At the same time, all Peter's successors, like Peter himself, promoted the centrality of Orthodoxy to the Russian way of life, exploiting religion as an element in foreign policy when appropriate. Foreigners were free to worship in their own churches – there was no official revival of the old Muscovite ghetto mentality – but attempts to convert Russians were strictly outlawed. Peter never intended to secularise Russia or to throw it open to proselytising by other faiths, only to limit the church's power to those areas which the state deemed to be the church's business. For the mass of the people the church, its calendar and its culture continued to play much the same central role in their lives as they had done for their Muscovite ancestors. From Nicholas I onwards, the term 'Holy Russia' (rarely, if ever, heard in the eighteenth century) was revived and Orthodox principles were vigorously promoted in élite circles, too.

Peter's impact on the Russian economy is more controversial. The jury is still out on the question of whether he accelerated or slowed the development of capitalism in Russia. On the face of it, he produced success stories – the two dozen or so factories in operation when Peter came to the throne grew to almost 200 by his death. He did not accumulate a foreign debt. Russia was

self-sufficient in some areas of arms and textile manufacture and poised to
become the world's leading producer of pig iron by the 1740s. The opening
of new sea and river routes, the acquisition of ports, the development of a
merchant marine – all should have fostered wealth-creating trade. However,
private enterprise remained weak, little capital was accumulated, much trade
was in the hands of foreigners, as were insurance and banking, and towns
were underdeveloped. There was no 'great leap forward'. Peter's economy
operated in a traditional framework: war or defence created its momentum,
autocracy and serfdom allowed Peter to cope with military demands. It boiled
down to making the most of Russia's 'backwardness' by applying absolute
power to extract service, labour and taxes from all parts of the population,
with the bulk coming from the 90 per cent who were peasants. The state
played a disproportionate role in industrial growth and continued to do so for
the rest of the tsarist era. Under Peter's immediate successors the biggest
improvements to the national economy came not in industry but in agriculture, when expansion into the black-earth steppe lands in Catherine II's reign
produced a surplus of grain and other produce for export. The winners
tended to be those nobles who successfully exploited the manorial economy
rather than industrialists, the most successful of whom aspired to become
nobles. Ironically, some of the most successful private entrepreneurs were Old
Believers, who accumulated capital by mutual self-help and thrift without
aspiring to join the imperial establishment.

World power

Ultimately, the sacrifices made by all sections of the population were justified by international success. Peter made Russia a great power, which it
remained by and large, until very recently. (To assess whether currently
Russia is going up in the world or coming down is beyond the scope of this
book.) When the Senate in its address to Peter in October 1721 boasted that
Russia had 'joined the community of political nations' it had in mind
nations high up in the international pecking order and in control of their
own destinies. 'Political' nations concurred that Peter's Russia was a force in
world politics, not only its immediate neighbours, but also France, Spain and
particularly Britain, which feared the effect of Russian expansion on its Baltic
trade. 'Thanks to him Russia, the name of which was unknown not long
ago,' wrote Campredon in 1723, 'now has become the object of attention of
the greater part of European powers who seek her friendship, some for fear
of seeing her hostile to their interests, others for the sake of the benefits
which they hope to obtain through an alliance.'[11] In 1726 Russia signed a
defensive alliance with Austria, which proved to be a cornerstone of international politics.

But Russia's relationship with the wider world is also one of the most controversial aspects of Peter's legacy. His notorious 'Testament', first published in France in 1812, was long ago unmasked as a forgery. Even so, for all its absurdities, this plan for expansion inspired by unbridled ambition reflected certain tendencies in Russia's imperial policy in the eighteenth century. Peter built on or laid the foundations of policies – participation as a full partner in world diplomacy and in European dynastic politics, keeping Poland weak, expansion towards the 'natural' boundaries of coastlines and/or fellow Orthodox populations, probes into alien territory for exploration and trade – which were to bring Russia into conflict with other powers and give birth to the image of the aggressive Russian 'bear', intervening on behalf of the Orthodox in the Ottoman empire, partitioning Poland, playing the 'great game' in Central Asia.

Some modern historians have argued that of all Peter's legacies, great power status, the most glorious according to the rhetoric of eighteenth-century power politics, was the most destructive. Expansion fuelled by autocracy and serfdom created demands which perpetuated these two institutions, keeping the Russian people poor and enslaved. The impetus for devoting most of the national budget to defence was created by fear not only of foreign enemies across the borders, but also of disaffected subjects inside the expanding empire. The growth of empire created 'strategic overstretch' in a country without overseas colonies whose most easily exploitable natural resource was its own population. In order to justify sacrifices, even in peacetime a strong army and navy were equated with national pride, boasted about in official publicity and displayed on ceremonial occasions. All Russia's emperors from Peter onwards presented themselves primarily as soldiers and preferred to be surrounded by military and naval men. Even the eighteenth-century empresses sometimes donned the uniform of the guards.

In his intense personal involvement in things military Peter set a dangerous precedent, particularly in respect of the fleet, which became a vital component in the myth of Peter's fashioning of Russia 'out of nothingness', a feat with biblical resonances. 'He was your first Japhet!' declared Prokopovich in his funeral oration. 'He has accomplished a deed hitherto unheard of in Russia: the building and sailing of ships, of a new fleet that yields to none among the old ones. It was a deed beyond the whole world's expectations and admiration and it opened up to thee, Russia, the way to all corners of the earth and carried thy power and glory to the remotest oceans.'[12] In Peter's time this enthusiasm was not widely shared. 'The Russian nation has little inclination for naval affairs but rather regards it all as an unnecessary expense,' commented Georg Grund. 'The fleet is regarded more as a whim of the tsar's than an essential for Russia's military strength.'[13] Peter's immediate successors lacked the personal commitment and resources to keep the fleet going and by the 1730s Russia to all intents and purposes lacked a viable fleet. 'The Muscovites do not seem to be such a terrible people as they were when the Czar was living,' wrote Vice-Admiral Sir Charles Wagner in 1726.[14] Yet as an essential component in Russia's great power status the fleet was not easily abandoned and was revived under Catherine II. The Russian historian Evgeny Anisimov has compared the cost of building and maintaining a navy in the early modern world with that of developing a space programme in the later twentieth century. It is an apt analogy, especially in the Russian context. Both Peter's navy and the USSR's space rockets generated a host of symbols above and beyond their immediate function, conveying the clear message that Russia was a major contender on the world stage, equipped with the means of conquering worlds beyond its immediate frontiers. At the same time, both attracted criticism for wasting public funds which might have been put to better use.

Window on the West

Perhaps the longest-running debate about Peter's legacy concerns Russian national identity. Peter never called St Petersburg his 'window on the West' (the phrase seems to have originated with the Italian traveller Francesco Algarotti's reference in 1739 to 'this great window recently opened in the north through which Russia looks on Europe'[15]) but more than anything else he created, the city became associated with his vision of making Russia more Western. Sankt-Piter-Burkh (strictly speaking, the city of St Peter rather than 'Peter's city') was Peter's creation, even if he left just the vision and outline of his 'Paradise' rather than the finished product. The everyday reality in 1725 and for years to come was a sort of ribbon development, with splendid buildings jostling for space on the embankments and behind them wretched hovels and general squalor. Rural disorder always threatened to disrupt the symmetry of the model city. A series of edicts issued during the tsar's lifetime warned residents not to allow cows, goats, pigs and other livestock to wander around the streets unless accompanied by herdsmen, but repetitions of the orders show that no one paid much attention to them. The Russian countryside was never far away, even in the capital.

When Peter died St Petersburg was only twenty-two years old and most of its major buildings less than fifteen years old. Few of its inhabitants had lived there for much more than ten years, yet their lives had been transformed, especially those of the élite. Memoirs of the period immediately after Peter's death show that the lifestyle introduced under Peter did not change: fireworks, illuminations, balls, mixed company were the order of the day, even if Peter's 'democratic' assemblies were abandoned in favour of more exclusive gatherings. For upper-class women in particular there was to be no return to the segregated *terem* (how could there be, with empresses on the throne?), even if a woman's function in society, like that of her Western counterparts, was still to make a suitable marriage, be a decorative companion and produce children. There was some talk among conservatives, it is true, of a return to Moscow, after Peter II's court was based there throughout his short reign. A writer in the *British Journal* in March 1730 voiced fears that inland trade would not be revived 'unless the Empire of Russia rouses itself from under the lethargic slumber, which it is now fallen into; their furred Gowns and long Petticoats will return upon them; and all the sordid affectation of a singularity from all the world, which made them so truly contemptible before, will do the like again ... '[16] These fears (or hopes, for those European neighbours who would have preferred to see Russia marginalised) were unfounded. After her coronation in 1731 Empress Anna returned the court to St Petersburg and sponsored aspects of Western culture which were barely developed in Peter's reign, such as ballet and opera. Peter's successors built on his cultural legacy, extending it more widely through the empire, as for example in Catherine II's programme for reconstructing the centres of provincial capitals in the classical style, although the mass of the population were unaffected.

Secular publishing, especially of practical manuals, experienced a sharp decline once Peter's personal sponsorship was removed. Several presses were closed and by 1728 as a result of huge deficits and unsold stock Peter's publishing operation was all but dismantled. In the late 1720s only about twenty books were published each year. But as their service requirement was reduced, some of the élite had more time to devote to reading and in some cases writing. The Academy of Sciences became a major publisher of scientific and scholarly literature and in Elizabeth's reign, and particularly in Catherine II's, translations of major works of European literature and philosophy became available in print, as well as works by Russian authors. Peter's project for an Academy of Arts was finally realised in 1757, when Russian artists were trained to work in areas of the figurative arts such as sculpture and history painting which in Peter's reign had been practised almost exclusively by foreigners. Peter did not secularise Russian culture, although he changed the priorities of high culture irrevocably. There continued to be a strong demand for religious art and architecture and most Western-trained Russian artists working in the capitals painted icons as well as secular works. In 1764, for example, the painter A. P. Antropov sent a petition to Catherine II requesting payment for an icon of the Nativity of Christ, two shrouds with Christ's image and two portraits of the empress which he had painted for her coronation, a characteristic mix of the sacred and secular.

Peter, as we know, regarded Western dress as a signifier of civilisation, and at court and in upper-class homes Western norms were firmly established. The Russian male élite remained clean-shaven until beards came back into fashion in the latter half of the nineteenth century. Alexander III was the first Romanov since the seventeenth century to wear a beard, in his case a deliberate signifier of his Russianness. Outside St Petersburg, of course, dress rules were often flouted. In 1726 the authorities learned that officers and non-commissioned officers on leave or in retirement were going around with beards and wearing old-fashioned Russian dress. Peter's decree was reiterated, with the concession that in the absence of a barber the beard could be trimmed with scissors. Infringements met with fines or flogging and deprivation of patents of nobility for any officer who committed a fourth offence.[17] Even some leading nobles were reluctant to throw away their old clothes. An inventory of the belongings of Princes A. G and I. A. Dolgoruky made as a result of their banishment in 1730 contained large quantities of men's and women's pre-reform clothing, easily recognised by the different vocabulary used to describe it. In the reign of Catherine II, Old Russian dress in stylised form began to make a comeback for ladies at court for special occasions. In 1826, an observer at Nicholas I's coronation ball commented approvingly on women wearing what he described as 'patriotic attire', recalling a time 'when Russians were not ashamed of their splendid dress, proper for the climate, which had a national character and was incomparably more beautiful than foreign dress'.[18] Even so, 'Russian style' remained a sort of fancy dress reserved for grand special occasions.

It has been argued on the one hand that Peter's cultural reforms led to a loss of national identity and created a deep rift between the élite and the mass of the population; on the other, that his over-ambitious experiment in cultural engineering produced only a superficial imitation of European civilisation. The picture of noble life in the provinces in the seventeenth century as one of 'almost unrelieved rudeness and coarseness, with a frequently repeated motif of drunkenness and violence' probably changed little in the decades after Peter's death.[19] For a few Russians, however, 'becoming Europeans' had more profound implications than just wearing Western dress and speaking bad French, which, incidentally, became the language of the court in the latter part of the eighteenth century, not in Peter's reign. Becoming more like an Englishman or a Frenchman or a Pole meant demanding a parliament, a free press, corporate rights, a constitutional or elective monarchy. Peter himself had challenged the old Orthodox medieval world view, valid for boyar and peasant alike, in which behaviour was determined by authority and custom, while access to other worlds, either through books or travel, was severely restricted. He encouraged selected Russians to travel abroad, promoted exploration and scientific enquiry, had Western books translated and published and encouraged the learning of foreign languages. Such policies produced at least a handful of questioning individuals, of which Peter himself represented a striking example. The walls of the citadel of medieval Muscovy, in which subjects were locked in and women were locked up, were breached, both by foreigners coming in and Russians going out. The superiority of old Russia, once upheld unquestioningly by guardians of the true faith, was challenged by the need to study at the feet of 'heretics'. But what gave the reforms their impetus – the example of the tsar himself and his challenge to the traditional image of the Orthodox ruler – also set the limits, for this was reform from above.

Peter enjoyed absolute power, ruling without limitation by any elected or corporate bodies. A succinct formula, borrowed from the Swedish, appears in both the Military and Naval Statutes: 'His Majesty is a sovereign monarch, who is not answerable to anyone in the world in his affairs, but holds the power and authority to rule his realms and his lands as a Christian monarch by his own will and good opinion.'[20] Here at least he left no experiment to be discarded or amended by his successors. The fact that he chose sometimes to defer to the Prince-Caesar or dress like a shipwright emphasised his power rather than detracted from it. Pluralism, the glimmerings, however feeble, of civil society, was killed at birth because the demands of war, which required everyone's efforts to be harnessed, did not allow Peter to break with authoritarian rule. Ironically, the Russian nation's new-style mobility – young men sent abroad to study, women forced to come out and socialise in public, nobles and their families uprooted from Moscow to St Petersburg, whole villages of peasants transferred *en masse* to work on major new projects – was regarded as just as oppressive as the Moscow-centred ethos of Old Russia.

Few of Peter's successors were as good as he was at getting what they wanted, but they all ruled as autocrats. Two attempts by élite circles to limit autocracy – in 1730 when a small group of top nobles tried to impose a set of conditions on Empress Anna and in 1825 when the Decembrists gathered around the Bronze Horseman statue to demand the abolition of autocracy and serfdom – ended in disgrace or death for the rebels. When autocracy was finally limited, in 1906, Nicholas II (urged by his wife to 'be Peter the Great') pretended that it hadn't been and almost got away with clawing back concessions until war and revolution swept the old regime away. The long life of Russia's particular brand of absolute monarchy, on which Peter set an indelible seal, suggests that the system was effective as long as Russia was successful.

Reformer or revolutionary? Views of Peter from the 1720s to the 1980s

To conclude this chapter, let us return to the broad outlines of the debate about Peter over the centuries. (For a much fuller treatment of this topic readers should consult the invaluable works of Nicholas Riasanovsky.) Frederick Weber began his influential book on Russia thus: 'It must be owned not only by all who have been in Russia themselves, but also by those who have any Notion of the Affairs of the North, that for about these twenty Years past Russia has been entirely reformed and changed.'[21] Ivan Nepliuev, looking back on Peter's reign in old age, wrote: 'This monarch brought our fatherland to a level with others; he taught us to recognise that we are people too;

in a word, whatever you look at in Russia, all has its beginnings with him and whatever is done henceforth will also derive its source from that beginning.'[22] As we have seen, neither of these statements is entirely true. Autocracy was not limited, the mass of the Russian population remained enserfed, small towns and villages hardly changed at all and many of the changes that did occur – in the armed forces, the church, culture – were heralded in the reigns of Peter's predecessors. But, viewed with the eyes of a foreigner who witnessed the growth of St Petersburg and the external transformation of its population at first hand or a servitor from an old noble family who was sent on naval training and became a diplomat, Peter must have seemed like a revolutionary. Men in the thick of things like Weber and Nepliuev experienced the full force of the rhetoric which presented Peter as a creative genius and they also encountered the man in the flesh, whose energetic commitment to change was so palpable that both those who welcomed change and those who feared it were convinced he really did have the power to transform Russia, for good or ill, by his own will. What is remarkable is that this impression has never been erased. Apart from a brief interlude during Soviet times, the debate about Peter always starts from the premise that he made a difference.

The view from above, which prevailed for much of the eighteenth and nineteenth centuries, is epitomised in a laudatory speech composed in 1755 by the first full-time member of the Russian Academy of Sciences, Mikhail Lomonosov, himself a beneficiary of Peter's educational reforms, in which he imagines a man leaving Russia at the beginning of Peter's reign and returning much later. On seeing new buildings and customs, the fleet, the arts, knowledge, even rivers altered in their courses, this man would conclude 'that he had been on his travels many centuries, or that all this had been achieved in so short a time by the common efforts of the whole human race or by the creative hand of the Almighty, or, finally, that it was all a vision seen in a dream'.[23] The notion that Peter accomplished in a few decades what otherwise would have taken centuries, belief in the power of one strong individual to transform a whole country were variously expressed in the imagery of turning darkness into light, non-existence into being, or raw stone into a statue. It remained a central pillar of official ideology until the collapse of the empire. As the historian M. P. Pogodin wrote in 1841:

> The Russia of today, that is European Russia, diplomatic, political, military, commercial, industrial, scholarly, literary – is the creation of Peter the Great. Wherever we look, everywhere we encounter that colossal figure, which throws a long shadow over our entire past, and even eliminates old history from our field of vision – a figure which is still stretching, as it were, its arms over us, and which, it seems, will never disappear from sight, no matter how far we advance in the future.[24]

The first writer seriously to question the benefits of Peter's legacy was Prince Mikhail Shcherbatov (1733–90), who knew the Petrine era better than most of his contemporaries as a result of his work in Peter's archive. Shcherbatov conceded that without Peter Russia would have needed another two hundred years to reach the level of development it had achieved. He praised Peter's promotion of science and rejection of ignorance, his attacks on xenophobia, his conquest of coasts, his ports and fleet. But he also deplored his cruelty, his subordination of the nobility, his treatment of Alexis and the succession, his attacks on religion and custom, and his neglect of Moscow. Shcherbatov's particular target was the 'corruption of morals': women, who in Muscovy had been 'unaware of their beauty, began to realise its power; they began to try to enhance it with suitable clothes, and used far more luxuries in their adornments than their ancestors'. Men, too, in their desire to be attractive to women, strove after self-adornment and 'voluptuousness and luxury'. There was a high price to pay for Westernisation, both literally and figuratively.[25]

Russia's first major historian, Nikolai Karamzin (1766–1826), an admirer of Peter in his youth but influenced by new thinking about national identity and national spirit later in life, assessed the impact of Peter's reforms even more radically than Shcherbatov. In his view, without Peter Russia would have needed six hundred years to catch up. But he too believed that 'progress' had been bought at a high price:

> Family customs were not spared by the impact of the tsar's activity. The lords opened up their homes; their wives and daughters emerged from the impenetrable *teremy*; men and women began to mingle in noise-filled rooms at balls and suppers; Russian women ceased to blush at the indiscreet glances of men, and European freedom supplanted Asiatic constraint .... We became citizens of the world but ceased in certain respects to be citizens of Russia. The fault is Peter's.[26]

Alexander Pushkin, who was at heart an admirer of Peter, gathering material for an unfinished history of his reign, gave poetic form to the doubting voice, notably in *The Bronze Horseman* (1833) which weighs up Peter's magnificent achievement as epitomised by St Petersburg against the lost happiness of the humble clerk, Evgeny, who dares to challenge the 'idol' on the horse.

The issue of Peter and Russian national identity was developed more fully in the debate between the Westernisers and the Slavophiles in the 1830s–50s, which was inaugurated by the claim of Peter Chaadaev (1794–1856) in his first 'Philosophical Letter' (published in 1836) that once 'a great man wanted to civilize us, and in order to give us a foretaste of enlightenment, he threw us the mantle of civilization: we took up the cloak but did not so much as touch civilization'. Chaadaev was unpatriotically scathing about Russia's lack of achievements, but in a later work he conceded that, since Peter, Russia's path had been irrevocably Western – 'In his hand Peter found only a blank sheet of paper, and he wrote on it: Europe and the West' – and acknowledged the advantages of backwardness which would allow Russia in time to surpass the West; for 'if we have come after others, it is in order to do better than the others'.[27] Some Westernisers like Vissarion Belinsky (1811–48) adulated Peter – 'the greatest phenomenon not only of our history, but also of the history of all mankind; he is the divinity that called us to live, breathing a living soul into the body of the old Russia, colossal but plunged in deathly slumber'[28] – convinced that Peter's work was incomplete and that further radical political and social reform was needed. In particular, civilisation must be brought to the peasants. Slavophiles, on the other hand, stressed the destructive nature of Peter's reforms, which they deplored as the essentially non-Russian products of Western rationalism, of which artificial St Petersburg was the worst manifestation. They were thankful that the peasants at least had retained their national character, as expressed through their pure Orthodox faith and the peasant commune. In the words of Konstantin Aksakov (1817–60), the government 'must understand the spirit of Russia and embrace Russian principles, which have been rejected since Peter's day'.[29] He and his fellow Slavophiles painted an idyllic picture of Muscovite Russia, with its allegedly harmonious relationship between tsar and people and its indigenous religious culture. Peter was cast in the role of villain, to the extent that the Slavophile Peter Kireevsky loathed his own name.

In the latter half of the nineteenth century professional historians such as S. M. Solov'ev (1820–79) and V. O. Kliuchevsky (1841–1911) revealed much more fully the Muscovite roots of many of Peter's reforms, as well as chronicling and analysing Peter's reign on the basis of scholarly research on primary sources, which tended to reveal the often chaotic and piecemeal nature of his activities. They took a pragmatic, warts and all, view of Peter himself (some of the most famous passages in Kliuchevsky's history described his violent, drunken habits) but they still maintained that Peter spelled Progress, allowing Russia to achieve its rightful status as a world power. 'Not one nation has ever achieved such a feat as the one achieved by the Russian nation under the leadership of Peter,' wrote Kliuchevsky.[30] Only towards the end of the tsarist era did academic historians such as Paul Miliukov (1859–1943), working on the basis of extensive primary research on the economy in particular, dwell on the violence, the arbitrariness and the sacrifices, 'the paucity of the results compared with the magnitude of the wasted resources'.[31] Even in Miliukov's work and that of other late tsarist historians, Peter remained central to debates about Russia's place in the world and its destiny. Works of fiction, too, like Dmitry Merezhkovsky's *Antichrist (Peter and Alexis)* (1904–5) based on a metaphysical scheme involving the juxtaposition and clash of opposites – pagan and Christian values – represented the clash between Peter and Tsarevich Alexis as a battle for Russia.

After 1917 this emphasis looked set to change: the lives of the pre-revolutionary great and good, especially Russian tsars who had 'exploited the masses', surely would have no place in the new ideological framework, which stressed the collective over the individual, the common man over the monarch. Following the toppling of monuments to tsars, which we consider in our final chapter, in the late 1920s/early 1930s there were attempts to write 'great' men out of the narrative and replace them with economic forces and class warfare. The enormously influential historian and Party activist M. N. Pokrovsky (1869–1932) based his Marxist analysis of the 'Petrine' era on the rise of merchant capital, of which Peter was the agent. Peter himself was stripped of all heroism and charisma. Another influential historian, M. A. Rozhkov, identified the 'gentry revolution' as the key element, allotting little space to Peter himself, except to underline his crudeness. If some early Soviet historians made Peter less interesting, some avant-garde literature of the 1920s, when censorship was still perfunctory, cast aside all restraints to produce a grotesquely over-the-top image. Boris Pil'niak, for example, presented Peter as 'an abnormal man, always drunk, a syphilitic, neurasthenic, who suffered from psychotic fits, fits of despair and violence, who strangled his son with his bare hands, a man absolutely without a sense of responsibility, contemptuous of everything, who to the end of his life failed to understand either the historical logic or the physiology of national life. A maniac. A coward.'[32]

Both these trends were short-lived, as early Soviet pluralism was restricted and Stalin's regime embraced the exemplary lives, even the cults, of living and recently dead new heroes, together with the selective revival of some key figures from the more distant past. As Stalin said, 'Marxism does not at all deny the role of outstanding individuals.' Revived heroes from the past were carefully refashioned to meet ideological needs, to serve as role models for citizens or historical prototypes for party leaders. Stalin did not admire Peter as much as he admired Ivan the Terrible, but he appreciated certain parallels between Peter and himself. 'When Peter the Great, who had to deal with more developed countries in the West, feverishly built works and factories for supplying the army and strengthening the country's defences,' wrote Stalin in 1928, 'this was an original attempt to leap out of the framework of backwardness.'[33] It was a commonplace of Marxist-Leninist thinking that Russia had to 'catch up' with (and eventually overtake) the West, whatever the cost. Hence Peter's reformed government, army and navy, factories and education were all to the good. In the Second World War the hero of Poltava and Hangö was harnessed to the cause. Most importantly, Peter's example seemed to demonstrate that people could be changed, but that in order to create new men and women, you had to get rid of the old. Of course, Marxist–Leninist historians were bound to denounce Peter's exploitation of the peasantry and praise popular rebels such as Bulavin. Peter's 'cosmopolitanism' was also roundly condemned. Cultural historians stressed native achievements over foreign borrowings. This bipolar view of Peter and his reforms prevailed for the rest of the Soviet era.

Oddly enough, it was difficult for Soviet historians to tackle the 'bizarre' phenomena of Peter's life because they were difficult to integrate and to reconcile with the rational, teleological approach to his reign as one of modernisation grounded in materialism and class interest, viewed with reference to Russia's fundamental needs in respect of the expansion of empire, international relations and economic, social and cultural development. When 'anti-behaviour' was mentioned at all in orthodox Soviet works, it was usually given a didactic interpretation: Peter was providing lessons, examples and models of how *not* to behave or exercises in satire, mocking and undermining the old and the traditional in the interests of modernisation. His 'modesty' and his 'simplicity' were taken at face value: he could be the 'people's tsar' (Lenin and Stalin enjoyed a similar reputation) at the same time as he chastised the people for their own good.

In the 1980s the old Soviet certainties began to crumble. Mikhail Gorbachev conceived his perestroika as broadly 'Petrine' in outline and a number of commentators in Russia and abroad spotted the analogies between Peter and Gorbachev as reforming leaders who 'acted alone'. Gorbachev's visits to the West, his economic reforms, his borrowing of Western technology, even his 'imitation' of the dress and manners of Western statesmen, seemed to recall the opening of Peter's 'window' on Europe. Yet it was argued that, like Peter, Gorbachev was motivated less by concern for people than by love of empire and that his main goal was the preservation of the USSR's superpower status under the one-party state. He had no more intention of discarding Communism than Peter had of discarding autocracy. In respect of this analogy, Peter was the more successful of the two.

A contributory factor to the collapse of Communism in Russia was Gorbachev's new openness or *glasnost*, which gave rise, among other things, to new historical writing and attempts to fill in the gaps (in Russian, 'white spots') in the historical record. Although the most spectacular revelations related to twentieth-century Russia, there was also some new thinking about Peter's reign, notably with reference to certain negative parallels with Communist Russia which previously could only be hinted at. The St Petersburg historian Evgeny Anisimov characterised Peter as 'the creator of the administrative-command system and the true ancestor of Stalin', who laid the foundations of the totalitarian state, treating subjects like children with 'the pedagogy of the cudgel' in order to achieve progress in the name of the 'common good'. He argued that Peter destroyed alternatives ('civil society'), notably the church, and created the 'well-regulated police state' with its reliance on spying mechanisms and controls. Referring to the debate about capitalism in Russia, a central issue in the experimental economic climate of the 1980s, Anisimov argued that Peter weakened individual enterprise by increasing 'the overriding role of the state in the life of society as a whole'. What was missing were competition and freedom.

Some of the most stimulating writing on Peter's reign produced in this period occurred in the work of semioticians of the Tartu school, led by Iury Lotman, who offered an approach to culture through the study of signs. Their Peter was not just a conventional military commander with exclusively practical goals, but a master of ceremonies, a leading actor or 'player' with the power to 'toy' with armies, fleets, towns and people. Wars, battles and sieges, diplomacy with its elaborate conventions and rituals, not to mention courtly life could be approached as masquerade, role play and theatricalisation; Peter's deference to Prince-Caesar was presented as a semiotic struggle, a polemic with the traditional Muscovite concept of how a true tsar should behave. Very much at odds with the rational, materialistic approach to history still favoured in official academic circles, at the time the work of the Russian semoticians probably influenced Western scholars more than their Russian counterparts.

It is significant that Lotman was based at Tartu in Estonia, a republic which enjoyed higher standards of living and more freedom of expression than the Russian heartland. In 1991 Estonia and the other Baltic states, which had been the main pickings of Peter's wars, declined to join Gorbachev's Commonwealth of Independent States and the USSR itself was swept away. How Peter himself has fared in post-Soviet Russia we shall return to at the end of our final chapter.

XII

Commemorating Peter
1725–2002

In the 1840s a mad government clerk called Timofeev was arrested for climbing on to the Bronze Horseman statue and trying to knock the figure off the horse, on the grounds that he, Timofeev, was Peter I and the horseman was an impostor. Nicholas I asked to see the madman, who kept shouting 'I want to sit on the bronze horse!' Nicholas ordered a wooden horse to be made to look like the Falconet statue, painted bronze and taken to the hospital. Timofeev calmed down and spent many days sitting on the horse in the pose of Falconet's Peter.[1]

Paintings and statues: 1725–1917

No other Russian ruler has been depicted so often and commemorated over such a long period of time as Peter, whose familiar visage, the first consistently recognisable likeness of any Russian ruler, stares out from paintings, prints, illustrations, statues, busts, enamels, carvings, tapestries, artefacts, medals, coins, banknotes and, more recently, advertisements. Stalin and Lenin had more statues, paintings and memorabilia dedicated to them, but the phenomenon of 'Leniniana' and 'Staliniana' was short-lived, whereas the production of images of Peter continues to the present day. The proliferation of Peter's image owed much to the fact that his successors were anxious to present themselves as his heirs and also, in ways less easy to define, reflected his popularity (or notoriety) with different sections of Russian society. Visual representations, places where he lived and stayed, museums dedicated to him, objects which belonged to him or which he made, anniversaries celebrating landmarks in his life and career, have arguably contributed as much to his image over the centuries as the writings of historians, novelists and poets, but they have not been so systematically catalogued and analysed. They gave Peter a visible, palpable, but often ambiguous afterlife and make a fitting conclusion to our portrait of Russia's most influential and controversial ruler.

A striking early example was Rastrelli's wax figure, which, dressed in the suit that Peter had worn at Catherine's coronation in 1724, seemed to express silent approval of her succession. In its reincarnation as a museum exhibit it drew curious crowds, who were intrigued by the figure's uncannily lifelike qualities and by rumours that it contained a mechanism which allowed it to stand up and sit down. Rastrelli's 1723 bronze bust of Peter was perhaps even more influential in inspiring numerous copies in metal, marble and plaster for displaying in public places. In imperial Russia Peter's portraits stood or hung in places of honour in all the royal residences, copies (often bad ones) of well-known works painted from life by Caravaque, Dannhauer, Kneller, Kupetsky, Moor, Nattier, Nikitin and others rubbing shoulders with new compositions, which in turn were reproduced as prints for wider dissemination and to illustrate the copious literature, both factual and fictional, devoted to Peter and his reign. In his magisterial study of Russian engraved portraits D. S. Rovinsky devoted 778 entries to Peter, each with numerous subdivisions of portrait types. In the nineteenth century, artists and sculptors brought the Petrine era to life in historical compositions on such themes as the boy Peter discovering his first boat, Peter punishing the strel'tsy and the ever-popular Peter rescuing the sailors.

A systematic study of posthumous portraits of Peter is beyond the scope of this book, so let us focus on a selection of the more interesting ones. One of the most important was Jacopo Amigoni's large allegorical composition of Peter Victorious (1732–37), which hangs in the small throne room of the Winter Palace. The themes are war and victory: Peter looks self-assured, even self-satisfied, his booted right foot placed firmly on a mortar. To his right lie drums, to his left a pile of books rests on a map of a fortress, indicating conquests, while behind him stands Minerva/Victory holding a spear and gesturing at warships in the background, her head inclined admiringly towards the hero. Above the two figures, hovering putti place a laurel wreath on Peter's head. The painting, produced in the reign of Anna, contains an allusion to female rule (Anna/ Elizabeth/ Catherine as Minerva became a cliché), as well as to Russia's adulation of her manly protector, who watches over her still.

The most famous of all images of Peter must surely be Etienne Falconet's equestrian statue, unveiled in St Petersburg in 1782 and inscribed with the words TO PETER THE FIRST FROM CATHERINE THE SECOND in Russian and Latin, the first public monument to be erected in Russia. One of Peter's personae, as we have seen, was that of a sculptor, who takes a raw, shapeless block of stone and gives it form. In the Petrine discourse, the raw block was Old Russia (barbarism, disorder), the resultant beautiful statue New Russia (civilisation, order), which itself was Peter's monument. Falconet gave a brilliant twist to this discourse of imperial creative genius pitted against popular barbarism by incorporating an actual raw block of stone into his composition. The boulder known as the 'Thunder Stone' on which the horse stands, its shape also appropriately reminiscent of a wave, was said to be a rock on which Peter often stood to look out over the Finnish gulf. It took more than five months in 1769–1770 to drag it from the forest to Senate Square, a heroic feat of suitably Petrine proportions. The original rock, incidentally, was much rougher and cruder, but Falconet could not resist smoothing and polishing it.

For his horse and rider Falconet rejected the rather static 'Marcus Aurelius' model usually favoured for public monuments to conquering heroes and created a new type of iconography, more dynamic and technically daring. The serpent being trampled beneath the horse's hooves complemented the metaphor of the unhewn rock by suggesting opposition (cunning, malice, envy), with a hint of St George's dragon. It and the horse's tail also provided essential support for the rearing steed, which appears to stand only on its hind legs. Peter is dressed not in a Muscovite caftan or in contemporary dress, but in something allegorical, which Falconet rather vaguely characterised as 'the clothing of all time, in a word, heroic clothing'. Falconet wasn't so good at doing faces. Peter's head, crowned with a laurel wreath, was modelled by his pupil Marie Collot, who worked from a life mask which Carlo Rastrelli took from Peter in 1719, to produce the slightly protruding eyes, pointed nose, and sharply outlined chin familiar from other sources.

At the unveiling in August 1782 canvas screens 12 metres high fell away and 'the carved image of the immortal Monarch appeared as though rising from the bowels of the earth. ... The Great Woman greeted the Great Man.'[2] Cannon fire boomed out from the fortress and from ships on the river and troops fired guns and beat drums as the Preobrazhensky and Semenovsky guards marched along the Neva embankment. Sons and grandsons of men who had seen the living Peter inspected his image and medals were handed out. Catherine, ever eager to confirm her own Petrine credentials, later wrote to her friend Friedrich Melchior Grimm: 'He [Peter] was too far away to speak to me but he seemed to have an air of contentment which encouraged me to do better in the future if I could.'[3] Probably more than any other work of art, the Bronze Horseman imprinted Peter's image, later filtered through Pushkin's poetic evocation, on the Russian consciousness.

Not everyone appreciated the statue's message of enlightenment. Some critics argued that Peter was forcing Russia to rear up, rather than to move forward. Taking a cue from Pushkin, whose poem brings the bronze 'idol' to life to pursue a hapless clerk, doubters have identified the serpent bent help-lessly beneath the trampling hooves with the victims of power rather than the forces of reaction or evil, and the bearskin on which the horseman sits with the bear-like Russian peasants, crushed under the burdens imposed by tsarism. After Catherine's death her son Paul brought Rastrelli's equestrian statue of Peter, cast in 1744 then hidden away, out of storage and added the inscription TO THE GRANDFATHER FROM THE GRANDSON, 1800, with the intention of removing Falconet's monument and replacing it with Rastrelli's, which Catherine apparently hated. Assassination intervened, but Rastrelli's statue still stands outside Paul's former residence, the Mikhailovsky fortress.

In the nineteenth and early twentieth centuries sculptors favoured more realistic, if still idealised, historical detail, as in Mark Antokol'sky's famous statue, modelled in 1872, of Peter in the uniform of the Preobrazhensky guards and the three-cornered hat from Poltava, holding a cane in his right hand and a telescope in his left. He looks purposefully into the distance and prepares to step forth, the sense of motion emphasised by his wind-blown garments. The statue was cast in bronze for the grounds of Peterhof in 1883 and for the bicentenary (1898) of the founding of Taganrog, where it was unveiled in 1903. Copies were produced for further Petrine anniversaries and in 1898 an engraving of the head and shoulders appeared on the 500-rouble banknote

Its nineteenth-century equivalent on canvas was P. Delaroche's much-reproduced portrait of Peter the conqueror, his right hand resting on a cannon barrel and holding a sword which points towards a map of the Baltic spread out over a boulder on which Peter rests his left arm. His expression is confident, stern and manly, his figure much broader and better proportioned than in real life. (Peter's surviving clothes and shoes indicate that he had narrow shoulders and small feet.) Informal group portraits featuring Peter as shipwright and sailor – working in the docks at Amsterdam or Deptford, relaxing with foreign sailors and so on – were also popular in the nineteenth century and no less part of the myth than the many studies of Peter as war hero. J. B. Michel's engraving from a painting by Wapper (1858) of Peter with shipbuilders in Zaandam has Peter gestering towards a model of a ship, a book open on the table in front of him, which is strewn with mathematical instruments. Such images were didactic in tone and popular for illustrating Russian children's history books.

Petrine subjects painted abroad sometimes had a different agenda. The Irish painter Daniel Maclise's historical composition *Peter at Deptford* (1857), for example, is a testament to the Victorian enthusiasm for the dignity of labour. The brawny tsar-carpenter (his features based on Kneller's portrait) posing with sleeves rolled up ready to do some vigorous sawing is contrasted with the slightly puny-looking, velvet-clad figure of William III, who has come to pay a visit. The painting also illustrates some of the exotic elements in Peter's entourage, which aroused gossip at the time – a monkey (said to have jumped at King William), a dwarf, and one of Peter's mistresses. By and large, Russian painters eschewed such 'unseemly' details.

Only in the last decades of tsarism did a few artists refuse to glamorise Peter, drawing on contemporary accounts of Peter's 'two faces' which so fascinated writers like Merezhkovsky, for example, the Duc de Saint-Simon's memorable evocation (1717) of an appearance imbued with 'intelligence, reflectiveness and grandeur', which for seconds at a time and without warning would be disfigured by muscular spasms that struck fear into the onlooker, giving Peter a 'wild and terrible air'.[4] The successful portraitist Valentin Serov described Peter as 'frightful-looking: long, on weak, spindly little legs and with a head so small in relation to the rest of his body that he must have looked more like a sort of dummy with a badly stuck on head than a live person'.[5] His own reconstructions of the Petrine era included *Peter the Great* (1907), which captured brilliantly Peter's great loping strides and his grim determination to keep walking in the face of a St Petersburg gale, as servants and officials struggle to keep pace, and *The Great Eagle Cup* (1904), in

which Peter leads a throng of courtiers, men and women, to one of his puni-
tive drinking sessions.

These slightly irreverent studies co-existed with the thoroughly idealised
images still favoured in official circles, which received a great boost from a
string of Petrine anniversaries in the first decades of the twentieth century.
The bicentenary of the battle of Poltava in 1909 inspired two more
Antokol'sky copies, one in front of the Cathedral of St Samson (also a Petrine
foundation), which was presented by two descendants of Peter's famous general B. P. Sheremetev, and another by the hospital of the Preobrazhensky regiment. In 1909–10 the historical compositions *Peter the Great Saving
Shipwrecked Fishermen* and *Tsar Carpenter*, both commissioned by Nicholas
II from the sculptor Leopold Bernshtam, were unveiled in front of the eastern wing and central arch of the Admiralty respectively.

In 1910 several Baltic towns conquered two hundred years previously
received Peter monuments in affirmation of their continued allegiance to
emperor and empire. The monument in Riga (Peter, it will be recalled, derived
much pleasure from the city's capitulation) was especially formidable, an
equestrian statue by the German sculptor Gustav Schmidt-Kassel set on a very
high plinth. Evacuated before the advancing German army in 1915, the statue
was lost in a shipwreck and raised from the bottom in 1934. The statue
unveiled in Reval in 1910 was removed from its central site in 1922 when
Estonia became independent, then reduced to just head and shoulders and
subsequently melted down during the Second World War. One of the most
chequered histories belongs to Bernshtam's statue of Peter in Viborg. In 1918,
when Russia ceded Viborg to Finland, it was replaced by a Finnish independence monument, which the Red Army removed in 1940 to make way for Peter
again, but in August 1941 the Nazis toppled Peter's statue, which lost its head.
It was repaired and restored by the Soviets in 1954, its fate and that of its fel-
lows illustrative of rival claims in the Baltic and the significance attached to
monuments in the conflicting quests for imperial expansion and national
independence. We return to the fate of other monuments later in this chapter.

Perhaps the most widely distributed of any of the late imperial images of
Peter was a copy of Jacobus Houbraken's famous engraved version of Moor's
1717 portrait (allegedly Peter's own favourite), which appeared in 1912 on the
new 500-rouble note. Set to the left of the note in an oval frame topped with
a crown and surrounded by fanciful swags and elaborate columns (a deterrent
to forgers), Peter's armour-clad image seems intended to reinforce confidence
in the currency and provide a reminder of the roots of Russia's prosperity
(suggested by the fecund-looking allegorical female figure representing Russia
opposite) in the expansion of empire and military might which Peter sponsored. These banknotes were in circulation for only a few years before the
Provisional Government and then the Bolsheviks replaced them with new
symbols and images.

Peter's places

A number of buildings and sites closely associated with Peter acquired the status of virtual shrines, where patriots could pay homage and young people imbibe Petrine virtues. The first memorial museum was inaugurated by Peter himself, who had a keen awareness of posterity. In 1723, the same year that he transferred the 'grandfather' of the fleet from Moscow to St Petersburg and set it on a plinth, Peter ordered the construction of a protective casing around his first St Petersburg cabin. By the middle of the eighteenth century visitors to this 'cradle of the Russian empire' could view the bench on which Peter sat to admire his fast-growing city, his skiff, workman's tools and objects made by him. Peter's preference for small wooden houses was, of course, a component in the myth of his self-effacing modesty. The author of the first Russian guide to St Petersburg devoted several pages to an exposition of the theme of 'Why such a Great Monarch should have chosen to dwell in such a small and wretched little house ... which, however, little though it was, was more exalted than the splendid palace of Emperor Cyrus, the many-chambered mansion of Solomon and as worthy of honour as splendid Versailles.'[6] The discourse of greatness achieved through humility dominated virtually all subsequent guides to the little house.

Pavel Svin'in, author of a pioneering early nineteenth-century description of the sights of St Petersburg, advised his readers to begin their city tour there, for 'nowhere perhaps does this Great man appear more worthy of respect and wonderment than in this humble cabin. . . . From this hut he, the Conqueror of Charles, forced arrogant Europe to respect him.' The cabin's very simplicity aroused a sense of deep reverence, fitting easily into the Sentimentalist/Romantic landscape and offering a lesson in aesthetics (the simple hut viewed against a picturesque background) as well as virtue.[7] Visitors were advised to combine a visit to the cabin with one to Peter's little boat in its neoclassical boathouse in the Peter-Paul Fortress, commissioned by Catherine II in 1766, where a similar lesson about modest beginnings could be appreciated.

Nicholas I was particularly generous to the little house, funding a new brick outer casing, ventilation and drainage channels. An 1838 children's guide to St Petersburg detailed the response expected of those who entered:

Why does this structure of simple architectural design stand among all these splendid buildings ? My friends, show reverence to this structure, for its walls conceal the little house of Peter the Great! We must remove our hats for we are approaching one of our country's holy places. . . . We cross the threshold and I see on your faces an expression of that holy rapture with which your pure, noble Russian souls overflow. You are struck dumb by the satisfaction of having the good fortune to be in the hut in which our immortal Peter lived.[8]

The children were admonished to kiss the boat which Peter made and to pray to the icon which he revered.

Peter's image was thus none too subtly refashioned to satisfy the requirements of Official Nationality (Orthodoxy, Autocracy, National Feeling), in which religious sentiment was a vital component. From Nicholas's reign onwards the cabin's focal point became the chapel in one of its rooms, which housed Peter's icon of the Saviour. 'Hundreds of candles flicker before the miraculous image and indeed a marvel worthy of the Great Peter is accomplished,' wrote the author of a much-reprinted guide to the cabin: 'it is as if his humble dwelling were transformed into a holy church for all those grieving, embittered and seeking God's mercy.'[9] Apparently a visit to the chapel was popular with students before examinations in April and May. In the words of a 1903 guide (the cabin was decorated for the bicentenary), the cabin was 'dear to the heart of every Russian person'.[10] Peter's modest example may not always have reflected well on his descendants, however. A 1914 handbook for rural teachers preparing their classes for a trip to the capital advised them to show their pupils a postcard of Peter's little house (many views were readily available for a few kopecks), drawing attention to its 'modest dimensions', then later to compare it with a picture of the Winter Palace. The visit to the little house was the recommended first stop. Later when they visited the Winter Palace, the author anticipated that some of the children themselves would make the comparison between the opulent residence and the simple cabin, but if not, the teacher was to do so.[11]

Some Petrine places were more elusive. In 1872 there was talk of erecting a monument on the spot where Peter died. But where was it? The old Winter Palace had been incorporated into the west wing of the palace extended by Catherine I, which in the 1770s was itself partly demolished and formed the foundations for Quarenghi's Hermitage Theatre. In the 1830s one A. L. Maier, whose mother had been born in the very same room (or a least that was what she was told), calculated that the 'sacred spot' was on the first floor in the second room along from the Neva on the corner of the Neva and Zimnaia Kanavka. A later investigator, using one of Quarenghi's plans, concluded that the study had disappeared, but that a portion of its outer wall, visible from the street, survived. A plaque was attached.[12]

A more tangible memorial site was Peter's tomb to the right of the altar in the Peter-Paul Cathedral, the first permanent version of which, as we saw, dated from Anna's reign. Lomonosov's project for a memorial in the form of mosaic panels to mark the fiftieth anniversary of the battle of Poltava in 1759 never materialised (only one Poltava mosaic was assembled and can be seen today in the St Petersburg Academy of Sciences) and the tomb remained more or less as it is now. The present white Italian marble sarcophagus was one of fifteen designed in 1865–67 by the architect A. A. Puaro and fitted with new metal plaques, after Alexander II discovered that the old tombstones

under their fabric covers were unpolished and chipped. Doing homage at
Peter's tomb was a must for visitors to the capital. Svin'in instructed his patriotic traveller to gaze at the cold stone, to recall the words of Prokopovich's
funeral sermon and remember Peter's great deeds for the happiness and glory
of millions, with feelings of love, respect and reverence.[13] Children using the
1838 guidebook referred to earlier were commanded: 'Get down on your
knees, children, before the tomb of Peter and with hot tears let us bedew this
monument and recall the deeds of the one who is hidden beneath this stone.'
Following Metropolitan Platon's example 'we too ask him to rise up and view
the achievements of his successors who try to imitate him'.[14] 'How many holy
thoughts and reminiscences well up in the soul with a single glance at the sar-
cophagi, made from simple stone without any decoration and clad in brocade
covers,' wrote another guide.

> Beneath them rest our crowned heads. Walking past a long row of graves
> of ordinary people one feels dejection and with involuntary sadness you
> look into the distance, at the empty plot which, perhaps, will receive your
> mortal remains; but standing above the tomb of the ruler of millions of
> subjects, who encompassed in his designs all the world, the father of the
> fatherland, you are struck by a strange sensation, which you experience
> fully but cannot express in words.[15]

Ordinary folk's encounters with dead great men were calculated to reinforce
the natural order of things.

Over the centuries the tomb was decorated with trophies, standards,
poems and medals. In the 1850s these included the flag from Chesme laid
there by Catherine in 1770, an 1803 medal, the measuring icon of St Peter in
a gold case and the bone chandelier made by Peter for the Martsial'nye
springs in 1724. On the eve of the First World War a guide recorded four icon
lamps, six medals (placed there for various anniversaries, including two in
1909), and seventeen silver wreaths. On the wall there was a bas-relief of
Antokol'sky's statue in Taganrog. Much of this paraphernalia was swept away
after 1917.

St Petersburg did not have a monopoly on Petrine shrines. In Voronezh, for
example, in the early 1830s there was a proposal to convert the only building
dating from Peter's time into a museum, filled with suitable furniture, portraits and other items (preferably belonging to Peter) and a book cupboard
containing books about his life and times. On a nearby hill, cleared of the
hovels which spoilt the view, an obelisk monument to Peter in a memorial
park was planned, In 1834 the new house-museum complex was officially
opened and a patriotic eyewitness was moved to enthuse about Petrine principles in his own time. Nicholas I, as he pointed out, came to the throne a
hundred years after Peter's death:

In our imagination we were transported back to that time when just over a hundred years previously, amidst these very walls, on the order of the benefactor of the Fatherland Peter the Great work was in full swing and those wise undertakings which subsequently formed the basis of Russia's glory and greatness were being implemented.... My Russian heart was enflamed with a sensation of national pride and beat strongly at the thought that Russia, my fatherland, has attained such a level of greatness and glory of which one cannot find another comparable example in all History. Was there ever and will there ever be another State of such gigantic size, inhabited by millions of people, confessing a single faith, speaking one language, ruled by a single set of laws and obeying a single Sovereign?[16]

The project for raising an obelisk to Peter was halted by lack of funds, however, and only in 1860 was a statue unveiled of Peter leaning on an anchor with his left hand and pointing forward with his outstretched right arm.

One of the oldest of the surviving houses where Peter stayed was originally at Archangel. After suffering fire and storm damage in the 1760s, it was protected by boarded cladding in order to preserve the remains for posterity. It continued to decay, however, causing one patriot to deplore the fact that 'in the chamber where this great man deigned to rest from his labours and devised ways of improving the welfare of his people, in that place where trophies should stand, now his ungrateful descendants allow senseless four-legged beasts into this forgotten temple'.[17] In the nineteenth century the wooden house was transferred to safer ground and in 1909 moved to the square in front of the cathedral for the celebration of the 200th anniversary of the battle of Poltava.

At Poltava itself, the house where Peter stayed after the battle was demolished in the early nineteenth century and its site marked by an obelisk, as was the church of the Transfiguration built in 1711. In 1837, however, the older church of the Saviour, where Peter prayed, was preserved with stone cladding by order of the future Alexander II, taking a leaf out of his father's book. (One of the stops on his educational tour of Europe was the little house at Zaandam.) In 1849 the site of the house was marked by a more substantial monument with the inscription PETER I RESTED HERE AFTER HIS EXERTIONS ON 27 JUNE 1709 and a separate plaque ERECTED IN THE REIGN OF NICHOLAS I.

In Vologda the assembly of the nobility and town council restored another of Peter's small houses, which opened as a museum on 30 May 1872. People in their best clothes flocked to the cathedral where the bishop conducted a liturgy in Peter's memory. There was a military parade followed by a grand banquet in the noble assembly rooms, where a choir performed patriotic and religious songs and toasts were drunk to the imperial family, accompanied by the inevitable rapturous cries of 'Hurrah' and speeches about Peter's deeds. There is a postscript to this story. In June 1885 Grand Duke Vladimir

Aleksandrovich visited the house. Accounts of this event give a vivid impression of the significance attached to royal visits in providing 'outreach' from the capital to the provinces and binding provincials closer in loyalty to the crown, in this case by the further sanctification of a 'Petrine place'. To make a more specific link with the senior cabin in St Petersburg, they installed a copy of the icon of the Saviour. Thereafter, as in St Petersburg, a chapel was in operation in the house, apparently visited by huge crowds, especially on 30 May, 29 June and 28 January. On the first anniversary of the consecration of the chapel, the marshal of the nobility delivered a speech, which linked the loyal subjects of Vologda to the centre of empire and to other Russian towns through a shared history and shared concern for the preservation of historical memory and monuments.

The author of an article dedicated to the occasion thanked the Lord that the plan devised in 1872 had been brought to fruition, but now dreamed of acquiring one of Peter's uniforms, a sword and a hat for the museum. (One suspects that they were running rather short of genuine Petrine uniforms at this point.) On 29 June 1887, the Petrovsky Invalid Home in Memory of the 200th Anniversary of the Birth of Peter the Great was opened in the building. The biography of Peter supplied in the handsome guides published in 1887 stressed that the common folk loved Peter because he had sanctified physical labour by working as a simple carpenter; intellectuals loved him because he founded schools; women because he emancipated them from their 'servile position'; and so on. The heart of every genuinely Russian person was allegedly overflowing with inexpressible gratitude to the 'Great Worker', who by visiting Vologda four times showed that 'he did not scorn even the most far-flung corners of Russia'.[18]

The literary treatment of Petrine places in the capital and outside demonstrated several dominant themes. Peter's shrines were 'temples' to his modest tastes, to hard work and self-sacrifice and in preserving them or visiting them his royal descendants showed their own 'Petrine' solicitude for the welfare of the great family of Russian people. Like Christ, who was born in a stable and brought up in a carpenter's cottage, Peter exalted himself by making himself humble. Even visitors to the Grand Palace at Peterhof were reminded that Peter preferred to stay in the more intimate Monplaisir, while at nearby Strel'na palace, equally grand but neglected, they were directed to the smallish wooden palace next door: 'Here is yet another holy place, here is a precious relic of things which once belonged to Peter! Look upon this bed with pillows and cover, look upon this walnut cupboard in which stand the Dutch teacups of the immortal Peter.'[19] In the grounds in the 1830s trees planted by Peter's own hands still grew, known as 'Peter's nurslings' and very carefully preserved. At the same time, the authorities did not hesitate to celebrate the imperial Peter, lover of grand victory parades. In 1833 Nicholas I commissioned Auguste Montferrand to design the Peter the Great Memorial

Room (small throne room) in the Winter Palace, which as its centrepiece featured Amigoni's grand portrait behind a silver throne and at the sides paintings of the battles of Lesnaia and Poltava. The decorations included Latin monograms, crowns and thousands of double eagles against a background of red velvet. There were times when it was more appropriate to evoke the spirit of the great emperor on his steed than the modest workman at his lathe.

Peter's possessions

Besides portraits and sculptures, most of Peter's places displayed objects owned or made by Peter, which after his death were carefully preserved as virtual cult objects. Much survived in his own Kunstkamera in a section known as Peter I's Cabinet, where from 1732 Rastrelli's wax model seated on a simple throne presided over stuffed effigies of Peter's horse and dogs and assorted items of Petrine memorabilia – the worn boots, 'whose decrepitude demonstrates this monarch's great thrift', which were said to have been bought out of wages earned on a shift at an ironworks;[20] stockings, allegedly darned by the monarch himself; the hat from Poltava shot through by a bullet; his lathes and some of the handiwork produced on them; mathematical instruments; and much more. Peter's collection of rarities and curiosities, including his preserved babies and two-headed sheep and Nicolas Bourgeois's stuffed effigy, were in adjacent rooms. His clothes, some 300 items ranging from richly embroidered tunics to linen underpants, were kept in the Marly palace at Peterhof. In 1848 Nicholas I ordered Peter's belongings to be collected together from various museums and royal residences and installed in the Peter the Great Gallery in the Winter Palace. An inventory made in 1865 indicates that the wax model, the stuffed horse and dogs occupied the centre, surrounded by portraits of Peter and his family and circle and some of his collection of Dutch paintings. Large objects such as a carriage, desk and lathes were also displayed.[21]

A special exhibition was held in 1903 for the bicentenary of St Petersburg, where visitors could see Peter's travelling medicine chest, his collection of extracted teeth, an ivory chandelier made by him, items of his clothing and his spectacles, chairs, dinner services, glassware and coins. There were gifts presented to him by various people – a cup from Catherine to mark the launching of a ship, an amber-framed mirror from Frederick William of Prussia – and gifts made by him for others, for example, a coconut with a gold rim with Peter's monogram and a Russian eagle (for the disgraced Prince Gagarin) and a snuffbox for Lieutenant Botov.

In 1909, Poltava year, complaints about the cramped premises and restricted public access to the Petrine collections in the Winter Palace prompted the creation of a special section in the old Kunstkamera. Two thousand two hun-

dred and sixty-seven items were transferred to the Museum of Anthropology and Ethnography, which opened its four-roomed memorial museum in May 1912. It included not only items from Peter's time but also later commemorative objects, such as models of the statues at Kronstadt and Poltava, a doll based on the landlady of the Zaandam house and two models of the house itself.

Petrine anniversaries

The paintings and statues, palaces and artefacts all came into their own on Petrine anniversaries, which in their turn prompted new visual tributes. Russia's rulers staged ceremonies around monuments to the tsar-reformer in order to denote their own commitment to enlightenment, modernity, military victory or whatever current policies required and to provide a focus for collective endorsements. Such celebrations, accompanied often by presentation booklets and souvenirs, were largely a creation of the later nineteenth century, Russia's version of the 'invention of tradition' centred on royal houses, although a few were observed earlier. The centenary of the founding of St Petersburg on 16 May 1803, for example, was marked by quite modest ceremonies, confined mainly to the centre of the city along the banks of the Neva and emphasising Russia's naval heritage. Ships, including Peter's little boat, and buildings were decorated with banners and pennants and there were illuminations at night. On the following day members of the Synod and Senate, on Alexander I's orders, laid a medal on Peter's tomb with the inscription: 'Look down from on high, Great Man, and see how your descendants place on your ashes a sign of their grateful spirits. Your services [to your country] continue to bear fruit even from the tomb.'[22] In 1811 the centenary of the battle of Poltava was marked by the building of a victory monument, an eagle on a high column.

Nicholas I was no doubt frustrated by the fact that no major Petrine anniversaries fell within his reign, but he commemorated his hero in any event. A statue at Kronstadt was unveiled on Poltava day (27 June) 1841. Celebrating the bicentenary of Peter's birth in 1872 fell to his son Alexander II. For Alexander, who had escaped an assassination attempt in 1866 and was experiencing a crisis of public confidence in his reforms, inviting comparisons with his tsar-reformer predecessor was a calculated risk which seems to have paid off. The celebrations in the capital on 30 May centred on processions linking together Petrine places and memorabilia. A 21-gun salute from the fortress signalled the start of the day, which began with delegations from city organisations and priests collecting the icon of the Saviour from the cabin, joining another line from the Trinity Cathedral and converging on the Peter-Paul Cathedral, where representatives of Peter's army and navy were lined up. Here on three gold cushions Peter's uniform, breastplate and hat, the sword from Poltava and his Order of St Andrew were laid out. A scroll bore an extract from his (probably apocryphal) speech to the troops before the battle. On another cushion lay a medal issued in Peter's honour which the emperor would place on his tomb after a requiem mass held there. Then a procession set off for the Nevsky gates and quay of the fortress; here a flotilla was waiting to escort the icon and memorabilia across the river to the festooned Bronze Horseman statue, where another religious ceremony took place.

The key roles in the ceremonies were reserved for the élite, but the intention was to involve and enthuse the ordinary public, who in St Petersburg were treated to a series of 'popular readings' on Peter with edifying pictures displayed to illustrate Peter's fearlessness and unselfishness, for example Peter standing up in a boat during a storm while all around his companions panic and the inevitable tale of Peter saving the drowning sailors. The bicentenary inspired events and publications all over the empire, highlighting the progressiveness of Peter's descendants and their fostering of Petrine virtues for the good of the whole nation. In Moscow the celebrations focused on the opening on 30 May of the great Politechnical Exhibition, which commemorated Peter's fostering of industry and technology, his encouragement of enlightenment and his hard work and dedication to duty. The 'grandfather' of the Russian navy put in an appearance, accompanied by the emperor's brother Grand Duke Constantine. Other towns with Petrine connections, such as Petrozavodsk, unveiled statues.

The first two decades of the twentieth century witnessed a cluster of Petrine tercentenaries, a mixed blessing at a time when past glories proved useful for diverting attention from present crises and humiliations (notably the Russo-Japanese war), yet the reigning monarch, Nicholas II, was lukewarm towards his Petrine inheritance, preferring Moscow to St Petersburg. Even so, Nicholas responded positively to selected Petrine motifs, especially military and naval ones. His son Alexis was usually photographed wearing a sailor suit and was given his own 'play' regiment; this spawned a movement in schools and churches, where boys did military drill and gymnastics, sang patriotic songs and indulged in other activities, in imitation of the British Boy Scouts. In 1910 the magazine *Play Troops (Poteshnye)* was launched. All this was a cruel irony given that Alexis's haemophilia prevented him from being more than a token solder or sailor. For those of a pessimistic persuasion, the choice of name of Nicholas's only heir was also unfortunate, given the fate of Tsarevich Alexis Petrovich.

For the St Petersburg bicentenary in 1903 the city was decorated in the then fashionable baroque-classical revival style, with copious garlands and painted backdrops. Theatrical spectacles recreated the assemblies, balls and masquerades of Peter's time, and there were gatherings around the Bronze Horseman, *tableaux vivants* on Trinity Square and replica ships on the Neva. Voluntary organisations such as the Vasil'evsky Island Society of Popular Entertainments and the Board of Guardians of Popular Sobriety joined in to stage public events on the Field of Mars and other open spaces, where people could enjoy fairground amusements. Souvenirs on sale, some based on items produced for Queen Victoria's various jubilees, included pewter drinking cups featuring Petrine places (the little cabin, the Summer Gardens), and small brass busts of Peter with '1703–1903' stamped on the base.

People all over the empire were expected to mark the capital's birthday. In the Tsar Alexander Gymnasium in Reval, the head of history A. V. Belgorodsky delivered a lecture to his pupils about 'that true hero, that true epic warrior of the Russian land', praising Peter's self-sacrifice and faith in God and stressing that the building of St Petersburg had been accomplished by the whole nation.[23] A circular printed in Kazan' declared: 'Now on the day of this most solemn anniversary, recalling with a sense of national pride the glorious historical past and the service rendered by Petersburg by implanting new European culture, the duma of the town of Kazan', one of the oldest towns in Russia, sends greetings from the distant East to the capital city and warm wishes that it may long remain the centre of Russian culture, the focal point of the administrative and spiritual life of Russia.'[24] Of all the Petrine anniversaries, the bicentenary of the battle of Poltava, 27 June 1909, received the most official backing, coinciding as it did with the apparent restoration of Romanov authority following the survival of tsarism after the 1905 revolution and the restrictions imposed in 1907 on the franchise and other liberties conceded in 1905–6. Nicholas II could relate more easily to Peter's military victories than he could to his Westernising reforms and lusty habits. Commemorative booklets described his visit to Poltava in lyrical tones. Even the sun knew its duty, it seems, 'bathing the participants in its gentle rays, as the people greeted their Little Father Tsar'. On 26 June Nicholas reviewed the troops, mingling with officers of the Preobrazhensky guards, among them three descendants of officers who fought with Peter, and visited the communal graves of Russian victims. A new monument to Commandant Kellin, the defender of Poltava, was unveiled. On the 27th there was a service in the church of St Samson and a procession of the cross on to the site of the battle-field, accompanied by the ringing of church bells, the firing of guns and the beating of drums. In the afternoon there was a further ceremony at the eagle-topped Glory monument. This was as much Nicholas's day as Peter's. Official descriptions focus more on the enthusiastic reaction of the people to their Little Father, their responses ranging from tears of joy to rapturously powerful and mighty hurrahs, than on the historical events of 1709. In a speech the emperor underlined the need for all true Russians to support and love their tsar and serve their country and he expressed his faith in the people.

Not only in St Petersburg, where a number of celebratory volumes were printed by imperial command, but all over the country loyal presses vied with each other to sing the praises of Russia's past feats of arms. Typical of the material produced for display in public buildings were large illustrated wall sheets, at the centre of which, above a picture of Swedes surrendering, was an engraving of Delaroche's portrait of Peter, and above it a portrait of Nicholas II. The two tsars are surrounded by leading churchmen of the Petrine era and Peter's command-ing officers to suggest the combined forces of state and church.[25]

Poltava was the first of a series of major anniversaries – Borodino (1812), the Romanov tercentenary (1613) and the battle of Hangö (1714) – which kept official Russia in a more or less permanent state of self-congratulation. The sense of tsar and people united which these occasions conveyed, in some cases genuine popular enthusiasm for the ceremonies in question, bolstered Nicholas's faith in his own popularity and in the power of a direct link with his people to overcome all obstacles. In the words of a booklet published in 1909: 'The Japanese war and its grave consequences – that was our sin. At Poltava we repented and now we can boldly say that a strong, rich and pop-ulous Russia *will be unconquerable* for ever as long as it remains a believing, pious *Holy* Rus.'[26] In 1914–17 such sentiments were to prove dangerous.

Soviet Peter

After 1917, when many effigies of emperors and empresses fell victim to the fury of urban mobs and Futurist iconoclasts, statues of Peter proved to be far from sacrosanct. The best-known victims of Lenin's 1918 Decree on Monumental Propaganda, which ordered the removal of monuments set up 'in honour of tsars and their servants', were the Moscow memorials to Alexander II and Alexander III, the toppling of whose heads symbolised the fall of tsarism. Less publicised was the removal of Bernshtam's *Tsar Carpenter* and *Peter the Great Saving Shipwrecked Fishermen*, both destroyed in January 1919, and V. V. Lishev's statue of Peter in front of the Arsenal, which was not saved by the fact that it had been sponsored by workers for the Arsenal's bicentenary in 1914. Other victims included a stone bust by an unknown author in the lower park at Strel'na, Ilia Gintsburg's 1911 bust of Peter in front of the church of the Holy Spirit in Greater Okhta (a district once inhabited by carpenters) and a bronze figure of Peter in working clothes with an axe at Strestroretsk. If acts of demolition during the civil war were sanctioned by revolutionary iconoclasm, in the late 1920s–1930s the industrialisation of the country supplied a pretext. A surviving copy of the Tsar Carpenter in the Summer Gardens was destroyed in 1930 for its metal content and several of Antokol'sky's statues of Peter were demolished, including the ones in front of the Cathedral of St Samson and the Preobrazhensky guards hospital. In the early Soviet period, when some radicals argued that on key national sites all buildings and monuments built more than ten years before should be destroyed, only monuments with something above and beyond a tsar's image, even Peter's, could survive. Falconet's Bronze Horseman, for example, owed its preservation to its unique design and technical ingenuity, as well as to its associations with Pushkin and the Decembrists. It became even more the symbol of Peter's (as opposed to Lenin's, from 1924) city in Soviet times as a result of the destruction or removal of all other outdoor monuments to Peter, with the exception of Rastrelli's equestrian statue.

The various Petrine museum collections survived the first decade of Soviet power more or less intact, but were inevitably caught up in the new thinking about museums and what was termed 'the growing interest of the masses of the people in history'. Peter's cabin was placed under the protection of the new Museums Authority in 1918. In 1930 the chapel was 'liquidated' and the little house restarted life as a 'valuable monument of material culture, an interesting monument of architecture characterising the initial stage of construction and life in the town'.[27] Its presentation as a 'military-camp structure' was emphasised by the items selected for display – saws and other tools, draughtsmen's instruments and so on. This practical approach stripped the house of most of its associations with Peter as a personality. Peter's wooden house at Archangel was moved to Kolomenskoe (also a Petrine place), where it too functioned as a museum to labour. One guide claimed that it was the 'direct predecessor of the cabin of Peter I in St Petersburg, better because it was built by local Russian masters'.[28] Under the influence of M. N. Pokrovsky, it was decreed that separate commemorative displays dedicated to pre-revolutionary leaders were 'alien to the spirit of the times' and that exhibits should be distributed to different museums under such impersonal labels as 'Feudal-Serf-Owning Russia' and the 'History of the USSR. XVIII century'.[29] However, Stalin's slightly grudging approval of Peter prevented him from disappearing from the picture altogether.

Peter's places and statues came back into their own during the Second World War, along with other pre-revolutionary monuments and buildings. In 1941 mountaineers and steeplejacks camouflaged the steeple of the Peter-Paul Cathedral, which, as a Romanov mausoleum, had been neglected in the years following the revolution. The cathedral spire became the measure of the courageous defence of the city and inevitably evoked its creation 'from nothing'. The Bronze Horseman survived the blockade behind wooden casing and sandbags. Apart from the difficulty of moving it, there was a legend that it must remain or the city would fall. In the words of a slim pamphlet published towards the end of the war:

In the days of the Great Fatherland War the significance of the statue to Peter I is especially evident. This most precious artistic treasure of Russia symbolises the immeasurable creative forces which lurk within her, the greatness of a state created by the Russian people and transformed by Peter. Recalling Peter's victorious struggle with foreign intervention, his monument unites the renowned glory of Russian arms and the military heroism of our own days. In the city which endured unprecedented sufferings and victories in 1941–44, the monument has remained unscathed amidst the dangers which threatened it. A strong case, reminiscent of a military defence, protected it from enemy shells and air raids during the blockade. Heroic Leningrad was able to defend the statue of its founder, just as it succeeded in defending its honour, freedom and historic fame.[30]

As the Nazis approached the city and threatened to raze it, Peter's first house became a potent symbol, too. In 1941 its contents were evacuated and a round-the-clock guard was mounted on the camouflaged building. Soldiers of the Soviet army departing for the front in 1944, took their oath there, vowing to fight just as heroically for the Motherland as Peter I's soldiers had fought.[31] Despite suffering bombardments, it was the first Leningrad museum to reopen after the blockade.

In 1942 orders were given to repair and redecorate Peter's tomb in time for the October Revolution anniversary on 7 November, likewise the tombs in other parts of the city of Alexander Nevsky and Generals Suvorov and Kutuzov, which were all hurriedly tidied up and embellished as rallying points in the struggle against Fascism. A new display was designed, including a sculpted head based on Collot's study for the Bronze Horseman. New recruits came to the tomb, where they could read the words allegedly spoken by Peter to his troops before Poltava: 'Of Peter know only that he sets no worth on his own life if only Russia and Russian piety, glory and well-being may live.'

The greatest impetus to the revival of Peter's reputation was undoubtedly the wanton destruction of so much of his heritage outside St Petersburg. In particular, the Nazis reduced the Grand Palace at Peterhof to rubble; its fountains and cascades were mined and surrounding pavilions, including Peter's favourite Monplaisir, were gutted. After the war their rebirth from the ashes became a potent symbol of Soviet Russia's regeneration. In the Hermitage an exhibition on Peter's Russia, including many items of Petrine memorabilia transferred there just before the war, opened in November 1947. The Summer Palace and Gardens reopened their doors to the public in the same year. Statues destroyed or damaged in the war, like the one at Voronezh, were repaired or recast and restored to their pedestals. The publication of Peter's letters and papers, which began in 1887 and halted in 1918, resumed in 1946 with a volume of notes for documents from the year 1708 (and currently has still only reached 1713). New museums opened on previously neglected sites, for example, in 1946 the Martsial'nye Springs open-air museum 54 kilometres from Petrozavodsk, incorporating the former church of SS Peter and Paul and a wooden pavilion over the springs, built in 1833. No trace remained of Peter's original 'palace' or spa buildings. The first exhibits included chairs with backs worked by Peter on his lathe alongside displays on the 'self-sacrificing struggle of the Karelian peasants against the Swedish aggressors'.[32] The spa was revived and in 1964 a sanatorium began to admit patients.

The parameters within which Peter could be depicted or celebrated were still restricted. On the one hand, he must not be praised too much (he had, after all, fleeced the peasants and been a little too welcoming to foreigners) and he was not as great as Lenin in the Soviet hierarchy of leaders; on the other, he was a Russian national hero and could not be denigrated or ridiculed. The tercentenary of Peter's birth in 1972 was, in the words of an American historian who witnessed it, 'almost an event'.[33] Celebrations were left in the hands of individual organisations, rather than the Party and Soviet authorities, who two years previously had pulled out all the stops to mark the centenary of the birth of Lenin in spectacular fashion. In Leningrad there were exhibitions in the Russian Museum (the most comprehensive ever staged on the portraiture of the Petrine period), the public library and the coffee house in the Summer Gardens. In Moscow, the Shchusev Museum of Architecture displayed contemporary materials on early St Petersburg and exhibitions were held in the Petrine halls of the State Historical Museum, the Kremlin Armoury, the cabin at Kolomenskoe, and the Tret'iakov Gallery. In general, the message was a positive one – Peter was a 'man of his time', which included serfdom, torture and other horrors, but he was also 'progressive', a predecessor of the Bolsheviks in his application of reason, sponsorship of science and technology and prioritising of the common good. As visitors to Peter's tomb in the 1970s–90s will recall, his was the only one among the Romanov graves to be regularly supplied with fresh flowers and marked out with a sculpted portrait and a military standard. The bipolar view of Peter remained the official one up to the collapse of the USSR, although in the works of a few bold historians Peter the first Bolshevik metamorphosed into Peter the first Stalinist.

Post-Soviet, post-modern Peter

In September 1991, just a few weeks after the abortive coup to overthrow Mikhail Gorbachev which accelerated the rise of Boris Yeltsin and three months before the USSR formally ceased to exist, the inhabitants of what was then Leningrad voted in a referendum to restore the city's original name and on 7 November, hitherto devoted to the October Revolution, crowds gathered on Palace Square to celebrate. Speakers addressed the assembled crowds on such themes as the reopening of Peter the Great's 'Window on Europe' and the Petrine origins of the armed forces. Across the boat-filled

River Neva in the Peter-Paul fortress a 12-gun salute was fired and flares were lit, both on the ramparts and on the lighthouses on the spit of Vasil'evsky Island, recalling the waterscape of Peter's time and his love of sailing, fireworks and loud explosions. Yet it was not all adulation, for together with new freedoms of expression and travel came freedom to demystify and debunk old heroes, a process from which Peter was not exempted.

In the 1990s a number of historians followed Anisimov's lead. Rejecting the received wisdom that Peter made Russia 'leap forward', for example, Iakov Vodarsky asserted that he actually put a brake on Russia's progress and created conditions for holding it back for one-and-a-half centuries, while Anatoly Lanshchikov called Peter 'the Bolshevik emperor', arguing that he decelerated Russia's development by accentuating those features – tyranny and servitude – that separated it from Europe, turning the whole country into one huge hierarchical GULAG.[34] Other writers, deeply critical of post-Soviet politics and politicians, have emphasised not only Peter's cruelty and arbitrariness, but also the moral corruption of virtually all who served him, hence studies of Menshikov as the founder of the Russian Mafia. The following item was published in *Moscow News* in 1998:

In November the leader of Russia received an anonymous letter. 'Reforms', wrote the correspondent, 'have led to corruption on a monstrous scale, to theft and crime throughout the country. Your inner circle, men whom you call your closest associates, men dedicated to the cause of reform (members of the high court, commanders of the armed forces and executive power, including even the leaders of your administration), firstly, have soiled their hands with bribe-taking; secondly, are guilty of embezzlement; thirdly, are implicated in protecting criminals and undermining the judicial processes.'

Readers were surprised to hear that the recipient of this letter, a few months before his death, was not Boris Yeltsin but Peter I. 'Embezzlement on a huge scale right under the leader's nose, millions stashed away in Western banks, the incredible greed of the new elite! And we thought all this was just a feature of life today. It seems we just don't know the history of reform well enough,' wrote the author.[35]

Another current in post-Soviet history writing responds to popular curiosity about the private lives of semi-sacrosanct figures of the past, unearthing previously suppressed information about their health (physical and mental), tastes, sexual orientation and family relations, a trend which extended even to such previously untouchable historical figures as Lenin, whose childhood, sex life and last illness were explored in lurid detail. With regard to pre-revolutionary monarchs, customer demand has fuelled a mini-industry in such compendia as *The House of the Romanovs* and other genealogies. Peter addicts have been catered for partly by reprinting works by pre-revolutionary writers

such as M. A. Semevsky, A. G. Brikner and A. Waliszczewski and partly by
articles in popular journals. One series in *Science and Religion* portrayed Peter
as a sex maniac, who indulged in indiscriminate sexual relations with men
and women, including his own sister Natalia and his niece the duchess of
Mecklenburg. Elsewhere somewhat less sensational articles have examined the
shadowy figures of Tsaritsa Evdokia and Anna Mons. New, more sympathetic
treatments of Tsarevich Alexis (in Stalinist histories vilified as the figurehead
of a band of 'enemies of the people', in later Soviet views a necessary sacrifice
for the common good) include the film *Peter and Alexis,* which explores the
father–son relationship from Alexis's point of view while stressing the agony
of Peter's position.

By and large, the general public does not seem to have been much influenced by attempts to present Peter's unheroic side. In an opinion poll conducted by Radio Free Europe in 1993 to discover 'Russia's most notable
political figure', Peter got 44 per cent of the votes with Lenin a poor second
at 16 per cent,[36] while in another poll conducted in Moscow in 1994 on the
question 'Which era of Russian history can Russians be most proud of?' 54
per cent chose Peter's reign. (Stalin's was second, with about 20 per cent.)
These results seem to have been prompted in part by popular longing for a
strong man to intervene and take charge, but without the taint of the recent
past, in part by popular perceptions of the Petrine era as a time when Russia
was strong. 'Peter helped to create the military-patriotic consciousness of the
Russian people and shaped their attitude towards service, honour and dignity,' declared the journal *Armiia.* 'It is useful to remember this Petrine lesson
today.'[37] Interviews with 'ordinary' people reveal analogous views. Maxim,
aged seventeen, told an American sociologist: 'Peter had enormous strength
of will; he slept only four hours a day, the rest of the time he gave over to
work. Peter brought about a strengthening of the Russian fleet, won back
some lands which belonged to Russia. It was a prosperous country then.'[38]
The continuing saga of the decay of the Russian armed forces and fleet only
seems to increase nostalgia for Peter's time.

The public has been resistant to deviations from the standard Petrine
iconography, the chief visual expression of which is a controversial statue by
the Russian émigré sculptor Mikhail Shemiakin, set up in June 1991 right in
the middle of the Peter-Paul fortress, which portrays the tsar as an ill-formed
freak, unnaturally small-headed, bald, bug-eyed and spindly-limbed. It draws
freely on Rastrelli's wax model (minus its wig), which Shemiakin often saw in
his pre-emigration days working as a porter in the Hermitage (a 'bearer of culture', as he joked) and also on unflattering descriptions of Peter by his contemporaries. The inscription echoes Catherine II's dedication on Falconet's
monument: TO THE FOUNDER OF THE GREAT RUSSIAN CITY EMPEROR PETER I
FROM THE ITALIAN SCULPTOR CARLO RASTRELLI AND THE RUSSIAN ARTIST
MIKHAIL SHEMIAKIN. The seated figure always attracts a cluster of onlookers,

not least because a legend has grown up that if you touch the model's index finger your wish will come true. Shemiakin himself has expressed satisfaction that his work has created a new St Petersburg legend. Tourists like to be photographed next to it, although the more traditionally minded can have their pictures taken just a few paces away with a live Peter look-alike in guards uniform.

The wider context of Shemiakin's work is the exploration of the 'laughter culture of Old Russia', carnival and the modern avant-garde, a principle which he has also expressed in a new monument to Peter by the Thames at Deptford, London, unveiled in June 2001. There were rumours that the sculptor's initial idea of surrounding the tsar with jesters displaying their bare bottoms was vetoed by the organising committee as incompatible with the aims of the Peter the Great Foundation set up to help young people in south London, for whom hard-working Peter is held up as a role model. Staff at the London embassy's reception for Russian National Day, a week after the unveiling, were keen to dissociate themselves from the new monument, which they found too stylised, too *modern*; the face was not an accurate likeness of Peter, 'whom every Russian can recognise'. Similar opinions have been expressed about the St Petersburg statue: it offends because it does not resemble the Peter whom people think they know. Peter the man of many faces, masks and disguises, Peter the freak, has not really gained currency.

Guides and curators in the many museums with Petrine associations continue to take an admiring and reverential view, while being aware that there is another. 'Peter was a complex character,' admitted the guide at the end of a recent tour of the Summer Palace. Then, after short pause, 'But he did a lot for Russia, perhaps best of all creating St Petersburg.' An exception was a curator who had worked for many years at Peterhof and ventured the view, on a private tour, this time, that Peter suffered from mental illness and psychoses. In his opinion, Peter's various joke fountains in the park, which drench the unwary, and the replica of a great eagle cup among the exhibits in Monplaisir palace were no laughing matter, but rather examples of Peter's perverted sense of humour and disregard for human dignity. He was *nenormal'nyi*.

Carnivalesque Peter and mad Peter appeal to a small minority, but traditional Peter – hero, worker, teacher – is more in evidence than ever. A copy of Bernshtam's *Tsar-Carpenter*, cast from a version in Amsterdam, has been restored not far from its original place on the Neva embankment in front of the west wing of the Admiralty. Even more striking, in the busy entrance hall of the Moskovsky railway station on Insurrection Square a statue of Lenin has been replaced by a large copy of Rastrelli's bronze bust of Peter on a plinth. Whereas in the old days people made arrangements to meet 'by Lenin', now they meet by Peter, who greets visitors arriving in *his* (no longer Lenin's) city. Meanwhile, inside the Peter-Paul Cathedral, just a short walk from

Shemiakin's statue, Peter's tomb is draped with the flag of St Andrew (now restored to the ships of the Russian fleet) and covered with copies of medals. Next to it the small sculptural group *Deposition from the Cross* by the Italian sculptor Zorzoni is back in its place. Brought to St Petersburg in 1717 as part of a job lot for display in the Summer Gardens, at some point after Peter's death it was placed in the cathedral, allegedly on Peter's orders, and was transferred to Peter's tomb in 1872, but removed in 1972 to the storeroom of the Museum of the History of St Petersburg. (New scholarship on the foreign artists who created the religious art in Peter's cathedral is being published.)

The relatively new art of Russian commercial advertising also utilises Peter's image in various ways, for example, to suggest strength and authority. Peter himself never got round to founding banks, but advertisements for the Menatep Bank ('a strong bank for a strong country') feature Peter's portrait and the Petrovsky bank on Nevsky Prospekt has a bust of Peter over its entrance. The pack of top-selling 'Peter I' cigarettes (which, of course, Peter never smoked, although he enjoyed a pipe) gets the message across to millions: 'These unique cigarettes of highest quality have been created using superior types of tobacco which were purveyed to the court of Peter I from Europe and are capable of satisfying the most discriminating connoisseur who believes in the revival of the traditions and greatness of the Russian land.' The 'Peter I' logo, with its double-headed eagle on a black background is everywhere – on awnings, posters, parasols on street cafés, cars. Other cigarette packs also display Peter's portraits. This sort of advertising is not new. In pre-revolutionary Russia, 'Imperatorskie' cigarettes were popular. Petrine associations are used (along with images of Old Russia and an idealised Russian countryside of butter-churning milkmaids) to promote other Russian products: 'Petrovskoe' beer, with its Bronze Horseman logo, made at the Stenka Razin factory in St Petersburg, is one of several brands in competition with foreign beers and lagers, and 'Peter the Great' original Russian vodka made in St Petersburg 'of the finest grain spirit and pure natural soft water' features the head and shoulders of Nattier's portrait in a medallion surrounded by weaponry over a ribbon in the new Russian national colours. Commercial interests can use the patriotic Peter, urging self-sufficiency and preferring wholesome Russian products, or Westernising Peter, encouraging new technology and Western fashions.

Peter's enhanced status as local St Petersburg hero is hardly unexpected, but Moscow, too, has taken advantage of the lucky (some would say unlucky) coincidence of a series of Petrine anniversaries to raise Peter's flag on its own mast and pre-empt some of the forthcoming St Petersburg-based celebrations for 2003. As Moscow's Mayor Iury Luzhkov wrote in the preface to the catalogue for the Kremlin exhibition 'Peter the Great and Moscow' (1998), here were born 'the schemes of Russia's future transformation': the fleet was founded, the Grand Embassy set off and the first victories of the Northern

War were celebrated. In their foreword the directors of the participating museums expressed the hope that the exhibition, which brought together more than 400 exhibits, would help boost confidence in the 'Great Future of our Fatherland'.[39]

Moscow now also boasts the biggest Peter the Great statue in the world, Zurab Tsereteli's 98-foot Monument to the Tercentenary of the Russian Fleet. It stands on its own small island in the river, to the west of the Kremlin, and is linked by a short walkway to the bank in front of the Red October sweet factory, but in 2001 no one walked across to sit on the attractive benches around the monument's base, since public access was barred following threats to blow it up by neo-Bolsheviks protesting against monuments to tsars. Instead of the usual plinth, Peter is standing on a galleon (which he dwarfs) which is supported by an ornate structure of piled-up prows bearing metal wind-vanes in the shape of the St Andrew's flag. Peter stands erect, turning a ship's wheel with his left hand and brandishing a rolled-up map in his right. The face is recognisably his, but this has not appeased the monument's critics.

Muscovites have protested about the cost (an estimated $11 million), the inappropriateness (Peter hated Moscow), the lack of consultation and the ugly intrusiveness of the towering ensemble. They also object to being fobbed off with a second-hand design, for if Peter's clothes look a bit more fifteenth-century than eighteenth – strange armoured shoes and a sort of doublet – this may be because the monument was based on Tsereteli's design for a giant statue to Christopher Columbus, which now stands in San Juan, Puerto Rico, where locals apparently call it 'Chris Kong'. To its detractors, Peter-Columbus seems to be crushing the ship beneath him (a reference to the crushing burdens imposed by Russia's leaders), while the map in his right hand looks like a human bone, hinting at cannibalism: Peter devours Russia. In general, the statue's size and ostentation recall the worst excesses of the Soviet predilection for gigantic monuments of 'Egyptian' proportions. Many regard it not only as part of the 'Tsereteli-isation' of Moscow (the much-decorated Zurab – People's Artist, Academician, Laureate, President of the Academy of Arts etc. – is the author of numerous high-cost projects, including fairytale fountains in Manezh Square and the Poklonnaia gora memorial complex on the outskirts) but also as a gross example of Mayor Luzhkov's plan to impose his own vision on the city and to create a pedestal for himself. In honouring Peter, Luzhkov may also have been honouring Boris Yeltsin, who repeatedly declared himself an admirer and emulator of the first emperor. Luckily for the mayor, Yeltsin's successor, Vladimir Putin, is also a fan of Peter's brand of firm government from above. St Petersburger Putin is even planning a new presidential residence in Peter's palace at Strel'na.

For the new establishment, the Moscow monument has a positive message; its iconography evokes the idea of a voyage of exploration, of Peter the discoverer of new lands steering the New Russian ship, a metaphor for far-sighted leadership from above. Peter looks towards the West, the inspiration for much of Luzhkov's new Moscow. At the same time the monument arouses nostalgia for a lost empire. On 6 September 1997 the *St Petersburg News* announced:

> Yesterday at the opening of the monument there was much talk about Russia's place in the modern world, about its power and lost position, its glory and its future. The speakers, major figures of the Russian state and country's fleet, emphasised that Russia's independence and its security are impossible without the strengthening of its naval traditions, which were begun three centuries ago by the young Peter.[40]

In this respect, it is ironic that one of the (unverified) explanations for the tragic sinking of the submarine *Kursk* in August 2000, in which 118 submariners perished, was that it was hit by a shell from the *Peter the Great*, the biggest ship afloat in the Russian navy, part of a discourse which blames the country's rulers for indifference to the fate of ordinary citizens. In the popular imagination, as we know, Peter is associated with *saving* men from drowning and, it is said, would have rushed to the site of the disaster in the Barents Sea to help in the rescue operation.

Tsereteli's monument is interestingly juxtaposed with other post-Soviet monuments. To the north rises New Moscow's most grandiose restoration project, the rebuilt Cathedral of Christ the Redeemer, which can accommodate 10,000 worshippers. The original, blown up on Stalin's orders in 1931, was founded in 1839 by Nicholas I, Peter's great admirer, to fulfil the pledge of Alexander I to erect a memorial church to the victims and heroes of the Napoleonic wars. One of the best views of the Peter monument can be had from its roof gallery. If you approach the statue from Krymsky Val to the south-west, walking past the exhibition halls, it appears at first to be part of the open-air sculpture park popularly known as the 'graveyard' of Communist monuments, although in fact it is separated from it by a road and the river. After the collapse of the USSR, many redundant statues were brought here and laid on their sides, sometimes in several pieces, including the toppled monument to Feliks Derzhinsky from opposite KGB headquarters on Lubianka Square and several statues of Stalin. Admirers of Peter could think of him rising triumphant above the fallen idols of the failed Soviet experiment. More recently, however, some of the Soviet statues in the park have been raised, causing people to muse on the fact that Russia can never get rid of its leaders, or its attachment to strong leaders, who have a nasty habit of coming back to life just when you think they are dead and gone.

Moscow's contemporary symbolic landscape contains many such references and allusions to times and places outside itself, a vital element in its reconfiguration and reinvention in the 1990s both as capitalist city and as city of Orthodoxy and heritage, as religious replicas resurrected from the past rub shoulders with genuine monuments in a landscape of shopping malls, McDonald's and Pepsi Cola signs. It was Peter who opened up Russia to their early eighteenth-century equivalents, creating his own New Russians and his own model city albeit in another location, so it is not surprising that the chronological correspondence of Russia's latest reinvention of itself to events of Peter's time three hundred earlier has led to the late twentieth/early twenty-first century being dubbed a new Petrine era without the military victories.

Poets have often used the image of the Bronze Horseman, looking down from his pedestal at the new life going on around him, and even climbing down to explore it, to suggest questions about Russia's past and future. In Vladimir Maiakovsky's poem 'The Last St Petersburg Fairy Tale' (1916), Peter, the horse and the serpent climb down from their rock and go to the nearby Astoria hotel (where someone apologises for stepping on the serpent's tail), but are forced to return to the places allotted to them for all time. The last lines evoke the dejection on the horse's face and the frustration of Peter, an emperor 'without a sceptre', at being a prisoner fettered in his own city. A modern poet has the horseman casting a 'gloomy look' at a girl in jeans (recalling his first meetings with his Kate) and asking what the hell's going on as he scans the banks, exchanges and down-and-outs (*banki, birzhi, bomzhi*) and longs to leap down from his 'dead horse' as he contemplates the approach of the twenty-first century.[41] No doubt Tsereteli's giant Peter will similarly be brought to life to walk the streets of the city which he never much cared for and to discover that almost three centuries after his death no one has replaced him as the pivotal point for discussions about Russia's past and future and that many of the issues he grappled with still await a resolution.

Abbreviations

Alekseeva: M. A. Alekseeva, *Graviura petrovskogo vremeni* (L., 1990)

Bantysh-Kamensky: N. N. Bantysh-Kamensky, *Obzor vneshnikh snoshenii Rossii s derzhavami inostrannymi*, 4 vols (M., 1894–1902)

Bassewitz: H-F. Bassewitz, 'Zapiski grafa Bassevicha, sluzhashchie k poiasneniiu nekotorykh sobytii iz vremeni tsarstvovaniia Petra Velikogo (1713–1725)', *Russkii arkhiv*, 3 (1865)

Bergholz, I: *Dnevnik kamer-iunkera Fridrikha-Vil'gel'ma Berkhgol'tsa 1721–1725.* (M., 2000) (1721–22)

Bergholz, II: *Dnevnik kammer-iunkera Berkhgol'tsa, vedennyi im v Rossii v tsarstvovanie Petra Velikogo s 1721–1725 g.* 3rd ed. (M., 1902–3) (1723–25)

Bespiatykh: *Peterburg Petra I v inostrannykh opisaniiakh*, ed. Iu. Bespiatykh (L., 1991)

BP: Bumagi imp. Petra I, izdannye akademikom A. Bychkovym (SPb, 1873)

BRAPG: Britain and Russia in the Age of Peter the Great. Historical Documents, ed. S. Dixon et al. (London, 1998)

CASS: Canadian-American Slavic Studies

CMRS: Cahiers du monde russe et sovietique

Consett: *For God and Peter the Great. The Works of Thomas Consett, 1723–1729,* ed. J. Cracraft (Boulder, 1982)

CSP: Canadian Slavonic Papers

DPPS: Doklady i prigovory sostoiavshiesia v pravitel'stvuiushchem Senate v tsarstvovanie Petra Velikogo, vols I–VI (SPb, 1880–1901)

DR: Dvortsovye razriady, 4 vols (SPb, 1852–55)

Esipov: G. V. Esipov, *Raskol'nich'i dela XVIII stoletiia,* 2 vols (SPb, 1861)

Garrard: J. Garrard, ed. *The Eighteenth Century in Russia* (Oxford, 1973)

Golikova: N. B. Golikova, *Politicheskie protsessy pri Petre I* (M., 1957)

Golombievsky: A. A. Golombievsky, *Sotrudniki Petra Velikogo* (M., 1903)

Gordon: Patrick Gordon's diary, Tsentral'nyi Gosudarstvennyi Voenno-Istoricheskii Arkhiv, f. 846, op. 15, ed. khr. 1–7

Grebeniuk: ed. V. P. Grebeniuk, *Panegiricheskaia literatura petrovskogo vremeni* (M., 1979)

GRM: Gosudarstvennyi Russkii Muzei

Grund: Georg Grund, *Bericht über Russland in den Jahren 1705–1710* (Account of Russia in the Years 1705–1710) ed. Iu. N. Bespiatykh (SPb, 1992)

JGO: Jahrbücher für Geschichte Osteuropas

Juel: Just Juel, 'Iz zapisok datskogo poslannika Iusta Iuliia', *Russkii arkhiv,* 30 (1892), books 1–3

Klein: J. Klein et al. eds, *Reflections on Russia in the Eighteenth Century* (Cologne, Weimar, Vienna, 2001)

Korb: J.-G.Korb, *Diary of an Austrian Secretary of Legation at the Court of Czar Peter the Great*, trans. and ed. Count MacDonnell, 2 vols (London 1863/1968)

Kurakin: B. A. Kurakin, 'Gistoriia o tsare Petre Alekseeviche', in *Rossiiu podnial na dyby*, vol. I (M., 1987)

L.: Leningrad

LOI: Leningradskoe otdelenie instituta istorii Akademii Nauk, f. 270 (Letters and Papers of Peter I) (Now: Sankt-Peterburgskii Filial Instituta Rossiiskoi Istorii Rossiiskoi Akademii Nauk)

M.: Moscow

Medals: I. G. Spassky and E. Shchukina, *Medals and Coins of the Age of Peter the Great* (L., 1974)

MIGO: *Materialy dlia istorii Gangutskoi operatsii*, 3 vols (Petrograd, 1914)

Muller: A. Muller, ed. and trans. *The Spiritual Regulation of Peter the Great*, (Seattle, 1972)

Nartov: *Rasskazy Nartova o Petre Velikom*, ed. L. N. Maikov (SPb, 1891)

Nepliuev: *Zapiski Ivana Ivanovicha Nepliueva (1693–1773)* (SPb, 1893)

Neuville: F. de la Neuville, *A Curious and New Account of Muscovy in the Year 1689*, ed. L. Hughes (London, 1994)

OV: *Osmnadtsatyi vek. Istoricheskii sbornik izdannyi P. Bartevenym*, 4 vols (M., 1869)

Perry: John Perry, *The State of Russia* (1716) (London, 1967)

Peterson: C. Peterson, *Peter the Great's Administrative and Judicial Reforms* (Stockholm, 1979)

PGW: *Peter the Great and the West: New Perspectives*, ed. Lindsey Hughes (Basingstoke, 2000)

PiB: *Pisma i bumagi Imperatora Petra Velikogo*, I: 1689–1701 (1887); II: 1702–3 (1889), III: 1704–5 (1893); IV: 1706 (1900); V: 1707, Jan.–June (1907); VI: 1707, July–Dec. (1912); VII (i): 1708, Jan.–June (1918); VII (ii): 1708, Jan.–June, notes (1946); VIII (i): 1708, July–Dec. (1948); VIII (ii): 1708, July–Dec., notes (1951); IX (i): 1709 (1950) and (ii): 1709, notes (1952); X: 1710 (1956); XI (i): 1711, Jan.–June (1962) and (ii): 1711, July–Dec. (1964); XII(i): 1712 (1975) and XII (ii): 1712 (1977); XIII (i): 1713, Jan.–June (1992)

PRO: Public Record Office

PRG: *Pisma russkikh gosudarei i drugikh osob tsarskogo semeistva*, 3 vols (M., 1861)

PSZ: *Polnoe sobranie zakonov rossiiskoi imperii*, I–II (1649–88); III (1689–99); IV (1700–12); V (1713–19); VI (1720–22); VII (1723–27) (SPb, 1830)

PV: *Petr Velikii. Vospominaniia. Dnevnikovye zapisi. Anekdoty*, ed. E. Anisimov (SPb, 1993)

PZh: *Pokhodnye zhurnaly Petra I 1695–1726* (SPb, 1853–55) (separate vols for each year)

RGADA: Rossiiskii (formerly Tsentral'nyi) gosudarstvennyi arkhiv drevnikh aktov

Riasanovsky: Nicholas Riasanovsky *The Image of Peter the Great in Russian History and Thought* (Oxford, 1985)

RNB: Rossiiskaia Natsional'naia Biblioteka, St Petersburg

RR: Russian Review

RRP: Russia in the Reign of Peter the Great: Old and New Perspectives, ed. A. G. Cross (Cambridge, 1998)

RWEC: Russia and the World of the Eighteenth Century, eds R. Bartlett et al. (Columbus, Oh., 1988)

Sbornik: *Sbornik vypisok iz arkhivnykh bumag o Petre Velikom* 2 vols (M., 1872)

SEER: Slavonic and East European Review

SGECRN: Study Group on 18th-century Russia Newsletter

SIRIO: *Sbornik imperatorskogo rossiiskogo istoricheskogo obshchestva*

Solov'ev: S. M. Solov'ev, *History of Russia*, vol. XXVI *Peter the Great. A Reign Begins 1689–1703*, trans. L. Hughes (Gulf Breeze, 1994)

SPb: St Petersburg

SR: *Slavic Review*

SSH: Soviet Studies in History

Stählin: Jacob Stählin, *Podlinnye anekdoty o Petre Velikom* (L., 1990)

Ustrialov: N. Ustrialov, *Istoriia tsarstvovaniia Petra Velikogo*, 6 vols (SPb., 1858–69)

VI: *Voprosy istorii*

Viktorov: A. Viktorov, *Opisanie zapisnykh knig i bumag starinnykh dvortsovykh prikazov, 1613–1725*, 2 vols (M., 1883)

Weber: F. C. Weber. *The Present State of Russia*, 2 vols (London, 1722–23)

Whitworth: Charles Whitworth, *An Account of Russia as it was in the Year 1710. Rossiia v nachale XVIII veka. Sochineniia Ch. Uitvorta* (M.-L., 1988)

WOR: A Window on Russia: Papers from the V International Conference of the Study Group on Eighteenth-Century Russia, Gargnano, 1994, eds M. di Salvo and L. Hughes (Rome, 1996)

ZA: A. Voskresensky, *Zakonodatel'nye akty Petra I*, vol. I (M.-L., 1945)

200-letie: *200-letie Kabineta ego imp. velichestva 1704–1904* (SPb, 1911)

Russian archival references follow Russian practice: f. = fond [collection], op. = opis' [section]; d. = delo [file], kn. = kniga (book), l. = list [folio] (ll. = listy)

Notes

Preface

1 ZA, 115.
2 Anthony Cross, 'Petrus Britannicus: the Image of Peter the Great in 18th-century Britain', *WOR*, 8.

I Growing Up 1672–89

1 P. Krekshin, 'Kratkoe opisanie blazhenykh del velikogo gosudaria, imperatora Petra Velikogo, Samoderzhtsa Vserossiiskogo', in *Zapiski russkikh liudei.* ed. N. Sakharov (SPb., 1841), 8–9.
2 *PiB*, XI, 281.
3 *PSZ*, I, no. 607.
4 'Stoglav', in *Russkoe zakonodatel'stvo X–XX vekov*, vol. II (M., 1985), ch. 20.
5 Stählin, no. 92, 141–3.
6 Philip Longworth, *Alexis. Tsar of All the Russias* (London, 1984), 229.
7 Neuville, 15.
8 S. Medvedev, 'Sozertanie let kratkoe 7190, 91 i 92', *Chteniia v Imperatorskom Obshchestve Istorii i Drevnostei Rossiiskikh*, 1894, book 4, 65–6.
9 'Istoriia o vere i chelobytnaia o strel'tsakh Savvy Romanova', *Letopisi russkoi literatury i drevnosti*, ed. N. Tikhomirov, 5 (1863), part II, 111–48.
10 *Vosstanie v Moskve 1682 g. Sbornik dokumentov*, ed. V. I. Buganov and N. G. Savich (M., 1976), 113–17.
11 Ibid., 104–6.

12 Lindsey Hughes, *Sophia, Regent of Russia* (New Haven, 1990), 140–1.
13 E. Kämpfer, 'Diarium itineris ad aulam Moscoviticam indeque Astracanum suscepti anno MDCLXXIII', in K. Meier-Lemgo, *Englebert Kämpfer, der erste deutsche Forschungsreisende 1651–1716* (Stuttgart, 1937), 13.
14 *Relation du voyage en Russie fait en 1684 par Laurent Rinhuber* (Berlin, 1883), 230.
15 Quoted in F. Adelung, *Kritish-literärische Übersicht der Reisenden in Russland bis 1700*, vol. II (SPb and Leipzig), 270–1.
16 Neuville, 59.
17 A. Babkin, 'Pis'ma Frantsa i Petra Lefortov o "Velikom posol'stve"', *VI*, 1976, no. 4, 122–3.
18 Kurakin, 386.
19 J. Banks, *A New History of the Life and Reign of Czar Peter the Great, Emperor of All Russia, and Father of his Country* (London, 1740), 48.
20 Ustrialov, I, 99; Kurakin, 364–5.
21 *PSZ*, II, no. 1186, 770–86.
22 Whitworth, 60.
23 'The Story of the Ship's Boat which gave his Majesty the Thought of Building Ships of War', in Consett, 210.
24 Kurakin, 369.
25 *PRG*, III (M., 1861), 68–9.
26 *PSZ*, II, no. 1258, 889.
27 Ustrialov, I, 370.
28 *Rozysknoe delo o Fedore Shaklovitom i ego soobshchnikakh*, III (SPb, 1893), 1–2.
29 Gordon, V (unpaginated).

30 Solov'ev, 173–4.
31 Nartov, 100–1.
32 *PiB*, I, 13–14.

II *Prelude to Greatness* 1689–97

1 *PiB*, I, 36.
2 Kurakin, 375.
3 *PSZ*, III, no. 1358, 46–7 (29 Oct., 1689).
4 Testament of Patriarch Joachim, 17 March 1690, in G. Vernadsky, *A Source Book for Russian History*, vol. II (New Haven, 1972), 361–3.
5 *DR*, IV, 527–30.
6 Kurakin, 379.
7 *Russkii Biograficheskii Slovar'*, 25 vols (SPb, 1896–1918), 352.
8 Kurakin, 379.
9 *DR*, IV, 552–4.
10 Kurakin, 381–2.
11 *Sbornik*, I, 116–17.
12 Ibid., I, 133–5.
13 *DR*, IV, 577–9, 590. *PSZ*, III, no. 1381, 71 ff.
14 Kurakin, 384.
15 I. A. Zheliabuzhsky, 'Zapiski', *Rossiia pri tsarevne Sof'e i Petre I*, ed. A. B. Bogdanov (M., 1990), 221.
16 *DR*, IV, 821–2.
17 M. M. Bogoslovsky, *Petr I. Materialy dlia biografii*, vol. I (M., 1940), 161–3.
18 *DR*, IV, 840–51.
19 Ibid., IV, 853–6.
20 *PiB*, I, 21.
21 Ibid., IV, 379.
22 Kurakin. 389.
23 Consett, xxxiii.
24 Nartov, 138; Stählin, no. 97, 150.
25 Whitworth, 64–5.
26 G. V. Esipov, 'Zhizneopisanie kniazia A. D. Menshikova', *Russkii arkhiv*, 1875, no. 7, 236; D. Serov, 'Pervonachal'noe nakoplenie kapitala: tainy imperii kniazia Menshikova', *Russkaia Aziia*, 41, no. 11, 1994, 3.
27 *PiB*, I, 331; II (1703), 126; III (1704), 94, 159, 321.
28 Ibid., III, 700.

29 Ibid., II, 220–1.
30 Ibid., IV, 184.
31 Korb, II, 6.
32 *PSZ*, III, no. 1536, 220–3.
33 N. A. Baklanova, ed. 'Tetradi startsa Avramiia', *Istoricheskii arkhiv*, 7 (1951), 143–55; Golikova, 78–86.
34 Golikova, 131–2.
35 Gordon, VI, 96r–96v.
36 Gordon; Zheliabuzhsky, 'Zapiski', 257. Golikova, 87–101.

III *The Grand Embassy* 1697–99

1 Solov'ev, 137.
2 A. Babkin, 'Pis'ma Frantsa i Petra Lefortov o "Velikom posol'stve" ', *VI*, 1976, no. 4, 124–5.
3 Anthony G. Cross *Peter the Great through British Eyes. Perceptions and Representations of the Tsar since 1698* (Cambridge, 2000), 8.
4 Babkin, 'Pis'ma', 126–7.
5 Bantysh-Kamensky, IV, 208.
6 Quoted in L. Oliva, *Peter the Great. Great Lives Observed* (Englewood Cliffs, NJ, 1970), 108.
7 A. Arkhangel'sky, *Domik Petra Velikogo v Saardame* (Kazan', 1901), 7, 11.
8 Cross, *Peter the Great*, 10–11.
9 RGADA, f. 9, kn. 53, l. 635, 637.
10 Consett, 210.
11 Quoted in L. Loewenson, 'People Peter the Great Met in England. Moses Stringer, Chymist and Physician', *SEER*, 37 (1959), 459.
12 A. G. Cross, 'Petrus Britannicus: The Image of Peter the Great in 18th-century Britain', *WOR*, 4–5.
13 Wolfgang von Schmettau and Joseph Hill writing in June 1697, quoted in Janet Hartley, 'England "Enjoys the Spectacle of a Northern Barbarian". The Reception of Peter I and Alexander I', *WOR*, 12.
14 A. Vasil'chikov, 'O novom portrete Petra Velikogo', *Drevniaia i novaia Rossiia*, no. 3, 1877, 325–6.
15 *BRAPG*, 22.

16 Loewenson, 'People Peter the Great Met', 462.

17 Perry, 164. Nartov, no. 7, 10.

18 Journal for 1698, in F. Tumansky, *Sobranie raznykh zapisok i sochinenii* (SPb, 1788), III, 67–8.

19 M. M. Bogoslovsky, 'Petr I v Anglii v 1698', *Institut istorii. Moskva. Trudy*, I (1926), 399.

20 *BRAPG*, 13–14; *Bishop Burnet's History of His Own Time*, IV (Oxford, 1833), 407.

21 J. Barrow, *The Life of Peter the Great*, 3rd edn (London, n.d.), 97; A. Gaedeke, 'Peter der Grosse in England im J. 1698', *Im neuen Reich. Wochenschrift für das Leben des deutschen Volkes*, I (Jan.–June, 1872), 223.

22 Nartov, no. 6, 10.

23 A. Lentin, *Peter the Great: his Law on the Imperial Succession. The Official Commentary* (Oxford, 1996), 208–10.

24 Nartov, no. 82.

25 *BRAPG*, 16 (expenses claim from Andrew Styles: 'eighteen pairs of stockings for the blacks').

26 Austrian envoy Hofmann, in Gaedeke, 'Peter der Grosse', 217–24.

27 See *Diary of John Evelyn*, ed. John Bowle (New York, 1983), 403–4. *BRAPG*, 15.

28 Gaedeke, 'Peter der Grosse', 224–5 (Graf von Auersperg).

29 O. Beliaev, *Dukh Petra Velikogo* (SPb, 1798), 22–3; Ustrialov, III, 142.

30 S. O. Androsov, 'Petr I v Venetsii', *VI*, 1995, no. 3, 129–35.

31 Korb, I, 155–6.

32 Ibid., 156; Imperial envoy Ignatius von Guarient to Emperor Leopold I, 12 Sept. 1698, in Ustrialov, III, 621–3.

33 Korb, I, 159–60.

34 Perry, 195, 196–7.

35 PRO, State Papers 91/4 part II, ff. 112–13 (20 Feb./3 March 1706 to Secretary of State).

36 Korb, I, 257.

37 Esipov, II, 171–2.

38 Ibid., 87.

39 B. A. Uspensky, 'Historia sub specie Semioticae', in H. K. Baran, ed., *Semiotics and Structuralism. Readings from the Soviet Union* (New York, 1976), 71.

40 Korb, I, 194; II, 92.

41 Grund, 133.

42 Juel, III, 6.

IV War with Sweden 1700–8

1 *PSZ*, III, no. 1735, 680–1, no. 1736, 681–2.

2 Ibid., IV, no. 1741, 1.

3 Perry, 197–8; Cornelius de Bruyn, *Travels into Muscovy, Persia, and Part of the East Indies; containing an Accurate Description of what is most remarkable in those Countries*, 2 vols (London, 1737), I, 46.

4 Esipov, II, 176–7.

5 *PiB*, IX, 69 (3 Feb. 1709).

6 P. Shafirov, *A Discourse Concerning the Just Causes of the War between Sweden and Russia: 1700–1721*, ed. W. E. Butler (Dobbs Ferry, NY, 1973), 348.

7 [Daniel Krman], 'Maloizvestnyi istochnik po istorii severnoi voiny', *VI*, 1976, no. 12, 107.

8 Korb, II, 134.

9 Stählin, no. 89, 137–8.

10 Preface to the Military Statute, *PSZ*, V, no. 3006.

11 *PSZ*, III, no. 1747, 3.

12 Golikova, 200.

13 I. A. Zheliabuzhsky, 'Zapiski', in A. Bogdanov, *Rossiia pri tsarevne Sof'e i Petre I* (M., 1990), 283–5.

14 Solov'ev, 250.

15 Stählin, no. 88, 136–7.

16 *PSZ*, III, no. 1886, 181–2 (30 Dec. 1701).

17 Korb, II, 144; *SIRIO*, XXXIX, 24 Sept., to Harley.

18 *PiB*, II, 65 (5 June 1702).

19 Perry, 240.

20 Bruyn, *Travels*, I 25–6, 28.

21 *PSZ*, IV, no. 1907, 191–2 (3 April 1702).

22 Viktorov, II, 467–8, 469.

23 *PSZ*, IV, no. 1921, 201.

24 *Zhurnal ili podennaia zapiska Blazhennyia i vechnodostoinnyia pamiati gos. imp. Petra Velikago s 1698 goda, dazhe do zakliucheniia neishtatskogo mira*, vol. I (SPb, 1770–2), 69.

25 'O zachatii i zdanii tsarstvuiushchego grada Sanktpeterburga' (RNB OR Ermitazhnoe

sobranie, no. 359, ll. 3–13), in Bespiatykh, 258–62.

26 *PiB*, II, 204.

27 'O zachatii i zdanii tsarstvuiushchago grada', 259–60.

28 P. P. Pekarsky, *Nauka i literatura v Rossii pri Petre Velikom*, vol. I (SPb., 1862), 273–4.

29 *PiB*, III, 162; IV, 209.

30 Ibid., *PiB*, III, 385 (2 Oct.), 410 (30 Oct.).

31 Ibid., 283 (March 1705).

32 Ibid., 954.

33 G. Bogdanov, *Istoricheskoe, geograficheskoe i topograficheskoe opisanie Sanktpeterburga, ot nachala zavedeniia ego s 1703 po 1751 god.* (SPb, 1779), 283.

34 *PiB*, V, 13; *PRG*, I, 1.

35 *PV*, 157.

36 *SIRIO*, XXXIV, 102.

37 *200-letie.*, appendix II, 5.

38 Ibid., 14.

39 *PiB*, III, 312 (13 April 1705).

40 Ibid., 342 (14 May 1705).

41 A. V. Chernov, 'Astrakhanskoe vosstanie 1705–1706 gg.', *Istoricheskie zapiski*, 64 (1959), 196; Golikova, 226, 246–7.

42 *PSZ*, IV, no. 2015, 282–3 (16 Jan. 1705).

43 F. J. Strahlenberg, *Zapiski kapitana Filippa Ioganna Stralenberga ob istorii i geografii Rossiiskoi imperii Petra Velikogo*, trans. and ed. Iu. Besspiatykh et al. 2 vols (M.-L., 1985), I, 117, 138.

44 Esipov, II, 103.

45 PRO SP 91/4 part II, 20 Feb/3 March 1706, f. 112 to Secretary of State, Feb. 1706; *SIRIO*, XXXIX, 248–9.

46 *PiB*, III, 450.

47 Ibid., IV, 184, 751.

48 Quoted in A. Rothstein, *Peter the Great and Marlborough. Politics and Diplomacy in Converging Wars* (Basingstoke, 1986), 72.

49 V. N. Berkh, *Zhizneopisanie gen.-adm. F. M. Apraksina* (SPb., 1825), 8–9.

50 *PSZ*, IV, no. 2155, 383 (13 Aug. 1707).

51 *PiB*, VII (i), 28.

52 Ibid., VII (i), 43–4. *Pis' ma tsarevicha Alekseia Petrovicha, k ego roditeliu gosudariu Petru Velikomu, gosudaryne Ekaterine Alekseevne i kabinet-sekretariu Makarovu* (Odessa, 1849), 23.

53 *PiB*, X, 27, 476–7.

54 Ibid., VII (i), 128.

55 Ibid., 138 (14 April), 166 (14 May).

56 Nartov, 76–8.

57 *PiB*, VII (i), 600–2.

58 Ibid., 131–2.

59 Ibid., 167 (15 May 1708).

60 Ibid., VIII, 36–7 (23 July 1708).

61 V. S. Bobylev, *Vneshniaia politika Rossii epokhi Petra I* (M., 1990), 51.

62 Whitworth, *SIRIO*, L, 61–2.

63 *PiB*, VIII, 72–3 (9 Aug. 1708).

64 Ibid., 90 (17 Aug. 1708).

65 Ibid., IV, 185. Stählin, no. 96, 148–9.

66 Ibid., VI, 110, 117; VIII, 287.

67 Ibid., III, 760.

68 Ibid., XI (ii), 154–5 (28 Sept. 1711).

69 O. Subtelny, 'Mazepa, Peter I, and the Question of Treason', *Harvard Ukrainian Studies*, 2 (1978), 170–1, 175.

70 Whitworth, 14.

71 *PiB*, VIII, 237 (27 Oct. 1708).

72 Subtelny, 'Mazepa', 180; *PiB*, IX, 321.

73 Dispatches to Henry Boyle, PRO, State Papers Foreign, Sweden, SP 95, vol. XVII in T. Mackiv, *English Reports on Mazepa, 1687–1709* (New York, 1983), 129–30.

74 *PiB*, VI, 92 (12 Sept. 1707); IV, 27 (21 Jan. 1706).

V From Poltava to Pruth 1709–11

1 *PiB*, VIII, 334.

2 [Daniel Krman], 'Maloizvestnyi istochnik po istorii severnoi voiny', *VI*, 1976, no. 12, 98.

3 *PiB*, IX, 174 (to Menshikov, 9 May 1709).

4 Ibid., 167–8.

5 Ibid., 200.

6 Ibid., 226.

7 P. Englund, *The Battle of Poltava. The Birth of the Russian Empire* (London, 1992), 155.

8 *PiB*, IX, 236.

9 *Kniga Marsova ili Voinskikh del* (1713/1766), 71; *PiB*, IX, 258–62.

10 *PiB*, IX, 388.

11 Erebro Rasmus, quoted in E. Mosgovaia,

'Obraz Petra I-imperatora v proizvedeni-iakh tvorchestva Bartolommeo Karlo Rastrelii', *Monarkhiia i narodovlastie v kul'ture prosveshcheniia* (M., 1995), 3–4.

12 Juel, III, 134–5.

13 *PiB*, IX, 231; LOI, d. 107, ll. 254–5 (16 Aug. 1724).

14 V. Ger'e, *Sbornik pisem i memorialov Leibnitsa, otnosiashchikhsia k Rossii i Petru Velikomy* (SPb., 1873), 177–80.

15 *PiB*, X, 32.

16 Ibid., 35.

17 Ibid., 223.

18 Ibid., VIII, 460, 462.

19 Ibid., X, 361.

20 *Medals*, no. 46.

21 'Reskripty i ukazy Petra I k lifliandskim general-gubernatoram: Polonskomu, kn. Golitsynu i kn. Repninu', *OV*, VI, 34–5 (7 Feb. 1716).

22 Weber, II, 98.

23 *Zhurnal ili podennaia zapiska*, part 1, 251–2.

24 *PiB*, X, 57.

25 Juel, III, 18.

26 *PSZ*, IV, no. 2272, 494–7; *PiB*, X, 311–16.

27 *ZA*, 162.

28 Juel, III, 114.

29 Ibid., 113.

30 *PiB*, XI (i), 60.

31 *PSZ*, IV, no. 2328, 634–5; no. 2330, 635.

32 *PiB*, XI (i), 144.

33 *Istoriia pravitel'stvuiushego Senata za 200 let*, vol. I (SPb, 1911), 123.

34 *PiB*, XI (i), 218, 489.

35 Ibid., 237.

36 Ibid., 166.

37 Ibid., XI (ii), 112 (1 Sept. 1711).

38 Ibid., XIII (i), 93 (28 Feb. 1713).

39 *ZA*, 206–7 (2 July 1713).

40 *PiB*, XI (i), 84.

41 *PZh*, 1711, 308.

42 *PiB*, XI (i), 230, 496 (12 May).

43 Juel, III, 133.

44 Esipov, I, 134–55, 159–64.

45 *PiB*, XI (i), 151–2 (23 March 1711).

46 Quoted in B. Sumner, *Peter the Great and the Ottoman Empire* (Oxford, 1950), 44.

47 *PiB*, XI (i), 305.

48 Stählin, no. 17, 45–6.

49 *PiB*, XI (ii), 12.

50 Ibid., 41 (28 July).

51 Ibid., 137.

52 Quoted in Sumner, *Ottoman*, 40.

53 *PiB*, XI (ii), 138.

54 Ibid., 140.

55 Ibid., X, 281.

56 Ibid., XI (ii), 123, 124–5, 133.

57 Ibid., 170 (14 Oct. and 17 Sept. 1711).

58 S. V. Efimov, 'Tsarevich Aleksei v S. Peterburge', *Peterburgskie chteniia 96* (SPb, 1996), 56.

59 Weber, II, 105.

60 *PiB*, XII (i), 41, 120.

VI Peter in Europe 1712–17

1 *PiB*, XII (i), 9–10.

2 Ibid., 17–25.

3 Ibid., 37.

4 Ibid., 44–5.

5 Ibid., 81–2.

6 Ibid., 86, 361.

7 Ibid., 83.

8 V. I. Vasil'ev, *Starinnye feierverki v Rossii (XVII-perv. ch. XVIII v.* (L., 1960), 51.

9 *PiB*, XII (i), 114, 331; Weber, I, 92.

10 Ibid., 115–16.

11 Ibid., 133.

12 Ibid., 141.

13 Ibid., 180.

14 Ibid., XII (ii), 31.

15 Ibid., 54, 62.

16 Ibid., 135.

17 Ibid., 64.

18 Ibid., 167, 174–5.

19 *200-letie*, 9–10; LOI, f. 270, d. 72, f. 173.

20 *MIGO*, I (i), 16.

21 'Tsaritsa Ekaterina Alekseevna', *Russkaia starina*, 1880, 766.

22 *MIGO*, I (i), 47–8.

23 Grebeniuk, 72–4.

24 Bantysh-Kamensky, IV, 213; *MIGO*, I (ii), 19.

25 LOI, d. 73, l. 177 (19 Sept. 1713).

26 *PSZ*, V, (10 Jan, 1714); LOI, f. 270, d. 75, l. 10.

27 *Sbornik Mukhanova*, 2nd edn (SPb, 1866), 251.

28 Nartov, 83–4.

29 'Reskripty i ukazy Petra I', *OV,* IV, 22 (to Prince Golitsyn in Reval, 29 June 1714).

30 *MIGO*, I (ii), 209.

31 LOI, d. 76, l. 119.

32 Weber, I, 36.

33 Quoted in R. Warner, 'British Merchants and Russian Men-of-War', *PGW*, 109.

34 *MIGO*, I (i), 67.

35 Weber, I, 89–90. Thanks to Ernest Zitser.

36 *PSZ*, V, no. 2762 (20 Jan. 1714), 76; no. 2778 (28 Feb. 1714), 86.

37 Ibid., no. 2789.

38 Weber, I , 44, 105.

39 *The Tryal of the Czarewitz Alexis Petrowitz, who was condemn'd at Petersbourg, on the 25th of June, 1718* (London, 1725), 10.

40 Ustrialov, VI, prilozhenie, 346–8.

41 Ibid., 348–9.

42 M. I. Semevsky, *Tsaritsa Praskov'ia 1664–1724* (M., 1989), 69.

43 *DPPS*, VI (i), no. 388, 326–8.

44 Muller, 30, 40.

45 LOI, d. 101, ll. 705–705 rev. (1722).

46 V. S. Bobylev, *Vneshniaia politika Rossii epokhi Petra I* (M., 1990), 107.

47 John Barrow, *The Life of Peter the Great* (Edinburgh, 1894), 291.

48 *PRG*, I, no. 83; To Prince M. Golitsyn, LOI, d. 84, l. 24.

49 LOI, d. 84, ll. 19–20 (Jan. 4, 1717)

50 LOI, d. 86, l. 44.

51 Ibid., l. 67.

52 M. Poludensky, 'Petr Velikii v Parizhe', *Russkii arkhiv*, 1965, nos. 5–6, 2–27.

53 RGADA, f. 9, kn. 53, l. 84; Grebeniuk, 77–8.

54 LOI, d. 84, l. 179 (21 Oct. 1717).

55 Kurakin, 378–9.

56 *ZA*, 60.

57 Ibid., 270.

58 Ibid., 377; *PSZ*, no. 3261 (22 Dec. 1718).

59 *PSZ*, VI, no. 3947, 643 (6 April 1722).

60 M. I. Semevsky, *Slovo i delo 1700–1725 Ocherki i rasskazy iz russkoi istorii XVIII veka* (SPb, 1884), 297.

61 Ibid., 310; RNB, Otdel rukopisei, f. 450.

VII *Father and Sons* 1718–20

1 Ustrialov, VI, 388–9. For a detailed analysis of the politics of the Alexis affair, see P. Bushkovitch, *Peter the Great. The Struggle for Power, 1671–1725* (Cambridge, 2001), which appeared after the present book was being prepared for publication.

2 Ustrialov, VI, 411.

3 Texts in S. A. Prokhvatilova, *Neprotrebnyi syn. Delo tsarevicha Alekseia Petrovicha* (SPb, 1996), 335–42; Ustrialov, VI 442–4, *PSZ*, VI no. 3151, *ZA*, 164–9, 169–70.

4 Prokhvatilova, 343.

5 Ia. Gordin, 'Delo tsarevicha Alekseiai ili tiazhba o tsene reform', *Zvezda*, 1991, no. 11, 130.

6 Ibid., 134–5.

7 Ibid., 135.

8 Ibid., 140.

9 *PSZ*, V, no. 3159.

10 Stählin, no. 27, 58.

11 *200-letie*, 76. Pekarsky, *Nauka i literatura v Rossii pri Petre Velikom*, 2 vols. (SPb, 1862), I, 57.

12 *200-letie*, 247.

13 Pekarsky, *Nauka*, I, 56.

14 Nartov, 70.

15 Ustrialov, VI, 240.

16 *The Tryal of the Czarewitz Alexis Petrowitz, who was condemn'd at Petersbourg on the 25th of June 1718* (London, 1725), 74, 91.

17 O. F. Kozlov, 'Delo tsarevicha Alekseiia', VI, 1969, no. 9, 214.

18 Weber, I, 229.

19 *Kraevedcheskie zapiski. Issledovaniia i materialy, vyp. 2. Petropavlovski Sobor i velikokniazheskaia usypal'nitsa* (SPb, 1994), 63.

20 Weber, I , 229–31.

21 Dmitry Merezhkovsky, *Petr i Aleksei. Roman* (M., 1994), 136.

22 *ZA*, 164.

23 *PSZ*, V, no. 3241, 597–8.

24 Weber, I , 188.

25 Bergholz, II, 71.

26 N. D. Beliaev, 'Russkoe obshchestva pri Petre Velikom', *Den'* (1864), no 2, 5–6.

27 *BP*, 401–2.

28 Ibid., 432–3.
29 Ibid., 467.
30 Ibid., 458–9 (6 April 1722).
31 *PSZ*, VI, no. 3777, 382 (29 April 1721).
32 Ibid., no. 3676, 264 (16 Nov. 1720).
33 *BP*, 427.
34 *PSZ*, VI, no. 3585, 193–4 (20 May 1720. Repeat of 13 June 1718); no. 3799, 402–3 (24 June 1721).
35 Ibid., VI, no. 3799, 402–3.
36 Stählin, no. 33, 65.
37 Weber, I, 278.
38 *PSZ*, VI, no. 3494, 121; no. 3676, 264.
39 *BP*, 425–6 (28 June 1721).
40 *ZA*, 61–3; *PSZ*, V, no. 3244.
41 *PSZ*, V, no. 3294.
42 Ibid., no. 3380.
43 RNB, Otdel rukopisei, f. 480, op. 2, l. 1 (Podennye zapiski Kn. A. D. Menshikova).
44 LOI, d. 90, 2 Jan. 1719, l. 7.
45 Ibid., 13 Jan., l. 40, 16 Jan., l. 54.
46 Ibid., 27 Jan., l. 84.
47 Ibid., 12 Feb., l. 109.
48 *Petrovskoe vremia v litsakh* (SPb, 1999), 10.
49 LOI, d. 90, 23 Feb., l. 127.
50 *PSZ*, VI, no. 3338.
51 LOI, d. 90, 24 March, l. 224.
52 Weber, I, 265.
53 *PRG* I, 76, 80.
54 RNB Otdel rukopisei, f. 480, op. 2, ll. 35–35 v.
55 Weber, I, 266.
56 Stählin, no. 95, 146–8.
57 LOI, d. 90, l. 443.
58 *BRAPG*, 204–6.
59 LOI, d. 90, l. 20.
60 *PSZ*, V, no. 3464 (10 Dec.).
61 Bergholz, I, 52–3. *200–letie*, 76–7.
62 *PSZ*, VI, no. 3485, no. 3937.
63 Ibid., 2; *ZA*, 74.
64 *PSZ*, no. 3937, 526–637.
65 Ibid., no. 3534, 141–60 (28 Feb. 1720).
66 Ibid., VII, no. 4422, 205 (20 Jan.).
67 Peterson, 115.
68 *ZA*, 290.
69 M. I. Semevsky, *Slovo I delo, 1700–1725. Ocherki i rasskazy iz russkoi istorii XVIII veka* (SPb, 1884), 314–15; *PiB*, VI, 301–2; *PZh*, 1720, 13.
70 *PZh*, 1720, 29–30.
71 N. V. Kaliazina and G. N. Komelova, *Russkoe iskusstvo Petrovskoi epokhi* (L., 1990), ills. 167 and 173.
72 Grebeniuk, 236.
73 Nepliuev, 102–3.
74 *PZh*, 1720, 39–40.

VIII The Year of Nystad 1721

1 A. F. Bychkov, *Pis 'ma Petra Velikogo, khraniashchiesia v imp. Publ. biblioteke* (SPb, 1872), 78–9.
2 Kurakin, 386.
3 Weber, I , 90–1.
4 RNB, Otdel rukopisei, Ermitazhnoe, 450; M. I. Semevsky, *Slovo i delo 1700–1725. Ocherki i rasskazy iz russkoi istorii XVIII veka* (SPb, 1884), 313–14.
5 P. V. Verkhovskoi, *Uchrezhdenie Dukhovnoi Kollegii i Dukhovnyi reglament,* 2 vols (Rostov/Don, 1916) I, 155.
6 G. Vernadsky, *A Source Book for Russian History* (New Haven, 1972), I, 256.
7 Muller, 30–41.
8 Nartov, 57–8.
9 Quoted in translation in M. Raeff, ed. *Peter the Great Changes Russia* (Lexington, 1972), 39–43.
10 Stählin, no. 54, 92; no. 79, 126; no. 100, 154–5.
11 Esipov, I, 59–84.
12 Nartov, 70.
13 *PiB*, I, 95.
14 Ibid., IX (i), 331.
15 LOI, d. 107, ll. 254–5.
16 *PiB*, XI, 230, 241.
17 Nartov, 142.
18 *PSZ*, VI, no. 3485, 42–4 (on priests), 49–50 (on good behaviour on board ship).
19 Weber, I , 236.
20 *PSZ*, VI, no. 3759, 370–1.
21 Ibid., no. 3771, 377.
22 *ZA*, 168.
23 *SIRIO*, XV, 204–5.
24 J. Cracraft, *The Church Reform of Peter the Great* (London 1971), 22.

25 *SIRIO*, LX, 191–2.

26 Ibid. XL, 168–9.

27 LOI, d. 97, l. 233.

28 *PSZ*, IV, no. 2132, 363.

29 *SIRIO*, XL, 39–40; Bergholz, I, 136.

30 Bassewitz, 133, 197.

31 LOI, d. 97, l. 317 rev., 318, 329–40.

32 Ibid., d. 97, l. 353.

33 Ibid., d. 97, l. 352 (2 April 1721) and l. 360 (15 April).

34 Ibid., d. 97, l. 322, 421.

35 Ibid., d. 97, l. 115 to V. Dolgoruky.

36 *PZh*, 42–4.

37 *PSZ*, VII, no. 4912; LOI, f. 270, d. 97, l. 442 ff.

38 *SIRIO*, LII, 195; Bergholz, I, 178–84.

39 LOI, d. 98, l. 119.

40 *PZh*, 73.

41 Ibid. See S. O. Androsov, *Zhivopisets Ivan Nikitin* (SPb, 1998).

42 *PSZ*, VI, no. 3819, 420–31.

43 'Reskripty i ukazy Petra I', *OV*, IV, 68.

44 *PZh*, 1721, 75.

45 'Opisannoe samovidtsem torzhestvo, proiskhodivshee v S-Peterburge 22 okt. 1721 goda', *Syn otechestva*, 1849, book 2, 1–4.

46 *ZA*, 155–9.

47 V. I. Vasil'ev, *Starinnye feierverki v Rossii (XVII–perv. Ch. XVIII veka)* (L., 1960, 47–8.

48 Bergholz, I, 131.

49 Weber, I, 323.

50 LOI, d. 106, ll. 83–4. (14 Jan. 1724).

51 Bergholz, I, 189.

52 Stählin, 42.

53 Weber, I, 352.

54 *SIRIO*, XL, 348–9.

55 J. E. Clay, 'God's People in the Early 18th Century. The Uglich Affair of 1717', *CMRS*, 26 (1985), 107.

IX Ranks and Regulations 1722-23

1 Perry, 271, 274.

2 Bassewitz, 212–13.

3 *ZA*, 175–6; *PSZ*, VI no. 3893, 496–7.

4 LOI, d. 101, l. 120.

5 *PSZ*, VI no. 3947, 642–3.

6 Ibid., no. 3965, 653.

7 LOI, d. 106, l. 565.

8 Ibid., f. 270, d. 101, ll. 248–50, 613.

9 *PSZ*, VI, no. 3970, 656–7.

10 *ZA*, 124.

11 *PSZ*, V, no. 2876, 137.

12 Ibid., no. 3711, 311–12.

13 Ibid., VI, no. 3919.

14 Korb, II, 153.

15 *PSZ*, VI, no. 3979, 662–4.

16 Ibid., VII, no. 4507, 285–6.

17 Golombievsky, 15.

18 Ibid., 12.

19 Ibid., 16.

20 *PSZ*, VI, no. 3937, 544.

21 LOI, d. 101, ll. 204–7.

22 *PSZ*, VI, no. 4047, 726–36.

23 Ibid. VII, no. 4490, 276.

24 LOI, d. 101, l. 232.

25 *Sbornik*, II, 116, 120.

26 *ZA*, 182.

27 Nartov, no. 94, 64.

28 *PZh*, 1722, 192.

29 *BP*, no. 375, (30 Aug.).

30 *PZh*, 1723, 2.

31 *SIRIO*, XLIX, 321–3; Bassewitz, 221–2.

32 *Sbornik*, II, 96; LOI, d. 105, ll. 15, 16, 17.

33 Bassewitz, 222; *PZh*, 1723, 8, 32.

34 Grebeniuk, 236.

35 LOI, d. 105, l. 30.

36 Ibid. d. 103, l. 535.

37 RNB, Otdel rukopisei, f. 1003, d. 11, l. 373.

38 *BP*, 520–1.

39 T. Filippov, *Odin iz neizdannykh 'iurnalov' Petrovskogo tsarstvovaniia za 1723–1724* (Kiev, 1912), 17; *PZh*, 1723, 16–17.

40 Filippov, 22–3.

41 Bassewitz, 233. LOI, d. 103, l. 644.

42 *PZh*, 1723, 18–19, and 'Morskaia khronika', 26–8, *PSZ*, VII, no. 4562, 345.

43 LOI, d. 104, l. 24.

44 *PSZ*, VII, no. 4298, 110–12.

45 LOI, d. 101, ll. 244–4 rev.

46 Ibid., d. 104, ll. 32–32 rev. *PSZ*, VII, no. 4301.

47 *SIRIO*, XL, 281 ff.

48 Filippov, 22.

49 LOI, d. 104, ll. 163–4, 169; *ZA*, 131–2.
50 *PSZ*, VII, no. 4344, 147–50. 400.
51 Ibid., VII, no. 4345, 150–1.
52 LOI, d. 103, l. 292, 336–7, 517.
53 Weber, I , 247–8. Stählin, no. 23, 53.
54 Stählin, no. 48, 84.
55 V. Berkh, 'Zhizneopisanie gen.-leit. V. I. Gennina', *Gornyi zhurnal*, 1826, book 4, 128.
56 LOI, d. 1014, ll. 198, 200.
57 Ibid., d. 104, l. 495.
58 Ibid., d. 104, l. 459; d. 106, ll. 80–80 ob.
59 *ZA*, 179–80. *PSZ*, VII, no. 4366, 161–2.
60 Grebeniuk, 83–4.

X A Coronation and a Funeral 1724–25

1 *PZh*, 1724, 30–1.
2 LOI, d. 106, l. 36, 97–97 rev.
3 *PZh*, 1724, 35.
4 Bergholz, II, 16–17.
5 LOI, d. 106, ll. 132–4.
6 Bergholz, II, 10–11. Bassewitz, 242.
7 LOI, d. 106, ll. 197–207; *PSZ*, VII, no. 4443, 220–4.
8 Weber, I , 15–16.
9 LOI, d. 84, l. 60.
10 *PZh*, 1724, 37–8.
11 LOI, d. 106, ll. 468–9.
12 *PZh*, 1724, 4; S. Novoselov, *Opisanie kafedral'nogo sobora vo imia sviatykh Pervoverkhovnykh Apostolov Petra i Pavla* (SPb, 1857), 283–4.
13 LOI, d. 106, l. 496.
14 Ibid., d. 106, ll. 491, 492 , 516.
15 Ibid., d. 107, l. 581.
16 *PSZ*, VII, no. 4501, 281.
17 Alekseeva, 96–7.
18 Bergholz, II, 43.
19 LOI, d. 107, l. 39.
20 Ibid., d. 107, l. 148.
21 Ibid., d. 107, l. 189.
22 Ibid., d. 107, ll. 159–60 rev; *Petr Velikii. Pervyi ovtsevod na iuge Rossii* (M., 1872), 52.
23 LOI, d. 107, l. 184.
24 Ibid., d. 107, l. 255 = also book 63, l. 649.
25 Ibid., d. 107, l. 290; ZA, 148.
26 L. N. Semenova, 'Inostrannye mastera v Peterburge v pervoi treti XVIII v.', *Nauka i kul'tura Rossii XVIII v. Sbornik statei* (L., 1984), 207.
27 Ivan Pososhkov, *The Book of Poverty and Wealth*, ed. and transl. A. Vlasto and L. Lewitter (London, 1987), 282.
28 *PSZ*, VI, no. 3937, 539.
29 *PiB*, XIII (i), 178.
30 LOI, d. 104, l. 531 (Dec. 1723).
31 Nartov, 34.
32 Nepliuev, 107.
33 *SIRIO*, XL, 273–4.
34 Grebeniuk, 85–6.
35 *SIRIO*, III, 387–8.
36 LOI, d. 107, 328–328 rev.
37 Stählin, no. 110, 170–3.
38 Villebois, quoted in N. Pavlenko, 'Strasti u trona Ekateriny I', *Rodina*, 1993, no. 10, 109.
39 *PZh*, 1724, 22–3.
40 Bergholz, II, 75.
41 O. Neverov, ' "His Majesty's Cabinet" and Peter I's Kunstkammer', in O. Impey and A. McGregor, eds, *The Origins of Museums. The Cabinet of Curiosities in 16th–17th-Century Europe* (Oxford, 1985), 58.
42 *SIRIO*, LII, 358–9.
43 LOI, d. 107, l. 468 *PZh*, 1724, 24.
44 Ibid., d. 109, l. 2.
45 *PZh*, 1725, 1–3.
46 LOI, d. 109, l. 24. Stählin, no. 111, 174–5.
47 *SIRIO*, LII, 437ff.
48 Bassewitz, 257.
49 T. A. Lebedeva, *Ivan Nikitin* (M., 1975), 88; S. O. Androsov, *Zhivopisets Ivan Nikitin* (SPb, 1997), 83–4.
50 V. Iu. Matveev, 'Raznykh zhudozhestv mastera', *Nauka i kul'tura Rossii XVIII. Sbornik statei* (L., 1984), 154.
51 *O smerti Petra Velikago. Kratkaia povest'* (SPb, 1727 [1726]), 4.
52 RNB Otdel rukopsei: 'Tseremoniia o pogrebenii ego imperatorskogo velichestva Petra I i gosudaryni tsarevny.'
53 Novoselov, *Opisanie*, 283–4.
54 Ibid., 23.

XI Legacy

1 N. Tikhomirov, *V pamiati Petra Velikogo. Sbornik literaturnykh proizvedenii, otnosi-ashchikhsia k Petru Pervomu, izdannyi po povodu 200-letniago iubileia rozhdeniia tsaria-preobrazovatelia* (SPb, 1872), 321–2.

2 E. Shmurlo, *Petr Velikii v otsenke sovremen-nikov i potomstva* (SPb, 1912), primechaniia, 39. Ia. Grot, 'Petr Velikii kak prosvetitel' Rossii', in *Sbornik otdeleniia russkogo iazyka i slovestnosti imp. Akademii Nauk*, X (1872), no. 3, 42–3.

3 Nepliuev, 122.

4 Quoted in Janet Hartley, 'Changing Perspectives: British Views of Russia from the Grand Embassy to the Peace of Nystad', *PGW*, 66.

5 *SIRIO*, XV, 252 (Mardefeld); LII, 427 (Campredon).

6 *200-letie*, appendix II, 57.

7 Grebeniuk, 298.

8 M. Cherniavsky, *Tsar and People: Studies in Russian Myths* (New York, 1961), 86.

9 S. Novoselov, *Opisanie kafedral'nogo sobora vo imia sviatykh Pervoverkhovnykh Apostolov Petra i Pavla* (SPb, 1857), 253–6.

10 J. Vrieze ed., *Catherina de keizerin en de kunsten* (Zwolle, 1996), 145.

11 *SIRIO*, XV, 313–14.

12 Feofan Prokopovich, *Sochineniia*, ed. I. P. Eremin (M.-L., 1961), 126.

13 Grund, 35–6.

14 Hartley, 'Changing Perspectives', 67.

15 *Lettres du comte Algarotti sur la Russie* (London and Paris, 1769), 64.

16 Hartley, 'Changing Perspectives', 67.

17 *PSZ*, VI, no. 4944.

18 R. Wortman, *Scenarios of Power. Myth and Ceremony of the Russian Monarchy*, 2 vols (Princeton, 1995–2001), I, 136, 293.

19 Valerie Kivelson, *Autocracy in the Provinces: the Muscovite Gentry and Political Culture in the Seventeenth Century* (Stanford, 1997), 38.

20 *PSZ*, V, no. 3006, 325; VI, no. 3485, 3.

21 Weber, I, preface.

22 Nepliuev, 122.

23 'Panegyric to Peter I' (1755), in M. Raeff, ed., *Russian Intellectual History. An Anthology* (New York, 1966), 42–8.

24 'Essay on Peter the Great', quoted in Riasanovsky, 111.

25 M. M. Shcherbatov, *On the Corruption of Morals in Russia*, ed. and trans. Antony Lentin (Oxford, 1969), 145–7.

26 *Karamzin's Memoir on Ancient and Modern Russia*, ed. Richard Pipes (New York, 1966), 123–4.

27 R. T. McNally, *The Major Works of Peter Chaadaev* (Notre Dame and London, 1969), 37, 205.

28 Quoted in Riasanovsky, 127.

29 'On the Present State of Russia' (1855), in L. Jay Oliva, *Peter the Great. Great Lives Observed* (Englewood Cliffs, N.J., 1970), 152.

30 See Riasanovsky, 166–76.

31 P. Miliukov, *Ocherki po istorii russkoi kul'-tury*, part 3 (SPb, 1903), 165–6.

32 *Sochineniia*, 1924, vol. 3 (Kara-Murza, 208).

33 19 Nov. 1928, speech to plenum of Central Committee.

XII Commemorating Peter
1725–2002

1 S. F. Librovich, *Istoriia mednogo vsadnika* (Petrograd & M., 1916), 86.

2 P. Svin'in, *Dostoprimechatel'nosti Sankt-peter-burga i ego okrestnostei*, 5 parts (SPb, 1816–28), I, 32.

3 I. Bischoff, 'Etienne Maurice Falconet', *RR*, 24 (Oct. 1965), 385.

4 *Memoirs of Louis XIV and the Regency*, quoted in M. Raeff, ed., *Peter the Great Changes Russia* (Lexington, 1972), 20.

5 I. Grabar', *V. A. Serov. Zhizn' i tvorchestvo* (M., 1913), 248–9.

6 G. Bogdanov, *Istoricheskoe, geograficheskoe i topograficheskoe opisanie Sanktpeterburga, ot nachala zavedeniia ego s 1703 po 1751 god.* (SPb, 1779), 54–5.

7 Svin'in, *Dostoprimechatel'nosti Sanktpeter-burga*, III, 44–51.

8 V. Bur'ianov, *Progulka s det' mi po S.-Peterburgu*, 3 parts (SPb, 1838) I, 75–80.

9 D. G. Bulgakovsky, *Domik Petra Velikogo i ego sviatynia v S. Peterburge* (SPb, 1891), 30.

10 *Putevoditel' po S.-Peterburgu. Obrazovatel'nye ekskursii* (SPb, 1903), 157–79.

11 *Putevoditel' po S.-Peterburgu. (Ekskursii nachal'nykh shkol)* (SPb, 1914), 10, 28, 33.

12 F. Litvinov, *K voprosu, v kakoi palate skonchalsia imp. Petr Velikii* (SPb, 1913).

13 Svin'in, *Dostoprimechatel'nosti Sanktpeterburga*, III, 23–4.

14 Bur'ianov, *Progulka*, I, 83–99.

15 I. Pushkarev, *Kafedral'nyi sobor sv. apostol Petra i Pavla*, (Sankt-Peterburgskikh vedomostei, otdel vtoroi. Chast' neoffitsial'naia) n.d., 39.

16 *Vysochashe podverzhdennyi proekt o sooruzhenii pamiatnika v gorode Voronezhe imp. Petru Velikomu* (M., 1834).

17 N. D. Naumova and G. A. Kvashina, *Domik Petra I v Kolomenskom* (M., 1990), 11–12.

18 *Domik Petra Velikogo v Vologde* (SPb, 1887).

19 Bur'ianov, *Progulka* III, 16–17.

20 O. Beliaev, *Kabinet Petra Velikogo*, 3 vols (SPb, 1800), I, 15, 47–8.

21 *Pamiatniki russkoi kul'tury pervoi chetverti XVIII veka v sobranii Gos. ordena Lenina Ermitazha. Katalog* (L.-M., 1966), 16.

22 RNB, no. 18.151.2.322. One sheet.

23 A. V. Belgorodskii, *Maloe slovo o velikom (po povodu 200-letiia osnovaniia Peterburga* (Reval, 1903), 6.

24 RNB, no. 34. 84. 9.105. One sheet.

25 *Dvukhsotletie slavnoi Poltavskoi pobedy oderzhennoi Russkimi voiskami nad Shvedami* (SPb, 1909).

26 *Tsar' na Poltavskikh prazdnestvakh 26–27 iunia 1909 g.* (SPb, 1909), 47.

27 N. G. Rogacheva, comp. *Domik Petra I na Petrogradskoi storone* (L., 1941), 16.

28 *Domik Petra I v muzee zapovednike 'Kolomenskom'* (M., 1966).

29 *Pamiatniki russkoi kul'tury*, 24.

30 A. Romm, *Pamiatnik Petru I v Leningrade* (M.-L., 1944), 24.

31 L. K. Ziazeva, *Domik Petra I. Putevoditel' po muzeiu* (L., 1983), 57.

32 *Muzei zapovednik, 'Martsyal'nye vody'* (Petrozavodsk, 1980).

33 James Cracraft, 'The Tercentenary of Peter the Great in Russia', *CASS*, 8 (1974), 319.

34 Ia. E. Vodarskii, 'Petr I', *VI*, no. 6 (1993), 77. Anatoly Lanshchikov, 'Imperatorbol'shevik', *Rodina*, no. 3 (1992), 86–92.

35 Natalia Davydova, 'The Horror of Historical Analogies', *Moscow News*, 13–20 Dec. 1998, on a series of lectures for teachers on 'The Tragedy of Reform in Russia'.

36 N. V. Riasanovsky, 'The Image of Peter the Great in Russian History and Thought and its Present Condition', in G. Szvak, ed. *The Place of Russia in Europe* (Budapest, 1999), 184.

37 'Rasskaz o tom, kak Petr I reformiroval rossiiskuiu armiiu', *Armiia*, 1992, nos. 11–12, 70–2.

38 Deborah Adelman, *The Children of Perestroika. Moscow Teenagers Talk about their Lives and Future* (New York, 1992), 143.

39 *Petr Velikii i Moskva. Katalog vystavki*, ed. N. S. Vladimirskaia (M., 1998), preface.

40 Anatolii Agragenin and Iurii Trefilov, 'Den' Peterburga', *Sankt-Petersburgskie vedomosti*, 6 Sept. 1997.

41 Gennady Morozov, 'Imperator', *Mednyi vsadnik*, no. 1, 1998, 59–60.

Select Bibliography

The bibliography provides both a guide to further reading on Peter and his era in English and an indication of the major English-language secondary sources consulted during the writing of this book, in addition to the citations given in the Notes and the Abbreviations. It concentrates on works published in the last twenty years, although older works of continuing usefulness are included. General histories of Russia and general reference works are not included. A final section lists some recent works (1996–2001) published in Russian. A fuller bibliography of earlier Russian scholarship will be found in my *Russia in the Age of Peter the Great* (1998).

The Seventeenth-and Eighteenth-Century Background

Avrich, P. *Russian Rebels 1600–1800* (New York, 1972).

Baehr, S. *The Paradise Myth in Eighteenth-Century Russia* (Stanford, 1991).

Baron, S. and Kollmann, N. *Religion and Culture in Early Modern Russia and Ukraine* (DeKalb, Ill. 1997).

Billington, J. *The Icon and the Axe* (New York, 1966).

Black, J. L. *Citizens for the Fatherland. Education, Educators and Pedagogical Ideals in Eighteenth-Century Russia* (Boulder, Colo., 1979).

Boss, V. *Newton and Russia: the Early Influences 1698–1796* (Cambridge, Mass., 1972).

Brown, W. *A History of Eighteenth-Century Russian Literature* (Ann Arbor, 1978).

Cherniavsky, M. *Tsar and People: Studies in Russian Myths* (New York, 1961).

Cross, A. G. 'By the Banks of the Neva'. *Chapters from the Lives and Careers of the British in Eighteenth-Century Russia* (Cambridge, 1996).

—— 'By the Banks of the Thames'. *Russians in Eighteenth-Century Britain* (Cambridge, 1980).

Crummey, R. O. *Aristocrats and Servitors: the Boyar Elite in Russia, 1613–1689* (Princeton, 1983).

Dixon, S. *The Modernisation of Russia 1676–1825* (Cambridge, 1999).

Duffy, C. *Russia's Military Way to the West* (London, 1981).

Dukes, P. *The Making of Russian Absolutism 1613–1801* (London and New York, 1990).

Freeze, G. *The Russian Levites. The Parish Clergy in the Eighteenth Century* (Cambridge, Mass., 1977).

Fuller, W. C. *Strategy and Power in Russia 1600–1914* (New York, 1992).

Givens, R. D. *Servitors or Seigneurs: The Nobility and the Eighteenth-Century Russian State* (Michigan, 1984).

Hartley, J. *A Social History of the Russian Empire 1650–1825* (London, 1999).

Hittle, J. *The Service City. State and Townsmen in Russia 1600–1800* (Cambridge, Mass., 1979).

Karlinsky, S. *Russian Drama from its Beginnings to the Age of Pushkin* (Berkeley, 1985).

Keep, J. *Soldiers of the Tsar: Army and Society in Russia 1462–1874* (Oxford, 1985).

Kivelson, V. *Autocracy in the Provinces. The Muscovite Gentry and Political Culture in the Seventeenth Century* (Stanford, 1997).

Kollmann, N. *By Honor Bound. State and Society in Early Modern Russia* (Ithaca, NY, 1999).

LeDonne, J. P. *Absolutism and Ruling Class. The Formation of the Russian Political Order, 1700–1825* (Oxford, 1991).

—— *The Russian Empire and the World, 1700–1917: the Geopolitics of Expansion and Containment* (Oxford, 1997).

Longworth, P. *Alexis Tsar of All the Russias* (London, 1984).

Marker, G. *Publishing, Printing and the Origins of Intellectual Life in Russia 1700–1800* (Princeton, 1985).

Michels, G. B. *At War with the Church. Religious Dissent in Seventeenth-Century Russia* (Stanford, 1999).

Moon, D. *The Russian Peasantry 1600–1930. The World the Peasants Made* (London and New York, 1999).

Okenfuss, M. *The Discovery of Childhood in Russia. The Evidence of the Slavic Primer* (Newtonville, Mass., 1980).

—— *The Rise and Fall of Latin Humanism in Early Modern Russia* (DeKalb, Ill., 1995).

Pintner, W. and D. K. Rowney, eds. *Russian Officialdom. The Bureaucratisation of Russian Society from the 17th–20th Century* (Chapel Hill, NC, 1980).

Pushkareva, N. *Women in Russian History: from the Tenth to the Twentieth Century*, ed. and trans. E. Levin (Armonk, NY, 1997).

Raeff. M. *Origins of the Russian Intelligentsia. The Eighteenth-Century Nobility* (New York, 1966).

—— *Understanding Imperial Russia. State and Society in the Old Regime* (New York, 1984).

Rogger, H. *National Consciousness in Eighteenth-Century Russia* (Cambridge, Mass., 1960).

Stevens, C. B. *Soldiers on the Steppe. Army Reform and Social Change in Early Modern Russia* (DeKalb, Ill., 1995).

Thyrêt, I. *Between God and Tsar. Religious Symbolism and Royal Women of Muscovite Russia* (DeKalb, Ill., 2001).

Vlasto, A. P. *A Linguistic History of Russia to the End of the Eighteenth Century* (Oxford, 1986).

Vucinich, A. *Science in Russian Culture. A History to 1860* (London, 1963).

Wirtschafter, E. K. *Structures of Society. Imperial Russia's 'People of Various Ranks'* (DeKalb, Ill., 1994).

Wortman, R. *Scenarios of Power. Myth and Ceremony in Russian Monarchy*, vol. I (Princeton, 1995).

Peter and his Reign: General

Anderson, M. S. *Peter the Great* (London and New York, 1995).

Anisimov, E. V. 'Peter I: Birth of Empire', in J. Cracraft, ed. *Major Problems in the History of Imperial Russia* (Lexington, Mass., 1994), 82–99.

—— *Progress through Coercion. The Reforms of Peter the Great* (New York, 1993).

Bushkovitch, P. *Peter the Great. The Struggle for Power 1671–1725* (Cambridge, 2001).

Cracraft, J., ed. *Peter the Great Transforms Russia* (Lexington, Mass., 1991).

De Jonge, A. *Fire and Water. A Life of Peter the Great* (London, 1979).

Hughes, L., *Russia in the Age of Peter the Great* (New Haven and London, 1998).

—— 'Peter the Great: A Hero of our Time?', *History Review*, 34 (1999), 42–7.

Kliuchevsky, V. *Peter the Great*, trans. L. Archibald (London, 1958).

Marshall, W. *Peter the Great* (London and New York, 1995).

Massie, R.K. *Peter the Great. His Life and World* (London, 1981).

Raeff, M., ed. *Peter the Great Changes Russia* (Lexington, Mass., 1972).

Soloviev, S. M. *A History of Russia* (Gulf Breeze, Fla.): vol. XXV, *Rebellion and Reform, 1682–89,* ed. L. Hughes (1989); vol. XXVI, *Peter the Great. A Reign Begins. 1689–1703,* ed. L. Hughes (1994); vol. XXIX *Peter the Great. The Great Reforms Begin,* ed. K. Papmehl (1981).

Sumner, B. *Peter the Great and the Emergence of Russia* (London, 1958).

Peter: Historiography, Image and Myth

Alexander, J. 'Comparing Two Greats: Peter I and Catherine II', *WOR*, 43–50.

Anisimov, E.V. 'Progress through Violence: from Peter the Great to Lenin and Stalin', *Russian History*, 17 (1990), 409–18.

Black, C. E. 'The Reforms of Peter the Great', in C. E. Black ed., *Rewriting Russian History* (New York, 1956), 232–59.

Cracraft, J. 'More about Peter the Great', *CASS*, 14, 1980, 535–44.

—— 'The Tercentenary of Peter the Great in Russia', *CASS*, 8 (1974), 319–26.

—— 'Kliuchevsky on Peter the Great', *CASS*, 20 (1986), 367–81.

Gasiorowska, X. *The Image of Peter the Great in Russian Fiction* (Madison, Wisc. 1979).

Hughes, L. 'Biographies of Peter', *RRP*, 13–24.

—— 'From Tsar to Emperor: Portraits of Peter the Great', in G. Szvak, ed. *The Place of Russia in Eurasia* (Budapest, 2001), 221–32.

—— 'Images of Greatness: Portraits of Peter I', in *PGW*, 250–70.

—— ' "Nothing's Too Small for a Great Man": Peter the Great's *domiki* and the Creation of the Petrine Myth' (*SEER*, forthcoming).

—— 'Peter the Great and the Fall of Communism', *Irish Slavonic Studies*, 17 (1997), 1–18.

Lewitter, L. R. 'Peter the Great and the Modern World', in P. Dukes ed. *Russia and Europe* (London, 1991), 92–107.

Marker, G. 'Soloviev's Peter', in Klein, 73–83.

McNally, R. 'Chaadaev's Evaluation of Peter the Great', *SR*, 23, (1964), 31–44.

Platt, K. 'Antichrist Enthroned: Some Demonic Visions of Russian Rulers', in P. Davidson, ed. *Russian Literature and its Demons* (New York and Oxford, 2000), 87–124.

Rasmussen, K. 'Catherine II and the Image of Peter I', *SR*, 37 (1978), 57–69.

Riasanovsky, N. *The Image of Peter the Great in Russian History and Thought* (Oxford, 1984).

—— 'The Image of Peter the Great in Russian History and Thought and its Present Condition', in G. Szvak, ed. *The Place of Russia in Europe* (Budapest, 1999), 180–7.

Family and Favourites

Alexander, J. 'Catherine I, her Court and Courtiers', *PGW*, 227–49.

Bushkovitch, P. 'Power and the Historian: the Case of Tsarevich Aleksei 1716-1718 and N. G. Ustrialov 1845–1859', *Proceedings of the American Philosophical Society*, 141 (1997), 177–212.

Hughes, L. 'A Note on the Children of Peter the Great', *SGECRN*, 21 (1993), 10–16.

Longworth, P. *The Three Empresses: Catherine I, Anna and Elizabeth of Russia* (New York, 1972).

McLeod Gilchrist, M. 'Aleksei Petrovich and Afrosin'ia Fedorovna', *Slavonica*, 1 (1994), 47–66, and 2 (1995/6), 61–4.

Monas, S. 'Anton Divier and the Police of St Petersburg', in M. Halle et al. eds. *For Roman Jakobson. Essays on the Occasion of his Sixtieth Birthday* (Hague, 1956), 361–6.

Petschauer, P. 'In Search of Competent Aides: Heinrich von Huyssen and Peter the Great', *JGO*, 26 (1978), 481–502.

Rougle, W. 'Antonio Manuel de Vieira and the Russian Court 1697–1745', *RWEC*, 577–90.

Primary Sources (See also works listed in Abbreviations)

Dmytryshyn, B. *Imperial Russia: a Source Book 1700–1917* (New York, 1967).

Hellie, R. ed. and trans. *The Muscovite Law Code (Ulozhenie) of 1649*, part I: Text and Translation (Irvine, Ca., 1988).

Kaiser, D. and Marker, G., eds. *Reinterpreting Russian History* (Oxford, 1994).

Oliva, L. J. *Peter the Great. Great Lives Observed* (Englewood Cliffs, NJ, 1970).

Peter the Great: his Law on the Imperial Succession. The Official Commentary, ed. A. Lentin, (Oxford, 1996).

Pososhkov, I. *The Book of Poverty and Wealth*, ed. and trans. L. Lewitter and A. Vlasto (London, 1987).

The Prerogative of Primogeniture ... Written on the Occasion of the Czar of Muscovy's Reasons in His Late Manifesto for the Disinheritance of his Eldest Son from the Succession to the Crown (London, 1718).

Prokopovich, F. 'Sermon on Royal Authority and Honour' (1718), in M. Raeff, ed. *Russian Intellectual History. An Anthology* (New York, 1966).

Shafirov, P. P. *A Discourse Concerning the Just Causes of the War between Sweden and Russia: 1700–1721*, ed. W. E. Butler (Dobbs Ferry, NY, 1973).

The Travel Diary of Peter Tolstoy, ed. M. Okenfuss (DeKalb, Ill., 1987).

The Tryal of the Czarewitz Alexis Petrowitz, who was Condemn'd at Petersbourg, on the 25th of June, 1718 (London, 1725).

Vernadsky, G. *A Source Book for Russian History*, vol. II (New Haven, 1972).

The Regency of Tsarevna Sophia

Hughes, L. ' "Ambitious and Daring above her Sex": Tsarevna Sophia Alekseevna (1657–1704) in Foreigners' Accounts', *Oxford Slavonic Papers*, 21 (1988), 65–89.

—— *Russia and the West: the Life of Prince V. V. Golitsyn* (Newtonville, Mass., 1984).

—— 'Sofia Alekseevna and the Moscow Rebellion of 1682', *SEER*, 63 (1985), 518–39.

—— 'Sophia, "Autocrat of All the Russias": Titles, Ritual and Eulogy in the Regency of Sophia Alekseevna (1682–89)', *CSP*, 28 (1986), 266–86.

—— *Sophia Regent of Russia, 1657–1704* (New Haven and London, 1990).

Smith, A. 'The Brilliant Career of Prince Golitsyn', *Harvard Ukrainian Studies*, 19 (1995), 639–54.

Zelensky, E. ' "Sophia the Wisdom of God": The Function of Religious Imagery during the Regency of Sofiia Alekseevna', in L. Fradenburg, ed. *Women and Sovereignty* (Edinburgh, 1992), 192–211.

Politics and Political Theory. Government, Law

Benson, S. 'The Role of Western Political Thought in Petrine Russia', *CASS*, 8 (1974), 254–73.

Bushkovitch, P. 'Aristocratic Factions and the Opposition to Peter the Great: the 1690s', *Forschungen zur osteuropäischen Geschichte*, 50 (1995), 80–120.

Cracraft, J. 'Did Feofan Prokopovich Really Write *Pravda Voli Monarshei*?', *SR*, 40 (1981), 173–93.

—— 'Empire versus Nation: Russian Political Theory under Peter I', *Harvard Ukrainian Studies*, 10 (1986), 524–41.

—— 'Opposition to Peter the Great', in E. Mendelsohn and M. Schatz, eds. *Imperial Russia 1700–1917: State, Society, Opposition* (DeKalb, Ill., 1988), 22–34.

Dukes, P. 'Some Aberdonian Influences on the Early Russian Enlightenment', *CASS*, 13 (1979), 436–51.

Hassell, J. 'Implementation of the Russian Table of Ranks during the 18th century', *SR*, 29 (1970), 283–95.

Lentin, A. 'Public Law and the Idea of the "Reguliarnoe gosudarstvo" ', *RRP*, 41–52.

Madariaga, I. de 'Tsar into Emperor: the Titles of Peter the Great', in R. Oresko et al. eds, *Royalty and Republican Sovereignty in Early Modern Russia* (Cambridge, 1996), 351–81.

Medushevskii, A. 'Administrative Reforms in the Russian Empire: Western Models and Russian Implementation', *PGW*, 36–50.

Peterson, C. *Peter the Great's Administrative and Judicial Reforms* (Stockholm, 1979).

Petschauer, P. 'The Philosopher and the Reformer: Peter I, Leibniz and the College System', *CASS*, 13 (1979), 473–87.

Schafly, D. 'The Popular Image of the West in Russia at the Time of Peter the Great', *RWEC*, 2–21.

Uspensky, B. 'Echoes of the Notion "Moscow as the Third Rome" in Peter the Great's Ideology', in Iu. Lotman and B. Uspensky, eds, *The Semiotics of Russian Culture* (Ann Arbor, 1984), 53–64.

—— 'Historia sub specie Semioticae', in H. K. Baran, ed. *Semiotics and Structuralism. Readings from the Soviet Union* (New York, 1976), 66–7

Whittaker, C. 'The Reforming Tsar: the Redefinition of Autocratic Duty in 18th-century Russia', *SR*, 51 (1992), 77–98.

Wortman, R. 'Peter the Great and Court Procedure', *CASS* , 8 (1974), 303–10.

Society: Nobles and Peasants

Anisimov, E. 'Changes in the Social Structure of Russian Society at the End of the 17th to the Beginning of the 18th Century', *SSH*, 28 (1989), 33–58.

—— 'The Struggle with Fugitives During the Reform Period', *SSH*, 28 (1989), 59–77.

Bartlett, R. 'The Peasantry and Serfdom in the Time of Peter the Great: Recent Research', *RRP*, 53–64.

Crummey, R. O. 'Peter the Great and the Boyar Aristocracy, 1689–1700', *CASS*, 8 (1974), 274–87.

Madariaga, I. de 'The Russian Nobility in the 17th and 18th Centuries', in H. M. Scott, ed. *The European Nobilities 1600–1800* (London, 1995), 223–73.

Meehan Waters, B. *Autocracy and Aristocracy. The Russian Service Elite of 1730* (New Brunswick, NJ, 1984).

—— 'The Muscovite Noble Origins of the Russian Generalitet of 1730', *CMRS*, 12 (1971), 28–75.
—— 'The Russian Aristocracy and the Reforms of Peter the Great', *CASS*, 8 (1974), 288–302.

Economy, Trade and Industry. Towns

Anisimov, E. 'Remarks on the Fiscal Policy of Russian Absolutism' [on the poll tax], *SSH*, 28 (1989), 10–32.

Baron, S. 'The Fate of the Gosti in the Reign of Peter the Great', *CMRS*, 14 (1973), 488–512.

Blanc, S. 'The Economic Policy of Peter the Great', in W. Blackwell ed. *Russian Economic Development from Peter the Great to Stalin* (New York, 1974), 21–49.

Frederiksen, O. 'Virginia Tobacco in Russia under Peter the Great', *SEER*, 21 (1943), 40–56.

Kahan, A. 'Observations on Petrine Foreign Trade', *CASS*, 8 (1974), 222–36.

—— *The Plow, the Hammer and the Knout* (Chicago, 1985).

Lewitter, L. R. 'Ivan Pososhkov (1652–1726) and "The Spirit of Capitalism"', *SEER*, 51 (1973), 524–53.

Matley, I. M. 'Defence Manufactures of St Petersburg 1703–1730', *Geographical Review*, 71 (1981), 411–26.

O'Brien, C. 'Ivan Pososhkov. Russian Critic of Mercantilist Principles', *SR*, 14 (1955), 503–11.

Foreign Policy, Diplomacy and Wars

Altbauer, D. 'The Diplomats of Peter the Great', *JGO*, 28 (1980), 1–16.

Anisimov, E. 'The Imperial Heritage of Peter the Great', in H. Ragsdale, ed., *Imperial Russian Foreign Policy* (Cambridge, 1993), 21–35.

Bagger, H. 'The Role of the Baltic in Russian Foreign Policy 1721–1773', ibid., 36–55.

Bennigsen, A. 'Peter the Great, the Ottoman Empire and the Caucasus', *CASS*, 8 (1974), 311–18.

Englund, P. *The Battle of Poltava. The Birth of the Russian Empire* (London, 1992).

Frost , R. I. *The Northern Wars, 1558–1721* (Harlow, 2000).

Herd, G. 'Peter I and the Conquest of Azov: 1695–1696', *PGW*, 161–76.

Kaminski, A. *Republic vs Autocracy. Poland, Lithuania and Russia 1686–1697* (Cambridge, Mass., 1993).

Kirby, D. 'Peter I and the Baltic', *PGW*, 177–88.

Konstam, A. *Poltava 1709. Russia Comes of Age* (London, 1994).

Lewitter, L. 'The Apocryphal Testament of Peter the Great', *Polish Review*, 6 (1966), 27–44.

—— 'Peter the Great. Poland and the Westernisation of Russia', *Journal of the History of Ideas*, 14 (1958), 493–506.

—— 'Russia, Poland and the Baltic, 1697–1721', *Historical Journal*, 2 (1968), 3–34.

—— 'The Russo-Polish Treaty of 1686 and its Implications', *Polish Review*, 9 (1964), no. 3, 5–29; no. 4, 21–37.

Mancall, M. *Russia and China: Their Diplomatic Relations to 1728* (Cambridge, Mass., 1971).

Subtelny, O. 'Mazepa, Peter I, and the Question of Treason', *Harvard Ukrainian Studies*, 2 (1978), 158–84.

—— *The Mazepists: Ukrainian Separatism in the Early Eighteenth Century* (Boulder, Col., 1981).

—— 'Peter I's Testament: a Reassessment', *SR*, 33 (1974), 663–78.

—— 'Russia and Ukraine: the Difference that Peter I Made', *RR*, 39 (1980), 1–17.

Sumner, B. *Peter the Great and the Ottoman Empire* (Oxford, 1950).

Army and Navy

Deane, J. *History of the Russian Fleet during the Reign of Peter the Great* (London, 1899).

Hellie, R. 'The Petrine Army: Continuity, Change, Impact', *CASS*, 8 (1974), 237–253.

Hughes, L. 'Peter the Great: a Passion for Ships', in M. Cornwall and M. Frame, eds, *Scotland and the Slavs: Cultures in Contact, 1500–2000*, (Newtonville, Mass., 2001), 3–20.

Konstam, A. and Rickman, D. *Peter the Great's Army 1: Infantry* (London, 1993); *2: Cavalry* (London, 1993).

Phillips, E. J. *The Founding of Russia's Navy. Peter the Great and the Azov Fleet 1688–1714* (Westport, Conn., 1995).

Ryan, W. F. 'Navigation and the Modernisation of Russia', in R. Bartlett ed., *Russia in the Age of Enlightenment: Essays for Isabel de Madariaga* (London, 1990), 75–105.

—— 'Peter I's English Yacht', *Mariner's Mirror*, 69 (1983), 65–87.

—— 'Peter and English Maritime Technology', *PGW*, 130–58.

Sarantola-Weiss, M. 'Peter the Great's First Boat, "Grandfather of the Russian Navy" ', *WOR*, 37–42.

Stevens, C. 'Evaluating Peter's Military Forces', *RRP*, 89–104.

Warner, R. 'British Merchants and Russian Men-of-War: the Rise of the Russian Baltic Fleet', *PGW*, 105–17.

—— 'The Kožuchovo Campaign of 1697', *JGO*, 13 (1965), 487–96.

Russia and Britain

Anderson, M. S. 'English Views of Russia in the Age of Peter the Great', *SR*, 13 (1954), 200–14.

Barlow, P. 'Peter the Great in England', *Anglo-Soviet Journal*, 46 (1986), 6–10.

Bruce, M. 'Jacobite Relations with Peter the Great', *SEER*, 4 (1935–36), 343–62.

Chance, J. 'George I and Peter I after the Peace of Nystad', *English Historical Review*, 26, no. 102 (1911), 161–87.

Cross, A. G. *Anglo-Russica. Aspects of Cultural Relations between Great Britain and Russia in the 18th and early 19th Centuries* (Oxford and Providence, 1993).

—— *Peter the Great through British Eyes. Perceptions and Representations of the Tsar since 1698* (Cambridge, 2000).

—— ' "Petrus Britannicus": the Image of Peter the Great in Eighteenth-Century Britain', *WOR*, 3–10.

Fedosov, D. 'Peter the Great: the Scottish Dimension', *PGW*, 89–101.

Grey, I. 'Peter the Great in England', *History Today*, 6 (1956), 225–34.

Hartley, J. 'Changing Perspectives: British Views of Russia from the Grand Embassy to the Peace of Nystad', *PGW*, 53–70.

—— 'England "Enjoys the Spectacle of a Northern Barbarian". The Reception of Peter I and Alexander I', *WOR*, 11–18.

Lane, J. 'Diligent and Faithful Servant: Peter the Great's Apprentices in England', *PGW*, 71–88.

Loewenson, L. 'People Peter the Great Met in England. Moses Stringer, Chymist and Physician', *SEER*, 37 (1959), 459–68.

—— 'Some Details of Peter the Great's Stay in England in 1698. Neglected English Materials', *SEER*, 49 (1962), 431–43.

Rothstein, A. *Peter the Great and Marlborough. Politics and Diplomacy in Converging Wars* (Basingstoke, 1986).

Ritual and Ceremonial Culture. The Court

Anderson, M. S. 'The Court of Peter the Great', in A. Dickens, ed., *The Courts of Europe, Patronage and Royalty 1400–1800* (London, 1977).

Cross, A. G. 'The Bung College or the British Monastery in Petrine Russia', *SGECRN*, 12 (1984), 14–24.

Goldstein, D. 'Gastronomic Reforms under Peter the Great. Towards a Cultural History of Russian Food', *JGO*, 48 (2000), 481–510.

Hughes, L. 'The Courts of Moscow and St Petersburg', in J. Adamson ed., *The Courts of Europe during the Ancien Régime* (Cambridge, 1998), 294–313.

—— ' "For the Health of the Sons of Ivan Mikhailovich": I. M. Golovin and Peter the Great's Mock Court', in Klein, 43–51.

—— *Playing Games: the Alternative History of Peter the Great* (London, 2000).

—— 'The Petrine Year: Anniversaries and Festivals in the Reign of Peter the Great', in K. Friedrich ed., *Festival Culture in Germany and Europe from the Sixteenth to the Twentieth Century* (Lewiston, 2000), 148–68.

Zguta, R. 'P. I's "Most Drunken Synod of Fools and Jesters" ', *JGO*, 21 (1973), 18–21.

Zitser, E. 'A Royal Charivari: The Wedding of the "Prince Pope" and the Apotheosis of St. Petersburg', unpublished paper, 1999.

Art and Culture. St Petersburg

Androsov, S. 'Painting and Sculpture in the Petrine Era', *RRP*, 161–72.

Cracraft, J. *The Petrine Revolution in Russian Architecture* (Chicago, 1990).

—— *The Petrine Revolution in Russian Imagery* (Chicago, 1997).

Cross, A. G. 'Did Peter Sit for Kneller at Utrecht in 1697?', *SGECRN*, 28 (1998), 32–42.

Dolskaya-Ackerly, O. 'Choral Music in the Petrine Era', *RRP*, 173–86.

Egorov, I. *The Architectural Planning of St Petersburg* (Ann Arbor, 1969).

Hibbert, C. 'St Petersburg in the Days of Peter the Great', in *Cities and Civilizations* (New York, 1986), 152–61.

Hughes, L. 'Close Shave: a Pogonic History of Petrine Russia', *SGECRN*, 23 (1995), 3–4.

—— 'German Specialists in Petrine Russia: Architects, Painters and Thespians', in R. Bartlett and K. Schönwälder, eds, *The German Lands and Eastern Europe* (Basingstoke, 1999), 72–90.

—— 'Russia's First Architectural Books: a Chapter in Peter the Great's Cultural Revolution', in C. Cooke, ed., *Russian Avant-Garde Art and Architecture* (London, 1983), 4–13.

Jones, R. E. 'Why St Petersburg?', *PGW*, 189–205.

Kaganov, G. 'As in the Ship of Peter', *SR*, 50 (1991), 754–67.

Likhachev, D. S. 'The Petrine Reforms and the Development of Russian Culture', *CASS*, 13 (1979), 230–4.

Marcialis, N. 'The Linguistic Situation in the Petrine Era', *RRP*, 133–46.

Marker, G. 'The Petrine "Civil Primer" Reconsidered: a New Look at the Publishing History of the "Grazhdanskaia azbuka 1708–27" ', *Solanus* (1989), 25–39.

—— 'Publishing and Print Culture', *RRP*, 119–132.

Marsden, C. *Palmyra of the North. The First Days of St Petersburg* (London, 1942).

Spassky, I. and Shchukina, E. *Medals and Coins of the Age of Peter the Great* (L., 1974).

Women

Alexander, J. 'Amazon Autocratixes: Images of Female Rule in the Eighteenth Century', in P. Barta, ed., G*ender and Sexuality in Russian Civilization* (London, 2001), 33–54.

Hughes, L. 'Between Two Worlds: Tsarevna Natal'ia Alekseevna and the "Emancipation" of Petrine Women', *WOR*, 29–36.

—— 'From Caftans into Corsets: The Sartorial Transformation of Women during the Reign of Peter the Great', in P. Barta, ed. *Gender and Sexuality in Russian Civilization* (London, 2001), 17–32.

—— 'Peter the Great's Two Weddings: Changing Images of Women in a Transitional Age', in R. Marsh ed., *Women in Russia and Ukraine* (Cambridge, 1996), 31–44.

Kollmann, N. S. 'The Seclusion of Elite Muscovite Women', *Russian History*, 10 (1983), 170–87.

Marrese, M. 'Women and Westernization in Petrine Russia', *RRP*, 105–18.

Schafly, D. 'A Muscovite Boiarynia Faces Peter the Great's Reforms: Dar'ia Golitsyna between Two Worlds', *CASS*, 31 (1997), 249–65.

Religion and the Church

Bissonette, G. 'Peter the Great and the Church as an Education Institution', in J. Curtiss, ed., *Essays in Russian and Soviet History in Honour of G. T. Robinson* (Leiden, 1963), 3–19.

—— 'Feofan Prokopovich', Garrad, 75–105.

—— 'Feofan Prokopovich: a Bibliography of his Works', *Oxford Slavonic Papers* (1975), 1–36.

Cracraft, J. *The Church Reform of Peter the Great* (London, 1971).

Crummey, R. *The Old Believers and the World of Antichrist. The Vyg Community and the Russian State 1694–1855* (Madison, 1970).

Lewitter, L. 'Peter the Great's Attitude towards Religion', *RWEC*, 62–77.

Serech, J. 'Stefan Yavorsky and the Conflict of Ideologies in the Age of Peter the Great', *SEER*, 30 (1951), 40–62

Zhivov, V. 'Church Reforms in the Reign of Peter the Great', *RRP*, 65–78.

Education and Science

Alexander, J. 'Medical Developments in Petrine Russia', *CASS*, 8 (1974), 198–221.

Haigh, B., 'Design for a Medical Service – Peter the Great's Admiralty Regulation (1722)', *Medical History*, 19 (1975), 129–46.

Hans, N. 'The Moscow School of Mathematics and Navigation (1701)', *SEER*, 29 (1951), 532–6.

Nesterov, O. ' "His Majesty's Cabinet" and Peter I's Kunstkammer', in O. Impey and A. McGregor, eds, *The Origins of Museums. The Cabinet of Curiosities in 16th–17th-Century Europe* (Oxford, 1985), 54–61.

Okenfuss, M. 'The Jesuit Origins of Petrine Education', in Garrard, 103–30.

—— 'Russian Students in Europe in the Age of Peter the Great', ibid., 131–45.

—— 'Technical Training in Russia under Peter the Great', *History of Education Quarterly*, 13 (1973), 325–45.

Rieber, A. J. 'Politics and Technology in Eighteenth-Century Russia', *Science in Context*, 8 (1995), 341–68.

Shaw, D. 'Geographical Practice and its Significance in Peter the Great's Russia', *Journal of Historical Geography*, 22 (1996), 160–76.

—— 'Recent Studies of the Cartography and Geography of Peter the Great's Reign', *RRP*, 79–88.

Recent Works on Peter and his Reign in Russian (1996–2001)

Abbasov, A. M., *Po mestam deianii Petra (Putevoditel')* (M., 1996).

Androsov, S. O. *Zhivopisets Ivan Nikitin* (SPb, 1998).

Borodkina, N. N., *Tserkov', obshchestvo i godudarstvo v epokhu Petra Velikogo* (Saratov, 1997).

Burlaka, D. K., and Kara-Murza, A. A. *Petr Velikii: pro et contra* (SPb, 2000).

Burykin, A. D., 'Petr I kak vospitatel' russkogo obshchestva', *Istoricheskie lichnosti Rossii* (SPb, 1998), 12–14.

Chirikov, V., *Strannyi monarkh* (Voronezh, 1996).

Efimov, S. V., 'Tsarevich Aleksei v S. Peterburge', *Peterburgskie chteniia 96* (SPb, 1996), 54–7.

Galanov, M. M. 'Semeistvo Naryshkinykh i politicheskaia bor'ba Rossii v poslednei chetverti XVIII v.', *VI*, 1999, 6, 145–9.

Godizhenko, N. V., *Reformy Petra I* (Noril'sk, 1998).

Kaliazina, N., ed. *Gosudarstvennyi Ermitazh. Iz istorii petrovskikh kollektsii* (SPb, 2000).

Kareeva, N., *Pervonachal'nyi dvorets Petra Velikogo. Putevoditel'. Domik Petra I* (SPb, 1998).

Karpov, G. M., *Velikoe Posol'stvo Petra I* (Kaliningrad, 1998).

Kopaneva, N. et al. (eds), *Petr I i Gollandiia. Russko-gollandskie nauchnye i khudozhestvennye sviazi v epokhu Petra Velikogo* (SPb, 1997).

Kotin, I. Iu., 'Petr Velikii v Oksforde', *Trudy gos. muzeiia istorii Sankt-Peterburga*, 3 (SPb, 1998), 49–54.

Kretinin, G. V., *Prusskie marshruty Petra Pervogo* (Kaliningrad, 1996).

Krotov, P. A. *Gangutskaia bataliia 1714 goda* (SPb, 1996).

K 300-letiiu Velikogo posol'stva Petra I v zapadnuiu Evropu (M., 1999).

Lelina, E. I., 'Novoe o khorosho izvestnom. (K voprosu o nachale stroitel'stva Petro-pavlovskogo sobora)', *Peterburgskie chteniia 96*, (SPb, 1996), 65–8.

Likhacheva, O. 'Obraz Petra I v iubileinykh torzhestvakh Peterburga (1803–1903)', *Istorizm v kul'ture. Materialy mezh. nauchnoi konferentsii v S-Peterburge 24–25 noiab. 1997g.* (SPb, 1998), 168–75.

Makogonova, M. *Petropavlovskaia krepost'* (SPb, 1998).

Mezin, S. A., *Vzgliad iz Evropy. Frantsuzskie avtory XVIII veka o Petre I* (Saratov, 1999).

Nemiro, O. V., 'Iz istorii prazdnovaniia 100-letiia i 200-letiia osnovaniia Sankt-Peterburga', *Peterburgskie chteniia 96* (SPb, 1996), 429–33.

Petr Velikii i Moskva. Katalog vystavki (M., 1998).

Putilov, N., ed., *Petr Velikii v predaniakh, legendakh, anekdotakh, skazkakh, pesniakh* (SPb, 2000).

Shenkman, G. S., *Velikii Petr* (SPb, 1999).

Strukov, A. *Epokha Petra I glazami uchenykh* (Voronezh, 1999).

Tsar Petr i korol' Karl. Dva pravitelia iz naroda. Sb. statei (M., 1999).

"Vechera s Petrom Velikim": Nravstvennye uroki istorii (SPb, 2001).

Zagorovskii, V. P., *Petr Velikii na Voronezhskom zemle* (Voronezh, 1996).

Zolotarev, V. and Kozlov, I. A., *Petr Velikii i morskoe mogushchestvo otechestva* (M., 1996).

Index

Most personal proper names and a limited selection of general subject headings are listed. Towns, rivers and other geographical locations are included when they were the sites of battles and treaties, when Peter spent time there, and so on. There are selected thematic entries for Moscow, St Petersburg, Sweden and for Peter himself